Approaches to Predicative Possession

Bloomsbury Studies in Theoretical Linguistics

Bloomsbury Studies in Theoretical Linguistics publishes work at the forefront of present-day developments in the field. The series is open to studies from all branches of theoretical linguistics and to the full range of theoretical frameworks. Titles in the series present original research that makes a new and significant contribution and are aimed primarily at scholars in the field, but are clear and accessible, making them useful also to students, to new researchers and to scholars in related disciplines.

Other titles in the series:

Agreement, Pronominal Clitics and Negation in Tamazight Berber, Hamid Ouali

A Neural Network Model of Lexical Organisation, Michael Fortescue

Contrastive Studies in Morphology and Syntax, edited by Michalis Georgiafentis, Giannoula Giannoulopoulou, Maria Koliopoulou and Angeliki Tsokoglou

Deviational Syntactic Structures, Hans Gotzsche

First Language Acquisition in Spanish, Gilda Socarras

Grammar of Spoken English Discourse, Gerard O'Grady

Pragmatic Syntax, Jieun Kiaer

The Semantic Representation of Natural Language, Michael Levison, Greg Lessard, Craig Thomas and Matthew Donald

The Syntax and Semantics of Discourse Markers, Miriam Urgelles-Coll

The Syntax of Mauritian Creole, Anand Syea

Approaches to Predicative Possession

The View from Slavic and Finno-Ugric

Edited by
Gréte Dalmi
Jacek Witkoś
Piotr Cegłowski

BLOOMSBURY ACADEMIC
LONDON · NEW YORK · OXFORD · NEW DELHI · SYDNEY

Bloomsbury Academic
Bloomsbury Publishing Plc
50 Bedford Square, London, WC1B 3DP, UK
1385 Broadway, New York, NY 10018, USA
29 Earlsfort Terrace, Dublin 2, Ireland

BLOOMSBURY, BLOOMSBURY ACADEMIC and the Diana logo
are trademarks of Bloomsbury Publishing Plc

First published in Great Britain 2020
Paperback edition published 2021

Copyright © Gréte Dalmi, Jacek Witkoś, Piotr Cegłowski and Contributors, 2020

Gréte Dalmi, Jacek Witkoś and Piotr Cegłowski have asserted their right under the Copyright, Designs and Patents Act, 1988, to be identified as Editors of this work.

All rights reserved. No part of this publication may be reproduced or transmitted in any form or by any means, electronic or mechanical, including photocopying, recording, or any information storage or retrieval system, without prior permission in writing from the publishers.

Bloomsbury Publishing Plc does not have any control over, or responsibility for, any third-party websites referred to or in this book. All internet addresses given in this book were correct at the time of going to press. The author and publisher regret any inconvenience caused if addresses have changed or sites have ceased to exist, but can accept no responsibility for any such changes.

A catalogue record for this book is available from the British Library.

A catalog record for this book is available from the Library of Congress.

ISBN: HB: 978-1-3500-6246-7
PB: 978-1-3502-7793-9
ePDF: 978-1-3500-6247-4
eBook: 978-1-3500-6248-1

Series: Bloomsbury Studies in Theoretical Linguistics

Typeset by Integra Software Services Pvt. Ltd.

To find out more about our authors and books visit www.bloomsbury.com and sign up for our newsletters.

Contents

List of Contributors		vi
Editors' Note		vii
1	Introduction *Gréte Dalmi*	1
2	Genitive of Negation (GoN) in Polish possessive and locative existential sentences: A testing tool for case overwriting, case projections and derivational phases *Jacek Witkoś*	11
3	Extraction of possessive NP-complements and the structure of the nominal domain in Polish *Piotr Cegłowski*	40
4	The Definiteness Effect in Russian existential and possessive sentences *Olga Kagan*	61
5	Predicative possession in Belarusian, a mixed BE/HAVE language *Egor Tsedryk*	80
6	Predicative possession as a clause type in Finnish *Maria Vilkuna*	113
7	The argument structure of BE-possessives in Hungarian *Gréte Dalmi*	136
8	Existential possession in Meadow Mari *Alexandra Simonenko*	162
9	Predicative possession in Permic *Nikolett F. Gulyás*	186
10	Predicative possessive constructions in Selkup dialects *Beáta Wagner-Nagy*	205
11	Conclusion *Gréte Dalmi, Jacek Witkoś and Piotr Cegłowski*	221
Index		224

Contributors

Piotr Cegłowski
Associate Professor of Linguistics, Adam Mickiewicz University, Poznań, Poland

Gréte Dalmi
Part-time Lecturer of English, University of Technology, Budapest, Hungary

Nikolett F. Gulyás
Assistant Professor of Linguistics, Eötvös Loránd University, Budapest, Hungary

Olga Kagan
Adjunct Professor of Linguistics, Ben Gurion University, Beersheba, Israel

Alexandra Simonenko
Postdoctoral Research Fellow of Linguistics, Research Foundation Flanders (FWO) & Ghent University, Ghent, Belgium

Egor Tsedryk
Associate Professor of Linguistics, Saint Mary's University, Halifax, Canada

Maria Vilkuna
Associate Professor of Linguistics, University of Helsinki, Finland

Beáta Wagner-Nagy
Professor of Linguistics, University of Hamburg, Germany

Jacek Witkoś
Professor of Linguistics, Adam Mickiewicz University, Poznań, Poland

Editors' Note

We, the editors, express our gratitude to the contributors, reviewers, graphic designers and production experts, who made this volume possible. First and foremost, we are grateful to Bloomsbury Academic, and its editors, who whole-heartedly supported this enterprise from the very beginning. Second, we are grateful to the authors in this book, who produced fascinating chapters on various aspects of predicative possession in Slavic and Finno-Ugric languages. We sincerely hope that with the nine chapters included in this volume, we can make an important contribution to understanding cross-linguistic variation in general, and the variety of forms possessive sentences may take in human languages, in particular.

Slavic and Finno-Ugric languages have long historical ties. They mutually influence each other, especially in areas where the two language families are in contact. Yet, it is interesting to see how different the linguistic structures expressing predicative possession may be in these two language families. While Slavic languages tend to use the *HAVE*-type of predicative possession, Finno-Ugric languages predominantly use *BE*-possessives.

Theoretical linguists try to find the unifying properties of individual human languages and search for general rules and principles to describe them. In the present case, event structure, argument mapping, definiteness and case marking are the key features in finding these unifying properties. We, as editors, are convinced that studying predicative possession in the individual languages presented in this volume will lead us to a better understanding of possession relation in general.

Editing a volume with a collection of contributions on typologically diverse languages is impossible without involving a number of experts on the topic, as reviewers. We wish to express our gratitude to the reviewers for their thorough and conscientious work:

Artur Bartnik (KUL, Lublin)
Gréte Dalmi (University of Technology, Budapest)
Gabi Danon (Tel Aviv University, Tel Aviv)
Marcel Den Dikken (ELTE, Budapest)
Itamar Frances (University of Chicago, Chicago)
Ljudmila Geist (University of Stuttgart, Stuttgart)
Thomas Angelo Grano (Indiana University, Bloomington)
Alexander Grosu (Tel Aviv University, Tel Aviv)
Anders Holmberg (Newcastle University, Newcastle)
Gerson Stefan Klummp (Tallin University, Tallin)
Malgorzata Krzek (Newcastle University, Newcastle)
Jaakko Leino (University of Helsinki, Helsinki)
Inna Livitz (New York University, New York)

Edith Moravcsik (University of Wisconsin, Milwaukee)
Neil Myler (Berkeley University, Boston)
Genoveva Puskás (University of Geneva, Geneva)
Marta Ruda (Jagellonian University, Cracow)
Radek Simik (Humboldt University, Berlin)
Balázs Surányi (PKKE, Piliscsaba)
Maria Vilkuna (University of Helsinki, Helsinki)
Beata Wagner-Nagy (Hamburg University, Hamburg)

Last, but not least, we are thankful to the technical editors, who meticulously edited and re-edited our manuscripts according to our request. For technical reasons, we moved all footnotes to the end of each chapter, according to the publisher's regulations.

Gréte Dalmi
Jacek Witkoś
Piotr Cegłowski

1. Introduction

Gréte Dalmi

There are at least two reasons to devote special attention to this book. The first one is that the languages discussed here are still relatively under-represented in the recent syntactic and semantic literature. The second reason is typological in nature. Cross-linguistically, predicative possession materializes either as HAVE-possessives or as BE-possessives (see Heine 1997; Stassen 2009; Creissels 2014). While Slavic predominantly uses HAVE-possessives, BE-possessives are more prevalent in Uralic. In some of these languages, the two types are used with certain semantic differences between them. This raises the question whether the two major forms of predicative possession are derivationally related or whether the choice in a given language is accidental and should be described in terms of parametric variation.

1.1. Topic and structure of the volume

The volume is based on the papers presented at the Predicative Possession Panel of BASEES in March 2017 at Fitzwilliam College, Cambridge, which were later complemented by some Finno-Ugric studies on the topic. The editors are pleased to offer this extended collection of papers now to a wider audience.

The chapters of the book centre around the syntactic phenomenon of predicative possession. The approaches taken to this construction in the volume vary from minimalist, nano-syntactic, cartographic, constructionist, formal semantic, typological, and comparative. What makes this collection a unique enterprise is that it relies on the facts of typologically distinct, though geographically overlapping language families, notably, Slavic and Finno-Ugric. Although the two language families are genealogically unrelated, there is a fair amount of interaction between them, especially in areas where they are in direct contact. One obvious example of such interaction is found in Balto-Slavic. Balto-Slavic languages employ both HAVE-possessives and BE-possessives, to express predicative possession, and thus represent a borderline case (see McAnnalen 2011; Mazzitelli 2017).

The first four chapters discuss the facts of Slavic possessives. West Slavic is represented by two chapters discussing Polish possessives. The next chapter offers a semantic account of Russian existential and possessive sentences, representing East Slavic. The last chapter in the Slavic block is a study of Belarusian possessive sentences, representing the Balto-Slavic mixed pattern. The following four chapters give a representative sample of possessive sentences in Finno-Ugric languages, including Finnish, Hungarian, Meadow Mari and Permic. The last chapter deals with Selkup, a Samoyedic language closely related to Komi and Udmurt. The volume is accompanied by a reference list and an index.

1.2. Theories of predicative possession

Stassen (2009) establishes four major forms of predicative possession, out of which three employ existential BE and only one uses possessive HAVE. There are two main theories concerning the choice of HAVE vs. BE in possessive constructions, which will be referred to here as the derivational vs. the lexicalist theory.

The derivational approach, dating back to Benveniste (1966), takes it that possessive HAVE-sentences and possessive/exististential BE-sentences are all derivable from copular BE-sentences. This idea is resurrected in Freeze's (1992) study. He addresses the question whether possessive HAVE, existential BE and copular BE can be derived from a unified underlying structure. Kayne (1993), relying on Szabolcsi's (1983, 1985, 1994) work on Hungarian possessive NPs, also takes a derivational approach and assigns possessive HAVE-sentences and copular BE-sentences the same underlying structure. In his analysis, all these verbs take a single argument. The possessor raises to the canonical subject position of possessive HAVE just like the theme argument does in copular BE-sentences. This view is also reflected in Belvin & Den Dikken (1997) and Den Dikken (1997, 1998, 1999, 2006).

In some Slavic and several Finno-Ugric languages, possessive sentences are built on existential BE; in these sentences the possessor bears oblique case (see Stassen 2009). This poses an immediate problem for the derivational approach. On the one hand, the oblique possessor cannot target the same canonical [Spec, IP] subject position that nominative subjects do, as the former cannot have its features licensed in that position. On the other hand, the oblique possessor is VP-internally more prominent than the nominative theme in possessive BE-sentences. Furthermore, under the derivational approach, copular BE must undergo transitivization in order to materialize as possessive HAVE. This issue has been recently taken up by Jung (2011) and Myler (2016).

Myler (2016), building on Jung (2011), argues that 'copulas exist to "sentencify" fundamentally non-sentential syntactic units'. The copula is usually realized as BE. If, however, the rest of the structure is transitive, the copula is realized as HAVE. To achieve this, Myler (2016) introduces the VoiceP functional projection, surmounting the lexical layer of copular BE and he employs the mechanism of 'delayed gratification' to introduce the possessor in this functional projection. The differences between existential/possessive BE-sentences vs. copular BE-sentences in his theory are not attributed to the BE-predicate itself, even in languages with morphologically distinct BE-predicates in this domain; rather, to the different functional layers and the syntactic mechanisms employed in them. The same meaningless BE verb is involved in each case, and the existential/possessive content comes from elsewhere.

As was pointed out in a series of studies by Partee & Borschev (2002, 2008), Paducheva (2000) and Błaszczak (2007, 2010), BE-possessives share a whole range of syntactic and semantic properties with BE-existentials but not with copular BE-sentences in Slavic languages. The Definiteness Restriction in affirmative sentences, GEN NEG in Slavic negated sentences, anaphoric binding, case marking on the possessor and the possessee segregate existential and possessive BE-sentences from copular BE-sentences.

Under the lexicalist approach, BE-possessives and HAVE-possessives are structurally distinct constructions, though both have two event participants, the possessor and the possessee (see Paducheva 2000; Blaszczak 2007; Partee & Borschev 2008).

Paducheva (2000) proposes that in addition to copular BE, Russian also has an existential BE. Existential BE-sentences share several properties with possessive BE-sentences. The author argues that the Russian existential BE appears in existential and possessive BE-sentences alike and it invariably takes two arguments: a location and a theme in the former, and a possessor and a theme in the latter. To support her claims, she offers semantic, syntactic and prosodic tests, including Definiteness Restriction, GEN NEG, sentence stress and word order.

Błaszczak (2007) distinguishes three different meanings of BE, each of which has its own selectional properties/argument structure. The postulation of three different types of BE, Błaszczak (2007) argues, can help us explain the puzzling phenomenon of GEN NEG.

Partee & Borschev (2002, 2007, 2008) assume that existential BE also appears in possessive BE-sentences. They derive the difference between locative copular sentences and locative existential sentences from their different perspectival centre. While in locative copular sentences the subject is interpreted as definite/specific, existential and possessive sentences impose the Definiteness Restriction, whence the theme argument must be indefinite/non-specific. Genitive of Negation is found in negated existential and possessive BE-sentences, but never in copular BE-sentences.

1.3. An overview of the chapters

1.3.1. The introductory chapter attempts to give an insight into the current accounts of predicative possession. On the one hand, it surveys some mainstream theories that view possessive sentences akin to copular sentences, in which the copular predicate selects a single small clause; it also discusses some lexicalist approaches, which start out with an existential/possessive unaccusative predicate, taking two distinc arguments.

1.3.2. The contribution by **Jacek Witkoś** is concerned with Genitive of Negation (GoN) in locative existential and possessive and constructions in Polish. Following a brief presentation of the key data, the author discusses current accounts of the problem, with special emphasis on two types of locative constructions in Polish. In generative syntactic approaches, GoN has served as a testing tool for syntactic theories (see, for example, Babby 1980, 1990; Willim 1989; Tajsner 1990; Franks 1994, 1995; Witkoś 1998, 2003a, b; Brown 1999; Przepiórkowski 1999; Błaszczak 2001; Bailyn 2004; Kagan 2013). The author follows this suit and lists two recent proposals to the GoN test. The chapter provides a rudimentary presentation of two recent approaches to case theory: Pesetsky's (2013) case overwriting theory and Caha's (2009) case projection approach. It is shown that they both offer interesting views on the engineering details of the GoN but the nano-syntactic theory of case projections seems to give a straightforward answer to the question why only structural cases (accusative and nominative) are replaced by genitive in the scope of clausal negation. The case overwriting theory cannot, in principle, independently constrain the case replacement process in hand unless it resorts to a fairly liberal application of Spell-Out. In the final section of the chapter, the long-distance version of the GoN is briefly treated as a diagnostic for the notion of a derivational phase and its extension.

1.3.3. **Piotr Cegłowski**'s chapter presents a possible scenario for the extraction of possessive (genitive) NP-complements that sets a more elaborate architectural setting than the one put forward by Bošković (2014a,b, 2015a, b) in his labelling account. The proposal draws on the assumption that the nominal structure (NP) in Polish is insulated with a number of functional projections (see also Rutkowski 2002, 2007; Migdalski 2001, 2003; Rappaport 2001a, b). The argumentation is based on the observation that Polish does not consistently observe the characteristics of an 'NP-language' in the sense of Bošković (2008, 2009) and is additionally supported with the relevant results of an acceptability survey of the selected types of extraction (Left Branch Extraction, deep extraction, extraction of possessive [genitive] NP-complements across numerals, among others). A closer look at the data obtained in the course of the study enables us to make interesting insights into the mechanics of extraction that substantiate the observation that this sort of operation is to a large extent discourse-driven. Given the size and the number of postulated projections, it is argued that the account of Antilocality in the spirit of Grohmann (2003, 2011) seems better suited than that of Bošković's (2014a,b, 2015a, b) in dealing with the displacement phenomena involving extraction and fronting.

1.3.4. The next chapter by **Olga Kagan** deals with the Definiteness Effect in Russian existential and possessive sentences. Existential sentences display the so-called Definiteness Effect in a range of languages. Strong DPs, including definite expressions, cannot occur in the position of the pivot, in contrast to their weak, indefinite counterparts. The Russian data pose a challenge to this generalization. While in positive existential sentences, the Definiteness Effect is present, negative ones easily allow strong pivots. Crucially, the pivot in negative existential sentences is obligatorily marked genitive. Building on previous work on GoN, the author argues that this case marks a DP as property-denoting and signals its shift to the property type. In turn, a DP that denotes a property is acceptable in existential sentences irrespective of its (in)definiteness. Russian possessive BE-sentences do exhibit the Definiteness Effect even under negation, despite their structural similarity to BE-existentials.

1.3.5. The last chapter in the Slavic block by **Egor Tsedryk** discusses some fascinating data from Belarusian. This language uses both BE and HAVE to express possession at the clausal level (Isačenko 1974). In the generative tradition, dating back to influential analyses proposed by Freeze (1992) and Kayne (1993), the BE/HAVE alternation could be a result of a syntactic transformation relating both surface forms to a common underlying structure. More recently, Myler (2016) has shown that multiple possessive forms, including the BE/HAVE alternation, are a result of a limited number of functional heads, which have different morpho-phonological realizations because of different syntactic environments. That is, different surface forms do in fact indicate different syntactic structures. The author approaches BE/HAVE alternation in Belarusian from this second perspective. He shows that there is no binary split between BE and HAVE, but a tripartite variation between (i) existential BE, (ii) copular BE and (iii) HAVE. Copular and existential BE are in strict complementary distribution, whereas HAVE can alternate with either of them. In fact, HAVE does not alternate with a verb BE (copular or existential), but with the preposition *u* 'at'. Assuming Distributed Morphology (Halle & Marantz 1993 et seq.), the author proposes that both *u* 'at' and HAVE are allomorphs of the same spatio-temporal root, $\sqrt{AT}$, in different syntactic environments. Based on a cognitive definition of possession (Langacker 1993, 2009), he assumes that $\sqrt{AT}$ encodes inclusion (Bjorkman & Cowper 2016) and offers a unified morpho-syntactic and semantic analysis of BE/HAVE predicative possession in Belarusian.

1.3.6. **Maria Vilkuna** discusses predicative possession as a clause type in Finnish in the framework of Construction Grammar. The concept of clause type, often used in Finnish grammar, and its status as a construction, are introduced and explained in this chapter. Typologically, the Finnish pattern represents the locational possessive (Stassen 2009). It is a crystallized subtype of the so-called existential clause type, which displays an 'inverse' encoding of figure-ground relations. Finnish existential clauses challenge most notions of subjecthood, and this is even clearer in the possessive clause. The chapter analyses the structural features common to existentials and possessives and those features that distinguish the two. The effect of negation on the marking of the possessee is explored to discuss further semantic distinctions and borderline cases. Although canonical instances of the possessive and existential patterns are distinctive enough, their exact borders are harder to draw. By giving a thorough description of the possessive clause, the author attempts to clarify the criteria for drawing these lines.

1.3.7. **Gréte Dalmi**'s analysis of Hungarian BE-possessives reveals that the argument structure of these sentence types patterns with that of BE-existentials rather than with that of copular BE-sentences. The chapter takes a lexicalist approach, in which existential and possessive BE, just like possessive HAVE, select two distinct arguments (see Chvany 1975; Paducheva 2000; Błaszczak 2007, 2010; Partee & Borshev 2008). These predicates, therefore, must be segregated from copular BE-predicates, which select only a single small clause (see Stowell 1981; Chomsky 1995; Bowers 2001; Den Dikken 2006). As the author points out, existential and possessive BE-sentences observe the Definiteness Restriction (see Milsark 1979) in several languages, which copular BE-sentences never do. Taking this and a whole range of related syntactic and semantic properties into consideration, the chapter argues for the segregation of existential and possessive BE-sentences from copular BE-sentences in Hungarian. It discusses some problems arising in the current accounts of Hungarian BE-possessives and relates posssessive BE to the *piacere* 'please'-class of *psych*-predicates (see Belletti & Rizzi 1988; Grimshaw 1990; Harley 2002).

The dative possessor occupies a more prominent VP-internal position than the nominative theme in Hungarian BE-possessives. There is a null pronominal possessor inside the possessive DP (see Den Dikken 1999), which is bound by the dative possessor. Coreference between them is indicated by the agreement suffix on the possessee. In discourse-semantically marked sentences, this DP-internal null possessor may become overt and can co-occur with the overt dative possessor. These facts force the dyadic unaccusative analysis of BE-possessives.

1.3.8. **Alexandra Simonenko** provides a semantic account of existential possessive constructions in Meadow Mari. This language is a member of the Volgaic branch of the Finno-Ugric language family. The chapter proposes that the semantics of the construction has two loci: genitival NPs relativizing existential assertion to a domain controlled by a particular individual ('the possessor') at the event time introduced by the existential predicate, on the one hand, and possessive suffixes introducing a salient relation holding with respect to a situation defined independently of the main predicate. It also argues that Milsark's Definiteness Effect, characterizing this construction, is due to an irreconcilable conflict between the existential presupposition of certain determiners and the informativity condition associated with existential constructions (Zucchi 1995; Partee 1999). Possessive suffixes are argued to be immune to DE due to their lack of existential presupposition.

1.3.9. **Nikolett F. Gulyás**'s chapter investigates predicative possession in two Permic languages, Komi-Permyak and Udmurt, from a typological point of view. In both languages, possessive clauses belong to the locational subtype according to Stassen's (2009) typology. The clauses are encoded in similar ways. Both nominal and pronominal possessors are marked by the genitive case in these languages and they are followed by *em* 'be' in Komi-Permyak and *vań* 'be' in Udmurt. These verbs are inflected for tense and also for number in Komi-Permyak. Possessees are unmarked in Komi-Permyak, while the possessive suffix can hardly be omitted in Udmurt. This variation may be due to Russian and Turkic influence. Under certain syntactic criteria, the marking of the possessee can deviate from the above patterns. Semantic properties of the possessee seem to have no effect on the encoding of the clause type in Komi-Permyak but in Udmurt one can find at least fragments of a former system that can be considered semantically motivated. There are some questionable, possession-like instances in both languages but on the basis of the data presented, all of them can be treated as real instances of possession.

1.3.10. The last chapter of the volume by **Beáta Wagner-Nagy** gives a classification of predicative possessive constructions in Selkup. It also shows the different strategies employed in these constructions in the different Selkup dialects. Selkup knows only one verb which is used in locational, possessive and existential sentences, i.e. *ɛːqo* 'be'. Thus, in all three sentence types this verb is the connecting element between the locational adverbial part (coda) and the theme (pivot). The structure of a possessive sentence differs from the existential or locative sentence only in marking the possessor (adverbial part). This topic is examined based on corpus data.

1.3.11. The concluding chapter evaluates the importance of the volume and its place in the existing works on this topic. It also explains in which areas of linguistics it can be best used for theoretical and educational purposes.

1.4. Summary

The volume is a collection of contributions investigating possessive constructions in two genealogically unrelated and typologically remote language families. Although HAVE-possessives are typically found in Slavic and BE-possessives are more common in Finno-Ugric, there is a handful of properties relating them. Thus, the Definiteness Restriction is found in both sentence types, which follows from the existential requirement, imposed by these predicates on their theme argument. Next, GoN in Slavic negated possessive sentences is the manifestation of the same existential requirement appearing as the Definiteness Requirement elswhere. This segregates HAVE-possessives and BE-possessives from copular BE-sentences, where such semantic requirements are never found. Finally, oblique possessors, found in some Slavic and several Finno-Ugric languages, are mapped to a position higher than the designated subject position of agentive clauses. This follows from the fact that they occcupy a more prominent VP-internal position than the theme. In Finno-Ugric BE-possessives, the theme argument often shows person/number agreement with the oblique possessor, due to a silent anaphoric possessor inside the theme argument, for which the oblique possessor serves as an antecedent.

References

Babby, L. 1980. *Existential Sentences and Negation in Russian*. Ann Arbor, MI: Karoma Publishers.
Babby, L. 1990. The syntax of surface case marking. In: Harbert, W. & Herschensohn, J. (eds), *Cornell Working Papers in Linguistics* 1, 1–32. Ithaca, NY: Cornell University Press.
Bailyn, J. F. 2004. The case of Q. In: Arnaudova, O. (ed.), *Proceedings of Formal Approaches to Slavic Linguistics: The Ottawa Meeting 2003*, 1–36. Ann Arbor, MI: Michigan Slavic Publications.
Belletti, A. & Rizzi, L. 1988. *Psych*-verbs and theta-theory. *Natural Language and Linguistic Theory* 6: 291–352.
Belvin, R. & Dikken Den, M. 1997. There, happens to, be, have. *Lingua* 101: 151–183.
Benveniste, E. 1966. *Être* et *avoir* dans leurs fonctions linguistiques. In: Benveniste, E. (ed.), *Problèmes de linguistique générale*. vol. 1, 187–207. Paris: Gallimard.
Bjorkman, B. & Cowper, E. 2016. Possession and necessity: from individuals to worlds. *Lingua* 182: 30–48.
Błaszczak, J. 2001. *Covert Movement and the Genitive of Negation in Polish* (Linguistics in Potsdam 15). Potsdam: Universitätsbibliothek.
Błaszczak, J. 2007. *Phase Syntax. The Polish Genitive of Negation*. Potsdam: University of Potsdam. Habilitation treatise.

Błaszczak, J. 2010. A spurious genitive puzzle in Polish. In: Fanselow, G. & Hanneforth, T. (eds), *Language and Logos. Studies in Theoretical and Computational Linguistics. Festschrift for Peter Staudacher for his 70th Birthday* (Studia Grammatica 72), 17-47. Berlin: Akademieverlag.
Bošković, Ž. 2008. What will you have, DP or NP? *Proceedings of the North East Linguistic Society* 37: 101-114.
Bošković, Ž. 2009. More on the no-DP analysis of article-less languages. *Studia Linguistica* 63: 187-203.
Bošković, Ž. 2014a. More on the edge of the edge. In: Chapman, C., Kit, O. & Kučerová, I. (eds), *Formal Approaches to Slavic Linguistics: The McMaster Meeting 2013 (FASL 22)*. Michigan, 44-66. Michigan: Michigan Slavic Publications.
Bošković, Ž. 2014b. Now I am a phase, now I am not a phase: on the variability of phases with extraction and ellipsis. *Linguistic Inquiry* 45(1): 27-89.
Bošković, Ž. 2015a. From the Complex NP Constraint to everything: on deep extractions across categories. *Linguistic Review* 32: 603-669.
Bošković, Ž. 2015b. On the timing of labeling: deducing Comp-trace effects, the Subject Condition, the Adjunct Condition, and tucking in from labeling. http://ling.auf.net/lingbuzz/002452.
Bowers, J. 2001. Predication. In: Baltin, M. & Collins, C. (eds), *The Handbook of Contemporary Syntactic Theory*, 299-333. Oxford: Blackwell.
Brown, S. 1999. *The Syntax of Negation in Russian: A Minimalist Approach*. Stanford, CA: CSLI Publications.
Caha, P. 2009. Nanosyntax of case. PhD dissertation. University of Tromsoe.
Chomsky, N. 1995. *The Minimalist Program*. Cambridge, MA: MIT Press.
Chvany, C. 1975. *On the Syntax of BE-sentences in Russian*. Cambridge, MA: Slavica.
Creissels, D. 2014. Existential predication in typological perspective. *Paper presented at the 46th Annual Meeting of the Societas Linguistica Europaea*. Revised version. http://www.deniscreissels.fr/index.php?pages/autres-documents-téléchargeables
Den Dikken, M. 1997. The syntax of possession sentences and the verb *have*. *Lingua* 101: 129-150.
Den Dikken, M. 1998. Anti-agreement in DP. In: Bezooijen, R. & Kagen, R. (eds), *Linguistics in the Netherlands*, 95-107. Amsterdam: Benjamins.
Den Dikken, M. 1999. On the structural representation of possession and agreement: the case of anti-agreement in Hungarian possessed nominal phrases. In: Kenesei, I. (ed.), *Crossing Boundaries: Theoretical Advances in Central and Eastern European Languages*, 137-178. Amsterdam: John Benjamins.
Den Dikken, M. 2006. *Relators and Linkers*. Cambridge, MA: MIT Press.
Franks, S. 1994. Parametric properties of numeral phrases in Slavic. *Natural Language and Linguistic Theory* 12: 597-674.
Franks, S. 1995. *Parameters of Slavic Morphosyntax*. New York: Oxford University Press.
Freeze, J. 1992. Existentials and other locatives. *Language* 68(3): 553-595.
Grimshaw, J. 1990. *Argument Structure*. Cambridge, MA: MIT Press.
Grohmann, K. 2003. *Prolific Domains: On the Anti-locality of Movement Dependencies*. Amsterdam: John Benjamins.
Grohmann, K. 2011. Anti-locality: too-close relations in grammar. In: Boeckx, C. (ed.), *The Oxford Handbook of Linguistic Minimalism*, 260-290. Oxford: Oxford University Press.
Halle, M. & Marantz, A. 1993. Distributed morphology and the pieces of inflection. In: Hale, K. & Keyser, S. J. (eds), *The View from Building 20: Essays in Linguistics in Honor of Sylvain Bromberger*, 111-176. Cambridge, MA: MIT Press.

Harley, H. 2002. Possession and the double object construction. In: Pica, P. & Rooryck J. (eds), *The Yearbook of Linguistic Variation* Vol 2, 21–69. Amsterdam: John Benjamins.

Heine, B. 1997. *Possession: Cognitive Sources, Forces, and Grammaticalization*. Cambridge: Cambridge University Press.

Isačenko, A. 1974. On *have* and *be* languages: a typological sketch. In: Flier, M. (ed.), *Slavic Forum: Essays in Linguistics and Literature*, 43–77. The Hague: Mouton.

Jung, H. 2011. *The Syntax of BE-possessives. Parametric Variation and Surface Diversities*. Amsterdam: Benjamins.

Kagan, O. 2013. *Semantics of Genitive Objects in Russian: A Study of Genitive of Negation and Intensional Genitive Case*. Dordrecht: Springer.

Kayne, R. 1993. Towards a modular theory of auxiliary selection. *Studia Linguistica* 47: 3–31.

Langacker, R. 1993. Reference-point constructions. *Cognitive Linguistics* 4: 1–38.

Langacker, R. 2009. *Investigations in Cognitive Grammar*. Berlin: Mouton De Gruyter.

McAnnalen, J. 2011. The history of predicative possession in Slavic: internal development vs. language contact. PhD dissertation. UCL, Berkeley.

Mazzitelli, L. F. 2017. Predicative possession in the languages of the Circum-Baltic area. *Folia Linguistica* 51(1): 1–60.

Migdalski, K. 2001. A Determiner Phrase approach to the structure of Polish nominals. In: Przepiórkowski, A. & Bański, P. (eds), *Generative Linguistics in Poland: Syntax and Morphosyntax*, 135–148. Warsaw: IPIPAN.

Migdalski, K. 2003. N-to-D raising in Polish. In: Staniulewicz, D. (ed.), *Papers in Language Studies. Proceedings of the Ninth Annual Conference of the Polish Association for the Study of English. Gdańsk 26-28 April 2000*, 187–193. Gdańsk: Wyd. UG.

Milsark, G. 1979. *Existential Sentences in English*. London: Routledge.

Myler, N. 2016. *Building and Interpreting Possessive Sentences*. Cambridge, MA: MIT Press.

Paducheva, E. 2000. Definiteness Effect: the case of Russian. In: von Heusinger K. & Egli, U. (eds), *Reference and Anaphoric Relations*, 133–146. Dordrecht: Kluwer.

Partee, B. 1999. Weak NP's in HAVE sentences. In: Gerbrandy, J., Marx, M., de Rijke, M. & Venema, Y. (eds), JFAK [a Liber Amicorum for Johan van Benthen on the occasion of his 50th Birthday], 39–57. Amsterdam: University of Amsterdam.

Partee, B. & Borschev, V. 2002. Genitive of Negation and Scope of Negation in Russian existential sentences. In: Toman, J. (ed), *Annual Workshop on Formal Approaches to Slavic Linguistics: The Second Ann Arbor Meeting* (FASL 10), 181–200. Ann Arbor: Michigan Slavic Publications.

Partee, B. & Borschev, V. 2007. Pros and cons of a type/shifting approach to Russian Genitive of Negation. In: Cate, B.D. & Zeevat, H. W. (eds), Proceedings of TbiLLC. 166/188. Berlin: Springer.

Partee, B. & Borschev, V. 2008. Existential sentences, BE and GEN NEG in Russian. In: Comorowski, I. & von Heusinger, K. (eds), *Existence: Semantics and Syntax*, 147–191. New York: Springer.

Pesetsky, D. 2013. *Russian Case Morphology and the Syntactic Categories*. Cambridge: MIT Press.

Przepiórkowski, A. 1999. Case assignment and the complement-adjunct dichotomy: A non-configurational constraint-based approach. PhD dissertation. Tübingen: The University of Tübingen.

Rappaport, G. 2001a. Extraction from Nominal Phrases in Polish and the Theory of Determiners. In: Willim, E. & Bański, P. (eds), *Formal Approaches to Polish Syntax*. Special edition of *Journal of Slavic Linguistics* 8(3): 139–198.

Rappaport. G. 2001b. The geometry of the polish nominal phrase: problems, progress, and prospects. In: Bański, P. & Przepiórkowski, A. (eds), *Generative Linguistics in Poland: Syntax and Morphosyntax*, 173–181. Warsaw: Polish Academy of Sciences.

Rutkowski, P. 2002. Noun/pronoun asymmetries: evidence in support of the DP hypothesis in Polish. *Jezikoslovlje* 3(1–2): 159–170.

Rutkowski, P. 2007. Hipoteza frazy przedimkowej jako narzędzie opisu składniowego polskich grup imiennych. PhD dissertation. Warsaw University.

Stassen, L. 2009. *Predicative Possession*. Cambridge: Cambridge University Press.

Stowell, T. 1981. The origin of phrase structure. PhD dissertation. Massachusetts Institute of Technology.

Szabolcsi, A. 1983. The possessor that ran away from home. *Linguistic Review* 3: 89–102.

Szabolcsi, A. 1985. Functional categories in the noun phrase. In: Kenesei, I. (ed.), *Approaches to Hungarian* 2: 167–189.

Szabolcsi, A. 1994. The noun phrase. In: Kiss K. É., & Kiefer, F. (eds), *The Syntactic Structure of Hungarian*. Syntax and Semantics 27, 179–274. New York: Academic Press.

Tajsner, P. 1990. Case Marking in English and Polish: A Government and Binding Study. PhD dissertation. Adam Mickiewicz University, Poznań.

Willim, E. 1989. *On Word Order. A Government-Binding Study of English and Polish*. Kraków: Wydawnictwo Naukowe Uniwersytetu Jagiellońskiego.

Witkoś, J. 1998. *The Syntax of Clitics: Steps Towards a Minimalist Account*. Poznań: Motivex.

Witkoś, J. 2003a. Nominative-to-genitive shift and the negative copula *nie ma/not is*: implications for the checking theory. *Journal of Slavic Linguistics* 10: 174–199.

Witkoś, J. 2003b. Some notes on single cycle syntax and Genitive of Negation. In: Bański, P. & Przepiórkowski, A. (eds), *Generative Linguistics in Poland: Morphosyntactic Investigations*, 167–182. Warsaw: Instytut Podstaw Informatyki Polskiej Akademii Nauk.

Zucchi, Alessandro. 1995. The ingredients of definiteness and the Definiteness Effect. *NaturalLanguage Semantics* 3: 33–78.

2. Genitive of Negation (GoN) in Polish possessive and locative existential sentences: A testing tool for case overwriting, case projections and derivational phases

Jacek Witkoś

1. Core data of the Genitive of Negation (GoN)[1]

The Polish Genitive of Negation is an obligatory process of the case shift from accusative to genitive on direct objects of transitive verbs triggered by clause negation. Thus, (1b) and (1d) show GoN, while (2) does not, as only constituent negation is involved:[2]

(1) a. Maria   czyta   gazet-ę.
        Maria.NOM reads   newspaper-ACC
        'Maria is reading a newspaper.'

    b. Maria   nie   czyta   *gazet-ę   / gazet-y.
        Maria.NOM NEG   reads   *newspaper-ACC /   newspaper-GEN
        'Maria is not reading a newspaper.'

    c. Maria   ma   gazet-ę.
        Maria.NOM has   newspaper-ACC
        'Maria has a newspaper.'

    d. Maria   nie   ma   *gazet-ę   / gazet-y.
        Maria.NOM NEG   have.3SG   *newspaper-ACC /   newspaper-GEN
        'Maria doesn't have any newspaper.'

(2)   Maria   czyta   nie   gazet-ę   ale   książk-ę.
        Maria.NOM reads   NEG   newspaper-ACC   but   book-ACC
        'Maria is not reading a book but a newspaper.'

No other cases on nominal complements of transitive verbs (here dative and instrumental) are affected by the presence of clausal negation:

(3) a. Maria   pomaga   córc-e.
       Maria.NOM   help.3SG   daughter-DAT
       'Maria is helping her daughter.'

   b. Maria   nie   pomaga   córc-e   / *córk-i.
       Maria.NOM   NEG   help.3SG   daughter-DAT / *daughter-GEN
       'Maria is helping her daughter.'

(4) a. Maria   spekulowała   akcj-ami.
       Maria.NOM   speculated   stock-INST
       'Maria speculated on stock.'

   b. Maria   nie   spekulowała   akcj-ami.
       Maria.NOM   NEG   speculated   stock-INST
       'Maria did not speculate on stock.'

Prepositional objects in accusative are not affected by clausal negation, either:

(5) a. Jan   patrzy   na   Mari-ę.
       Jan.NOM   look.3SG   on   Maria-ACC
       'Jan is looking at Maria.'

   b. Jan   nie   patrzy   na   Mari-ę /   *Mari-i.
       Jan.NOM   NEG   look.3SG   on   Maria-ACC / *Maria-GEN
       'Jan is not looking at Maria.'

In addition, the subject of locative existential constructions in Polish also changes to genitive in the scope of clause negation:

(6) a. Na stole   jest   piwo.
       on table   is   beer.NOM
       'There is beer on the table.'

   b. Na stole   nie   ma   *piwo / piw-a.
       on table   NEG   have.3SG   *beer.NOM / beer-GEN
       'There is no beer on the table.'

Interestingly, as was observed in a series of publications by Błaszczak (2008a, 2008b, 2010), the subject of 'agentive' locative constructions does not undergo GoN:

(7) a. Na przyjęciu   BYŁ   Jan.
       at party   be.PAST.3SG.M   Jan.NOM
       'As for the party, Jan was there.'

   b. Na przyjęciu   NIE   było   Jan-a.
       at party   NEG   be.PAST.3SG.N   Jan-GEN
       'As for the party, Jan was not there.'

(8) a. Jan   był   na przyjęciu.
       Jan.NOM   be.PAST.3SG.M   at party
       'Jan was at the party.'

   b. Jan   nie   był   na przyjęciu.
      Jan.NOM   NEG   be.PAST.3SG.M   at party
      'Jan was not at the party.'

In contrast to the Russian GoN, exemplified in (9), in Polish the arguments of unaccusative verbs are not subject to GoN.[3] Compare:

(9) a. V klase   pojavilis'   student-y.
       in class   appeared.3PL   student-PL.NOM
       'Students appeared in class.'
       (Russian, Borschev & Partee 2002)

   b. V klase   ne   pojavilos'   student-ov.
      in class NEG   appeared.3SG.N   students-PL.GEN
      'No students appeared in class.'

(10) a. Na zajęciach   pojawili   się   studenci.
        in class   appeared.3PL   RFL   student.PL.NOM
        'Students appeared in class.'

   b. Na zajęciach   nie   pojawili   się   studenci.
      in class   NEG   appeared.3PL   RFL   student.PL.NOM
      'No students appeared in class.'

GoN can also apply long distance, that is, negation in the main clause causes the case shift on the nominal direct object in the embedded infinitive (both in Control and Raising constructions). This is the so-called long-distance GoN (see Witkoś 1998). The presence of lexical material in the CP area (either the Complementizer or a *wh*-phrase) excludes long GoN:

(11) a. Maria$_i$ kazała Jan-owi$_j$ [PRO$_j$ czytać   listy]
        Maria.NOM   told Jan-DAT   read.INF   letters.ACC
        'Maria told Jan to read letters.'

   b. Maria$_i$ nie   kazała Jan-owi$_j$ [PRO$_j$ czytać   *list-y /
      Maria.NOM   NEG   told Jan-DAT   read.INF *letters-ACC /

      list-ów]
      letters-GEN
      'Maria did not tell Jan to read letters.'

c. Maria   nie   pozwoliła   [żeby   Jan   coś /
   Maria.NOM   NEG   allow   that   Jan.NOM   something.ACC /

   *czegoś   zabrał].
   *something.GEN took
   'Maria did not let Jan take anything.'

d. Maria   nie   wie   [komu   czytać
   Maria.NOM   NEG   know.3SG   who.DAT   read.INF

   bajki   / *bajek].
   bedtime stories.ACC   / *bedtime stories.GEN
   'Maria doesn't know whom to read bedtime stories.'

As expected, the dative nominal in the scope of negation does not shift to genitive (Jan-DAT in 11b). Interestingly, a single occurrence of clausal negation can cause multiple GoN when the indirect object is marked for accusative:

(12) a. Maria   nauczyła   Basi-ę   czytać   cyrylic-ę
        Maria.NOM   taught   Basia-ACC   read.INF   cyrillic script-ACC
        'Maria taught Basia to read the Russian alphabet.'

     b. Maria   nie   nauczyła   Bas-i
        Maria.NOM   NEG   taught   Basia-GEN

        czytać   cyrylic-y.
        read.INF   cyrillic script-GEN
        'Maria did not teach Basia to read the Russian alphabet.'

In the remainder of this chapter, I shall present a number of proposals accounting for these facts which are descriptively adequate and draw from different conceptual inspirations, couched in a broadly conceived minimalist framework. In the process, a number of alternatives are considered and an impact of the long-distance GoN for the notion of the derivational phase (Chomsky 2000, 2001, 2008) is assessed briefly.[4]

2. Genitive of Negation and two types of locative constructions

Witkoś (1998, 2003a, b) proposes a technical account of GoN based on the idea of the 'split' probe: Neg and v constitute two halves of a probe and they both jointly act upon the NP object in their c-domain:

(13) a. Maria   ma   gazet-ę.
        Maria.NOM   have.3SG   newspaper-ACC.F
        'Maria has a newspaper.'

     b. Maria   nie   ma   gazet-y.
        Maria.NOM   NEG   have.3SG   newspaper-GEN.F
        'Maria does not have a newspaper.'

(14) a. [Neg [v [V NP]]]
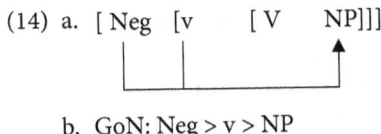

b. GoN: Neg > v > NP

So the GoN appears in the following configuration: Neg > v > NP; Neg locally c-commands v, which locally c-commands NP, where 'locally' implies that the NP goal and the 'split' probe Neg/v are placed in the same derivational domain. This scenario is obvious for (1) and the plain transitive possessive construction. It also tacitly assumes that there is a non-trivial difference between Polish and English, where only v and T are structural case probes. Oblique cases do not show the GoN in this account, as their status is very different. This is in line with Chomsky (1981) and Babby (1980). These cases are intrinsically connected with thematic relations holding between the predicates and their arguments and so, as markers of these thematic relations, they remain unaffected by any structural or grammatical factors.

Locative existential constructions receive a slightly different treatment in Witkoś (2003a), where the theme NP is taken to originate in [Spec, PP] of the PP location. In the affirmative variant *być* 'be' is unaccusative and does not license any case on the theme NP as a bare V, see (15). In the negative variant, a French-type *pro* appears, which, unlike expletive *there*, bears a full set of φ-features (3SG.NEUT), has its case valued as nominative by T and values its uninterpretable φ-features in return. The existential verb is more complex, as it is a v-V complex head licensing partitive case on the theme NP. The placement of Negation creates the configuration consistent with (14) above and genitive surfaces on the NP:

(15) a. Na stole   była   szklanka.
     on table   be.PAST.3SG.F   glass.3SG.F.NOM
     'There was a glass on the table.'

b. [ToP PP Top [TP T [VP be-V [PP NP [PP]]]]]
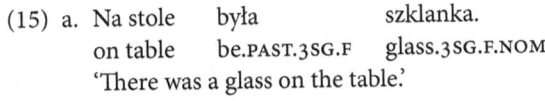

(16) a. Na stole   nie   było   szklanki.
     on table   NEG   be.PAST3.SG.N   glass.3SG.F.GEN
     'There was no glass on the table.'

b. [ToP PP Top [TP T [NegP Neg-nie [vP pro v[PART] [VP be-V [PP NP [PP]]]]]]]
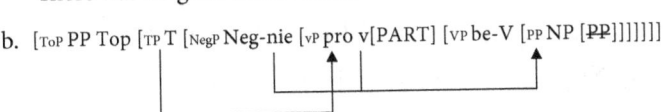

In this analysis, both (15) and (16) show two general versions of existential locative constructions. The affirmative sentence in (15) shows the version with unaccusative *be* and the subject that bears NOM, licensed by $T_{[Fin]}$ via Agree (the English style existential construction, see Chomsky 1986, 1995). The negated sentence in (16b) shows the Romance-type existential construction, in which the expletive (*pro*) bears NOM and the verb licenses partitive (genitive) on the associate (*szklanki* 'glass'). For similar analyses, see Belletti (1988), Lasnik (1995) and Hornstein & Witkoś (2003).

Significantly, in both analyses the associate starts in the object position which is c-commanded by both Neg and v (two halves of the split probe).[5]

However, Witkoś (1998, 2003a) excludes cases such as (8b) from the scope of investigation. Here, NP does not shift to genitive and this type of locative construction is discussed extensively in Błaszczak (2008a, b, 2010). Błaszczak observes that locative existential constructions must be distinguished from what she calls 'agentive' locative constructions. She proposes the following underlying representations for both, where v-V spells out as *być* 'be':

(17) a. $[_{vP} PP_{LOC} [_{v'} v [_{VP} V NP_{THEME}]]]$

b. $[_{vP} NP_{AGENT} [_{v'} v [_{VP} V PP_{LOC}]]]$

She treats (17a-b) as a syntactic expression of two alternative conceptual representations of existential/locative constructions proposed in Borschev & Partee (2002) and based on the notion of the Perspectival Centre. These authors claim that in structures with BE (and its close verbal cognates referring to existence or location) two participants are obligatory, THING and LOC:

(18) *Perspective Structure:*

In the following the underlined participant constitutes the Perspectival Centre:

a. Be (<u>THING</u>, LOC): structure of the interpretation of a Locative (Declarative) sentence;

b. Be (THING, <u>LOC</u>): structure of the interpretation of an Existential sentence.

Additionally, Borschev & Partee (2002) assume that the Perspectival Centre must be presupposed to exist, so it is in a way thematic by default. Their broad conceptual-semantic representation in (18a) corresponds to Błaszczak's agentive locative construction and its syntax in (17b), whereas their representation in (18b) corresponds to the syntax of the existential locative construction in (17a). In some sense, the representation in (18b/17a) says that location, expressed by the PP, has (contains) or does not have the THEME NP in it. It is immediately clear that our GoN licensing formula in (14) predicts that the GoN should apply in (19a) but not in (19b):

(19) a. $[_{NegP} Neg [_{vP} PP_{LOC} [_{v'} v [_{VP} V NP_{THEME}]]]]$ locative existential

b. $[_{NegP} Neg [_{vP} NP_{AGENT} [_{v'} v [_{VP} V PP_{LOC}]]]]$ 'agentive' locative

In (19a) the NP_{THEME} is c-commanded by both halves of the 'split' probe Neg/v, while in (19b) it is not: NP_{THEME} is c-commanded by Neg but it c-commands v-V (Neg > NP > v > V). Thus, an engineering account for lack of GoN in (8) is provided, but a principled justification for the difference between (19a) and (19b) is required.

The syntactic representation suggested in (19) is also supposed to match a semantic distinction between elements showing existential presupposition and the ones that do not show it. This is known from the discussion of GoN in Russian in Kagan (2013), where it is compared to the Genitive of Irrealis[6]:

(20) a. Ivan   iščet   ubežišče.
       Ivan   seeks   shelter.ACC
       'Ivan is looking for a/the shelter.'

   b. Ivan   iščet   ubežišča.
      Ivan   seeks   shelter.GEN
      'Ivan is looking for a shelter.'

The use of accusative in (20a) implies that Ivan has a particular location in mind (specific/definite), while the use of genitive in (20b) implies that any shelter will do. Kagan submits that the genitive or nominative on the subject in the locative construction is also a reflex of one's commitment to the existence of a given person/object at a particular location. In (21a) Ivan's existence at a particular location is not presupposed, while in (21b) Ivan's existence is presupposed by the speaker but his exact location in the room is denied:

(21) a. Ivana   ne   bylo   v komnate.
       Ivan.GEN   not   was3.SG.N in room
       'There was no trace of Ivan in the room.'

   b. Ivan   ne   byl   v komnate.
      Ivan.NOM   not   was3.SG.M in room
      'Ivan not was in the room.'

I believe that the assumption of a structure such as (19) allows us to formulate a syntactic explanation matching the semantic one put forward by Kagan: nominal elements (DP/NP) which are interpreted as presupposed/specific/definite occupy a different syntactic position from the non-presupposed/nonspecific/indefinite ones at a relevant step in the derivation. Hence, different interpretations are fed by distinct representations. For instance, placement of an argument within VP and interpretation of its A-chain there is a steadfast syntactic indication of what is to come in semantics: non-presuppositionality/non-specificity/indefiniteness, see Diesing (1992). Such is the position of the argument in (19a). On the other hand, placement of the nominal argument outside VP, as in example (19b), allows for its presupposed/specific/definite reading.

Furthermore, it is a well-known fact that the distinction in terms of specificity shows in the Russian GoN, too:

(22) a. Boris   ne   cital   pismo.
       Boris.NOM   not   read   letter.ACC
       'Boris did not read the letter.'

   b. Boris   ne   cital   pisma.
      Boris.NOM   not   read   letter.GEN
      'Boris did not read a letter.'

   c. [$_{TP}$ Boris T [$_{NegP}$ Neg [$_{vP}$ pismo [$_{v'}$ Boris [$_{v'}$ v [$_{VP}$ V pismo]]]]]]

One of the possible structural accounts for the interpretive difference here is to propose that the definite NP/DP participates in A-movement that carries it from the thematic position within VP to its case position in [spec,vP/AgroP], outside VP, see (22c). This is in fact the gist of the classic proposals in Bailyn (1995) and Brown (1999).[7] Thus, a structural parallel outlined in example (19) and in (25) below should hold. The contrast in (22) is absent from Polish, where the local GoN is obligatory and independent of the specificity/definiteness status of the DP/NP.[8]

Błaszczak (2008a, b, 2010) convincingly shows that the 'agentive' locative BE-construction differs from the locative existential one in a number of ways. First, it appears with the *po-* prefix, which, according to Piňon (1994) implies an agent. Significantly, GoN cannot apply to the NP argument here, see (23b), and the agentive interpretation is compatible with nominative in the context of clausal negation, see (23c)[9]:

(23) a. Bożenka   po-była   wczoraj   u Irenki.
       Bożenka.NOM   PFX-was   yesterday   at Irenka
       'Bożenka was at Irenka's place for a while yesterday.'

   b. *Bożenk-i   nie   po-było   wczoraj   u Irenki.
       Bożenka-GEN NEG   PFX-was3SG.N   yesterday   at Irenka
       ('intended: Bożenka was not at Irenka's place for a while yesterday.')

   c. Bożenka   nie   po-była   wczoraj   u Irenki
       Bożenka.NOM NEG   PFX-was3SG.N   yesterday   at Irenka

       ani   na chwilę.
       not   for minute
       'Bożenka was not at Irenka's place yesterday even for a while.'

Second, the 'agentive' locative construction is compatible with agent-oriented adverbs[10]:

(24) a. Jan   chętnie   był   w domu.
       Jan.NOM   willingly   be.PAST3SG.M   at home
       'Jan was at home willingly.'

   b. Jan   nie   był   chętnie   w domu.
       Jan.NOM   NEG   be.PAST3SG.M   willingly   at home
       'Jan was not at home willingly.'

   c. ??W domu   chętnie   był   Jan.
       at home   willingly   be.PAST3SG.M   Jan.NOM
       'At home, Jan was willingly.'

   d. *W domu   nie   było   chętnie   Jan-a.
       at home   NEG   be.PAST3SG.N   willingly   Jan-GEN
       'At home, there was no Jan willingly.'

   e. *Jan-a   nie   było   chętnie   w domu.
       Jan-GEN   NEG   be.PAST.3SG.N   willingly   at home
       'At home, there was no Jan willingly.'

Third, the subject of the 'agentive' locative construction can function as controller for PRO in a purpose adverbial infinitive clause, as in (25a). The regular theme NP showing GoN cannot perform this function, see (25b):

(25) a. Jan   nie   był   w szkole żeby [PRO
       Jan.NOM   NEG   be.PAST3SG.M   in school in order

       uniknąć   sprawdzianu].
       avoid.INF   test.GEN
       'Jan was (deliberately) not at school in order to avoid the test.'

   b. *Jan-a   nie   było   w szkole żeby [PRO
       Jan-GEN   NEG   be.PAST.3SG.N   in school in order

       uniknąć   sprawdzianu].
       avoid.INF   test.GEN
       'There was no (trace of) Jan at school in order to avoid the test.'

Furthermore, the agentive locative construction can feature the habitual form *bywać* 'be-HAB' while the locative existential cannot:

(26) a. Jan   bywał   na przyjęciach.
       Jan.NOM   be.PAST3SG.M.HAB   at parties
       'Jan was at parties from time to time.'

   b. Jan   nie   bywał   na przyjęciach.
       Jan.NOM   NEG   be.PAST3SG.M.HAB   at parties
       (Lit. 'Jan was not in the habit of going to parties.')
       'Jan didn't go to parties from time to time.'

   c. *Jan-a   nie   bywało   na przyjęciach.
       Jan-GEN NEG   be.PAST3SG.N.HAB   at parties
       (Lit. 'Jan was not in the habit of going to parties.')
       'Jan didn't go to parties from time to time.'

Finally, according to the theory of nominalization in Grimshaw (1990), nominalization, just like passivization, affects only unergative predicates and the 'agentive' locative copula, specifically in its habitual variant, looks like a good candidate for nominalization. At the same time, the unaccusative locative existential verb does not. This prediction is confirmed:

(27) a. Bywanie   Jan-a   w nocnych klubach   (zaskoczyło wszystkich).
       being   Jan-GEN   in night clubs   (surprised all)
       'Jan's frequent stays at night clubs surprised all.'

   b. **Bycie   gazet-y   na stole   (zaskoczyło mnie).
       being   newspaper-GEN on table   (surprised me)
       'The newspaper's being on the table surprised me.'

The five differences illustrated above warrant the assumption concerning the structural distinction between locative existential and 'agentive' locative constructions in Polish, with predictable consequences for the case licensing on the NP argument, despite the unfortunate circumstance that locative *być* 'be' in Polish projects vP whose head is bleached of any case licensing potential in the affirmative.[11] Let me then follow Błaszczak's analysis and settle for the following general picture of the GoN contexts, where (28a)–(28b) provide for the relevant configuration, whereas (28d) does not, and GoN does not apply to the 'agentive' subject of the locative construction[12, 13]:

(28) a. $[_{NegP}$ Neg $[_{vP}$ NP$_{AGENT}$ (POSSESSOR) $[_{v'}$ v$[_{vP}$ V NP$_{THEME}$]]]]
    transitive possessive

b. $[_{NegP}$ Neg $[_{vP}$ PP$_{LOC}$ $[_{v'}$ v $[_{vP}$ V NP$_{THEME}$]]]]
    locative existential

c. GoN: Neg > v > NP

d. $[_{NegP}$ Neg $[_{vP}$ NP$_{AGENT}$ $[_{v'}$ v $[_{vP}$ V PP$_{LOC}$]]]]
    'agentive' locative

3. GoN as a result of overwriting and 'peeling' of case projections

This section explores two recent approaches to the issue of nominal case: Pesetsky's (2013) case overwriting and Caha's (2009) case 'peeling'. Both approaches seem to depart from the typical current mainstream model of Agree-based minimalism and open new perspectives on how GoN should be dealt with.

3.1. Case overwriting (Pesetsky 2013)

In this section, the phenomenon of GoN is viewed from the perspective of a novel approach to case in Slavic offered by Pesetsky (2013). The core assumptions of Pesetsky's radical system is that particular grammatical categories bear certain cases as their signature property:

(29) a. N = GEN

b. D = NOM

c. V = ACC

d. P = OBL(ique)

These categories assign their case feature to all dependents they subcategorize for and merge with in line with the following principle:

(30) Feature assignment (Pesetsky 2013: 99):

    a. Copying: when α merges with β, forming [$_α$ α, β], if β has satisfied its complementation requirements and α is designated as a feature assigner for β, its prototype α* is immediately merged with β, forming [$_α$ α [$_β$ α* β]].

    b. Realization: A prototype x* is realized adjacent to the smallest element dominated by its sister.[14]

As Merge is cyclic and structure is built incrementally, every subsequent instance of merge overwrites the case assigned by a previous merge. Thus, in the oblique case environment, the relevant structure and history of derivation looks as follows:

(31) o   pjati   xorošix   devuškax
      about five.ABL good.ABL girls.ABL
      'about five good girls' (Russian)

(32) a. [NP$_{GEN}$ Q$_{GEN}$ AP$_{GEN}$ [NP$_{GEN}$]]

    b. [$_{DPNOM}$ [Q$_{NOM}$ - D$_{NOM}$] [NP$_{GEN}$ Q AP$_{GEN}$ [NP$_{GEN}$]]]

    c. P$_{OBL}$ → [DP$_{OBL}$ [Q$_{OBL}$ - D$_{OBL}$] [NP$_{OBL}$ Q AP$_{OBL}$ [NP$_{OBL}$]]]

In (31–32), locative is a concrete Spell-Out of the more general oblique case and it applies to the entire nominal sister constituent to P. In the process, it overwrites previous cases resulting from both internal and external merge: nominative on D (see 32b) and genitive on NP (32a). The case on every constituent that was merged in earlier is overwritten by subsequent applications of Feature Assignment unless a given constituent undergoes Spell-Out and is transferred out of the narrow syntax as a separate Spell-Out domain/phase.

An important strength of Pesetsky's (2013) approach shows in the extensive discussion of the puzzling pattern of case marking attested in nominal constructions with higher numerals (five and above) in Polish (the Genitive of Quantification, GoQ):

(33) a. pięć   studentek
         five.ACC students.GEN.F
         'five students'

    b. pięciu   studentkom
         five.DAT students.DAT.F
         'to five students'

This analysis of the Polish GoQ is modelled on Pesetsky's solution for an equivalent construction in Russian:

(34) QUANT-to-D movement in Polish GoQ modelled on (Pesetsky 2013: 26):

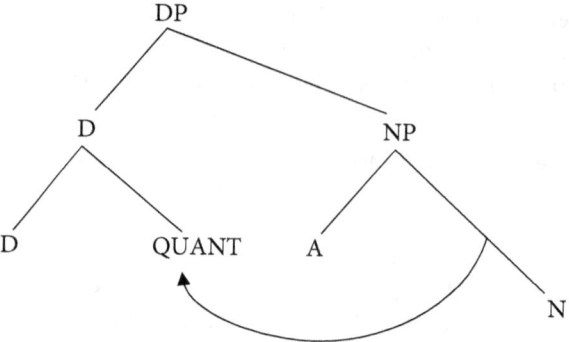

D selects for an NP complement but this does not satisfy its selection requirements (35a) and it attracts a higher numeral (QH) to (under)merge with it (35b):

(35) a. [$_{DP}$ D [$_{NP}$ A QUANT N]]

b. [$_{DP}$ [$_D$ D QUANT] [$_{NP}$ A ~~QUANT~~ N]]

Initially, D and NP merge but D bears a feature forcing the movement of QUANT to re-merge with it. Thus, QUANT moves from within NP and merges with D to satisfy this requirement. This form of movement is called UNDERMERGE. The numeral merges with D and satisfies its complementation requirements on the strength of (30), which results in feature copying. The numeral receives nominative, the signature property of D, while the (former complement) NP remains in its primary case (genitive) because upon merger with D it did not satisfy D's complementation requirements, and so feature copying did not apply.

It must be observed straight away that UNDERMERGE shows peculiar transfer-like consequences. A technical consequence of forming the complex object [$_D$ D QUANT] is to place the first-merged constituent (NP) in a limbo, out of the reach of Feature Application of D without spelling it out, though for all intents and purposes it is as if spelled-out and beyond the reach of D. But it is certainly not spelled-out in the standard sense, as shown in (31) and (32). Feature Application from P, a source of an oblique case, does indeed access both D and its NP-complement and overwrites the previous genitive case as oblique (here locative). We are then looking at a fairly uncommon syntactic context, where a given domain becomes opaque (island-like) with respect to a closer, more minimal Probe (NP is opaque to the complex [$_D$ D QUANT]) but opens up and becomes transparent to a more distant one (cf. 31–32).

Let me now try to construct a scenario in which the case overwriting account is applied to account for the GoN. It opens at least two possibilities for an analysis of GoN: one relies on sequential case overwriting within a stretch of structure that constitutes a single Spell-Out domain and applies UNDERMERGE:

(36) Sequential overwriting: GEN → ACC → GEN (see (1))
Maria   [$_{NegP}$ nie$_{GEN}$ [$_{VP}$ V$_{ACC}$ czyta [$_{NP}$ gazet-ę   / gazet-y]]].
Maria.NOM   not   reads   *newspaper-ACC / newspaper-GEN

(37) Neg undermerge

a. [$_{VP}$ VA$_{CC}$ [$_{NP}$ Neg N$_{GEN}$]]

b. [$_{VP}$ [$_V$ V$_{ACC}$ Neg] [$_{NP}$ ~~Neg~~ N$_{GEN}$]]

c. Maria   [$_{VP}$ V$_{ACC}$ czyta   [$_{NP}$ nie NEG gazet-y]]
   Maria.NOM   read   not   newspaper-GEN

d. Maria   [$_{VP}$ nie NEG V$_{ACC}$ czyta [$_{NP}$ ~~nie~~ NEG gazet-ę / gazet-y]]
   Maria.NOM   not   -reads   ~~not~~ *newspaper-ACC/newspaper-GEN
   'Maria is not reading a newspaper.'

Let me first turn to the application of UNDERMERGE in (37) in an attempt of assimilating the Genitive of Negation to the genitive of quantification.[15] In (37a) the negative element is first merged as a constituent of NP, which reflects the case of constituent negation in (2). Subsequently, the verb is merged in and it subcategorizes for the Neg element, possibly via an abstract NEG feature, necessary for derivation of negative clauses. As a result, the Neg element itself absorbs the accusative case feature of V, while the NP complement is left in its primary genitive, see (29). In the affirmative clause scenario there is no NEG element within the NP, as well as no NEG feature on V, so NP satisfies its subcategorization requirements and gets assigned the feature accusative, as a signature property of a transitive verb. In the scenario of constituent negation (2), there is no NEG feature on V (it is responsible for clausal negation), so again, the NP constituent [$_{NP}$ nie gazet-y] 'not newspaper-GEN' is subcategorized by the transitive verb and the primary genitive is overwritten with accusative.

There is, however, an obvious problem with applying UNDERMERGE to account for the GoN. As (11b) shows, the GoN has its long-distance variant, where negation placed on the main clause predicate forces genitive on the object of the embedded verb in infinitival constructions. As UNDERMERGE is related to selection and subcategorization, it is expected to apply only very locally across adjacent constituents. NEG-movement driven by long-distance subcategorization would be quite idiosyncratic.

The option of sequential overwriting in (36) appears to be more promising. In this derivation, the primary genitive on NP is overwritten by accusative assigned upon merge by the transitive verb, which in turn is overwritten by clausal negation subcategorizing for VP. On the face of it, (2) and (3) seem to pose a challenge here: why does Genitive of Negation not overwrite an accusative (or any other case) inside PP and why does it not overwrite cases other than accusative (and nominative in the existential/locative construction in 8b)? A possible answer is that these constituents are from independent phases. Pesetsky stresses the functional aspect of the phase, i.e. a constituent of a given category does not undergo transfer unless all relevant features within it have been checked and valued, which certainly depends on a wider syntactic context in which this constituent is placed. Pesetsky (2013: 89) defines the phase as follows:

(38) DP undergoes Spell-Out only after it is Vergnaud-licensed (i.e. case-marked).

He allows for a delay in the application of Spell-Out, which does not have to set in immediately, as soon as an appropriate configuration is formed. For instance, in the following construction involving a small clause, its DP-subject needs to wait to receive case for quite a few derivational steps: first, the DP must be constructed (and for Pesetsky DP bears nominative as its signature property, see (29)), next, it is embedded in the AP and, ultimately, in the matrix VP.

(39) Ja   sčitaju   [$_{AP}$ [$_{DP}$èt-u   lamp-u]   krasiv-oj]
     I   consider   this-ACC.F   lamp-ACC.F   beautiful.F.INST.SG
     'I consider this lamp beautiful.'
     (Russian, Pesetsky 2013: 36)

The definition in (38) recognizes a variable point of execution of Spell-Out and, in this respect, it is similar in spirit to the one in Svenonius (2004) and quite distinct from the rigid definition of the application of Spell-Out in Chomsky (2000, 2001, 2008, 2013, 2015):

(40) A straightforward assumption is that a phase is spelled out when all uninterpretable features on its head are checked (Svenonius 2004: 264).

In fact, Pesetsky's system must be even more liberal than (38) and (40), as the transfer does not apply as soon as the case features are checked/valued, as case overwriting implies multiple case feature satisfaction. The transfer cannot apply either too soon or too late, as examples (31) and (32) show. In particular, both GEN on the NP-complement and NOM on the DP are overwritten by an oblique case (locative) despite the fact that these domains have already been licensed for case(s). Thus, if Spell-Out were to apply to the NP or DP earlier, the oblique case could not spread over these domains. On the other hand, Spell-Out must apply relatively early in the case of adnominal genitive constructions:

(41) [$_{PP}$ k [$_{DP}$ D [$_{NP}$ krasiv-omu   stol-u   [$_{DP}$ molod-ogo   aktër-a]]]]
     to   beautiful-DAT.F   table-DAT.M   young-GEN.M   actor-GEN.M
     'to the young actor's beautiful table'

If it had not applied, the adnominal genitive should be overwritten by the case signature of an external category the containing DP is merged with, contrary to fact.

Thus, if a liberal policy towards the timing of the application of Spell-Out is a property of the theory of case designed in Pestetsky (2013), then assuming that PPs constitute derivational phases does not contradict the system.[16] Consequently, if we assume that PPs in general constitute separate phases and Spell-Out domains, then the

Genitive of Negation cannot overwrite any case assigned within a PP. What is more, if oblique cases are licensed by silent prepositions, the same solution applies to (3) and (4). So, it seems that Pesetsky's (2013) case overwriting approach can be employed to account for the core cases of the GoN, although a liberal application of Spell-Out detracts from the elegance of the system.

3.2. Case as a functional projection

The nano-syntactic model (see Starke 2009; Caha 2009, 2010, 2013) provides the means to derive various case patterns allowing for the movement of the NP within the set of case projections. The analysis of the position of the nominal head with respect to its satellites (demonstratives, numerals, adjectives) is based on Cinque (2005, 2010); certain types of movement are restricted, i.e. rightward and downward movements are forbidden, typically only a chunk of the structure including the nominal head can be moved. The essential component of the analysis is the premise that particular morphological cases are matched to precise positions within an articulated set of case projections which belongs to the extended projection of the noun (its Kase sequence, Kseq). In order to acquire a given case, typically expressed by a proper suffix in Slavic, the nominal merges in the structure uninflected and moves to a position c-commanding a given case head. The case sequence and ordering of cases is uniform across languages and is stated in the *Universal Case Contiguity* (Blake 1994; Caha 2009):

(42) comitative > instrumental > dative > genitive > accusative > nominative [noun]

(43) a. $[_{InstP}$ Inst $[_{DatP}$ Dat $[_{GenP}$ Gen $[_{AccP}$ Acc $[_{NomP}$ NP [Nom [~~NP~~]]]]]]]

b. $[_{InstP}$ Inst $[_{DatP}$ Dat $[_{GenP}$ Gen $[_{AccP}$ NP [Acc $[_{NomP}$ Nom [~~NP~~]]]]]]]

c. $[_{InstP}$ Inst [DatP Dat $[_{GenP}$ NP [Gen $[_{AccP}$ Acc $[_{NomP}$ Nom [~~NP~~]]]]]]]

d. $[_{InstP}$ Inst $[_{DatP}$ NP [Dat $[_{GenP}$ Gen $[_{AccP}$ Acc $[_{NomP}$ Nom [~~NP~~]]]]]]]

e. $[_{InstP}$ NP [Inst $[_{DatP}$ Dat $[_{GenP}$ Gen $[_{AccP}$ Acc $[_{NomP}$ Nom [~~NP~~]]]]]]]

As the structures in (42) and (43) show, nominative and accusative are placed as two adjacent lowest cases in the sequence, which indicates that they are the least marked cases set apart from the oblique ones, which are usually morphologically more complex (Caha 2009). Also, case syncretisms are predicted to occur on adjacent cases/nodes. In general, the nano-syntactic approach to case predicts that nominals in Slavic wear their cases on their sleeve in the sense that the NP moves overtly to a given position within the set of case projections (Kseq).

Caha (2009) develops a particular theory of case-driven movement called 'peeling'. In the position of the first merge in the thematic position NP appears with a full Kseq as in (44). Next, the case probe (K-selector in Caha's terms) forces a movement of the selected portion of the Kseq, including NP (as in Cinque 2005, 2010). So, v is a K-selector for AccP and an object of this size is moved to [Spec,vP], stranding ('peeling') all case projections above it to be spelled-out as some morphological material, possibly nought, see (45). All the projections below Acc are carried along to be spelled out as the accusative suffix after NP moves to B above the position of Acc, see (46):

(44) ([$_{vP}$ v ...[$_{VP}$ V [6 [$_{Com}$ F [5 [$_{Inst}$ E[4 [$_{Dat}$ D [3 [$_{Gen}$ C [2 [$_{Acc}$ B [1 [$_{Nom}$ [$_{NP}$ N...]]]]]]]]]]]]]]

(45) [$_{vP}$ [2 [$_{Acc}$ B [1 [$_{Nom}$ [$_{NP}$ N...]]]]] v [$_{VP}$ V [6 [$_{Com}$ F [5 [$_{Ins}$ E[4 [$_{Dat}$ D [3 [$_{Gen}$ C]]]]]]]]]

(46) [$_{vP}$ [[NP N...] [$_{Acc}$ B [1 [$_{Nom}$ [NP N...]]]]] v [$_{VP}$ V [6 [$_{Com}$ F [5 [$_{Ins}$ E[4 [$_{Dat}$ D [3 [$_{Gen}$ C]]]]]]]]]

For the analysis at hand, let me incorporate mostly the syntactic aspect of nano-syntax. As for the spell-out of case on concording modifiers, I take it to follow the general outline presented in Pesetsky (2013) and Norris (2014).

Let me adapt Caha's theory to the task of dealing with GoN in the following manner. I assume that the NP headed by the noun with [+N] feature has its case valued under Agree. The [+EPP] property of the head housing the probe (or the selector in Caha's terms) forces the raising of the relevant section of the Kseq, in line with (45). Next, the NP moves up to a given position within the case projection domain (Kseq). This movement constitutes the syntactic realization of case within the extended functional projection of the NP.[17] This is an attempt at incorporating the detailed syntax of case with the syntax of larger components including the nominal (the phrase and the clause) in a manner compatible with phase theory. I also propose the following extension to plain case valuation:

(47) Case licensing procedure:

  a. case valuation (Agree P, G)

  b. case realization (NP raising to the vicinity of the Probe and NP raising within domain within Kseq)

  c. case feature on NP active until realized

Upon the merger of an NP with a full inventory of cases (Kseq) with the probe, v-V or P, (a) the probe values case, and (b) once a concrete case is identified (depending on the probe/selector) a relevant Case Projection within Kseq becomes activated and attracts the NP. I assume that in this derivation the case head affects the entire phrase and the suffix must be appended not only to the final nominal position in the phrase but it must also spread onto the numeral/adjective/demonstrative, in the spirit of (30b) above. The step of case realization through the movement of NP plus assorted functional categories to the specifier of a given Case Projection is not as an additional device but it is a mandatory step for the process of NP-internal case concord to take place. The syntactic derivation hands over the NP structure to the morphological component of grammar following case realization.

In such an approach, GoN could be taken to constitute a correlation between valuation and realization of case:

(48) The two-step case licensing rule:

   a. structural case probes: v, T

   b. realize 'v case' as ACC, realize 'T case' as NOM

   c. NP is (case) active until its case is fully licensed (both valued and realized)

(49) Polarity Phrase:

   a. positive: realize valued 'v case' as it is (no extra upgrading step in NP movement)

   b. negative: preferably realize valued 'v case' as Gen (extra upgrading step in NP movement)

Thus, GoN would not be an independently valued case but rather it would be a realization of accusative and nominative under the scope of negation. Neg is not an independent probe/selector for case here but rather a modifier of the case valued by v. Although this position seems to complicate case relations, it has at least two advantages.

First, it means that the head of the Polarity Phrase is not a case probe, nor is it a component of a 'split' probe. Consequently, case valuation would look the same for Polish and English (with no split probes). Instead, the difference lies in the syntax of case realization (Kseq).[18]

Second, a uniform treatment of all verbal predicates in the context of negation is possible now, because the geometry of the Kseq allows for the realization of accusative as genitive but it does not allow for the realization of dative or instrumental as genitive, as these case positions are placed higher than the position for the genitive in the Kseq. As case realization is achieved via movement obeying the rules of syntax, lowering is not allowed. (50) illustrates the licensing of accusative, v is the Probe. It accesses NP in (50a) and requires its movement to [Spec, AccP] in (50b). The following merger of the positive variant of the head of the Polarity Phrase does not require the NP to be raised any further within the Kseq. Finally, v acts as the case-attractor triggering movement to [Spec, vP] of the NP object with the accusative-licensing section of the Kseq (AccP), see (50c). The Kseq structure c-commanded by NP spells out as the accusative suffix:

(50) a. Pol(Pos/Neg) v [Kseq ... [GenP Gen [AccP Acc [NomP Nom [NP]]]]]

   b. v [Kseq...[GenP Gen [AccP NP Acc [NomP Nom [N̶P̶]]]]]

   c. [$_{vP}$ [$_{AccP}$ NP [$_{NomP}$ Nom [N̶P̶]] Acc] v]

When the Polarity Phrase is headed by negation, it forces the extra step of movement for the NP from [Spec, AccP] to [Spec, GenP] at the stage of case realization, see (51a). Subsequently, GenP is raised to [Spec, vP] and the section of the Kseq c-commanded by NP spells out as genitive:

(51) a. Neg v   [...[$_{GenP}$ NP Gen [$_{AccP}$ N̶P̶ Acc [$_{NomP}$ Nom [N̶P̶]]]]

b. [$_{vP}$ [$_{GenP}$ NP [$_{Gen}$ [$_{AccP}$ N̶P̶ [$_{NomP}$ Nom [N̶P̶]] Acc] v]]]

However, the extra step of NP movement within the Kseq is not possible when the case licensing head selects for a case whose projection includes GenP, for instance dative. In this case, the extra step of case realization triggered by negation would have to involve a lowering movement, an option which is not provided for in this system:

(52) a. Pos v   [$_{DatP}$ NP Dat [$_{GenP}$ Gen [$_{AccP}$ Acc [$_{NomP}$ Nom [N̶P̶]]]]]

b. *Neg v   [$_{DatP}$ NP Dat [$_{GenP}$ Gen [$_{AccP}$ Acc [$_{NomP}$ Nom [N̶P̶]]]]]

The general geometry of the Kseq, the arrangement of case positions in a particular order and the movement of the NP within the Kseq make the nano-syntactic theory of case projections a credible vehicle for accounting for the local cases of the GoN. Unlike the theory of general case overwriting discussed in the previous section, the theory based on case projections makes a clear prediction as to which cases can be replaced by Genitive of Negation: only the ones whose projections are c-commanded by the projection of the genitive case.

At the same time, it is possible to find relations where NPs are moved from positions of 'larger' cases to positions of 'smaller' ones. Caha (2010) refers to such movement relations as sub-extraction; a coherent smaller sequence in the Kseq, including NP, is moved out of the entire Kseq. Typically, the higher the movement, the smaller the Kseq moved along, with passive serving as a perfect example where only the smallest bottom-most case projection is carried along while others are 'peeled off' and spelled out. Significantly, the 'smaller' case must be selected and called for by an independent higher selector.

For instance, such an intricate 'peeling' analysis is offered for the directional/locative preposition alternation in German in Caha (2010), corresponding to the case mentioned in fn. 11:

(53) a. [XP [P-LocP in] X [Asp-LocP [$_{DatP}$ dem Zimmer] [Asp-Loc' [P-LocP i̶n̶]]]]

b. [YP [XP in] Y [$_{PathP}$ [$_{AccP}$ das Zimmer [Path' Path [XP [P-locP i̶n̶] X [Asp-LocP [$_{DatP}$ d̶e̶m̶ ̶Z̶i̶m̶m̶e̶r̶] [Asp-Loc' [P-LocP i̶n̶]]]]

In the locative construction in (53a) the NP placed in the Dative Phrase initially occupies the position of the specifier of the locative projection [Spec, Asp-locP]. The locative adposition moves across it to XP. Next, once the directional element Path has been merged in (53b), it attracts the accusative NP to its specifier, which means that a section of the Kseq of DatP subextracts and AccP moves to [Spec, PathP], see (42) and (43). Subsequently, the remnant movement of XP brings it to [Spec,YP], where XP is spelled out as *in*. It is important to note that the sub-extraction of the [AccP NP] out of [DatP NP] is caused by movement to Path, a selector and target independent and separate from Location, calling for [DatP NP].

Now, let us return to GoN. According to the set of assumptions above, if NEG were an independent selector from the verb, a similar sub-extraction would be expected in (52) (so, in fact, a mirror image of GoN would emerge, where 'bigger' oblique cases feed sub-extraction, and GoN and 'smaller' structural do not). But lack of sub-extraction and no further peeling of Kseq layers here seem to show that NEG does not act as an independent case selector but only modifies the selection performed by the verb (v-V), as proposed above.

4. The long-distance GoN and the derivational phase

This final section is devoted to a discussion of the impact of long-distance GoN on the definition of the derivational phase. Consider a case below, where negation on the main clause predicate predictably impacts the case of the direct object of the embedded verb:

(54) Maria   nie   kazała   [Jan-owi   czytać   *list-y   / list-ów]
     Maria.NOM   NEG   told   Jan-DAT   read.INF   *letters-ACC / letters-GEN]
     'Maria did not tell Jan to read letters.'

(54) is taken to instantiate an Agree relationship between a probe (Neg) and a goal (the NP), which constitutes a prima facie challenge to the rigid formulation of the Phase Impenetrability Condition (PIC):

(55) *Phase Impenetrability Condition (PIC)*

    a. The domain of H is not accessible to operations at ZP (with ZP the smallest strong phase), only H and its edge are accessible to such operations (Chomsky 2001: 14).

    b. Interpretation / evaluation of phase α takes place uniformly at the next higher phrase, i.e. Ph1 is interpreted/evaluated at the next relevant phase Ph2 (Chomsky 2001: 13).

    c. $[_{ZP} Z...[_{HP} α [_H YP]]]$ with ZP and HP as strong phases (Chomsky 2001: 14).

When the CP projection and Polarity Phrase (the minimal maximal projection including both parts of the 'split' probe) are taken to constitute derivational phases, (54) has the following partial representation:

(56) 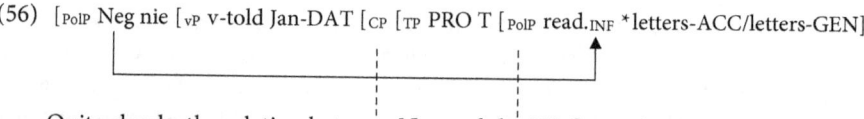[PolP Neg nie [vP v-told Jan-DAT [CP [TP PRO T [PolP read.INF *letters-ACC/letters-GEN]

Quite clearly, the relation between Neg and the NP flouts the PIC in (55).[19]

At this stage, several options present themselves. One alternative, ultimately adopted independently in Błaszczak (2001) and Witkoś (2003b), and related to postulates in Den Dikken (2007) and Gallego (2010), is to assume that the phase must be extended to accommodate (54):

(57) PIC holds of Agree but the phase must be extended, for instance: the phase is the smallest relevant convergent domain (PolP and CP).

This proposal is consistent with the definition proposed by Pesetsky (2013) and Svenonius (2004):

(58) DP undergoes Spell-Out only after it is Vergnaud-licensed (i.e. case-marked, JW) (Pesetsky 2013: 89).

(59) A straightforward assumption is that a phase is spelled out when all uninterpretable features on its head are checked (Svenonius 2004: 264).

But then the problem is that the derivation would sometimes have to wait for many steps for the features to be valued. In (54), they are valued when NegP is projected.[20] Given that, it would be tempting to tweak the definition of the phase instead:

(60) The PIC holds but it requires positive evidence for the phase status of particular heads.
Thus, in Polish:
a. only a 'contentive' CP is a phase (C-T_{Fin}, Cwh);
b. only NegP is a phase ([$_{PolP}$ NEG..])

This option may be conceptually inconvenient but empirically adequate.[21] Infinitival, affirmative CPs seem to be transparent to Agree (54) and Polarity Phrases with positive heads do not close off the NP case domain to external influence, while NegPs (see fn. 20) do. The problem is that a definition such as (60), and in fact any liberal definition like the ones proposed by Svenonius and Pesetsky, appear to bleach the notion of the phase altogether and lead to further complications.

Consider constructions combining both, a case of long-distance Agree and an independent instance of movement. Initially, only phase heads were allowed to have EPP features and drive movement to their specifier positions to provide for necessary escape hatches. Now, let us devise the movement dependency in such a way that an intermediate position is necessary for reconstruction, in the spirit of Fox (1999), Legate (2003) and Lebeaux (2009):

(61) a. Jan$_i$ nie   kazał   Mari-i$_j$ [PRO$_j$ pokazać   mu*$_k$
     Jan.NOM   NEG   told   Maria-DAT   show.INF   he.DAT

     [listów   Tomk-a$_k$ do siebie$_{i/j/k}$]]
     letters.GEN   Tom-GEN   to self
     'Jan$_i$ did not tell Maria$_j$ to show him Tom's letters to him/her/himself.'

b. [[ilu   listów   Tomk-a$_k$ do siebie$_{i/j/k}$]   Jan$_i$
    how many   letters.GEN   Tom-GEN   to self   Jan.NOM

    nie   kazał   Mari-i$_j$ [PRO$_j$ [$_{vP}$ t' pokazać   mu$_k$ t wczoraj]]]?
    NEG   told   Maria.DAT   show.INF   him.DAT   yesterday
    'How many of Tom's letters to himself did Jan$_i$ not tell Maria$_j$ to show him$_{i/*j}$ yesterday?'

(61a) shows that Neg in the main clause forces genitive on the direct object of the predicate in the embedded infinitive; it also shows three interpretation possibilities for the reflexive pronoun (Polish shows subject-oriented binding that respects the Tensed Sentence Condition, while it does not respect the Specified Subject Condition), where *siebie* 'self' can either be bound by the main clause subject *Jan*, or the embedded clause subject PRO, controlled by *Maria*, or even the possessive form of *Tomek*. Importantly, *Tomek* must be disjoint in reference with *mu* 'him', as the indirect object c-commands the direct one and a Principle C violation must be avoided. Thus, the stage is set for (61b), where *wh*-movement fronts the direct object to the main clause left peripheral position. Here, an additional interpretation appears, where *Tomek* can be coindexed with the indirect object of the embedded predicate. Now, assuming that one copy is interpreted at LF, this copy must be placed in such a position where the indirect object *mu* 'him' does not c-command *Tomek* and, at the same time, PRO c-commands the reflexive *siebie* 'self' to provide for the coreferential interpretation. What is this position? It is t' at the edge of the embedded vP (PolP) in (61b). Why does it come into being at all? The classic Phase Theory-inspired answer is: t' comes into being because the *wh*-phrase needs to move successive cyclically through phase edges and vP is a phase. But at the same time the embedded vP phase is the phase that the long-distance Agree relation between Neg and the embedded direct object cannot tolerate. The grammatical example in (61b) places contradictory requirements on the derivational machinery.[22] I expect it to show that phase extension may turn out to be an ultimately lethal medication for problems with phases. What next?

Now, we either turn to a theory where Spell-Out is non-simultaneous or we say that what is a phase for Move is not a phase for Agree. Marusić (2005, 2009) proposes that the section of the phrase marker fed to PF need not be of equal size to the section of the phrase-marker fed to LF. Applying this reasoning to (61b), the phrase marker including the main clause NegP and stretching to the embedded direct object NP is one PF-relevant Spell-Out domain. At the same time the embedded vP is an LF-relevant phase.

Bošković (2007) assumes that the PIC constrains Move but it does not constrain Agree:

(62) PIC holds for Move but it does not hold for Agree.

Bošković (2007: 613–614) points to languages that allow for agreement to reach into a finite CP, for instance Chukchee. In this language, the matrix v agrees with the object in the embedded clause, which clearly violates the PIC:

(63) ənən qəlyilu ləŋərkə-nin-et [iŋqun 0-rətəmŋəv-nen-at qora-t]
    he   regret.3 PL   that   3SG-lost-3-PL   reindeer-PL
    'He regrets that he lost the reindeers.'
    (Chukchee, Bošković 2007: 613)

Consequently, Bošković concludes that the PIC does not confine Agree. Thus, the Polish GoN looks like a less extreme version of the Chukchee long-distance agreement, as the long-distance GoN can reach only into infinitive complements.

5. Conclusions and outlook

This contribution concerned the issue of Genitive of Negation (GoN) in existential/locative, possessive and regular transitive constructions in Polish. As this topic is well known and has been discussed in a variety of generative frameworks and approaches, this presentation aimed at consolidating the factual basis and checking how various aspects of the GoN yield to novel accounts of the theory of case. Following a brief presentation of arguments put forward by Błaszczak in favour of two distinct structures for existential/locative vs. 'agentive' locative constructions in Polish, it was proposed that all cases of the GoN reflect a structural arrangement, where the NP argument is theme, placed in the complement position to V (both in the possessive/transitive 'object' case and the existential/locative 'subject' case). Subsequently, the phenomenon of the GoN was tested against two types of recent engineering solutions applied to theory of case. One is the case overwriting proposal in Pesetsky (2013), which seems to do well to cover the core GoN contexts, but it needs to employ an idiosyncratic mechanism of PP Spell-Out to avoid the overwriting of oblique cases with genitive. The other novel approach is the nano-syntactic theory of case projections put forward by Caha (2009, 2010, 2013), where a principled answer is provided to the question why only accusative and nominative alternate with genitive, although the procedure of case licensing needs to be complicated to provide for case valuation and realization. Finally, the long-distance version of the GoN was put under closer scrutiny in the context of the phase-based theory of syntax. The key point is that clausal negation on the main verb forces genitive on the direct object of the verb embedded in the infinitival complement. If NEG is taken to act, or co-act, as a probe on so remote a goal, this relation most likely violates the classic formulation of the Phase Impenetrability Condition stated in Chomsky (2001). It was shown that the attempt at expanding the phase to accommodate the long-distance GoN, advocated both in Błaszczak (2001) and Witkoś (2003b), fails to provide for other dependencies in the same domain. The safest conclusion appears to be that Agree (employed with the GoN) is less constrained than Move and a single universal principle such as the PIC, though very much welcome, cannot subsume their properties.

Notes

1. *Abbreviations*

ABL	ablative case	N	neuter gender
ACC	accusative case	NEG	negation
DAT	dative case	PAST	past tense
F	feminine gender	PFX	prefix
GEN	genitive case	PIC	Phrase Impenetrability Condition
GoN	Genitive of Negation	PL	plural number
INF	infinitive	PRES	present tense
INST	instrumental case	RFL	reflexive
HAB	habitual aspect	SG	singular number
M	masculine gender		

2. Unlike its Russian equivalent, the Polish Genitive of Negation does not show any sensitivity to the specificity/definiteness status of the affected NP. See Borschev & Partee (2002) and Kagan (2013) for a comprehensive review of the Russian GoN and Błaszczak (2008a, 2010) for differences between the Polish and the Russian GoN constructions.
3. Examples modelled on Błaszczak (2010).
4. As GoN has been a topic of animated debate in Polish and Slavic linguistics for several decades, it is impossible to provide even a brief summary of the most relevant accounts within the confines of this chapter. See Pesetsky (1982); Willim (1989); Tajsner (1990); Franks (1994, 1995); Brown (1999); Przepiórkowski (1999); Błaszczak (2001); Borschev & Partee (2002); Brown & Przepiórkowski (2006), etc.
5. A reviewer for this volume raises a question of why nominative themes in constructions with *psych*-predicates do not convert to genitive under negation if they are the lowest arguments remaining in its c-command:

   (i) Marii   spodobała   się   ta   sukienka.
       (to) Maria.DAT appealed   RFL   this   dress.NOM
       'This dress appealed to Maria.'

   (ii) Marii   nie spodobała   się   ta   sukienka.
        (to) Maria.DAT not appealed RFL   this   dress.NOM
        'This dress did not appeal to Maria.'

   They look like nominative objects, and are treated as such in Citko (2011). The point is well taken but its full discussion remains outside the scope of this contribution. Let me, however, outline two possible explanations. One is based on the gist of the proposal from Witkoś (2003a) shown in (14) above: GoN is licensed in the same configuration as accusative/partitive, so the split probe involved is Neg plus v, rather than T plus Neg. The analysis of GoN on the theme in the locative construction crucially requires its resemblance to the theme in the transitive construction in (16b). So the combination of T and Neg does not return genitive.

   The other possibility is linked to a specific placement of the nominative Theme in constructions with psychological predicates. For instance, Cuervo (2003) proposes to place the nominative Theme in [spec,vP], with the superior dative argument placed in a higher Applicative Phrase:

   (i) $[_{TP}$ T (Neg) $[_{ApplP}$ DP$_{DAT}$ [Appl $[_{vP}$ DP$_{NOM}$ [v $[_{VP}$ V]]]]]]

   Such an arrangement of arguments predicts that the configuration for GoN provided in ex. (14) is not met, with NegP placed anywhere between TP and vP, as the DP$_{NOM}$

6   I am grateful to a reviewer for this volume for pointing out this significant parallel between syntax/semantics of GoN.
7   Bailyn (2004) introduces a novel structural approach to genitive marking in Russian, unifying GoN and the Genitive of Quantification, among others. It is based on the division of labour between Negation itself (responsible for Negative Polarity Item licensing, among others) and feature Q(uantifier) responsible for the licensing of the genitive case:
(i) $[_{NegP}$ Neg $[_{vP[+Q]}$ NP$_{EXT}$ [v $[_{VP[+Q]}$ V $[_{QP}$ Q NP$_{INT}$]]]]
The Q-feature is selected for by Neg and percolates down the structure, in line with selection requirements of particular heads. This structure allows for a principled explanation for why external arguments of transitive verbs can easily serve as NPIs (they are c-commanded by Neg), but they do not undergo GoN. See Bailyn (2012) for a recent comprehensive account of this problem area.

is not c-commanded by the v (half) probe. And for GoN to apply, the nominal argument must be c-commanded by both halves of the split probe.

8   In fact, the Polish equivalent to (20) of the Genitive of Irrealis in Russian is grammatical only with the genitive form, just like the GoN. This would point to a possibility of an optional Object Shift in Russian in (22), feeding preservation of accusative in the scope of clausal negation as well as specific/definite interpretation and lack thereof in Polish. Further discussion of Polish/Russian differences in this respect is beyond the scope of this contribution.
9   Examples (23a) and (23b) come from Błaszczak (2008b).
10 The examples in (24) and (25) also come from Błaszczak (2008b).
11 This is a property it shares with the account presented in connection with the example in (15).
12 Where do unaccusative verbs fit into the picture of the GoN in Polish? As I show in (10), their sole arguments do not show the GoN. Our formula for the licensing of the GoN by a split probe in (14) predicts that these verbs should not fall under its scope if they do not have the vP level of structure. If they are only VPs one crucial part of the split [Neg – v] probe is consistently missing and thus their arguments, though c-commanded by Neg and V are not c-commanded by any case marker.
13 A reviewer for this volume expresses doubts as to whether or not Błaszczak's 'agentive BE' should project the vP level of structure and proposes the notion of the logical Operator introducing alternative, habitual/episodic states. I concur that this may look unorthodox if v is taken to correspond to the head licensing causation and structural accusative case only (Hale & Keyser 1993). Yet, it can be argued that the 'agentive BE' reflects the similarity between this type of BE and an unergative verb like *przebywać* 'stay', with the vP level projected. Furthermore, the structural account presented here remains operational as long as the nominal argument of BE in (28d) occupies a position in some functional projection outside VP. Its head may as well license an Operator introducing alternative states.
14 Realization of the prototype, for instance the adnominal genitive, is determined by morphological systems of individual languages. In one language it is realized through a preposition, in another through case spread and case concord within NP.
15 Bailyn (2004) presents an analysis along similar lines, where the feature Q(antitative) is taken to constitute a common denominator to three types of genitive constructions in Russian: partitive, negative and quantitative.

16   Pesetsky (2013: 75–80) introduces a caveat necessary to deal with cases where a preposition has both a locative and directional interpretation, each governing a different case and determined by the selecting verb:
   (i) Skała   leżała   na domu.
        rock.NOM   lay   on house.LOC
        'A rock was lying on a house.'
   (ii) Skała   upadła   na dom.
        rock.NOM   fell   on house.ACC
        'A rock fell on a house.'
   As the verb assigns accusative, just like in (29c), it needs to access the complement to P to assign case and such PPs cannot be separate phases. Pesetsky proposes to treat directional Prepositions (showing the location/direction case alternation) as complex constituents consisting of two heads: the DIR(ection) head and the LOC(ative) element. He takes the DIR head to belong to category Verb and proposes the following representation, where the locative P is not selected by DIR$_v$ as its complement but occupies the specifier position of a complement DP:
   [$_{DIRvP}$ DIRv [$_{DP}$ P$_{LOC}$ [$_{D'}$ D NP]]]

17   Arguments for a separate functional projection known as the Kase Phrase have been advanced in the field for some time now (cf. Willim 2000; Franks 2002; Norris 2014). Typically, this would be the locus for the reception of the case (feature) from an external source. Instead, I propose that a paradigmatically determined set of Case Projections insulates the NP core.

18   This weakening of the derivational function of Neg is also welcome for independent reasons. Typically, failure of feature valuation complicates the derivation but it seems that v and Neg are not always equal partners in the licensing of GoN. In colloquial Polish, some speakers show erosion of the otherwise obligatory GoN in the context of topicalization, where the topic bears accusative, rather than the expected genitive, see (ii):
   (i) Maria   nie   zauważyła tej   kobiety   /*tę   kobietę.
        Maria.NOM   NEG   noticed   this.GEN   woman.GEN   /*this.ACC woman.ACC
        'Maria did not notice this woman.'
   (ii) #Tę   kobietę   Maria   nie zauważyła t.
        this.ACC   woman.ACC   Maria.NOM   NEG noticed
        'This woman, Maria did not notice.'
   Such cases of variability are easier to deal with when Neg does not bear an independent feature but participates in the realization of case licensing performed primarily by v.

19   It would be tempting to say that the PIC holds for long-distance Agree in GoN through covert movement of the direct object. So, there would be an overt movement, with copy pronunciation at the bottom of the chain. This proposal is used to account for 'main V'/embedded DP$_o$' agreement in Hindi-Urdu (i) (see Bhatt 2005) and for similar facts in Tsez (ii) (see Polinsky & Potsdam 2001):
   (i) Ram-ne   [rotii   khaa-nii]   chaah-ii
        Ram.ERG   [bread.F eat.INF.F]   want.F.SG
        'Ram wanted to eat bread.'
   (ii) Ram-ne   [rotii   khaa-naa]   chaah-aa
        Ram.ERG   [bread.F eat.INF.M]   want.M.SG
        'Ram wanted to eat bread.'

Whenever the direct object is specific or definite, the main verb shows agreement with it, see (i). If the direct object is indefinite or non-specific, the main verb agrees with the head of the infinitive clause, see (ii). Applied to the GoN, this strategy would return the following LF representation:

(iii) [$_{PolP}$ Neg [$_{vP}$ v-told Jan-DAT [$_{CP}$ *letters-ACC/letters-GEN [$_{C'}$ C [$_{TP}$ PRO T

[$_{PolP}$ *letters-ACC/letters-GEN [$_{Pol'}$ read.INF *letters-ACC/letters-GEN]]]]]]

The problem with this proposal is that Polish, unlike Russian, requires the GoN of both non-specific and specific/definite NPs and no optionality is involved. A comprehensive discussion of the definition of the notion of the derivational phase and its consequences appears in Citko (2014).

20 The positive Polarity head does not affect GoN licensed in the lower clause:

(i) Jan [$_{PolP}$ Pos [$_{vP}$ kazał   Marii   [$_{NegP}$ nie [$_{vP}$ czytać
    Jan.NOM   told   Maria.DAT   NEG   read.INF
tego artykułu /*ten artykuł]]]
this.GEN article-GEN / *this.ACC article.ACC
'Jan told Maria to not read this paper.'

21 A similar position taken by Landau (2000) to allow for Exhaustive Control into wh-infinitives:

(i) John wonders [$_{CP}$ how [PRO to solve this puzzle t]]

Landau (2000) takes infinitive CPs not to constitute derivational phases. A suggestion similar in spirit to (60) is expressed in Landau (2008), Stepanov (2012) and Bošković (2011). These authors argue for island (phase) effects amelioration through head movement of the phase head: silent phase heads move to the selecting verb/head and, through movement, nullify the phase status of their maximal projections. On the strength of this hypothesis, only the non-silent contentive C$_{fin}$ (introduced by the obligatory lexical Complementizer że 'that') and Neg (nie 'not') head genuine phases, with other potential phases vanishing in thin air due to head movement.

22 It is possible to devise the notion of a phase relativized to a given relation holding between elements A and B. This would mean that the theory has turned a full circle; we used to have barriers relativized to particular relations (see Chomsky 1986; Manzini 1990; Rizzi 1990; Cinque 1991), and we now introduce relativized phases.

References

Babby, L. 1980. *Existential Sentences and Negation in Russian*. Ann Arbor, MI: Karoma Publishers.
Bailyn, J. F. 1995. A configurational approach to the Russian 'free' word order. PhD dissertation, Cornell University.
Bailyn, J. F. 2004. The case of Q. In: Arnaudova, O. (ed.), *Proceedings of Formal Approaches to Slavic Linguistics: The Ottawa Meeting 2003*, 1–36. Ann Arbor, MI: Michigan Slavic Publications.
Bailyn, J. F. 2012. *The Syntax of Russian*. Cambridge: Cambridge University Press.
Belletti, A. 1988. The case of unaccusatives. *Linguistic Inquiry* 19: 1–34.
Bhatt, R. 2005. Long-distance agreement in Hindi-Urdu. *Natural Language and Linguistic Theory* 23: 757–807.
Blake, B. J. 1994. *Case* (2nd edn). Cambridge: Cambridge University Press.

Borschev, V. & Partee, B. 2002. The Russian Genitive of Negation in existential sentences: the role of theme-rheme structure reconsidered. In: Hajicova, E. & Sgall, P. (eds), *Travaux de CNrcle LiSguistique de Pargue (novelle serie)*, vol. 4, 1–55. Amsterdam: John Benjamins.

Błaszczak, J. 2001. *Covert Movement and the Genitive of Negation in Polish* (Linguistics in Potsdam 15. Potsdam: Universitätsbibliothek.

Błaszczak, J. 2008a. Differential subject marking in Polish: the case of genitive vs. nominative subjects in 'X was not at Y'-constructions. In: de Hoop, H. & de Swarts, P. (eds), *Differential Subject Marking*. Studies in Natural Language and Linguistic Theory. 72, 113–149. Dordrecht: Springer.

Błaszczak, J. 2008b. What HAS to BE used? Existential, locative, and possessive sentences in Polish. In: Antonenko, A., Bailyn, J. & Bethin, C. (eds), *Formal Approaches to Slavic Linguistics 16: The Stony Brook 2006 Meeting*, 31–47. Ann Arbor: Michigan Slavic Publications.

Błaszczak, J. 2010. A spurious genitive puzzle in Polish. In: Fanselow, G. & Hanneforth, T. (eds), *Language and Logos. Studies in Theoretical and Computational Linguistics. Festschrift for Peter Staudacher for his 70th Birthday*. Studia Grammatica 72, 17–47. Berlin: Akademieverlag.

Bošković, Ž. 2007. On the locality and motivation of move and agree: an even more minimal theory. *Linguistic Inquiry* 38: 589–644.

Bošković, Ž. 2011. Rescue by PF-deletion, traces as (non)interveners and the that-trace effect. *Linguistic Inquiry* 42: 1–44.

Brown, S. 1999. *The Syntax of Negation in Russian: A Minimalist Approach*. Stanford, CA: CSLI Publications.

Brown, S. & Przepiórkowski, A. (eds). 2006. *Negation in Slavic*. Bloomington, IN: Slavica.

Caha, P. 2009. Nanosyntax of case. PhD dissertation, University of Tromsoe.

Caha, P. 2010. The German locative-directional alternation: a peeling account. *Journal of Comparative German Linguistics* 13: 179–223.

Caha, P. 2013. Czech numerals and no bundling. In: Shlonsky, U. (ed.), *Beyond Functional Sequence: The Cartography of Syntactic Structure*, vol. 10, 225–245. Oxford: Oxford University Press.

Chomsky, N. 1981. *Lectures on Government and Binding: The Pisa Lectures*. Dordrecht: Foris.

Chomsky, N. 1986. *Barriers*. Cambridge, MA: MIT Press.

Chomsky, N. 1995. *The Minimalist Program*. Cambridge, MA: MIT Press.

Chomsky, N. 2000. Minimalist inquiries. In: Martin, R., Michaels, D., Uriagereka, J. & Keyser, S. J. (eds), *Step by Step: Essays on Minimalist Syntax in Honor of Howard Lasnik*, 89–156. Cambridge, MA: MIT Press.

Chomsky, N. 2001. Derivation by phase. In: Kenstowicz, M. (ed.), *Ken Hale: A Life in Language*, 1–52, Cambridge, MA: MIT Press.

Chomsky, N. 2008. On phases. In: Freidin, R., Otero, C. P. and Zubizarreta, M. L. (eds), *Issues in Linguistic Theory: Essays in Honor of Jean-Roger Vergnaud*, 133–166. Cambridge, MA: MIT Press.

Chomsky, N. 2013. Problems of projection. *Lingua* 130: 33–49.

Chomsky, N. 2015. Problems of projection: extensions. In: Di Domenico, E., Hamann C. & Matteini, S. (eds), *Structures, Strategies and Beyond: Studies in Honor of Adriana Belletti*, 1–16. Amsterdam: John Benjamins.

Cinque, G. 1991. *A-Bar Dependencies*. Cambridge, MA: MIT Press.

Cinque, G. 2005. Deriving Greenberg's Universal 20 and its exceptions. *Linguistic Inquiry* 36: 315–332.

Cinque, G. 2010. *The Syntax of Adjectives: A Comparative Study*. Cambridge: MIT Press.
Citko, B. 2011. *Symmetry in Syntax: Merge, Move and Labels*. Cambridge: Cambridge University Press.
Citko, B. 2014. *Phase Theory*. Cambridge: Cambridge University Press.
Cuervo, M. C. 2003. *Datives at Large*. Cambridge, MA: MIT Press.
Den Dikken, M. 2007. Phase extension: contours of the theory of the role of head movement in phrasal extraction. *Theoretical Linguistics* 33: 1–41.
Diesing, M. 1992. *Indefinites*. Cambridge, MA: MIT Press.
Fox, D. 1999. Reconstruction, binding theory and the interpretation of chains. *Linguistic Inquiry* 30: 157–196.
Franks, S. 1994. Parametric properties of numeral phrases in Slavic. *Natural Language and Linguistic Theory* 12: 597–674.
Franks, S. 1995. *Parameters of Slavic Morphosyntax*. New York: Oxford University Press.
Franks, S. 2002. A Jacobsonian feature-based analysis of the Slavic numeric quantifier genitive. *Journal of Slavic Linguistics* 10: 141–181.
Gallego, A. 2010. *Phase Theory*. Amsterdam and Philadelphia, PA: John Benjamins.
Grimshaw, J. 1990. *Argument Structure*. Cambridge, MA: MIT Press.
Hale, M. & Keyser, S. J. (eds). 1993. *The View from Building 20*. Cambridge, MA: MIT Press.
Hornstein, N. & Witkoś, J. 2003. Yet another approach to existential constructions. In: Delsing, L-O., Falk, C., Josefsson, G & Sigurðsson, H. (eds), *Festchrift for Christer Platzak*, 167–184. Lund: Lund University Press.
Kagan, O. 2013. *Semantics of Genitive Objects in Russian: A Study of Genitive of Negation and Intensional Genitive Case*. Dordrecht: Springer.
Landau, I. 2000. *Elements of Control*. Dordrecht and Boston, MA: Kluwer.
Landau, I. 2008. Two routes of control: evidence from case transmission in Russian. *Natural Language & Linguistic Theory* 26: 877–924.
Lasnik, H. 1995. Case and expletives revisited: on greed and other human failings. *Linguistic Inquiry* 26: 615–633.
Lebeaux, D. 2009. *Where Does Binding Theory Apply?* Cambridge, MA: MIT Press.
Legate, J. 2003. Some interface properties of the phase. *Linguistic Inquiry* 34: 506–516.
Manzini, M. L. 1990. *Locality*. Cambridge, MA: MIT Press.
Marusić, F. L. 2005. On non-simultaneous phases. PhD dissertation. Stony Brook University.
Marusić, F. L. 2009. Non-simultaneous Spell-Out in the clausal and nominal domain. In: Grohmann, K. K. (ed.), *Interphases: Phase-Theoretic Investigations of Linguistic Interfaces*, 151–181. Oxford: Oxford University Press.
Norris, M. 2014. A theory of nominal concord. PhD dissertation. University of California: Santa Cruz.
Pesetsky, D. 1982. Paths and categories. PhD dissertation. Massachusetts Institute of Technology.
Pesetsky, D. 2013. *Russian Case Morphology and the Syntactic Categories*. Cambridge, MA: MIT Press.
Piñon, C. 1994. Aspectual composition and the 'pofective' in Polish. In: Avrutin, S., Franks, S. & Progovac, L. (eds), *Formal Approaches to Slavic Linguistics: The MIT Meeting 1993 (FASL 2)*, 341–373. Ann Arbor, MI: Michigan Slavic Publications.
Polinsky, M. & Potsdam, E. 2001. Long distance agreement and topic in Tsez. *Natural Language and Linguistic Theory* 19: 583–646.

Przepiórkowski, A. 1999. Case assignment and the complement-adjunct dichotomy: A non-configurational constraint-based approach. PhD dissertation. Universität Tübingen.
Rizzi, L. 1990. *Relativized Minimality*. Cambridge, MA: MIT Press.
Starke, M. 2009. Nanosyntax: a short primer to a new approach to language. *Nordlyd* 36: 1–6.
Stepanov, A. 2012. Voiding island effects via head movement. *Linguistic Inquiry* 43: 680–693.
Svenonius, P. 2004. On the edge. In: Adger, D., de Cat, C. & Tsoulas, D. (eds), *Peripheries: Syntactic Edges and their Effects*, 261–287. Dordrecht: Kluwer.
Tajsner, P. 1990. Case marking in English and Polish: a government and binding study. PhD dissertation. Adam Mickiewicz University, Poznań.
Willim, E. 1989. *On Word Order: A Government-Binding Study of English and Polish*. Kraków: Wydawnictwo Naukowe Uniwersytetu Jagiellońskiego.
Willim, E. 2000. On the grammar of Polish nominals. In: Martin, R., Michaels, D., Uriagereka, J. & Keyser, S. J. (eds), *Step by Step: Essays on Minimalist Syntax in Honor of Howard Lasnik*, 319–346. Cambridge, MA: MIT Press.
Witkoś, J. 1998. *The Syntax of Clitics: Steps Towards a Minimalist Account*. Poznań: Motivex.
Witkoś, J. 2003a. Nominative-to-genitive shift and the negative copula *nie ma/not is*: implications for the checking theory. *Journal of Slavic Linguistics* 10: 174–199.
Witkoś, J. 2003b. Some notes on single cycle syntax and genitive of negation. In: Bański, P. & Przepiórkowski, A. (eds), *Generative Linguistics in Poland: Morphosyntactic Investigations*, 167–182. Warsaw: Instytut Podstaw Informatyki Polskiej Akademii Nauk.

3. Extraction of possessive NP-complements and the structure of the nominal domain in Polish

Piotr Cegłowski

1. Introduction[1,2]

This chapter subscribes to the view that the nominal structure of Polish is composed of multiple functional projections located above the NP (e.g. Migdalski 2001, 2003; Rappaport 2001a, b; Rutkowski 2002, 2007). Following the general assumption that languages share a common functional nominal structure (Abney 1987), it differs considerably from structurally parsimonious models such as the one advocated by Bošković (2014a, b, 2015a, b) and Despić (2011), among others. Section 2 offers a brief overview of the selected (sometimes ignored) problems relating to the division of languages into two major 'camps', i.e. NP- and DP-. Section 3 scrutinizes the descriptive relevance of possessive (genitive) NP-complement extraction/fronting. Section 4 succinctly discusses the technical details of the empirical survey (procedure, data processing) and presents the results. In section 5, the relevance of discourse-related factors is revisited and a derivational mechanism underlying the structural setting proposed here (including its various implications) is suggested. Section 6 concludes the discussion.

2. NP- vs. DP-languages – a problematic distinction?

The debate concerning the structural composition of nominal expressions dates back to Szabolcsi (1983), Horrocks & Starvou (1987), among others, and is still an ongoing one. Ever since Abney's (1987) seminal work regarding the parallelisms between nominal structures and clauses, two major standpoints have emerged. These may crudely be represented as Universal DP-Hypothesis (1) and Small Nominal Hypothesis (2).

(1) *Universal DP-Hypothesis (DPH)*
    The presence of D(P) is universally attested (DP is part of UG)

(2) *Small Nominal Hypothesis (Norris 2014: 27)*
Nominals in all articleless languages are simply NPs
(i.e. they do not project functional structure)

In order to capture the difference between the so-called 'NP-' and 'DP-' languages, Bošković (2008, 2009) offers a detailed generalization based on a number of 'Greenberg-style' cross-linguistic implications some of which are presented in (3).[3]

(3) a. presence / absence of overt articles;
b. (un)availability of Left Branch Extraction (LBE);
c. (un)availability of scrambling;
d. presence / absence of adnominal genitives;
e. (un)availability of negative raising;
f. (un)availability of possessive binding.

A cursory glance at the list reveals that some languages recruited into the NP-camp due to the lack of overt articles will not uniformly follow the criteria, contrary to expectations. The one-way correlation between the absence of articles and the availability of LBE illustrates the point.

(4) Only languages without articles may allow LBE (Bošković 2008: 5)

It should be noted that (4) not only rules out LBE in DP-languages but also allows for the articleless (hence NP-) languages that still disallow LBE, for example Estonian and Korean (see Norris 2014: 29 and Kim 2011, respectively).[4] In other words, (4) does not explain why the two should pattern along with the other members of the DP-camp. Polish also seems significantly out of line with at least a few criteria proposed by Bošković, which arguably undermines its definite classification as an NP-language. Three representative examples presented as (3d)–(3f) are discussed here to exemplify the problem.

Thus, Bošković (2008) argues forcefully that 'double genitives' are only found in DP-languages (e.g. English, *John's collection of novels*). On the assumption that in Serbian/Croatian the D-layer is absent, there should be only one source of genitive case, which effectively renders the second possessor illicit. This expectation is not confirmed in Polish, though, consider the grammatical examples (5a)–(5c) discussed by Rozwadowska (1997: 36) and Rappaport (2001b: 6).[5]

(5) a. bochenek   chleba   Marka
    loaf.NOM   bread.GEN   Mark.GEN
    'Mark's loaf of bread'

b. wolność   wyboru   Polaków
   freedom.NOM choice.GEN   Poles.GEN
   'Poles' freedom of choice'

c. opis   zachodusłońca   Mickiewicza
   description.NOM sunset.GEN   Mickiewicz.GEN
   'Mickiewicz's description of the sunset'

Granted that the Theme argument is inherently endowed with genitive Case, Rappaport (2001a, b) argues that the source of the 'other' genitive, the Possessor-argument in (5a)–(5c), is actually D. In this sense, the D-N complex attested in the nominal structure in Polish resembles the (clausal) T-v/V configuration. Bošković (2008) aims to exclude double genitives in 'NP-languages' constraining the thematic types of adnominal, Genitive-marked arguments to agentive readings only. Still, such a constraint fails to exclude (5c), with *Mickiewicz* unambiguously interpreted as Agent.

In her analysis of the differences between the possessive binding in English and Serbian/Croatian, Despić (2011, 2013) attempts to explain why only the former that allows prenominal possessors of nouns placed in the subject position to bind beyond their binding domain, for example into the object, thereby causing the violation of binding principles B (6a) and C (6b) (Despić 2011: 31–32, (11)–(12)).

(6) a. *Kusturicin$_i$ najnoviji film ga$_i$ je zaista razocarao.
  Kusturica's latest film him is really disappointed
  'Kusturica's latest film really disappointed him.' (S/C)

 b. *Njegov$_i$ najnoviji$_i$ film je zaista razocarao Kusturicu$_i$.
  his latest film is really disappointed Kusturica
  'His latest film really disappointed Kusturica.' (S/C)

Despić takes the lack of the DP-layer in SC to be the reason why the possessors in (6a)–(6b) c-command 'out of the subject' and bind into the object.[6] However, a cross-linguistic comparison reveals that the argument does not hold, i.e. analogous sentences in Polish would be ranked differently (7a)–(7b).[7]

(7) a. */? Babcina$_i$ czapka dała jej$_i$ powód do radości.
  grandmother's cap gave her reason to joy
  'Grandmother's cap pleased her.'

 b. Tomka$_i$ dobry wynik końcowy / dobry wynik końcowy
  Tom.GEN good score final / good score final

  Tomka$_i$ zainspirował go$_i$ do dalszej pracy.
  Tom.GEN inspired him to further work
  'Tom's high semester mark motivated him to work further.'

Last but not least, consider the Negative Raising (NR) of the sort discussed by Bošković (2008) in sentences such as (8a)–(8b). Specifically, since words such as *until* and *at least* are taken to be negative polarity items (NPIs) requiring a clause-mate negation, the fact that the negation shows up as high as in the main clause indicates that the former must have been raised (Bošković 2008: 3, (12)).

(8) a. John didn't believe [that Mary would leave [$_{NPI}$ until tomorrow]]

 b. John didn't leave / *left until tomorrow.

Crucially, NR is argued to be disallowed in languages without articles. While the licensing relation depends on a number of factors (e.g. the structural configuration and the choice of the matrix predicate), there are cases where it clearly applies in Polish. Perhaps the most transparent picture of the phenomenon is provided by the so-called 'colloquial NPIs' that require strict clause-mate negation to preserve the idiomatic meaning, as in (9a)–(9b) (Modrzejewska 1981: 47, (28)–(29)). The presence of negation in the main clause in the grammatical examples presented as (9c)–(9d) implies that the former must have originated elsewhere, i.e. in the subordinate clause.

(9) a. Twój   szef   #(nie)   ruszy   palcem   by   ci   pomóc.
       your   boss   (not)   lift   finger   COMP   you.DAT   help
       'Your boss will (not) lift a finger to help you.'

   b. Piotr   #ma   złamany   grosz / nie   ma   złamanego   grosza.
      Peter   has   broken   cent / not   has   broken   cent
      'Peter has / doesn't have a red cent.'

   c. Nie   widziałem,   żeby   twój   szef   ruszył   palcem
      not   (I) see   so-that   your   boss   lifted   finger

      by   ci   pomóc.
      in-order-to   you   help.
      'I didn't see your lift a finger to help you'

   d. Nie   wydaje (mi)   się,   że   Piotr   ma   złamany   grosz.
      not   seem I.DAT   RFL   that   Peter   has   broken   cent
      'Peter doesn't seem to have a red cent.'

Although the inventory of 'NEG-raisers' in Polish is apparently smaller than in English, there seems to be some overlap. To conclude, the syntactic conduct of the idiomatic expressions presented in (9) (as well as other contexts involving the quantifier – negation interaction not discussed here for the sake of space) do not consistently toe the line set in Bošković (2008).

The three counterarguments presented in this section are generally limited to Polish and, in this sense, may perhaps be taken to show that it is indeed somewhat 'recalcitrant' but, after all, it constitutes an isolated case. While this contribution is not meant to make any claims with respect to other languages, it may be that a closer look at their syntactic behaviour will reveal some more loopholes in the (apparently not so robust) NP/DP classification.

3. NP-complement extraction – a descriptive sketch

While Bašić (2004: 34) observes that 'facts concerning the extraction of post-nominal complements seem to be much less clear and constant, with the amount of degradation varying considerably across speakers', Bošković (2014a: 48) takes a much more definite stance and claims that this type of extraction in NP-languages should be illicit for the same reason it is licit in DP-languages, i.e. due to the specific conflation of the *Phase Impenetrability Condition* (PIC, Chomsky 2001, 2008) and *Anti-locality*, consider his example from Serbian/Croatian (Bošković 2014a: 48, (17)).

(10) a. ?/*[Ovog grada]$_i$ sam   pronašla   [$_{NP}$ sliku t$_i$]
       this   city.GEN   am   found   picture
       'Of this city I found a/the picture'

   b. ? [Którego miasta]$_i$ znalazłeś   [zdjęcie t$_i$]?
        which.GEN city.GEN   found   picture
        'Which city did you find a picture of?'

   c. ... [$_{NP}$ t$_i$ [$_{NP}$ N t$_i$]]   # Anti-locality

   d. ... [$_{VP}$ t$_i$ V [$_{NP}$ N t$_i$]]   # PIC

For convenience, the relevant definitions are provided below.

(11) *Phase Impenetrability Condition (Chomsky 2001, 2008)*

   The domain of H is not accessible to operations outside HP; only H and its edge are accessible to such operations.

(12) *Anti-locality*

   a. (general version, paraphrased) - Movement must not be too local

   b. (Bošković 2015b: 3) - Movement of A targeting B must cross a projection distinct from B (where unlabelled projections are not distinct from labelled projections)

Assuming that Polish (like Serbian/Croatian) belongs to the NP-camp, it would be expected to exhibit the same pattern, i.e. (10b) should be ruled out either by the PIC or by Anti-locality.[8] In fact, native speakers of Polish do not uniformly reject sentences exemplified by (10b). Szczegielniak (1996: 6) (see also Borsley & Rivero 1994) offers examples where the possessor gets extracted out of a (fronted) nominal and subsequently merges with the auxiliary clitc –*ś*, analysed as a floating inflection in (13).

(13) (Ty) Ewy-ś   książkę   czytał.
     you Eve.GEN-2SG   book   read
     'You read Eve's book.'

Finally, on comparison of examples such as (10b) and (14), there is an intuition (shared even by those who do not unreservedly accept the former) that the latter seems at least slightly more acceptable.[9]

(14) [[TEGO   MIASTA]$_i$ zdjęciet$_i$]$_j$ znalazłem   t$_j$ w   gazecie.
     this.GEN city.GEN   picture.ACC   found   in   newspaper
     'I found a picture of this city in the newspaper.'

In his analysis of the interaction between the possessive and genitive forms in the grammar of Serbian/Croatian, Schoorlemmer makes analogous observations, consider the difference between (15a)–(15b) and (15c) (Schoorlemmer 2012: 2–3, (3)–(5)).

(15) a. [Kojeg svog saradnika]$_i$ je Petar sreo prijatelja t$_i$?
    which.GEN his.GEN co-worker.GEN is Petar met friend.ACC
    'Which co-worker did Peter met a friend of?'

   b. [Komunističke partije]$_i$ je Petar sreo člana t$_i$.
    communist party.GEN is Peter met member.ACC
    'Peter is a member of the communist party'

   c. *Kòga$_i$ je Petar sreo prijatelja t$_i$?
    who.GEN is Peter met friend.ACC
    'Who did Peter met a friend of?'

Last but not least, one should also revisit certain aspects of extraction across numerals (i.e. extraction from QP). Following the Genitive-of-Quantification scenario (Franks 1994; Bošković 2010, 2014a), the relevant structure is presented in (16).

(16) a. NP$_{GENi}$... [$_{QP}$ [$_{QP}$ NumP [$_{QP}$ Q [$_{FP}$ t$_i$ [$_{FP}$ F [$_{NP}$ [$_{NP}$ (AP) [$_{NP}$ N t$_i$]]]]]]]] # PIC

   b. NP$_{GENi}$... [$_{QP}$ t$_i$ [$_{QP}$ NumP [$_{QP}$ Q [$_{FP}$ t$_i$ [$_{FP}$ F [$_{NP}$ (AP) [$_{NP}$ N t$_i$]]]]]]] # Anti-locality

Once the technical details of the specific movements are scrutinized, the structure raises problems already attested in (10). Specifically, Anti-locality forces the movement of the NP-complement to the edge of FP. Given the presence of QP (the highest nominal projection – a phase now), the complement is bound to proceed through its edge to comply with the PIC. However, the movement from FP to QP is not anti-local. Interestingly, the Anti-locality – PIC mechanism should theoretically not preclude the extraction of prenominal (NP-adjoined) adjectival modifiers.[10]

To the extent that the presence of functional projections dominating the NP is relevant for the grammaticality judgements in examples featuring the extraction of NP-complements, a careful examination of native speaker grammaticality judgements may help verify the predictions regarding the structural composition of nominal structures in ('languages like') Polish and, possibly, shed some more light on the mechanics of extraction.

4. The data

4.1. The survey

In this section, the results of a study of acceptability of nominal extractions are presented and discussed in more detail. The data were collected by means of a questionnaire survey carried out in 2015 on the population of 183 native speakers of Polish. The participants were asked to fill in an online questionnaire comprising input sentences. While the time for completion was unlimited, a pilot study run on a small group of subjects had revealed that the average time needed to complete the survey was 15–20 minutes. Due to the specific character of the medium, the task had to be completed without interruption. The respondents were asked to evaluate the grammaticality of the input sentences using a 5-point Likert-type scale (1 – definitely incorrect; 2–rather incorrect; 3 – on the border of correctness; 4 – rather correct; 5 – definitely correct). For transparency, the procedure was additionally illustrated with relevant examples.

The input included eight types of extraction-related constructions including various types of LBE (LBE of adjectives, demonstratives and *wh-*), extraction of NP-complements, extraction across numerals, double AP LBE, deep LBE (deep extraction) and extraordinary LBE. For convenience, the discussion here will be restricted mainly to the extraction of possessive (genitive) NP-complements and touch upon extraction across numerals, the relevant examples are presented below.[11]

(17) SET G: extraction of possessive (genitive) NP-complements
Jeszcze w   szkole   średniej, jak sam   wspominał,
already in   school   high   as   (he) himself recalled

[$_{NP2}$ węgierskich pisarzy]$_i$ czytywał [$_{NP1}$ książki t] (z przyjemnością).
Hungarian   writers   (he) read   books   (with pleasure).
'Already in high school, as he himself recalls, he used to read the books of Hungarian writers with pleasure.'

(18) SET F: extraction across a numeral
Badacze   nie   mogli   uwierzyć [$_{AP}$ jak misternych]$_i$ udało im
researchers not   could   believe   how delicate   managed they.DAT

się   odkryć [$_{NP}$ siedem t$_i$ rękodzieł] z   epoki wczesnego Renesansu.
REFL   discover   seven   handicrafts   from era   Early   Renaissance
'The researchers could not believe that they had managed to discover seven (so) delicate handicrafts from the Early Renaissance.'

There were 5 items in each of the variable sets as well as 10 distractor sentences, resulting in 50 items altogether. In contrast to what is typically found in the literature, the sentences were relatively complex in order to effectively conceal the intentions of the researchers.[12] Nonetheless, the vast majority of the examples featured extractions within the same clause (72.5 per cent). Thus, the overall 'complexity' of the sentences did not serve to increase the distance between the extracted element and the extraction site. In that sense, the input sentences were assumed to be structurally comparable to the examples often encountered in this sort of linguistic studies.

4.2. Data processing

To obtain a statistically coherent picture of the data, central tendency (arithmetic mean, median, mode), dispersion (Standard Deviation, SD) and distribution (Skewed Distribution, SDis) were calculated. A brief look at the basic statistics allows to observe a marked difference in the acceptability of the specific extraction types. (19) represents the acceptability hierarchy based on the arithmetic mean obtained for the respective variable sets. In what follows, only the selected scores (i.e. extraction of genitive NP-complements, extraction of (prenominal modifiers) across a numeral, as well as both the highest and the lowest scores) will be discussed.

(19) LBE – *wh* (3.36) > LBE – adjectives (2.72) > **extraction of possessive (genitive) NP-complements (2.44)** > extraordinary LBE (2.40) > LBE – demonstratives (1.88) > extraction of an adjective across another adjective (double AP LBE) (1.86) > extraction across a numeral (1.69) > deep LBE (1.62)

As for LBE – *wh* (the highest score), the respondents' judgements were largely consistent for all the items within the respective sets. The mean result for SD (1.25) indicates that the judgements were generally concentrated around the mean score for each individual item. With the mean mode values reaching 4.00, SDis was negative (the majority of judgements was above the mean).

The results obtained for the extraction of NP-complements were worse, yet still fairly consistent.[13] The mean values for SD (1.21) and SDis (0.57) show that the judgements were not significantly dispersed, with the majority oscillating slightly below the mean score. It should crucially be noted that the respondents rated the items featuring the extraction of NP-complements across a numeral (Table 3.2, items 4 and 5, shaded) markedly higher, the scores comparable to LBE – *wh*.

While the scores for the sets presented in Table 3.2 may be regarded as either acceptable or marginally acceptable, the remaining ones, including the extraction of prenominal modifiers across a numeral (Table 3.3) and deep LBE (Table 3.4) fall sharply below the acceptability level. However, despite the low mean score, dispersion and concentration of scores still reveal a relatively consistent pattern. Although SD was relatively high in comparison with the mean score, SDis was positive for *all* the sets, thus indicating that the majority of the judgements were uniformly concentrated below the mean. The mean mode for the respective sets was 1.00, thus remaining in stark contrast with the equivalent values presented in Tables 3.1 and 3.2.

In most cases, the mean values for the specific items within a given set did not diverge significantly, which suggests that the subjects generally assessed the items within the respective sets alike. It may thus be concluded that individual differences between the specific items (e.g. the selection of the lexical verb, etc.) did not project on the acceptability judgements.

Table 3.1 LBE (-*wh*).

Statistics	Item 1	Item 2	Item 3	Item 4	Item 5	Mean (items 1–5)
Mean	3.42	2.66	3.79	4.34	3.29	3.36
SD	1.244708306	1.322468279	1.296118161	1.058715789	1.345271921	1.253456491
SDis	-0.482907483	0.174253342	-0.774510686	-1.791325446	-0.269983077	-0.62889467
Mode	4.00	1.00	5.00	5.00	5.00	4.00
Median	4.00	3.00	4.00	5.00	3.00	3.80

Table 3.2 Extraction of (genitive) NP-complements.

Statistics	Item 1	Item 2	Item 3	Item 4	Item 5	Mean (items 1–5)
Mean	2.21	1.58	2.01	3.11	3.26	**2.44**
SD	1.231813237	1.035992428	1.079683055	1.325071035	1.369237113	1.21
SDis	0.713267962	1.691161755	0.841184323	-0.103273081	-0.278170103	0.57
Mode	1.00	1.00	1.00	3.00	4.00	2.00
Median	2.00	1.00	2.00	3.00	3.00	2.20

Table 3.3 Extraction (of prenominal modifiers) across a numeral.

Statistics	Item 1	Item 2	Item 3	Item 4	Item 5	Mean (items 1–5)
Mean	1.70	1.92	1.58	1.74	1.49	**1.69**
SD	0.941314236	1.07138506	0.848344948	1.168983738	1.001365106	1.01
SDis	1.32224142	0.928789912	1.358169418	1.619237065	2.285134365	1.50
Mode	1.00	1.00	1.00	1.00	1.00	1.00
Median	1.00	2.00	1.00	1.00	1.00	1.20

Table 3.4 Deep LBE.

Statistics	Item 1	Item 2	Item 3	Item 4	Item 5	Mean (items 1–5)
Mean	2.05	1.55	1.42	1.58	1.53	**1.62**
SD	1.271347971	0.954937576	0.72227035	0.917189245	0.938148517	0.960778732
SDis	0.982941751	1.897178084	1.651201263	1.92586514	1.953484363	1.68213412
Mode	1.00	1.00	1.00	1.00	1.00	1.00
Median	2.00	1.00	1.00	1.00	1.00	1.20

4.3. A brief comment on the results of the survey

While the results generally support the observation that Polish allows LBE, they reveal a conspicuous discrepancy between the acceptability of its specific types. The relatively high acceptability of LBE -*wh* is somewhat expected given its 'discourse-sensitivity' (i.e. *wh*- elements are inherently 'prone to' (+Focus) marking[14]). However, the fact that the judgements obtained for the extraction of possessive (genitive) NP-complements (Table 3.2) fare as acceptable or marginally acceptable is rather unexpected given the definite claims regarding NP-complement extraction in article-less (NP-)languages (Bošković 2008, cf. Bašić 2004; Schoorlemmer 2012;

for Polish see Rappaport 2001a, b). Following the logic of the 'PIC & Anti-locality system' (Bošković 2014a, b, 2015a, b) it would not be unreasonable to assume that more structure should be included in the nominal domain above the NP to ensure that the NP-complement can move to the phase edge (PIC) without violating Anti-locality (cf. Abels 2003). This, however, renders a uniform analysis of the extraction of genitive possessors and deep LBE (extraction *out of* the NP-complement) inconceivable.

The data presented in this section allow us to observe that the 'PIC & Anti-locality system', while elegant in its simplicity, appears insufficient to deal with the Polish facts. At this point, it might also seem worthwhile to consider the reasons arguably underlying the ungrammaticality of NP-complement extraction in Serbian/Croatian (Bašić 2004; Schoorlemmer 2012) and Czech (Starke 2001). In his account of extraction in Czech, Starke (2001) observes that inherent case, i.e. genitive, dative or instrumental, marked nominals block complement extraction (20a). However, such a postulate is too strong for Polish, consider the acceptable (20b) and (20c).

(20) a. *Kterého herce bys sis rad vynadal priteli?
 which.GEN actor.GEN would you gladly scold friend.DAT
 'Whose actor's friend would you gladly scold?' (S/C)

 b. [Którego miasta]$_i$ przeczytałeś [opis t$_i$]?
 which.GEN city.GEN (you) read description.ACC
 'Which city did you read a description of?'

 c. [Którego miasta]$_i$ posłużyłeś się [opisem t$_i$]?
 which.GEN city.GEN (you) used REFL description.INST
 'Which city did you use a description of?' (Polish)

A different solution is entertained by Bašić (2004), who considers the GEN-ACC syncretism (triggering a specific 'garden path' effect) to be the source of the ungrammaticality of (21a)–(21b).

(21) a. *[Ovog studenta] sam pronašla knjigu?
 this.GEN student.GEN is found book.ACC
 'Of this student, I found the book?' (S/C)

 b. *Koga si pronašla knjigu?
 who.GEN is found book.ACC
 'Whose book did you found?' (S/C)

Specifically, the hearer automatically assigns ACC to the fronted NP-complement and gets confused once the actual ACC-marked object is introduced (Bašić 2004: 34, (72a)–(b)). To all intents and purposes, the prediction overgenerates even for Serbian/Croatian. Schoorlemmer (2012) discusses licit cases of NP-complement extraction exhibiting the GEN-ACC syncretism analogous to the one found in (21a)–(21b), consider (22) (Schoorlemmer 2012: 3, (3)).

(22) [Koje$_i$ svog saradnika]$_i$ je Petar sreo prijatela t$_i$?
    which.GEN his.GEN co-worker.GEN is Petar met friend.ACC
    'Which co-worker did Peter meet a friend of?' (S/C)

A closer look at the statistical data presented in Bašić's account reveals that the proposal is unlikely to hold for Polish, either. Out of the five examples featuring NP-complement extraction (Table 3.2), items (1) and (4) exhibit the 'problematic' syncretism. Thus, they should fare remarkably worse than the other, non-syncretic items. In fact, while item (1) indeed scores relatively low (SDis>0), item (4) appears to be second-best with SDis <0 (i.e. the majority of the respondents judgements was above the mean). As may be observed, the statistics for the 'syncretic' and the 'non-syncretic' items are comparably close.

5. The relevance of discourse-related factors

At this point, a related operation should also be taken into consideration, i.e. NP-internal complement fronting of the type shown in (23), an example from Polish.

(23) [[TEGO KRAJOBRAZU]$_i$ opis t$_i$]$_j$ odszukałem t$_j$ w starych materiałach.
    this.GEN landscape.GEN description.ACC found-I   in old   materials
    'I found a description of this landscape in archive materials.'

Several accounts have been offered to explain the peculiar nature of such NP-internal fronting. Thus, Witkoś (1993) analyses the surface order of [N NP$_{GEN}$] as resulting from the movement of N around the NP-complement to D in order to check the (covert) φ-features of N (see also Nowak 2000). Based on corpus data, specifically the discrepancy between the number of occurrences of [N NP$_{GEN}$] and the [NP$_{GEN}$ N] orders, Cetnarowska (2013: 4) considers this scenario implausible (24) (cf. Willim 1995).

(24) a. przyjazd   ojca   (no. of occurrences – 102)
       arrival.NOM father.GEN

    b. ojca   przyjazd   (no. of occurrences – 2)
       father.GEN arrival.NOM
       'father's arrival'

In turn, Rappaport (2001a, b) distinguishes between the derivation of subject and object genitive NP-complements and claims that the latter may only be fronted for stylistic purposes. Finally, Migdalski (2003) takes the base order to be [N NP$_{GEN}$] and explains the discrepancy pointed out in (24) by referring to the featural motivation underlying the derived order [NP$_{GEN}$ N]. As he suggests, NP-complement preposing is driven by the need to check the referentiality feature [REF], which apparently explains why non-referential complements cannot be preposed (25).[15]

(25) a. *Człowieka   prawa nie są przestrzegane w tym kraju.
         man.GEN   rights not are respected   in this country
         'Human rights are not respected in this country.'

   b. ?/*Tego   człowieka / Tomka   prawa były   już   wielokrotnie
         this   man.GEN / Tom.GEN   rights were   already   many times

      łamane.
      violated
      'This man's / Tom's rights have already been violated a number of times.'

While Migdalski's account correctly predicts the ungrammaticality of (25a), it apparently fails to explain the questionable status of (25b) despite the fact that the NP-complement is clearly referential. It may be, then, that the featural trigger for movement is more complex than just [REF]. At the same time, there is an intuition that (25b) sounds markedly better once the fronted nominal receives discourse-marked interpretation (FOC/TOP). The fact that the same interpretation does not rescue (25a) may suggest that a combination of features (e.g. REF, FOC/TOP) is at stake.

Following a similar track, Cetnarowska (2013) discusses a whole spectrum of discourse-sensitive movements of NP-complements in Polish. In her analysis of the definiteness and specificity effects in fronting, she takes them to be Topic-driven, as demonstrated by the example below (Cetnarowska 2013: 6, (19a)–(19b)).

(26) ??Każdej / KAŻDEJ   kobiety   obowiązkiem jest urodzić
      every.GEN / EVERY.GEN   woman.GEN   duty.INST   is   give-birth

     pięcioro   dzieci.
     five.DAT   children
     'Every woman's duty is to give birth to five children.'

Based on Rizzi's (1997) observation that quantifiers cannot occur as Topics (see Rizzi 1997), she argues for the Topic interpretation of the fronted expression in (26). Cetnarowska also considers different distribution of the fronted complements, i.e. before or after the demonstrative (Cetnarowska 2013: 8, (25a), (26a), glosses revised). Drawing on the typology of topics put forward by Frascarelli & Ramaglia (2013), she also classifies the fronted elements as G(iven) or C(ontrastive) / Aboutness-Shifted (AS) Topics (27) (Cetnarowska 2013: 8, (25a) and (26a), glosses adjusted).[16]

(27) a. ten Hanki   kolejny   narzeczony   (to   PIJAK)
        this Hanka.GEN   next   fiancé   COP   drunkard
        'this next fiancé of Hanka (is a DRUNKARD)'

   b. ?/* a Basi   ten   obecny mąż   to   PIJAK
         and Basia.GEN   this   current husband COP   drunkard
         'And as for Basia, her current husband is a drunkard.'

c. */? Marka   ta NAJSTARSZA córka   (wyszła za Hiszpana)
   Marek.GEN.TOP   this oldest.FOC daughter   (married a Spaniard)
   'This eldest daughter of Marek married a Spaniard.'

d. *Marka   ta   córka
   Marek.GEN.TOP   this   daughter
   'This Marek's daughter'

e. ta Marka   (najstarsza / NAJSTARSZA)   córka
   thisMarek.GEN   (eldest / ELDEST)   daughter
   'This eldest/ELDEST daughter of Marek's'

Apparently, though native speakers do not readily admit both the orders, i.e. Dem > NP-complement (27a), and NP-complement > Dem (27b), i.e. the latter is felt markedly worse. While Cetnarowska (2013: 8) assumes that the focused element serves to 'counterbalance' the fronted Topic, the remaining examples (27c)–(27d) do not fare any better.

Given the relevance of discourse marking for constructions exhibiting the fronting of possessive (genitive) NP-complements, incorporating discourse-related projections (Topic, Focus) in the cartographic representation of the left periphery of the nominal domain of Polish seems well-motivated. While the existence of such projections has already been well established in the literature on the nominal structure (Ihsane & Puskás 2001; Aboh 2004, among others), they seem potentially problematic for theories such as Bošković's (2014a, b, 2015a, b), that feature a very parsimonious model of the nominal left periphery.

5.1. Implementing the empirical observations

5.1.1. Step by step – demonstratives, prenominal adjectives and head nouns

In order to deal with the intricate fronting facts discussed in the preceding sections, the following 'base' structure including the demonstrative (DemP), a prenominal adjective (AP) / -wh and the head N is postulated (28).

(28)

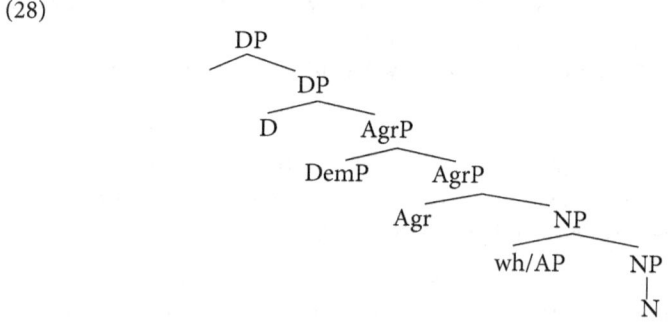

The proposal remotely follows Brugè (1996) and Giusti (1999/2002) (see also Progovac 1998) in that the demonstrative (DemP) is base-generated at the edge position of a functional projection AgrP (roughly corresponding to the Φ-Domain in the sense of Grohmann (2000/2003), i.e. the area where N-related agreement is established). The mechanism based on (28) dispenses with Cinque's (2005) descriptive observation that movement in the nominal domain always carries the NP along. It should be noted that Cinque himself provides for exceptions, such as contrastive Focus-driven movement of AP to a DP-initial position. Since most movements discussed in this chapter appear discourse-dependent (see also Fanselow & Ćavar 2002), such an alternative does not seem unreasonable. Finally, the proposal follows the path of analyses in the spirit of DPH (1) (see also Rappaport 2001a, b; Rutkowski & Progovac 2005; Rutkowski 2007; Pereltsvaig 2007).

Consider the way in which N agrees with the specific constituents of the nominal domain through AgrP (see Progovac 1998). The configuration in (28) offers two potential solutions at this point. Minimally, Agr and N enter into Agree, which results in N-to-Agr feature transfer / match (29, option 1) that does not induce movement. The transfer may optionally be accompanied by the pied-piping of the lexical material, triggering the movement of N to a higher functional projection, possibly D (29, option 2).

(29)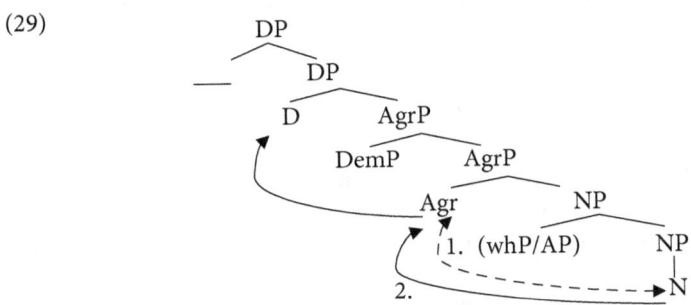

The movement of N-to-Agr may potentially be triggered by the referential features of D (Longobardi 1994) and eventually lead to N surfacing above the demonstrative, as in (30a), represented structurally in (30b) (cf. Rutkowski 2007).

(30) a. Sprzedawca   ten   (był już notowany).   (Polish)
         seller.SG.NOM. this.SG.NOM.   (was already noted)
         'This seller already had some criminal record.'

   b. [$_{DP}$ [$_D$ [$_{Agr}$ [$_N$ Sprzedawca]$_j$ Agr]$_i$ D] [$_{AgrP}$ [$_{DemP}$ ten] t$_i$ [$_{NP}$ t$_j$]]]

It is to be expected that DemP will agree with N regardless of which agreement option is selected by virtue of being base generated in Spec,AgrP.

The c-commanding sequence represented in (29) has the potential to account for the illicit extraction of prenominal AP across the demonstrative (DemP) on the grounds of the locality of movement, the relevant example illustrated in (31). Put differently, the movement of AP across DemP (a closer potential goal for the higher probe) renders the sentence ungrammatical.

(31) *Twierdzi, że uczęszczał na [nudny$_i$ [$_{AgrP}$ ten [$_{NP}$ t$_i$ wykład]]] (Polish)
(he) claims that (he) attended on boring this lecture
'He says that he attended this boring lecture.'

By the same logic, the presence or absence of DemP may be taken to determine the availability of possessive (genitive) NP-complement extraction (17) / fronting (27), the relevant details shown in (32).

(32) [$_{DP}$ [Tego miasta]$_i$ [$_{AgrP}$ (*to) [$_{NP}$ zdjęcie t$_i$]]] ukazało się wczoraj w gazetach
this.GEN city.GEN this picture appeared yesterday in newspaper
'A picture of this city appeared in the newspapers yesterday.'

Yet another look at (31) allows us to observe that the movement of the prenominal AP is sufficiently anti-local in view of Anti-locality as stated in (10). At the same time, an alternative solution to Anti-locality is available, consider Grohmann's (2000/2003) idea of clausal tripartition (33) applied to the nominal domain (see Ticio 2005 for Spanish).

(33) Grohmann (2000/2003: 180, paraphrased)
    a. [$_{\Omega \text{(roughly: CP)}}$ [$_{\Phi \text{(roughly: TP)}}$ [$_{\Theta \text{(roughly: vP)}}$]]]
    b. division of labour:
        i. Θ-Domain: part of the derivation where thematic relations are created
        ii. Φ-Domain: part of the derivation where agreement properties are licensed
        iii. Ω-Domain: part of the derivation where discourse information is established

Roughly speaking, movement carries the moved element along across domains and moving within the same domain is generally considered illicit. Assuming that domains Θ, Φ and Ω are, respectively NP, AgrP and DP, the instances of fronting / extraction of the prenominal AP (31) and the genitive NP-complement (32) are indeed anti-local. While both Bošković's and Grohmann's proposals seem equally effective at this point, in what follows the latter will be preferred due to its potential to deal with a substantial number of functional projections in the left periphery of the noun.

5.1.2. The discourse component

Once the cases of NP-complement extraction and fronting presented in the section above are analysed in detail, it seems evident that the two share a number of mutual characteristics. Primarily, both types of operations are 'discourse-sensitive', i.e. they are (at least partially) triggered by the same type of features. While an observation along these lines is not new (Giusti 1996; Rizzi 1997; Ihsane & Putskás 2001; Aboh 2004), its potentially novel aspect emerging from the considerations above is that the sentential triggers (Top/Foc) are 'synchronized' with the DP-internal stimuli in a way that allows us to view the two movements as the respective stages of a single operation (see also Svenonius 2003/2004). In order to capture this suggestion, the nominal structure put forward here includes the functional projections TopP and FocP. To illustrate the mechanics of the system, consider the derivation of (27a), repeated here as (34) and analysed in (35).

(34) a. ten   Hanki   kolejny narzeczony   to PIJAK
         this   Hanka.GEN   next   fiancé   COP drunkard
         'this next fiancé of Hanka is a DRUNAKRD'

(35)

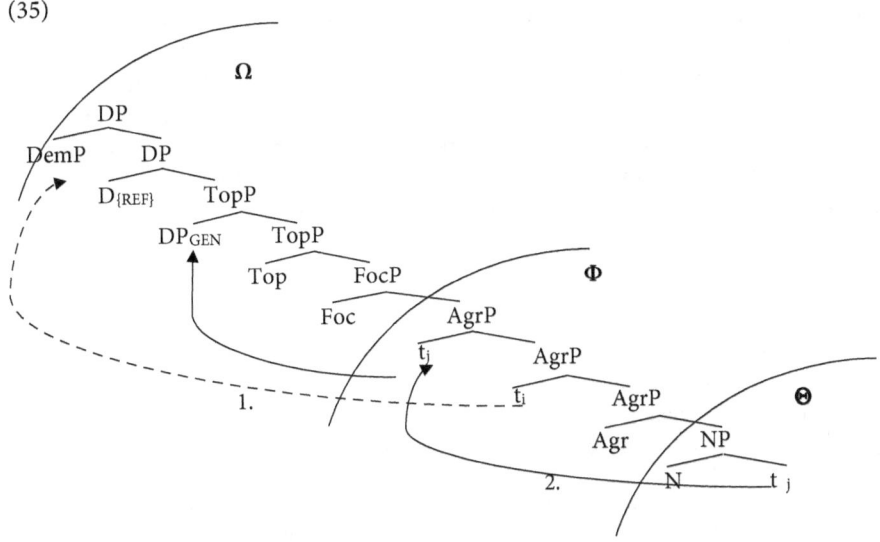

Provided that D is equipped with feature REF [EPP+], DemP moves to Spec,DP, which opens the way for the possessive (genitive) NP-complement to move cyclically through the Φ domain into TopP, where it receives the discourse-marked (Topic) interpretation. A potential problem at this point is that the sequence of operations in (34) does not strictly obey the Extension Condition (the movement of DP to TopP fails to extend the syntactic tree (see Pesetsky 1982; Kitahara 1997; Richards 2001; Chomsky 2008). However, the problem may be resolved by assuming that syntactic operations within the same phase are in effect simultaneous (see Chomsky 2008). In the absence of DemP, the possessive (genitive) NP-complement may serve as a goal for a DP-external probe, eventually triggering extraction and movement to the Topic position in the clausal structure, as in (36).

(36) [Tego miasta]$_i$ widziałem [$_{DP}$ t$_i$ [zdjęcie t$_i$]] we   wczorajszej   gazecie.
      this city.TOP   (I) saw   picture   in   yesterday's   newspaper
      'I saw a picture of this city in yesterday's newspaper.'

6. In lieu of a conclusion

The overarching aim of this chapter was to suggest a representation of the nominal structure of ('languages like') Polish that would constitute an alternative to the radically parsimonious account put forward by Bošković (2008, 2014a, b, 2015a, b). Such an alternative (a full-blown structural representation) is provided below:

(35) [$_{DP}$ D [$_{TopP}$ Top [$_{FocP}$ Foc [$_{AgrP}$ DemP [$_{AgrP}$ Agr [$_{QP}$ NumP [$_{QP}$ F$_Q$ [$_{NP}$ (wh/AP) [$_{NP}$ N]]]]]]]]]

Despite considerable complexity, the structure seems attractive for two major reasons. Firstly, it accounts for various types of extraction apparently attested in Polish (Section 4). Following the cartographic tradition, it also highlights the relevance of the Top-Foc component, placed in the left periphery of the nominal structure, performing as the locus of 'discourse marking'. In order to enable movement across domains consisting of a larger number of projections included in the area above the NP, it requires an alternative concept of Anti-locality (Grohmann 2000/2003, 2011).

Notes

1 *Abbreviations:*

ACC	accusative case	NEG	negation
AgrP	agreement phrase	NP	noun phrase
AP	adjective phrase	NR	negative Raising
COP	copula	NumP	number phrase
CP	complementiser phrase	PIC	phase impenetrability condition
D	determiner	Q	quantifier
DAT	dative case	QP	quantifier phrase
DemP	demonstrative phrase	REF	referentiality
DP	determiner phrase	RFL	reflexive
FOC	focus	S/C	Serbian/Croatian
FocP	focus phrase	SD	standard deviation
FP	functional phrase	SDis	skewed distribution
F$_Q$	quantifier (functional head)	TOP	Topic
GEN	genitive case	TopP	topic phrase
INST	instrumental case	TP	tense phrase
LBE	left branch extraction	vP (light)	verb phrase
N	noun	VP	verb phrase

2 This chapter is based on my talk given at BASEES 2017. I am grateful to the audience for insightful questions as well as the two anonymous reviewers for their extremely detailed and constructive feedback. The ideas and concepts contemplated here were extended and developed in Cegłowski (2017). This work was supported by grant no. 2012/07/B/HS2/02308 of the National Science Centre.

3 The list is not exhaustive, for an elaborate discussion see Bošković (2008).

4 See Fanselow & Féry (2013) for a comparative overview of the correlation between intervention effects and LBE in Slavic languages.

5   For interesting extensions, see Willim (1997, 2000) and Migdalski (2001).
6   Despić (2011: 34) also rejects the 'weaker' version of the Universal DP-Hypothesis that postulates the optional presence of the DP-layer in Serbian/Croatian (i.e. whenever demonstratives are present).
7   It should be noted that *babcina* in (7a) is an adjectival possessor, which makes it a relevant equivalent of *Kusturicin* in (6a). However, it must be pointed out that this form is considered archaic, which may affect the grammaticality judgements (see Witkoś & Dziubała-Szrejbrowska 2015). Given that an analogous observation can be made for Estonian (Norris 2014), Polish does not seem an isolated, idiosyncratic case in this respect.
8   Note that on the strength this account, NP (the topmost nominal projection) is taken to exhibit the properties of a phase in the sense of (11) (Bošković 2014a).
9   The NP-internal fronting of the nominal complement is relevant for its discourse-marked interpretation (e.g. contrastive).
10 Witkoś & Dziubała-Szrejbrowska (2015) offer a slightly different representation of the quantifier, which makes it possible to meet the strict criteria imposed by the PIC and Anti-locality (i). However, their analysis stems from independent sources and should not be used as an argument to feed/bleed Anti-locality by manipulating the number of projections in the nominal domain.
    i. $NP_{GENi} \ldots [_{QP} t_i [_{QP} NumP [_{QP} F_Q [_{NP} (wh/AP) [_{NP} N t_i]]]]$
11 Given space limitations, this section reports on the findings and presents selected input sentences only. For the full questionnaire, see Cegłowski (2017).
12 It may be observed that the data presented in the literature hardly ever match the flexibility that Slavic languages (as well as other languages exhibiting a relatively free word order) otherwise exert. In other words, the input examples that researchers typically use for collecting grammaticality judgements feature the constructions in question almost 'explicitly', which may bias the respondents and affect the reliability of the results.
13 As one of the reviewers correctly points out, the mean score 2.44 on the scale from 1 to 5 is relatively low and might indicate that speakers are unlikely to generate such sentences. At this point, one should consider the fact that these constructions are almost exclusively found in a specific context ('discourse-marking') and, as such, they are rather unlikely to be attested in a 'neutral' setting. As for the labels used in the Likert scale, these are meant to constitute an alternative to a standard 'binary opposition' whereby subjects have to choose between 'correct' and 'incorrect' ignoring the intuition that such a choice is too coarse and will not reflect their true native speaker judgements.
14 See Sabel (2000) for an elaborate typological overview of the correlation between *wh-* and Focus marking and Fanselow & Ćavar (2002) for a discussion of discourse-sensitive discontinuous structures in German, Polish and Croatian.
15 Cinque describes referentiality as 'the ability to refer to specific members of the set in the mind of the speaker, or pre-established in the discourse' (1990: 16). He also observes that referential *wh-*phrases can escape weak islands (See also Longobardi 1994; Öztürk 2005).
16 The exact distinction between the three types of topics is not directly relevant to the analysis presented here. For details, see Cetnarowska (2013); Frascarelli & Ramaglia (2013).

References

Abels, K. 2003. *Successive cyclicity, anti-locality and adposition stranding*. PhD dissertation. Storrs: University of Connecticut.
Abney, S. 1987. *The English noun phrase in its sentential aspect*. PhD dissertation. Boston, MA: MIT Press.
Aboh, E. 2004. Topic and focus within D. *Linguistics in the Netherlands* 21, 1–12. Amsterdam/New York: John Benjamins.
Bašić, M. 2004. Nominal subextractions and the structure of NPs in Serbian and English. MA thesis. Tromsø: University of Tromsoe.
Borsley, R. & M-L. Rivero. 1994. Clitic auxiliaries and incorporation in Polish. *Natural Language and Linguistic Theory* 12: 373–423.
Bošković, Ž. 2008. What will you have, DP or NP? *Proceedings of the North East Linguistic Society* 37: 101–114.
Bošković, Ž. 2009. More on the no-DP analysis of article-less languages. *Studia Linguistica* 63: 187–203.
Bošković, Ž. 2010. Phases and left-branch extraction. Talk presented at the Moscow Student Conference on Linguistics 5. Moscow State University, Moscow, Russia, 3–4 April 2010.
Bošković, Ž. 2014a. More on the edge of the edge. In: Chapman, C., Kit, O. & Kučerová, I. (eds), *Formal Approaches to Slavic Linguistics: The McMaster Meeting 2013 (FASL 22)*, 44–66. Michigan: Michigan Slavic Publications.
Bošković, Ž. 2014b. Now I am a phase, now I am not a phase: on the variability of phases with extraction and ellipsis. *Linguistic Inquiry* 45(1): 27–89.
Bošković, Ž. 2015a. From the complex NP constraint to everything: on deep extractions across categories. *The Linguistic Review* 32: 603–669.
Bošković, Ž. 2015b. On the timing of labeling: Deducing comp-trace effects, the subject condition, the adjunct condition, and tucking in from labeling. Available online: http://ling.auf.net/lingbuzz/002452.
Brugè, L. 1996. Demonstrative movement in Spanish: a comparative approach. *University of Venice Working Papers in Linguistics* 6, 1–53.
Cegłowski, P. 2017. *The Internal Structure of Nominal Expressions: Reflections on Extractability, Fronting and Phasehood*. Poznań: Wydawnictwo Naukowe UAM.
Cetnarowska, B. 2013. On topic movement within Polish noun phrases. Talk presented at the Poznań Linguistic Meeting, Poznań.
Chomsky, N. 2001. Derivation by phase. In: Kenstowicz, M. (ed.), *Ken Hale: A Life in Language*, 1–52. Cambridge, MA: MIT Press.
Chomsky, N. 2008. On phases. In: Freidin, R., Otero, C. P. & Zubizaretta, M. L. (eds) *Foundational Issues in Linguistic Theory: Essays in Honor of Jean-Roger Vergnaud*, 133–166. Cambridge, MA: MIT Press.
Cinque, G. 1990. *Types of A'-dependencies*. Cambridge, MA: MIT Press.
Cinque, G. 2005. Deriving Greenberg's universal 20 and its exceptions. *Linguistic Inquiry* 36(3): 315–332.
Despić, M. 2011. Syntax in the absence of determiner phrase. PhD dissertation. University of Connecticut.
Despić, M. 2013. Binding and the structure of NP in Serbo-Croatian. *Linguistic Inquiry* 44(2): 239–270.
Fanselow, G. & Ćavar, D., 2002. Distributed deletion. In: Alexiadou, A. (ed.), *Theoretical Approaches to Universals*, 65–107. Amsterdam: John Benjamins.

Fanselow, G. & Féry, C. 2013. A comparative perspective on intervention effects on left branch extractions in Slavic. In: Sulym, W., Smolij, M. & Djakiw, C. (eds), *Non Progredi est Regredi. Festschrift für Alla Paslwaska*, 266–295. Lwiw: Pais.
Franks, S. 1994. Parametric properties of numeral phrases in Slavic. *Natural Language and Linguistic Theory* 12: 570–649.
Frascarelli, M. & Ramaglia, F. 2013. DP-internal linkers at the interfaces. Talk presented at 23rd Colloquium on Generative Grammar, Madrid, Spain, 9–11 May 2013.
Giusti, G. 1996. Is there a FocusP and a TopicP in the noun phrase structure? *University of Venice Working Papers in Linguistics* 6(2): 105–128.
Giusti, G. 1999/2002. The functional structure of noun phrases: a bare phrase structure approach. In: Cinque, G. (ed.), *Functional Structure in DP and IP: The Cartography of Syntactic Structures 1*, 54–90. Oxford: Oxford University Press.
Grohmann, K. 2000/2003. *Prolific Domains: On the Anti-Locality of Movement Dependencies*. Amsterdam: John Benjamins.
Grohmann, K. 2011. Anti-locality: too-close relations in grammar. In: Boeckx, C. (ed.), *The Oxford Handbook of Linguistic Minimalism*, 260–290. Oxford: Oxford University Press.
Horrocks, G. & Starvou, M. 1987. Bounding theory and Greek syntax: evidence from wh-movement in NP. *Journal of Linguistics* 23: 79–108.
Ihsane, T. & Puskás, G. 2001. Specific is not definite. *Generative Grammar in Geneva* 2: 39–54.
Kim, S.-W. 2011. A note on the NP/DP parameter: left branch extraction in Korean. *Linguistic Research* 28(2): 257–269.
Kitahara, H. 1997. *Elementary Operations and Optimal Derivations*. Cambridge, MA: MIT Press.
Longobardi, G. 1994. Reference and proper names: a theory of N-movement in syntax and logical form. *Linguistic Inquiry* 25: 609–665.
Migdalski, K. 2001. A determiner phrase approach to the structure of Polish nominals. In: Przepiórkowski, A. & Bański, P. (eds), *Generative Linguistics in Poland: Syntax and Morphosyntax*, 135–148. Warsaw: IPIPAN.
Migdalski, K. 2003. N-to-D raising in Polish. In: Staniulewicz (ed.) *Papers in Language Studies. Proceedings of the Ninth Annual Conference of the Polish Association for the Study of English. Gdańsk 26–28 April 2000*, 187–193. Gdańsk: Wyd. UG.
Modrzejewska, E. 1981. NEG-raising predicates in English and Polish. *Poznań Studies in Contrastive Linguistics* 1981: 41–52.
Norris, M. 2014. A theory of nominal concord. PhD dissertation. University of California, Santa Cruz.
Nowak, A. 2000. On split PPs in Polish. Unpublished MS. Amherst: University of Massachusetts.
Öztürk, B. 2005. *Case, Referentiality and Phrase Structure*. Amsterdam: John Benjamins.
Pereltsvaig, A. 2007. On the universality of DP: a view from Russian. *Studia Linguistica* 61(1): 59–94.
Pesetsky, D. 1982. Paths and categories. PhD dissertation. Massachusetts Institute of Technology.
Progovac, L. 1998. Determiner phrase in a language without determiners. *Journal of Linguistics* 34: 165–179.
Rappaport, G. 2001a. Extraction from nominal phrases in Polish and the theory of determiners. In: Willim, E. & Bański, P. (eds), *Formal Approaches to Polish Syntax*. Special edition of *Journal of Slavic Linguistics* 8(3): 139–198.

Rappaport, G. 2001b. The geometry of the Polish nominal phrase: problems, progress, and prospects. In: Bański, P. & Przepiórkowski, A. (eds), *Generative Linguistics in Poland: Syntax and Morphosyntax*, 173–181. Warsaw: Polish Academy of Sciences.

Richards, N. 2001. *Movement in Language: Interactions and Architectures*. Oxford: Oxford University Press.

Rizzi, L. 1997. The fine structure of the left periphery. In: Haegeman, L. (ed.), *Elements of Grammar*, 281–337. Berkeley, CA: Kluwer.

Rozwadowska, B. 1997. *Towards a Unified Theory of Nominalizations: External and Internal Eventualities*. Wrocław: Wyd. Uniwersytetu Wroclawskiego.

Rutkowski, P. 2002. Noun/pronoun asymmetries: evidence in support of the DP hypothesis in Polish. *Jezikoslovlje* 3(1–2): 159–170.

Rutkowski, P. 2007. Hipoteza frazy przedimkowej jako narzędzie opisu składniowego polskich grup imiennych. PhD dissertation. Warsaw University.

Rutkowski, P. & Progovac, L. 2005. Classification projection in Polish and Serbian: the position and shape of classifying adjectives. In: Franks, S., Gladney, F. Y. & Tasseva Kurktchieva, M. (eds), *Formal Approaches to Slavic Linguistics: The South Carolina Meeting 2004*, 289–299. Ann Arbor: Michigan Slavic Publications.

Sabel, J. 2000. Partial *wh*-movement and the typology of *wh*-questions. In: Lutz, U., Müller, G. & von Stechow, A. (eds), *Wh-Scope Marking*, 409–446. Amsterdam: John Benjamins Publishing.

Schoorlemmer, E. 2012. Genitive noun complements in Serbo-Croatian: extraction and case. Talk presented at Formal Approaches to Slavic Linguistics 21, Bloomington, USA.

Starke, M. 2001. Merge dissolves into move. PhD dissertation. University of Geneva.

Svenonius, Peter. 2003/2004. On the edge. In: Adger, D., de Cat, C. & Tsoulas, G. (eds), *Peripheries: Syntactic Edges and their Effects*, 259–287. Dordrecht: Kluwer.

Szabolcsi, A. 1983. The possessor that ran away from home. *The Linguistic Review* 3: 89–102.

Szczegielniak, A. 1996. Deficient heads and long head movement in Slovak. In: Lindeseth, M. & Franks, S. (eds), *Formal Approaches to Slavic Linguistics: The Indiana Meeting 1996*, 312–331. Ann Arbor: Michigan Slavic Publications.

Ticio, E. 2005. Locality and anti-locality in Spanish DPs. *Syntax* 8(3): 229–286.

Willim, E. 1995. The syntax of noun phrases in Polish: linearization parameters. In: Palek, B. (ed.) *Proceedings of LP'94*, 166–189. Prague: Charles University Press.

Willim, E. 1997. *A Contrastive Approach to Problems with English*. Warsaw: PWN

Willim, E. 2000. On the grammar of Polish nominals. In: Martin, R., Michaels, D. & Uriagereka, J. (eds), *Step by Step: Essays on Minimalist Syntax in Honor of Howard Lasnik*, 319–346. Cambridge, MA: MIT Press.

Witkoś, J. 1993. Some aspects of phrasal movement in English and Polish. PhD dissertation. Adam Mickiewicz University, Poznań.

Witkoś J. & Dziubała-Szrejbrowska, D. 2015. A note on the genitive of quantification in Polish and derivational phases. *Poznań Studies in Contemporary Linguistics* 51(3): 433–462.

4. The Definiteness Effect in Russian existential and possessive sentences

Olga Kagan

1. The Russian Definiteness Effect puzzle[1]

1.1. Existential sentences and the Definiteness Effect (DE)

It has been known since at least Milsark (1974) that not all types of NPs (DPs in today's terminology) are acceptable in the post-verbal position of existential sentences (ESs). One factor that affects this acceptability is the quantifier or determiner the nominal contains. This is illustrated in (1) and (2) below.

(1) a. There are five chairs in the room.
 b. There are some chairs in the room.
 c. There is a / some chair in the room.
 d. There are no chairs in the room.

(2) a. *There is the chair in the room.
 b. *There are most chairs in the room.
 c. *There is every chair in the room.
 d. *There are both chairs in the room.
 e. *There is John in the room.

Following Francez (2007), among others, I will refer to the post-verbal nominal such as *five chairs* in (1a) as **the pivot** and to the optional expression such as *in the room* as **the coda**. It is worth noting that the pivot need not follow the verb in some languages (in fact, existential sentences in languages such as Russian and Hebrew lack a verb in the present tense altogether), while the coda often, but not necessarily, denotes location.

As can be seen in the above examples, existential sentences are compatible with nominals containing an indefinite article, numerals and quantifiers such as *some* or *no* but not with definite expressions (including proper names), nor with phrases containing such determiners as *every*, *most* or *both*. Following the terminology introduced by Milsark, nominals that are acceptable in the existential construction are called *weak* and the ones that are unacceptable, *strong*. The contrast between sentences such as (1) and (2) has also been called the 'Definiteness Effect' (DE), since definite nominals cannot appear in existential sentences, whereas (some of the) indefinite ones can.

Different analyses have been put forward in order to capture the nature of the strong/weak distinction. Some of the approaches (e.g. Milsark 1974; Barwise & Cooper 1981; Keenan 1987) concentrate on the semantics of the quantifier/determiner contained in the DP. For instance, Milsark proposes that weak quantifiers can have both cardinal and quantificational readings, whereas the strong ones can only be interpreted quantificationally. Existential sentences have a quantificational force of their own, hence they are compatible only with cardinally interpreted determiners, i.e. only with the weak ones. More generally, weak quantifiers have cardinal readings and are intersective and symmetric (Higginbotham 1987; Enç 1991). They are contrasted with purely proportional quantifiers, such as *every* and *most*, which are inherently strong.

However, Enç (1991) argues convincingly that the properties of quantifiers alone are insufficient to predict or account for the licensing of a nominal in an existential sentence. Specifically, even DPs with cardinal determiners become unacceptable in this construction if they are partitive. Thus, compare the grammatical sentences in (1) with their partitive counterparts in (3):

(3) a. *There are five of the chairs in the room.
    b. *There are some of the chairs in the room.
    c. *There is some of the chairs in the room.
    d. *There are none of the chairs in the room.

It follows that the strong/weak distinction should be applied to whole DPs rather than quantifiers in isolation. For instance, both expressions *five chairs* and *five of the chairs* contain the numeral *five*; however, only the former is acceptable in a ES. Enç further claims that the key property distinguishing the two types of nominals is specificity, analysed in the relevant part of her work as partitivity. Specific (partitive) DPs are strong, while the non-specific ones are weak. Crucially, all definite DPs and nominals with proportional quantifiers are predicted to be partitive (and specific) under her analysis. And since the pivots in (3) are overtly partitive, they are strong, too, which leads to the unacceptability of the sentences.

McNally (1998) further argues that the post-verbal nominal in ESs denotes a property or quantifies over properties (this analysis will be addressed in more detail below). Under this approach, the (un)acceptability of different types of nominals in ESs depends on the semantic type of these nominals. If the property denotation is unavailable for semantic or (sufficiently strong) pragmatic reasons, then the DP will be ruled out. Landman (2004) claims that the coda is an adjunct and proposes a 'flip-flop' mechanism that makes adjunction possible. Crucially, property-denoting nominals can undergo a shift to the adjunct type.

1.2. DE violations in Russian

The Definiteness Effect and the strong/weak distinction are observed in the existential construction in a range of languages. Negative existential sentences (NESs) in Russian seem to pose a problem since in these sentences, the Definiteness Effect turns out to be absent, or at least highly limited. (And, as we shall see later, affirmative existential sentences are different in this respect.)

(4) a. V   zale   net²   vrača.
        In   hall   NEG-BE   doctor.GEN.SG
        'There is no doctor in the hall.'

  b.   V   zale   net   stul'ev.
        In   hall   NEG-BE   chair.GEN.PL
        'There are no chairs in the hall.'

  c.   V   zale   ne   bylo   pjati   vračej.
        In   hall   NEG   was   five.GEN   doctor.GEN.PL
        'There weren't five doctors in the hall.' (NEG > 5) OR
        'Five doctors were not in the hall.' (5 > NEG)³

  d.   Dimy /   ego   net   doma.
        Dima.GEN   he.GEN   NEG-BE   at-home
        'Dima is not at home.'

  e.   Oboix   studentov   ne   bylo   v   zale.
        both.GEN   student.GEN PL   NEG   was   in   hall
        'Both students were not in the hall.' (BOTH > NEG)

  f.   Etogo   vrača   net   v   zale.
        this.GEN.SG   doctor.GEN.SG   NEG-BE   in   hall
        'This doctor is not in the hall.'

  g.   V   klase   ne   bylo   pjati   iz   étix   studentov.
        in   class   NEG   was   five.GEN   from   these   students
        'There weren't (even) five students in the class.' (NEG >5) OR:
        'Five of these students were not in the class.' (5 > NEG)

Examples in (4) reveal that not only weak DPs containing cardinal determiners (or no determiners whatsoever) are acceptable in Russian existential sentences. Rather, strong, definite DPs such as proper names, personal pronouns, expressions with a demonstrative, partitives and phrases with the quantifier *oba* 'both' are acceptable, as well. It can be seen from the above examples that a sentence-initial position is often preferable for such nominals; still, we clearly deal with an existential construction. This is revealed by the use of the negative existential item *net* (see fn. 2) in the present tense, by genitive case marking on the relevant DPs and by the lack of agreement between these DPs and the verb *byt'* 'be' in tenses other than the present (cf. 4e, in which the verb appears in the default neuter singular form, even though the (understood) subject is plural).

The problem becomes even more striking if we consider sentences with such potentially weak nominals as *pjati vračej* 'five doctors' (4c). The grammaticality of such sentences is not surprising: numerals are expected to be acceptable in the existential construction as long as they do not appear in a partitive phrase. The unexpected fact, however, is that the DP can take both wide and narrow scope over the negative operator. In other words, it can receive both a specific and a non-specific reading. For instance, (4c) is ambiguous between two interpretations, as is reflected in its translations above. Under one reading, the sentence asserts that there weren't even five doctors at the meeting, i.e. the number of doctors in the hall was lower than five. This is the non-specific, weak interpretation, quite natural for an existential sentence. However, an alternative reading is present according to which specific five doctors were absent at the meeting. In turn, the number of students who did attend could be quite high (e.g. thirty). The availability of this reading is quite surprising. The specific DP is presumably strong and it scopes above negation. Moreover, since negation, in turn, takes scope over the existential quantifier contributed by the existential construction, it follows that the DP takes scope over this quantifier. However, an existential sentence is supposed to assert (or negate) the existence of the entity denoted by the DP, at least its existence relative to some location (cf. Borschev & Partee 1998). Then how is it possible for the DP in question to scope above the existential operator?[4]

It is also worth noting that the strong, specific reading of (4c) is not only possible but also salient out of context.

1.3. Affirmative existential sentences and the Definiteness Effect

The range of facts discussed above seems to suggest that the Definiteness Effect is not observed in Russian. Should we conclude that Russian DPs do not exhibit the strong/weak distinction and/or that the Russian existential construction differs dramatically from its analogues in other languages?

The answer to this question is negative. A closer look reveals that Russian is not as different from English in the relevant respect as it may seem. First of all, some strong DPs are unacceptable even in Russian negative existential sentences:

(5) *V   zale   ne   bylo   každogo   studenta.
    in   hall   NEG   was   each.GEN SG   student.GEN SG
    'Each student was not in the hall.'/ 'Not every student was in the hall.'
    (*∀ > NEG) / (*NEG > ∀)

Secondly, it turns out that Russian affirmative existential sentences are 'well-behaved' in the sense that they exhibit the Definiteness Effect, or the strong/weak distinction, just as their counterparts in English do (cf. 6 below and Kondrashova 1996).

(6) a.   V   zale   jest'[5]   vrač.
         in   hall   BE   doctor.NOM SG
         'There is a doctor in the hall.'

    b.   V   zale   jest'   stul'ja.
         in   hall   BE   chair.NOM PL
         'There are chairs in the hall.'

c. V   zale   jest'   (minimum)   pjat'   vračej.
   in   hall   BE   (minimum)   five.NOM   doctors
   'There are (at least) five doctors in the hall.'

d. *Dima /   on   jest'   doma.
   Dima.NOM   he.NOM   BE   home
   'As for Dima, he is at home.'

e. *V zale   jest'   oba   studenta.
   in hall   BE   both.NOM   student
   'There are both students are in the hall.'

f. *V zale   jest'   étot   vrač.
   in hall   BE   this.NOM SG   doctor.NOM SG
   'There is this doctor in the hall.'

g. *V   zale jest'   pjat'   iz   étix studentov.
   in   hall BE   five.NOM   of   these students
   'There are five of these students in the hall.'

h. *V   zale   jest'   každyj   iz   étix   studentov.
   in   hall   BE   each.NOM   of   these   students
   'There is each of these students in the hall.'

(6) reveals that while weak DPs can appear in affirmative ESs, strong ones are unacceptable. The latter include proper names, personal pronouns, definite descriptions, partitive expressions and nominals that contain such inherently partitive quantifiers as *každyj iz* 'each of' and *oba iz* 'both of'.

It thus follows that Russian is, in fact, sensitive to the strong/weak distinction, and the semantics of the Russian existential construction does not differ dramatically from its counterparts in other languages. Rather, it is specifically Russian **negative** ESs that diverge from the regular pattern. This is demonstrated, for example, by the minimal contrast between the affirmative (and unacceptable) (6d)–(6g) on the one hand and their negative (and unexpectedly acceptable) counterparts in (4d)–(4g).

2. The negative/positive asymmetry: Explaining the data

An examination of such minimal contrasts reveals that affirmative and negative existential sentences differ in at least two ways. Firstly, and obviously, in their polarity. Secondly, in the case of the pivot. Thus, while in affirmative ESs the DPs appear in the nominative case, their counterparts in negative sentences are genitive. Genitive case marking is obligatory, as demonstrated in (7) below. The nominative case is not possible:

(7) V   zale   ne   bylo   studentov   / *studenty.
    in   hall   NEG   was   student.GEN.PL   / student.NOM.SG.F
    'There were no students in the hall.'

The phenomenon illustrated in (4) and (7) is known as Genitive of Negation (GoN). It is observed (with somewhat different distribution and restrictions) in numerous Balto-Slavic languages and involves genitive case marking of an internal argument that is typically expected to appear in the accusative or nominative case elsewhere. In what follows, I argue that it is precisely the genitive marking that makes (potentially) strong nominals acceptable in existential sentences. For this purpose, in the next subsection, I briefly discuss the phenomenon of GoN and semantic properties that characterize genitive arguments.

2.1. Genitive of Negation

In addition to the pivot in the existential construction, GoN marks objects of transitive verbs and subjects of certain intransitive ones (arguably, only as long as the latter are unaccusative). In these two environments, the genitive marking alternates with the accusative or the nominative, which distinguishes them from ESs. This results in genitive/accusative alternation with transitive verbs (8) and in genitive/nominative alternation with intransitive ones (9).

(8) a. Anna   ne   kupila knigi.
       Anna   NEG   bought books.ACC.PL
       'Anna didn't buy (the) books.'

   b. Anna   ne   kupila knig.
       Anna   NEG   bought book.GEN.PL
       'Anna didn't buy (any) books.' (Harves 2002)

(9) a. Otvet   ne   prišol.
       answer.NOM.SG   NEG   arrived.M
       'The answer did not arrive.'

   b. Otveta   ne   prišlo.
       answer.GEN.SG   NEG   arrived.N
       'No answer arrived.' (Babby 1978: 13)

Semantically, within the framework of such alternations, genitive arguments are known to be characterized by such properties as indefiniteness, non-specificity, non-referentiality, narrow scope and abstractness (in the sense that abstract nominals are more likely to appear in the genitive than concrete ones) (e.g. Timberlake 1986; Bailyn 1997; Pereltsvaig 1999; Harves 2002; Kagan 2013; Geist 2015 and references therein). Most of these generalizations correspond to tendencies, however, that can be overruled. Thus, definite, concrete and even specific nominals can, on certain conditions, receive genitive case. Even in (9b) above, the genitive subject may (and is even likely) to refer to an expected answer to a particular letter or request, which makes it at least in some sense specific.

More formally, two semantic properties have been recently proposed to characterize objects that appear in GoN: property-type denotation and absence of existential commitment.

(i) Partee & Borschev (2004) and Kagan (2005) argue that the genitive nominals are of the property type <e,t>. In contrast, their accusative or nominative counterparts are either of the quantificational or of the individual type, <<e,t>,t> or <e>, the more expected ones for the subject and object positions. This approach accounts for a whole range of narrower characteristics associated with GoN. For instance, property-denoting nominals are scopally inert. Therefore, not surprisingly, they cannot scope outside of negation. Further, since definite DPs are referential expressions, their most natural type is <e>. While a shift to the property type is not totally ruled out, it is expected to take place only under special circumstances. Thus, quite expectedly, such nominals will be accusative or nominative by default. The type of specific indefinites depends on the approach that one takes to specificity, but anyway, such nominals are unlikely to denote properties and, moreover, they are predicted to take a wide scope relative to the negative operator. Given that, they, too, are predicted not to appear in GoN. Finally, the property type approach is supported by the strong similarity between GoN and Intensional Genitive, i.e. the genitive marking of objects of certain intensional verbs (e.g. *xotet'* 'want', *ždat'* 'wait', *trebovat'* 'demand') and alternates with the accusative (cf. Neidle 1988; Kagan 2005, 2013; Borschev et al. 2008). As argued by Zimmermann (1993) and van Geenhoven & McNally (2005), objects of intensional predicates (or at least their subset) are property-denoting, which, in turn, strengthens the link between the property type and genitive-marking in Balto-Slavic.

(ii) A related, although by no means identical, property, argued to affect case-marking in Russian, is existential commitment. The sensitivity of object case to this property under negation, following intensional verbs or in both these environments, has been argued for by Grimm (2005), Kagan (2005), (2010), (2013), Borschev and colleagues (2008) and in other work by these researchers. The idea is that genitive case marks the objects whose referent is neither entailed nor presupposed to exist, or objects that quantify over a potentially empty set. To illustrate, (8b) above does not entail the existence of any contextually relevant books, and (9b) is compatible with a scenario under which the reply in question has never been written (in fact, this is the salient reading of the sentence). This analysis, too, captures a wide range of more specific generalizations (see Kagan 2013 for details).

An important specification is that *existential commitment* may, under certain conditions, be relativized to a particular version of reality or spatio-temporal location (cf. Borschev & Partee 1998, 2002; Kagan 2013). As far as GoN is concerned, this means that in certain environments, genitive marking signals the 'non-existence' (or absence) of a referent in a particular location (rather than the actual world in general). This is illustrated in the following minimal pair, taken from Padučeva (1997: 106):

(10) a. Maša ne vidna.
 Masha.NOM NEG seen.SG F
 'Masha can't be seen.'

b. Maši   ne   vidno.
   Masha.GEN   NEG   seen.SG.N
   'Masha can't be seen.' (meaning: Masha is not around at all.)

While (10a) suggests that Masha is present but hidden, for example behind a tree or behind some tall and fat person, (10b) essentially constitutes a way to state that Masha is not around. In other words, the alternation in case corresponds here to the opposition between presence versus absence, or the speaker's commitment to Masha's *existence* versus *non-existence*, within the speaker's field of perception. This kind of restriction becomes possible due to the presence of the perception predicate *viden* 'seen'.

2.2. Negative existential sentences: Semantics and case

Given the above discussion of the semantics of GoN, it is not surprising that we consistently observe this case marking in NESs. After all, these sentences (a) contain property-denoting pivots (as argued by McNally 1998) and (b) systematically entail the non-existence of an entity in a certain location (cf. Borschev & Partee 1998, 2002, who argue that NESs deny existence and that existence is always relativized, a generalization they call the 'Existence is Relative' Principle). Thus, the nominals in question both denote properties and lack (relative) existential commitment, which makes them ideal candidates for genitive case marking.

However, this fact on its own does not solve the apparent puzzle of losing the Definiteness Effect. How do we explain the special behaviour of Russian NESs? I propose that in such sentences, the Definiteness Effect is (almost) not observed because, due to their genitive case form, the nominals (even potentially strong ones) get interpreted as properties, which makes them acceptable in the existential construction. In contrast, in affirmative ESs, genitive marking is absent, and a shift to the property type interpretation is much more restricted, which results in the unacceptability of strong DPs.

I follow McNally (1998) in analyzing ESs as containing a property type argument and a one-place predicate, *be-instantiated*, which applies to properties. While I take the coda to play a significant part in existential sentences (cf. Zucchi 1995; Comorovski 1995; Keenan 2003), here I follow Francez (2007), among others, in treating it as an adjunct.[6] Simplifying somewhat, I assign the semantics in (12a) to the Russian existential verb *jest'*, roughly corresponding to the English 'there is' (tense ignored), and the semantics in (12b) to the existential sentence in (11).

(11) Byl   sil'nyj   dožd'.
     was   strong   rain.NOM.SG
     'It was raining cats and dogs', 'There was a heavy rain.'

(12) a. $\lambda P.$ be-instantiated (P)
     b. be-instantiated $(\lambda y.\text{heavy-rain}(y))$

I also follow Partee (1987) in assuming that nominal phrases can receive denotations of three different types: the individual type (e), the property type (<e,t>) and the quantificational type (<<e,t>,t>) (in fact, adding intensionality to the picture will result in an increased number of types), with a range of operations available that can change the type of an expression. The relevant type-shifting operations are the ones that turn a non-property to a property, i.e. **BE**, which turns quantifiers into properties, and **ident**, which turns individual-type expressions into properties.

Turning to the different kinds of nominals, weak DPs, such as *a boy, boys* or *three boys*, easily receive a property-type interpretation, which makes them perfect candidates for appearing in existential sentences. Thus, (11) with a bare pivot is interpreted as an assertion that the property of being a rain is instantiated in a contextually salient location, which, in turn, is equivalent to stating that there was a rain there. In contrast, strong DPs are either incompatible with the property type, or else, despite a potential compatibility, this type does not correspond to their natural interpretation. In the latter case, a shift to <e,t> is in principle possible but must be supported by lexical or contextual material. As a result, strong DPs are typically ruled out in ESs but can become acceptable under certain conditions, with an appropriate support. This is illustrated in (13).

(13)   a.   There was every kind of doctor at the convention.   (McNally 1998: 5)
        b.   There was the usual objection in the afternoon.   (Lumsden 1988: 153)

For instance, (13a) contains the proportional (strong) quantifier *every*, which makes the nominal an unlikely candidate for a postverbal position in an ES, given that it is expected to be of the quantificational type <<e,t>,t>. However, the lexical content of the DP (and specifically, the presence of the noun *kind*), reveals that in this instance, the quantifier ranges over properties rather than over individuals (particulars). This makes it appropriate for an existential sentence (cf. McNally 1998).

In turn, (13b) contains a definite DP, although definites are also normally treated as strong and tend to be ruled out in the existential construction. However, in this case, as discussed by Lumsden (1988), the DP gets interpreted as a specific temporal instantiation of the objection, or a stage of the objection (in the sense of Carlson 1977). This, in turn, causes the DP to receive a property-like (rather than referential) meaning. Roughly, the sentence asserts that the property of being the usual objection was instantiated in the afternoon. The definite nominal undergoes a natural shift to the property type, which, in turn, makes it acceptable in (13b).[7]

Russian has an additional way to facilitate the (potentially possible) type-shifting operation to trigger a property interpretation of a strong DP. This is done by marking the DP with Genitive of Negation. This case overtly marks the nominal as property-denoting. As a result, the shift becomes possible even in the absence of a particularly strong lexical or contextual support. Even a potentially strong nominal that appears in GoN undergoes a shift to the property type. Of course, if this shift is totally impossible for that kind of DP, the result will be an unacceptable sentence, as with *každyj* 'each' in (5), repeated below for the sake of convenience as (14).

(14) *V   zale   ne   bylo   každogo   studenta.
     in   hall   NEG   was   each.GEN.SG   student.GEN.SG
     'Every student was not in the hall.'

Here, we deal with a purely proportional, strong quantifier, which does not allow a property interpretation; it is only compatible with a quantificational one. It could still quantify over properties, as illustrated for English in (13a), but in order for such a meaning to be created, genitive marking is insufficient. In other words, in order for *student* to get interpreted as a **kind** of student, lexical support is needed (e.g. an analogue of the overt *kind of* in 13a). Moreover, since in Russian, it is the whole DP *každ-ogo student-a* (each-GEN student-GEN) that appears in the genitive case, it is the whole DP that is expected to be of the property type <e,t>. Since this is impossible, the sentence is unacceptable.

However, quite often, the property denotation is, though atypical, potentially possible for 'strong' DPs, and grammatical NESs result. In contrast, affirmative ESs do not contain a marker that would trigger, or enhance, the type-shift. Therefore, nominals that are not naturally interpreted as properties for independent reasons will be ruled out.

Let us now consider several acceptable examples.

(15) V   garaže   net   mašin.
     in   garage   NEG.BE   car.GEN.PL
     'There are no cars in the garage.'

The weak nominal *mašin* ('cars') is interpreted as a property of being a plurality of cars (type <e,t>), which, in turn, is entailed not to be instantiated in the parking lot. The sentence is acceptable similarly to its affirmative counterpart (16):

(16) V   garaže   jest'   mašiny.
     in   garage   BE   car.NOM.PL
     'There are cars in the garage.'

We can now turn to sentences that involve an apparent DE-violation. Let us begin with a proper name, an expression that is unambiguously definite even in an article-less language such as Russian:

(17) Dimy   net   doma.
     Dima.GEN   NEG.BE   home
     'Dima is not at home.'

While a proper name is most naturally interpreted as type *e*, it does in principle also have a property type denotation (cf. Partee 1987; McNally 1998; Zimmermann 1993, among others, for the property type of definite expressions). The DP *Dima* will then denote a property of being the specific individual Dima (18). Under an intensional approach, it will denote a function which for every possible world renders the same individual, Dima, as the value (i.e. it is a rigid designator).

(18) λx. x=dima

(17) then denies an instantiation of this property in a particular location (at Dima's home), i.e. it receives exactly the right kind of interpretation for an existential sentence. A property is entailed not to be instantiated in the location specified by the coda. Following Pereltsvaig's (1999) treatment of genitive proper names and Lumsden's (1988) discussion of definites in ESs, we may view this meaning as an assertion that no spatio-temporal instantiation of Dima, or no stage of Dima (in the sense of Carlson 1977), is present at Dima's home. This is a non-trivial statement, compatible with truth conditions of ESs.

Let us now consider the example (4c), repeated below as (19), which contains a numeral and is compatible with what seems like a wide-scope interpretation.

The acceptability of a weak DP in an existential sentence, whether affirmative or negative, is, again, not surprising. But, as discussed above, the strange observation is the availability of what looks like a wide-scope reading of *five doctors* over negation. The sentence is ambiguous between the two readings (i) and (ii).

(19) V   zale   ne   bylo   pjati   vračej.
     in   hall   NEG   was   five.GEN   doctor.GEN.PL
 (i) There were not even five doctors in the hall (only fewer than five). *NEG > 5*
 (ii) Five specific doctors were not in the hall.   *5 > NEG*

The way in which the first reading is derived is rather trivial. The genitive phrase is interpreted as a property of being five doctors (i.e. each instantiation of the property constitutes a set of five doctors). The sentence entails that this property was not instantiated in the hall. This, in turn, entails that the number of doctors present in the hall is lower than five (and, potentially, the set of doctors could be empty).

The surprising reading is (ii), in which the DP seems to take a wider scope than is presumably possible for it in an existential construction. I propose that, in fact, the wide scope is an illusion. In reality, the semantics of (19) under the second meaning is rather close to that of NESs that contain proper names, such as the one in (17). Here, the nominal *pjati vračej* (five doctors) receives a definite or specific interpretation (recall that Russian lacks articles and, therefore, semantic-pragmatic definiteness is typically not marked overtly). Roughly, the phrase is used by the speaker to pick up five particular individuals, for example Dr Who, Dr Jekyll, Dr House, Dr Livesey and Dr McCoy. Under the property type interpretation, the DP denotes the property of being **these particular five doctors**, similar to the way in which the DP *Dima* under the <e,t> type denotes the property of being the individual Dima. The shift to the property type, not quite natural for definite expressions or even specific indefinites, is facilitated by genitive case marking. Crucially, the DP does not take a wide scope, even under what looks like a wide-scope reading. The sentence has the same kind of meaning as any NES does. Specifically, a certain property (one of being a particular group of doctors) is entailed not to be instantiated in the hall. The wide-scope illusion is due to the definite/specific nature of the DP.[8]

(20) Oboix studentov ne bylo v zale.
 both.GEN student.GEN.PL NEG was in hall
 'Both students were not in the hall.' (BOTH > NEG)

In (20), the nominal *oboix studentov* 'both students' gets essentially interpreted as *the two students*, i.e. as a definite DP that under its property-type semantics denotes a property of being a set of two contextually specified individuals.

To sum up thus far, strong DPs are acceptable in Russian NESs due to the fact that GoN-marking facilitates their shift to the property type. If such a shift is totally impossible, however, the resulting sentences are unacceptable, as illustrated above for (5). This raises yet a different question. In particular, we know that typically, in non-existential sentences, GoN marks weak DPs (indefinite, non-specific, non-referential ones). If this case easily combines with strong DPs in NESs, what makes its distribution in other environments, for example in the object position, more restricted?

First of all, it should be emphasized that strong genitive DPs are, in fact, attested outside of NESs. This is illustrated in (21), taken from Kagan (2013):

(21) a. Ja ne videl tam Erielly.
    I NEG saw there Eriella.GEN
    'I didn't see Eriella there.'
    (Kurtz, K. 1992, *Hroniki Derini* 'The Chronicles of the Deryni')

 b. Tvoj otčot ne soderžit étix faktov.
    your report NEG contain these.GEN.PL facts.GEN.PL
    'Your report doesn't contain these facts.'

 c. Ja ne pomnju étogo razgovora.
    I NEG remember this.GEN.SG conversation.GEN.SG
    'I don't remember this conversation.'

Here, we see that GoN is compatible with definite objects. Still, it is true that such phrases are more likely to appear with the accusative marking.

Second, in the object position, there is an accusative alternative, which is more economical. Under the genitive version, the DP undergoes a shift to the property type, and then the verb (if extensional) has to undergo a type-shift as well, in order for type mismatch to be avoided. Originally, the verb looks for an e-type object, and a shift is needed in order for it to become compatible with an <e,t>-type one. Such a complexity must be motivated by semantic/pragmatic reasons, otherwise an accusative object with no type-shifting will be preferred. After all, typically, a definite expression of type e will render exactly the same truth conditions as its property-type counterpart. However, in NESs, (a) there is no need for a predicate to undergo a type-shift (as *be-instantiated* does, originally, look for a property-type nominal), and (b) there is no alternative for the DP, either semantic (only a property type DP is acceptable) or grammatical (neither accusative nor nominative nominals are possible, see (7)). Here, genitive case-marking and a shift to the <e,t> type is the only way to save the derivation. Hence, a genitive DP will be accepted unless a property interpretation is totally impossible for the given phrase.

3. Possessive BE-sentences: A puzzle

Let us now turn to the properties of possessive BE-sentences in Russian. Cross-linguistically, possessive BE-sentences share a range of characteristics with existential ones, including the presence of the Definiteness Effect (see, for instance, Freeze 1992 for discussion). Given that, the DE is not surprisingly observed in Russian possessive sentences. Here, strong DPs turn out to be disallowed, as expected, not only in affirmative but also in negative clauses. In other words, possessive BE-sentences are more well-behaved than their existential counterparts. In this section, I describe the puzzle, yet the solution is left for future research.

First of all, it is important to point out that Russian is a BE-language, i.e. the possessive construction in this language contains the existential *be* rather than a possessive verb analogous to English *have*. More precisely, in present tense the relevant sentences contain the existential verb *jest'* 'be' in the affirmative, and its negative counterpart *net* in negated sentences. In order to relate to the past and the future, the corresponding forms of *byt'* 'be' are employed.

Typical Russian possessive sentences are illustrated in (22). Note that the English translations contain the verb *have*, indicating that English is a HAVE-language.

(22) a. U   Koli   jest'   sobaka.
        at   Kolja   BE   dog.NOM.SG
        'Kolia has a dog.'

    b. U   Koli   net   sobaki.
        at   Kolja   NEG.BE   dog.GEN.SG
        'Kolja doesn't have a dog.'

Possessive sentences thus look quite similar to existential sentences in Russian (cf. Partee & Borschev 2008). They contain the same existential BE, the pivot is nominative in affirmative clauses and genitive under negation, and the coda is an *u*-DP 'at-DP' prepositional phrase, denoting the possessor.

The data turn out to be surprising once sentences with a definite or partitive pivot are considered. Strictly speaking, they are often not ungrammatical. However, they undergo a shift in interpretation that eliminates the combination of a possessive meaning with a referential reading of the DP. Two strategies are present. First, the sentences may receive an existential, locative, reading, with the coda interpreted as a location, not as a possessor. The strong DP is then acceptable in the same way and for the same reasons as discussed in the previous sections for NESs. Second, the strong DP may receive a type reading rather than token reading. Roughly, a phrase such as 'this car' will be understood as 'this kind of car', which will make its meaning not referential but rather very much property-like. This, in turn, makes the sentence perfectly compatible with an existential verb. Both alternatives are illustrated below.

For the sake of convenience, let us first consider an affirmative sentence and then turn to its negative counterpart. (Recall that with affirmative clauses, the Definiteness Effect is observed even in existential sentences.)

(23) U   menja   jest'   éta   kniga.
     at   me   BE   this.NOM.SG   book.NOM.SG
     'I have this book.'

Example (23), with a definite possessee (which contains a demonstrative), is perfectly acceptable with the possession reading. However, let us consider the readings it may and may not have.

i) 'I have a copy of this book.' The sentence has a reading according to which the speaker has a copy of a contextually specified book (where 'book' is treated as a content), for example *The Lord of the Rings*. Semantically, definiteness has to do not with a specific physical object but rather with a specific masterpiece. But the particular copy, the particular physical object that is owned by the speaker has not been previously mentioned in the context. In this case, the sentence is indeed possessive, but the possessed entity is not truly definite or specific. We deal with the **type-token** distinction (where a nominal may denote an abstract concept or an object that instantiates that concept), and the token possessed by the speaker is new rather than given. This makes a property type reading quite natural. 'This book' corresponds to a whole set of individual copies.

ii) 'I own this particular copy of the book.' This reading is absent. What (23) cannot mean is that the speaker possesses the specific copy of a book, the specific physical object that has been either mentioned or pointed at in the context.

In other words, (23) is compatible only with the interpretation under which 'this book' is treated as a kind of property (roughly, 'a book with this content'). The e-type interpretation whereby the nominal refers to a particular, previously mentioned, object is unavailable. In fact, if a reading along the line of (i) is absent for a given DP (for instance, when it is animate and thus cannot denote a set of copies), the sentence becomes unacceptable (24).

(24) ???U   menja   jest'   étot   rab.'
     at   me   BE   this.NOM.SG   slave.NOM.SG
     'I own this slave.'[9]

Let us now turn to a negative BE-possessive sentence. Interestingly, it has an additional acceptable reading, which is not available for (23). But most crucially, the analogue of reading (ii) above (one according to which the possession of a particular physical object is denied) is not available, showing that the Definiteness Effect is retained under negation.

(25) U   menja   net   étoj   knigi.
     at   me   NEG-BE   this.GEN.SG   book.GEN.SG
     'I don't have this book.'

Again, let us analyse the available and unavailable readings for this sentence.

i) 'I don't have a/any copy of this book.' Like in the first reading of (23), the speaker does not relate to a particular physical object but to a content, and asserts that she does not own any copy, any realization of the book in question. She denies possession of any token, not just of some particular token that is familiar from the discourse. Again, a property type interpretation of the DP is quite natural, in spite of its definiteness.

ii) 'This book is not at my place' (lit. 'not at me'). This is the second interpretation under which the sentence is perfectly acceptable. The familiar book (this time, a particular physical object that has been previously mentioned in the discourse) is not located in places that are characterized as the speaker's. For instance, it is not present in the speaker's bag or in the speaker's house. This interpretation is, for example, appropriate in a context in which a particular copy of the book is searched for.

Crucially, under this meaning, the sentence does not deny possession. It says nothing about who the book belongs to. It could belong to the speaker or to a different person. The statement has to do only with the book's **location**. It can thus be concluded that we deal with an existential, rather than possessive, sentence, in which location is specified by the *u*-phrase, i.e. the *u*-phrase is the coda. We already know that in Russian NESs, definite pivots are perfectly acceptable. Therefore, the acceptability of (25) under the existential (locational) reading is not surprising.

Interestingly, an analogous reading is not available for the affirmative sentence (23).

iii) 'I don't possess this (copy of the) book.' This reading is absolutely impossible, as the speaker cannot point at a specific book and use (25) to assert that it is not in her possession. In other words, if we concentrate on a particular copy of the book, the sentence becomes unacceptable as a possessive one. A definite DP is inappropriate and the Definiteness Effect is observed. For the sake of comparison, note that a similar sentence with an indefinite DP, such as (22b), is perfectly acceptable precisely under the possessive reading. Thus, (22b) asserts that Kolja does not own a(ny) dog. The contrast between (22b) and (25) under the third reading reveals that the Definiteness Effect is indeed present in Russian BE-possessive sentences.

We can thus conclude that in negative BE-possessive sentences, genitive case marking is not sufficient to cancel the Definiteness Effect, as shown in example (25) and the discussion of its interpretation. Definite possessees are only licensed as long as a type reading (as opposed to the token reading) is evoked. In this respect, affirmative sentences do not differ from their negative counterparts. The polarity-based asymmetry observed in ESs and discussed in Section 2 (and illustrated, for example, in the contrast between the negative (4d)–(4g) on the one hand, and the affirmative (6d)–(6g), on the other) is absent. This contrast between BE-existentials and BE-possessives remains to be accounted for. Why does Genitive of Negation, which facilitates a shift to a property-type interpretation, eliminate the Definiteness Effect in existentials but not in possessives? I leave this question open for future research.

4. Conclusion

To sum up, the Definiteness Effect is observed in Russian BE-sentences to a limited extent. In affirmative existential sentences, the facts are quite standard from a cross-linguistic perspective: weak DPs are licensed, while strong ones are typically disallowed in the position of the pivot. However, as soon as we turn to negative ESs, the picture changes dramatically, i.e. specific and definite pivots become totally acceptable, as well as DPs with the quantifier *oba* 'both', although certain strong quantifiers, such as *každyj* 'each' are still (predictably) disallowed. I have followed McNally's (1998) analysis in treating pivots in ESs as property-denoting and proposed that Genitive of Negation facilitates the shift of the pivot to the property type. This accounts for the contrast between Russian affirmative and negative ESs (since GoN is only checked in the latter) and one between Russian negative ESs and their counterparts in languages such as English. The latter lack a morphological tool such as GoN-marking and, therefore, exhibit the Definiteness Effect in a much clearer way.

In BE-possessive sentences, the configuration is different, even though there, too, the picture gets complicated by certain factors. Both in affirmative sentences and under negation, definite pivots are quite often acceptable but only under a *type* reading (as opposed to token reading). Otherwise, the sentences have to undergo a shift to an existential-locational meaning, losing their possessive character (in the present tense, this is only possible under negation). Thus, in order to retain a possessive interpretation, the possessee (pivot) has to be weak or, if definite, it must receive a property-like interpretation, which affects truth conditions in a transparent way. The mere genitive case marking is insufficient for the licensing of a definite nominal, a fact that reduces the asymmetry between negative and affirmative possessives and also makes the former quite different from NESs in the relevant respect.

Notes

1   *Abbreviations*

ACC	accusative case	GoN	Genitive of Negation
DE	Definiteness Effect	N	neuter gender
F	feminine gender	NOM	nominative case
GEN	genitive case	PL	plural number
NEG	negative marker	SG	singular number

2   In present tense, NESs contain the negative item *net*, which has been claimed to constitute a contraction of the negative marker *ne* 'not' and existential BE (e.g. Chvany 1975; Paducheva 2000; Partee & Borschev 2008).
3   The unexpected scope relations will be discussed in what follows.
4   The last problem arises if we assume that ESs contribute an existential operator. However, certain analyses do not involve such a quantifier (cf. McNally 1998), as will be discussed in more detail below.
5   The item *jest'*, originally a present tense form of the verb *byt'* (be), occurs only in existential and possessive BE-sentences. It is worth noting, however, that even in these constructions, its acceptability varies, and sometimes, a version without *jest'*

is preferred. See Kondrashova (1996) for a detailed discussion of the distribution of *jest'*. It is crucial to consider versions with *jest'*, however, since the alternatives in which this item is absent may (and are sometimes likely to) be interpreted as not existential but locative ones, for example *Dima is at home* rather than **There is Dima at home* (cf. Babby 1978 and Borschev & Partee 1998, 2002, for the discussion of the contrast between existential and locative/declarative sentences in Russian).

6. The analysis put forward in this chapter does not depend on this assumption.
7. Also, the fact that negative existential sentences can contain proper names is pointed out, for example, by van Rooij (2006).
8. The question of whether the DP should be treated as definite or rather as a specific indefinite under reading (ii) is not trivial, given that (a) the definiteness feature is not formally marked on such nominals in Russian and (b) the very term *specificity* is vague, subject to numerous interpretations and analyses (e.g. Farkas 2002; von Heusinger 2011; Kagan 2011 and references therein for discussion). For our current purposes, I assume that both readings are in principle possible and under both, the <e,t> type denotation corresponds to the property of being the same, specific, five individuals. Presumably, under the definite reading, both the speaker and the hearer know who these individuals are, whereas under the specific indefinite one, only the speaker does. Here, I follow the approach to specificity that is based on the concept of the speaker's knowledge, or speaker identifiability (Ioup 1977; Kagan 2011). I leave a more detailed investigation of the corresponding semantic-pragmatic properties of nominals such as *pjati vračej* (five doctors) in (19) to future research.
9. This sentence can, in fact, become acceptable under the meaning 'This slave is there to help me'. More generally, an interpretation of this kind tends to license definite DPs in existential sentences. Partee & Borschev (2008) call it the *dispositional* reading of possession.

References

Babby, L. 1978. *Negation and Subject Case Selection in Existential Sentences: Evidence from Russian*. Bloomington: Indiana University Linguistics Club.

Bailyn, J. F. 1997. Genitive of Negation is obligatory. In: Browne, W., Dornisch, E., Kondrashova, N. & Zec, D. (eds), *Annual Workshop on Formal Approaches to Slavic Linguistics: The Cornell Meeting*, 84–114. Ann Arbor, MI: Michigan Slavic Publications.

Barwise, J. & Cooper, R. 1981. Generalized quantifiers and natural language. *Linguistics and Philosophy* 4: 159–219.

Borschev, V. & Partee, B. 1998. Formal and lexical semantics and the genitive in negated existential sentences in Russian. In: Bošković, Ž., Franks, S. & Snyder, W. (eds), *Annual Workshop on Formal Approaches to Slavic Linguistics 6*, 75–96. Ann Arbor, MI: Michigan Slavic Publications.

Borschev, V. & Partee, B. 2002. The Russian Genitive of Negation in existential sentences: the role of theme-rheme structure reconsidered. In: Hajičová, E. & Sgall, P. (eds), *Travaux de Circle Linguistique de Prague (novelle serie)* 4, 185–259. Amsterdam: John Benjamins.

Borschev, V., Paducheva, E., Partee, B., Testelets Y. & Yanovich, I. 2008. Russian genitives, non-referentiality, and the Property-Type Hypothesis. In: Antonenko, A., Bailyn J. F. & Bethin C. Y. (ed.), *Formal Approaches to Slavic Linguistics: The Stony Brook Meeting (FASL 16)*, 48–67. Ann Arbor, MI: Michigan Slavic Publishers.

Carlson, G. 1977. Reference to kinds in English. PhD dissertation. University of Massachussets, Amherst.

Chvany, C. 1975 *On the Syntax of BE-sentences in Russian*. Cambridge, MA: Slavica.

Comorovski, I. 1995. On quantifier strength and partitive noun phrases. In: Bach, E., Jelinek, E., Kratzer, A. & Partee, B. (eds), *Quantification in Natural Languages*, 145–177. Dordrecht: Kluwer.

Enç, M. 1991. The semantics of specificity. *Linguistics Inquiry* 22: 1–25.

Farkas, D. F. 2002. Specificity distinctions. *Journal of Semantics* 19: 213–243.

Francez, I. 2007. Existential propositions. PhD dissertation. Stanford University, Stanford, CA.

Freeze, R. 1992. Existentials and other locatives. *Language* 68(3): 555–595.

Geenhoven, van, V. & McNally, L. 2005. On the property analysis of opaque complements. *Lingua* 115: 885–914.

Geist, L. 2015. Genitive alternation in Russian: a situation semantics approach. In: Zybatow, G., Biskup P., Guhl, M., Hurtig C., Mueller-Reichau O. & Yastrebova, M. (eds), *Slavic Grammar from a Formal Perspective*, 157–174. Berlin: Peter Lang.

Grimm, S. M. 2005. The lattice of case and agentivity. MSc thesis. University of Amsterdam.

Harves, S. 2002. Unaccusative syntax in Russian. PhD dissertation. Princeton University, Princeton, NJ.

Heusinger von, K. 2011. Specificity. In: von Heusinger, K., Maienborn, C. & Portner, P. (eds), *Semantics: An International Handbook of Natural Language Meaning*, vol. 2, 1025–1057. Berlin: de Gruyter.

Higginbotham, J. 1987. Indefiniteness and predication. In: Reuland, E. & ter

Ioup, G. 1977. Specificity and the interpretation of quantifiers. *Linguistics and Philosophy* 1: 233–245.

Kagan, O. 2005. Genitive case: a modal account. In: Falk, Y. (ed.), *Proceedings of Israel Association for Theoretical Linguistics* 21 (IATL 21).

Kagan, O. 2010. Genitive objects, existence and individuation. *Russian Linguistics* 34(1):17–39.

Kagan, O. 2011. On speaker identifiability. *Journal of Slavic Linguistics* 19(1): 47–84.

Kagan, O. 2013. *Semantics of Genitive Objects in Russian: A Study of Genitive of Negation and Intensional Genitive Case*. Dordrecht: Springer.

Keenan, E. 1987. 'A semantic definition of 'indefinite NP'. In: Reuland, E. & ter Meulen, A. (eds), *The Representation of (In)Definiteness*, 286–317. Cambridge, MA: MIT Press.

Keenan, E. L. 2003. The Definiteness Effect: semantic or pragmatic? *Natural Language Semantics* 11: 187–216.

Kondrashova, N. 1996. The Russian copula: a unified approach. In: Toman, J. (ed.), *Annual Workshop on Formal Approaches to Slavic Linguistics: The College Park Meeting 1994*, 171–198. Ann Arbor, MI: Michigan Slavic Publications.

Landman, F. 2004. *Indefinites and the Type of Sets*. Oxford: Blackwell.

Lumsden, M. 1988. *Existential Sentences: Their Structure and Meaning*. London: Croom Helm.

McNally, L. 1998. Existential sentences without existential quantification. *Linguistics and Philosophy* 21: 353–392.

Meulen ter, A. (eds), *The Representation of (In)Definiteness*, 43–70. Cambridge, MA: MIT Press.

Milsark, G. 1974. Existential sentences in English. PhD Dissertation. Massachusetts Institute of Technology.

Neidle, C. 1988. *The Role of Case in Russian Syntax*. Dordrecht: Kluwer Academic Publishers.
Padučeva, E. V. 1997. Roditel'nyj subjekta v otricatel'nom predloženii: sinaksis ili semantika? [Genitive of subject in a negative sentence: syntax or semantics?] *Voprosy jazykoznania* 2: 101–116.
Paducheva, E. 2000. Definiteness Effect: the case of Russian. In: Heusinger, von, K. & Egli, U. (eds), *Reference and Anaphoric Relations*, 133–146. Dordrecht: Kluwer.
Partee, B. 1987. Noun phrase interpretation and type-shifting principles. In: Groenendijk, J. A. G., de Jongh, D. & Stokhof, M. J. B. (eds), *Studies in Discourse Representation Theory and the Theory of Generalized Quantifiers*, 115–143. Dordrecht: Foris.
Partee, B. & Borschev, V. 2004. The semantics of Russian Genitive of Negation: the nature and role of perspectival structure. In: Watanabe, K. & Young, R. B. (eds), *Proceedings of SALT 14*, 212–234. Ithaca, NY: CLC Publications.
Parteee, B. & Borschev, V. 2008. Existential sentences, BE and the Genitive of Negation in Russian. In: Comorowski, I. & von Heusinger, K. (eds), *Existence: Semantics and Syntax*, 147–191. New York: Springer.
Pereltsvaig, A. 1999. The Genitive of Negation and aspect in Russian. In: Rose, Y. & Steele, J. (eds), *McGill Working Papers in Linguistics* 14: 111–140.
Rooij, van, R. 2006. *Attitudes and Changing Contexts*. Netherlands: Springer.
Timberlake, A. 1986. Hierarchies in the Genitive of Negation. In: Brecht, R. D. & Levine, J. S. (eds), *Case in Slavic*, 338–360. Ann Arbor, MI: Slavica Publishers, Inc.
Zimmerman, E. 1993. On the proper treatment of opacity in certain verbs. *Natural Language Semantics* 1: 149–179.
Zucchi, S. 1995. The ingredients of definiteness and the Definiteness Effect. *Natural Language Semantics* 3: 33–78.

5. Predicative possession in Belarusian, a mixed BE/HAVE language

Egor Tsedryk

1. Introduction[1,2]

This chapter investigates clausal possessive structures in Belarusian, an East Slavic language that Isačenko (1974: 44) considers to be in transition between a BE-possession language and a HAVE-possession language. I will focus on two general patterns that can be identified as Location and Action event schemas (Heine 1997: 47) or locational and HAVE possessives (Stassen 2009: 49, 62), as illustrated in (1a) and (1b), respectively.

(1) a. U   Hanny   ësc'   kvatèra.
        at   Hanna.GEN   be.$_{EXIST}$ apartment.NOM
        'Hanna has an apartment.'

   b. Hanna   mae   kvatèru.
       Hanna.NOM   have.3SG   apartment.ACC
       'Hanna has an apartment.'

The BE/HAVE alternation in (1) is an example of the so-called 'too-many-(surface)-structures puzzle' (Myler 2016: 2). This puzzle has been approached in two different ways in the generative literature. On the one hand, Freeze (1992) and Kayne (1993) have proposed a single underlying structure that may result in the BE or HAVE surface form, depending on the syntactic operations constrained by case and general properties of movement (see Myler 2016: 112–123, 307–328 for an overview and criticisms). On the other hand, Myler (2016) has recently shown that there is more than one underlying possessive structure, not only cross-linguistically but also within a given language. Crucially, these structural options are determined by a restricted inventory of functional heads and the lexical categories they combine with. I approach the BE/HAVE dichotomy in Belarusian from this second perspective. Thus, one of the fundamental questions concerns the inventory of syntactic heads and grammatical features that lead to multiple form-meaning pairings. In this respect, my ultimate goal is to identify these building blocks and to provide a unified account of BE and HAVE possessive structures in Belarusian.

There is yet another puzzle that Myler (2016: 2) identifies as the 'too-many-meanings' problem. For example, HAVE is well known for its multiple meanings in HAVE languages, such as English (see, e.g., Ritter & Rosen 1997: 296). With respect to Belarusian, I will show HAVE patterns with both existential and copular clauses. Does this mean that we should have an existential HAVE and a non-existential one? I will approach this question from a non-lexicalist perspective, adopting the framework of Distributed Morphology (Halle & Marantz 1993 et seq.). More precisely, my proposal is that we do not only have a single HAVE but that both BE and HAVE structures in Belarusian have a common spatiotemporal root labelled as $\sqrt{AT}$. This root encodes inclusion (cf. Bjorkman & Cowper 2016), and HAVE is just one of its morpho-phonological realizations, depending on the way this root is categorized in syntax. In fact, the actual alternation is not between BE and HAVE, but between HAVE and the preposition *u* 'at', which is the elsewhere form of $\sqrt{AT}$. Overall, my approach is strictly derivational: depending on the functional heads merged with the common spatiotemporal root, we end up with either a BE or a HAVE structure. Furthermore, an existential BE sentence (unlike a copular BE sentence) has an extra structural level created by an additional lexical root, $\sqrt{EXIST}$ (existential root, spelled out as *ësc'* in (1a)). In fact, this root derivationally has nothing to do with HAVE. I will show that the existential/copular dichotomy encodes two set-theoretic possibilities: partial inclusion (intersection of two sets) and maximal inclusion (inclusion of a set).

This chapter will unfold as follows. Section 2 starts with a theory-neutral overview of the data. Section 3 focuses on my theoretical assumptions, also presenting the inventory of functional heads, defining the copular verb and introducing the existential root. Section 4 provides a conceptual definition of possession, suggesting that a mixed BE/HAVE system encodes inclusion in a lexical root, not a functional head. Section 5 presents my analysis, illustrating both the semantic composition and spell-out rules of the attested BE and HAVE forms. This section also presents predicative possession from a set-theoretic perspective, differentiating between partial and maximal inclusion. I show that a single HAVE structure covers both relational types, whereas these two ontological variants are complementarily distributed between an existential BE and a copular BE structure (one with and the other without $\sqrt{EXIST}$). Finally, section 6 concludes the discussion.

2. The BE/HAVE alternation: An exploratory overview

The goal of this section is to present the BE/HAVE alternation in Belarusian from a pre-theoretical perspective. This overview consists of six parts. Section 2.1 presents BE and HAVE forms. Section 2.2 illustrates their distribution across various possessive relations (kinship, body parts, diseases, psychological conditions, etc.). Section 2.3 shows that neither the existential BE nor HAVE lexically encode ownership. Sections 2.4 and 2.5 focus on the Definiteness Effect and the patterns of case marking under the scope of negation, respectively. Section 2.6 summarizes the main findings.

2.1. BE/HAVE forms

Belarusian (like Russian) has two formal types of BE: an existential and a copular one. The existential BE can be recognized by the form *ësc'* in the present tense, as shown in (2),[3] which repeats (1a) with a full paradigm of BE forms. *Ësc'* is a non-agreeing form; agreement with the postverbal nominative can be observed in the past (agreement in gender) or in the future (agreement in person and number).

(2) U Hanny   ësc'   / by-l-a   / budz-e   kvatèra.
    at Hanna.GEN be$_{EXIST}$ / be$_{COP}$.PST.F / be$_{COP}$.FUT.3SG apartment.F.NOM
    'Hanna has / had / will have an apartment.'

In (3), I present a locative construction with the nominative in the preverbal position. The example depicts the copular BE, which has a null phonetic realization (Ø) in the present tense (excluding the form *ësc'*); otherwise, the same BE forms hold in the past and the future. In (4), I present the copular BE in a predicative structure. Again, the Ø/*ësc'* dichotomy is clearly seen in the present tense, and syncretic BE forms in the past/future[4] are attested. Table 5.1 presents the full paradigm of BE forms in Belarusian.

(3) Hanna   (zaraz) ësc'   / Ø   / by-l-a   / budz-e   u Minsku.[5]
    Hanna.F.NOM now   be$_{EXIST}$ / be$_{COP}$.PRS / be$_{COP}$.PST.F / beFUT-3SG in Minsk.LOC
    'Hanna is / was / will be (now) in Minsk.'

(4) Hanna   *ësc'   / Ø   / by-l-a   / budz-e   pryhožaja dzjaŭčyna.
    Hanna.NOM   be$_{EXIST}$ / be$_{COP}$.PRS / be$_{COP}$.PST.F / be$_{COP}$.FUT-3SG [beautiful girl].NOM
    'Hanna is / was / will be a beautiful girl.'

Table 5.1 Belarusian BE forms.

Tense Specification	Existential BE	Copular BE
Present	ësc'	Ø
Infinitive	by-c'	BE-INF
Past[6]	by-ŭ-Ø	BE-PST-M.SG
	by-l-a	BE-PST-F.SG
	by-l-i	BE-PST-PL
Future[7]	bud-u	BE.FUT-1SG
	budz-eš	BE.FUT-2SG
	budz-e	BE.FUT-3SG
	budz-em	BE.FUT-1PL
	budz-ece	BE.FUT-2PL
	bud-uc'	BE.FUT-3PL

I shall emphasize that the existential/copular distinction made here is purely formal (i.e. based on the surface forms). I will use it as a morpho-syntactic tool to probe the differences between possessive structures. That is, while considering BE-and HAVE-possessive clauses, it is important to keep the present tense as a 'litmus indicator' of the copular/existential contrast, following the generalization in (5).

(5) If *ësc'* cannot be overtly used in a present tense BE-possessive clause, this clause has a copular BE.

The relevant (and crucially, pre-theoretical) question to raise in the context of a mixed BE/HAVE system is the following: if HAVE alternates with BE, which BE does it alternate with, i.e. existential or copular BE? As we will see in section 2.2, HAVE alternates with both BE forms. More precisely, predicative possession in Belarusian has a tripartite variability relative to the observable surface forms: (i) existential BE, (ii) copular BE, and (iii) HAVE. Whether or not one wants to assume an additional BE verb is a matter of analysis. I do not distinguish 'possessive BE' as a special type because there is no separate possessive BE form in Belarusian. I also do not assume that possession necessarily underlies the existential BE *a priori*, leaving the observable linguistic contrasts to speak for themselves.

Finally, before turning to an overview of possessive relations in section 2.2, I shall mention that the negative form of *ësc'* is *njama* (cf. *net* in Russian and *nie ma* in Polish). This contracted form has the same stem as the present tense HAVE forms (see Table 5.2). The negative existential BE is etymologically related to HAVE (I do not have anything to say about this diachronic relationship). Nevertheless, from a synchronic perspective, *njama* is not part of the HAVE morphological paradigm for two reasons: (i) *njama* is inflectionally invariable (just like *ësc'*), and (ii) in nonpresent tense, it turns back into an inflected BE form (from Table 5.1), preceded by a negative particle *ne* (e.g. *ne by-c'* 'not be-INF', *ne by-l-a* 'not be-PST-F.SG', *ne bud-u* 'not be.FUT-1SG', etc.). In other words, the fact that *njama* has the same stem as a present tense form of HAVE is historically conditioned and does not necessarily imply that the present-day *ma-* (as a root of the present tense HAVE) lexically encodes an existential operator.

Table 5.2 Belarusian HAVE forms.

Tense Specification		HAVE
Present	ma-ju	HAVE.PRS-1SG
	ma-eš	HAVE.PRS-2SG
	ma-e	HAVE.PRS-3SG
	ma-em	HAVE.PRS-1PL
	ma-ece	HAVE.PRS-2PL
	ma-juc'	HAVE.PRS-3PL
Infinitive	me-c'	HAVE-INF
Past	me-ŭ-	HAVE-PST-M.SG
	me-l-a	HAVE-PST-F.SG
	me-l-i	HAVE-PST-PL

2.2. Existential BE, copular BE and HAVE across possessive relations

In (6), I show that the existential BE alternates with HAVE in the case of kinship relations. However, it is the copular BE that alternates with HAVE in the case of body parts and inanimate part-whole relations, as shown in (7)–(8). The existential BE also alternates with HAVE in the case of the so-called 'abstract possession' (Mazzitelli 2015: 94), as in (9). Finally, the examples in (10)–(11) show that neither the existential BE nor HAVE is possible with diseases and psychological conditions. Table 5.3 summarizes the state of affairs presented in (6)–(11). The whole picture can be described as follows: the existential BE is in complementary distribution with the copular BE, while HAVE alternates with either of them to the exclusion of diseases and psychological conditions.

(6) *Kinship*
    a. U Hèli   ësc'   dačka   i   syn.
        at Helja.GEN be$_{EXIST}$ daughter.NOM and son.NOM
        'Helja has a daughter and a son.'

    b. Hèlja   mae   dačku   i   syna.
        Helja.NOM has   daughter.ACC and son.ACC
        'Helja has a daughter and a son.'
        (adapted from S. Adamovič, 'Res publica Femina', *Naša Niva*, 1 December 1997)[8]

(7) *Body parts*
    a. U Hanny   *ësc' / Ø   pryhožyja vočy.
        at Hanna.GEN be.$_{EXIST}$ / be$_{COP}$.PRS [beautiful eyes].NOM
        'Hanna has beautiful eyes.'

Table 5.3 Distribution of BE and HAVE across possessive relations.

Categories	Existential BE	Copular BE	HAVE
Kinship	✓		✓
Body parts		✓	✓
Inanimate part-whole		✓	✓
Abstract possession	✓		✓
Diseases		✓	
Psychological conditions		✓	

b. Hanna mae pryhožyja vočy.
Hanna.NOM has [beautiful eyes].ACC
'Hanna has beautiful eyes.'

(8) *Inanimate part-whole*
 a. U hètaha drèva *ësc' / Ø mahutny stvol.
 at [this tree].GEN be.$_{EXIST}$ / be$_{COP}$.PRS [powerful trunk].NOM
 'This tree has a powerful trunk.'

 b. Hètaje drèva mae mahytny stvol.
 [this tree].NOM has [powerful trunk].ACC
 'This tree has a powerful trunk.'

(9) *Abstract possession*
 a. U mjane ësc' mara.
 at me.GEN be$_{EXIST}$ dream.NOM
 'I have a dream.'

 b. Ja maju maru.
 I.NOM have dream.ACC
 'I have a dream.'

(10) *Diseases*[9]
 a. U mjane *ësc' / Ø branxit.
 at me.GEN be$_{EXIST}$ / be$_{COP}$.PRS bronchitis.NOM
 'I have bronchitis.'

 b. *Ja maju branxit.
 I.NOM have bronchitis.ACC
 'I have bronchitis.'

(11) *Psychological conditions*
 a. U mjane *ësc' / Ø vjaliki sum pa radzime.
 at me.GEN be.$_{EXIST}$ / be$_{COP}$.PRS [great nostalgia].NOM for homeland
 'I am homesick.'

 b. ??Ja maju vjaliki sum pa radzime.
 I.NOM have [great nostalgia].ACC for homeland
 'I am homesick.'
 (Mazzitelli 2015: 166, (212))

There is undoubtedly a historical explanation of BE/HAVE alternation, as Belarusian is located in the areal zone between BE and HAVE languages (e.g., Russian and Polish; see Mazzitelli 2017 for an overview of the Circum-Baltic area).[10] Nevertheless, a language-internal explanation is also expected. What is interesting in the data presented thus far is that HAVE alternates with both the existential BE and the copular BE. Does this mean that there is more than one HAVE (one of which would lexically encode an existential operator)? For example, Tham (2004: 148, 2006: 218) differentiates a possessive HAVE, which takes an existential complement, a control HAVE and a focus HAVE. In section 2.3, I show that HAVE and the existential BE, used to express alienable possession, do not lexically encode ownership.

2.3. Lexical underspecification

Tham (2006: 138) notes that HAVE in English does not encode ownership either: this possessive relation is implied, but not entailed, which makes the cancellation in (12b) possible.

(12) a. Eliza has a mirror.
  b. Eliza has a mirror, but it doesn't belong to her.
  (Tham 2006: 138, (3))

HAVE in Belarusian is not an exception. However, this is not an exclusive property of HAVE: the ownership reading can be cancelled in both clauses in (1), the one with HAVE (13b) and the one with the existential BE (13a). The sentences in (13) mean that Hanna has an apartment at her disposal without necessarily being its formal owner.

(13) a. U Hanny ësc' kvatèra pad Minskam, ale ž
    at Hanna.GEN be$_{EXIST}$ apartment.NOM near Minsk.INST but EMPH

    hètaja kvatèra ëj ne naležyc'.
    [this apartment].NOM her.DAT NEG belong.3SG
    'Hanna has an apartment near Minsk, but this apartment doesn't belong to her.'

  b. Hanna mae kvatèru pad Minskam, ale ž
    Hanna.NOM have.3SG apartment.ACC near Minsk.INST but EMPH

    hètaja kvatèra ëj ne naležyc'.
    [this apartment].NOM her.DAT NEG belong.3SG
    'Hanna has an apartment near Minsk, but this apartment doesn't belong to her.'

In this regard, the existential BE and HAVE are different from the verb *valodac'* 'to own' in (14), whose root lexically encodes ownership, entailing a set of juridical rights, including the right to sell or to rent a property, not just availability of that property for Hanna's use.[11]

(14) #Hanna valodae kvatèraj pad Minskam, ale ž
    Hanna.NOM own.3SG apartment.INST near Minsk.INST but FOC

    hètaja kvatèra ëj ne naležyc'.
    [this apartment].NOM her.DAT NEG belong.3SG
    '#Hanna owns an apartment near Minsk, but this apartment doesn't belong to her.'

Nevertheless, the dispositional reading in (13) is very subtle. In fact, Belarusian speakers tend to associate HAVE with ownership, understood as prototypical possession (Mazzitelli 2015). The main point here is that the ownership reading is related to indefiniteness and, more precisely, to the existential closure of a possessee. Even though I do not offer a precise semantic account of this relationship in this chapter, I explore the origin of the existential closure with HAVE, claiming that it is not part of the verb's lexical entry. In section 5.2.1, I propose that the existential closure is provided in the course of the syntactic derivation as a default option, competing with a more marked contextual binding alternative. At this point, it is sufficient to mention that existentially closed possessees implicate a long-lasting control over an individual and, subsequently, reinforce the ownership (prototypical possession) implicature. Definiteness, on the other hand, is one of the factors that corroborates temporary possession and undermines the ownership reading of BE/HAVE. This correlation is illustrated in the next section, which presents definiteness as a type/token distinction.

2.4. Definiteness Effect

Existential *there*-clauses in English are known for a so-called 'Definiteness Effect' or 'Definiteness Restriction' on the postverbal DP (also known as 'pivot'), which can felicitously be headed by a weak determiner but not a strong/definite determiner (Milsark 1974, 1977; see other chapters in this volume for further references and discussion). An example of this effect is given in (15a). A similar restriction has also been observed with HAVE (Keenan 1987; Partee 1999; Tham 2004, 2006).

(15) a. There is a/*the dog in this house.
     b. John has an/*the older sister.

There is a substantive body of literature (see Ward & Birner 1995: 723) that has challenged indefiniteness as an absolute requirement in the existential sentences. The availability of the definite expressions in the existential *there*-clauses is contextually restricted and strongly depends on the availability of a discursive domain that an existential operator can quantify over. (16) exemplifies a definite DP instantiating a 'hearer-new token of a hearer-old type' (Ward & Birner 1995: 730). The existential operator quantifies over a domain of properties (i.e. hearer-old type) and picks up a hearer-new token from that domain (see Abbott 1997 for further discussion).

(16) There was the usual crowd at the beach today. (They were there yesterday too. Today for the first time they sat around a fire and roasted marshmallows.)
      (Ward & Birner 1995: 733, (24))

As for the Definiteness Effect in possessive HAVE clauses, it is also subject to contextual restrictions. There is nothing in principle that precludes a (syntactically) definite DP in the object position of HAVE, unless we differentiate different types of HAVE in the lexicon, as Tham (2004, 2006) does. For example, the sentence in (17b) (as an answer to (17a)) illustrates a control HAVE in Tham's lexical types of HAVE (her possessive HAVE is expected to select for an existential/indefinite possessee).

(17) a. Where are all the mirrors?
    b. Eliza has them.
       (Tham 2006: 144, (22a)–(22b))

I will now focus on the distribution of definite possessees in Belarusian BE/HAVE clauses. Like other East Slavic languages, Belarusian does not have articles. Therefore, I will use the demonstrative DP *hètaja kniha* 'this book' to show that it has a type reading with the existential BE and a token reading with the copular BE, while both readings are to a certain extent possible with HAVE.

Consider first (18). This utterance is possible in the context in which the speaker shows a book (i.e. we have a contextually definite DP), but it does not mean that she/he owns this particular book. The DP is interpreted as a particular kind of book (type reading).

(18) U mjane   taksama ësc'   hètaja kniha.
     at me.GEN also   be$_{EXIST}$ [this book].NOM
     'I also have this (kind of) book.'

Now suppose that two interlocutors talk about a book, which is part of their shared knowledge, and one of them wonders where this book could be, asking (19a). The answer in (19b) has a token reading, and the existential BE is precluded in this case.

(19) a. Ty vedaeš hdze   hètaja kniha?
       you know where [this book].NOM?
       'Do you know where this book is?'
    b. Hètaja kniha   zaraz *ësc' / Ø   u   mjane.
       [this book].NOM now   be$_{EXIST}$ / be$_{COP}$PRS at me.GEN
       'I have this book right now.'

Turning now to HAVE, it is used with a possessee interpreted as a type in (20) and as a token in (21b)[12] (given the context in (21a)). The first occurrence of HAVE patterns with the existential BE in (18) and its second occurrence is comparable with the copular BE in (19b). More generally, whenever the DP has a type reading, as in (18) and (20), the possessive relation tends to be ownership (permanent possession), while with a DP interpreted as a token, as in (19b) and (21b), it can only be temporary control (temporary possession).[13] These observations are summarized in Table 5.4 (the asterisk indicates incompatibility).

(20) Ja   taksama maju   hètuju knihu.
     I.NOM   also   have.1SG [this book].ACC
     'I also have this (kind of) book.'

Table 5.4 BE/HAVE and the type/token reading of the possessee.

Reading	Existential BE	Copular BE	HAVE
Type	ownership	*	ownership
Token	*	temporary control	temporary control (?)

(21) a. *Context*: Friends are sharing two books, *The Hobbit* and *The Three Musketeers*. They know who is the current reader of *The Hobbit*, but they have lost track of *The Three Musketeers*. When discussing this issue together, one of them utters (21b).

b. ?Ja   zaraz   maju   hètuju knihu.
   I.NOM   now   have.1SG   [this book].ACC
   'I have this book right now.'

2.5. The Genitive of Negation

The discussion of definiteness also touches upon the differences in case marking that can be observed under the scope of negation. Thus, I will provide some background with an example of genitive/accusative alternation observed with a non-possessive transitive verb in (22). The accusative in (22b) entails a particular discursively salient entity, while the genitive in (22a), known as 'the Genitive of Negation' (GoN), does not have this entailment.

(22) a. Hanna   ne   atrymala   kvatèry   u Minsku.
        Hanna.NOM NEG   get.PST.F   apartment.GEN in Minsk.LOC
        'Hanna didn't get an apartment in Minsk.'

    b. Hanna   ne   atrymala   kvatèru   u Minsku.
        Hanna.NOM NEG   get.PST.F   apartment.ACC   in Minsk.LOC
        'Hanna didn't get the apartment in Minsk.'

GoN in Belarusian is very similar to GoN in Russian: it has both structural and semantic properties.[14] In a nutshell, it normally affects internal arguments (those that form the inner verb phrase, excluding the logical subject) and can only alternate with a structural case (nominative or accusative), associated with surface syntactic positions, not specific semantic relations, marked by an idiosyncratic lexical case.[15] Finally, it structurally requires a sentential Neg (above the verbal phrase), which is able to take scope over an internal argument. On the semantic side, it is associated with properties and lacks existential commitment (Partee & Borschev 2004; Borschev et al. 2008; Partee et al. 2011; Kagan 2013, Chapter 4 in this volume). That is, GoN signals a DP of type <e, t> in (22a) ('property-type hypothesis', Partee et al. 2011: 150).

Returning now to the BE/HAVE alternation, if we negate an existential clause, such as the one in (18), GoN is mandatory, as shown in (23). The existentials indicate that the logical form required for GoN is the one in (24). That is, Neg must scope over an existential operator that binds a variable of type *e* (what is negated is the existence of an individual with a given property).

(23) U mjane njama hètaj knihi / *hètaja kniha.
at me.GEN not.be.EXIST [this book].GEN / [this book].NOM
'I don't have this (kind of) book.'

(24) $\neg \exists x_e . \text{property}(x)$

The copular BE presumably lacks the existential operator and, therefore, cannot feature GoN like the existential BE. However, there is a confounding factor. As can be observed in (25), which is the negated form of (19b), the lack of an overt verbal form creates the Neg + PP string in the phonetic form and makes the sentential Neg undistinguishable from a narrow constituent Neg (see Borschev et al. 2006 for discussion of similar cases in Russian).

(25) Hètaja kniha zaraz ne u mjane.
[this book].NOM now NEG at me.GEN
'It's not me (but somebody else) who has this book right now.'

HAVE, on the other hand, patterns with the existential BE in (26), but the accusative case is possible with a contextually salient particular book, as in (27b) uttered in the context of (27a) (with a raised pitch on the verb).

(26) Ja ne maju hètaj knihi.
I.NOM NEG have.1SG [this book].GEN
'I don't have this (kind of) book.'

(27) a. *Context*: Friends are sharing a book. At some point, the book is lost, and everyone suspects that Peter is its last reader. Peter wants to defend himself, uttering (27b).

b. ?Ja bolej ne maju hètuju knihu.
I.NOM anymore NEG have.1SG [this book].ACC
'I don't have this book anymore.'

Even though HAVE is a semantically marked option to express temporary possession (see fn. 13), the accusative case in (27b) is not as degraded as the nominative case in (23). It means that the possessee with HAVE is not coerced in the same way as it is with the existential BE. At the same time, postulating a special HAVE for (27b), different from HAVE in (26) (which requires an existential possessee), would create an unwelcome precedent for any other transitive verb that is subject to the genitive/accusative alternation, as the one in (22). That is, every such verb could also have an existential and a non-existential duplicate in the lexicon. Instead of deriving GoN from syntactic and compositional rules, it would just be left to the fate of lexical unpredictability.

2.6. Summary

To summarize, the BE/HAVE alternation in Belarusian (between the existential or copular BE and HAVE) has the characteristics compiled under (28).

(28) a. The BE/HAVE alternation in Belarusian is a tripartite alternation between (i) existential BE, (ii) copular BE, and (iii) HAVE.
 b. The existential and the copular BE are allomorphic in the nonpresent tense (Table 5.1) and are in complementary distribution across various possessive relations (Table 5.3).
 c. HAVE alternates with both the existential and the copular BE (except diseases and psychological conditions; see Table 5.3).
 d. BE and HAVE verbs do not lexically encode specific possessive relations (kinship, part-whole, ownership, temporary possession, etc.). These relations are inferred from the semantics of the nominal expressions.
 e. The possessee has a type reading with the existential BE, a token reading with the copular BE, and both type and token readings with HAVE.
 f. A token reading of alienable possessees requires extra-linguistic contextual support and correlates with the physical control reading (temporary possession).
 g. GoN is mandatory with the existential BE, absent with the copular BE, and can be overruled by the accusative case marking with HAVE (under a contextually marked token reading).

In section 5, I will address the variable behaviour of the verb HAVE, suggesting that it is in fact related to the preposition *u* 'at', but this relation is not derivational in nature (contra Freeze 1992 and Kayne 1993). HAVE is analysed as a contextual allomorph. In this regard, I follow Myler (2016), but from a slightly different perspective: Belarusian HAVE is derived from a lexical root, not a light verb. Section 3 presents my theoretical assumptions, motivated independently from the concept of possession. I return to the latter in section 4.

3. Beyond the realm of possession

Section 3.1 outlines the main theoretical premises. Section 3.2 sketches the functional spine of a transitive structure. Section 3.3 gives a morphosyntactic definition of the copula, and section 3.4 defines the existential function associated with the form *ësc'*.

3.1. General theoretical assumptions

Assuming the minimalist framework (Chomsky 2000 et seq.) and Distributed Morphology (Halle & Marantz 1993; Embick & Noyer 2007; Embick & Marantz 2008), I take syntax to be the only derivational engine responsible for the hierarchical structures of the language. These structures are created by a recursive application of Merge, which is the basic syntactic operation that takes two syntactic objects (which can be primitive or not) and creates a new one (a binary branching structure). The latter can be the input for the next application of Merge. There is no morphological derivation creating words before their insertion into syntax. That is, the lexicon does not have any derivational power; it is just a list of functional categories (with grammatical features) and lexical roots ($\sqrt{}$). Roots are category-neutral concepts that become nouns, verbs or adjectives in syntax when a root-containing structure is merged with a categorizing head (Marantz 1997; Embick & Marantz 2008; Alexiadou & Lohndal 2017). Little v is the categorial head that is central to the subsequent discussion. Its primary function is to verbalize the structure. For example in (29), little v verbalizes a root-containing structure ($\sqrt{P}$), creating a verb phrase (vP), but a verbalized structure may be without a root (see section 3.3).

(29)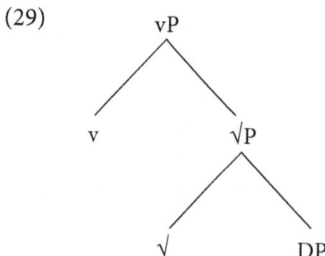

At some point in the derivation (call it 'Spell-Out'), a portion of the syntactic structure is associated with (transferred to) the interfaces that can be accessed by the sensorimotor and the conceptual-intentional systems. That is, terminal nodes (syntactic heads) are associated with a phonological form (PHON), on the one hand (30a), and with a semantic interpretation (SEM), on the other (30b). The association on the PHON side is known as (late) Vocabulary Insertion. To simplify, I will use an italicized transliterated form for PHON (head ↔ *transliterated form*). As for SEM, it is an interpretation function, shown by the double brackets ([[head]] = *logical form*).

(30) a. head ↔ PHON / __morphosyntactic context
      b. head ↔ SEM / __semantico-syntactic context

Both roots and functional heads are subject to contextual allomorphy (Marantz 2013: 97; Myler 2016: 34–35). That is, their Spell-Out depends on the surrounding morphosyntactic features. The same kind of variability is possible on the SEM side, in which case it concerns contextual allosemy (Marantz 2013: 101–106; Myler 2016: 40). The roots assumed in this chapter (to be introduced in sections 3.4 and 5.1) denote abstract spatiotemporal relations. They are subject to late insertion and, therefore, contextual allomorphy. However, they have fixed denotations; they are not subject to contextual allosemy, but they influence the semantics of their surroundings. Thus, in their context, little *v* does not need to introduce an eventuality variable. Overall, vP is one of the derivational phases when Spell-Out takes place. The interpretation function is applied to vP based on the semantic composition (from terminal to branching nodes). On the PHON side, it affects the syntactic objects embedded in the complement of little v. The root head-adjoins to v for categorization purposes and escapes early spell-out (this is how the form of the root may depend on tense features, introduced later in the derivation; see, e.g., Myler 2016: 34).

By definition, the roots do not have grammatical features (Embick & Noyer 2007: 295). Thus, spatiotemporal roots can denote relations between individuals, but they do not have case features, which would map abstract semantic relations onto grammatical relations. In other words, such roots need case-assigning heads in addition to their categorization. In this respect, little v may or may not be a structural case-assigner (i.e. be a transitivity marker). I assume that the structural accusative case is assigned under Agree (Chomsky 2000, 2001). More precisely, a case-assigning v has a bundle of unvalued agreement features, such as person, gender and number (ϕ-features),[16] in which case I label it as v_ϕ. This v probes the closest DP (downward) and initiates a process of mutual feature valuation, which applies only if the DP has an unvalued case. If the DP happens to receive a case value from a different source, the probing ϕ-features receive default values. In fact, I assume that the lack of feature values is a definitional property of uninterpretable features (Den Dikken 2014: 39). By transitivity, only valued features are interpretable.[17] That is, a feature cannot be interpreted at the interfaces as long as it remains unvalued. Thus, assignment of default values to ϕ-features is a last resort procedure that applies only if Agree cannot be applied.

3.2. The external argument introducer

In Belarusian (and East Slavic more generally), the accusative case can be assigned in the absence of a referential external argument (the logical subject), as can be observed in (31).[18] These constructions are known as 'transitive impersonal' constructions (Lavine 2010). Whether or not there is a null expletive in (31) is a separate issue. The main point here is that the case-assigning v_ϕ is not necessarily an argument-introducing head.

(31) a. I   tut   mjane   udaryla!
       and   here   me.ACC   hit.PST.N
       'And here I was hit!'
       (A. Bujnicki, 'Na kraju halaktyki' [On the edge of the galaxy], 2013)[19]

   b. (Šmat tam paljahlo   maladyx saldat), tam i   mjane   ranila.
      (a.lot there it.was.killed young   soldiers) there and me.ACC wound.PST.N
      '(Many soldiers were killed there), I was wounded there too.'
      (M. Koran, 'Kahanne na ŭsë žyccë' [Love for the whole lifetime], 2012)[20]

c. Mjane vanitue.
   me.ACC nauseate.3SG
   'I feel sick.'

Therefore, I assume an additional category, Voice, which introduces a referential external argument.[21] An extended transitive structure with an external argument is presented in (32). The subscript {D} on Voice indicates its selectional feature: Voice selects for a constituent of category D (this notation is adopted from Myler 2016).

(32)

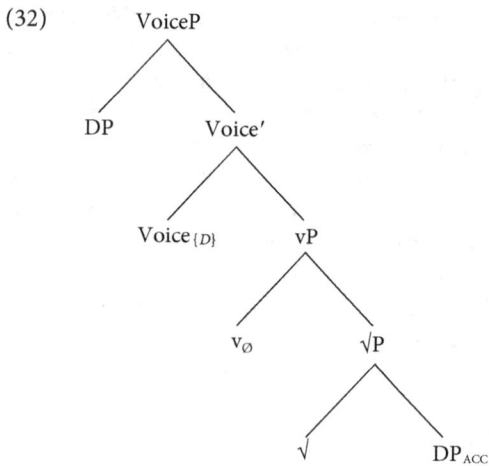

3.3. The copula verb

In the framework outlined above, I define the copula as a caseless v that verbalizes a small clause structure. For convenience, I label it as v_{be} to distinguish it from v_ϕ in (32). Small clauses in Belarusian come in two varieties, with or without the instrumental case, as in (33) ((33a) repeats (4) with the copula in the past tense).

(33) a. Hanna   byla   pryhožaja dzjaŭčyna.
        Hanna.NOM   be.PST.F   [beautiful girl].NOM
        'Hanna is / was / will be a beautiful girl.'

    b. Hanna   byla   pryhožaj dzjaŭčynaj.
       Hanna.NOM   be.PST.F   [beautiful girl].INST
       'Hanna is / was / will be a beautiful girl.'

Structurally, the instrumental case signals an asymmetrical structure projected from a predicational head (Pred), as in (34b). This structure is opposed to a headless small clause (SC) in (34a) (Pereltsvaig 2007: 12). Pred introduces an eventuality variable, which has to be bound by an existential operator in the aspectual projection (Roy 2013:

22; see also Matushansky 2000 and Richardson 2007: 208).²² The structure in (34a) supposedly lacks this variable.

(34)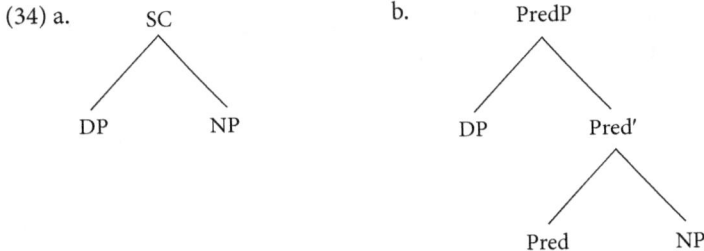

These structures are not verbal per se. In order to be verbalized, they have to be merged with little *v*, i.e. a vP would dominate SC in (34a) and PredP in (34b). Pred is detectable by the instrumental case on the predicate, but the head itself is phonetically null. With or without PredP, v_{be} is subject to the same Spell-Out rules, as in (35) (based on Table 5.1; T stands for tense).

(35) a. v_{be} ↔ *by-* / ___T[past] or [infinitive]
 b. v_{be} ↔ *bud(z)-* / ___T[future]
 c. v_{be} ↔ Ø/___(elsewhere)

One last comment is in order with respect to the branching node in (34a). SC is just a putative abbreviation for a syntactically undetermined label. The product of Merge cannot be properly labelled, since two maximal projections (phrases), forming a syntactic object, do not share formal features. Following Chomsky (2013), I assume that SC can only be labelled when DP moves.²³ More precisely, it moves to the specifier position of Tense Phrase (Spec,TP), as in (36). This movement creates a discontinuous element (with two copies), and the lower copy (marked by strikethrough) becomes irrelevant for labelling. As a result, SC is labelled as NP.

(36) [$_{TP}$ DP [$_{T'}$ T [$_{vP}$ v_{be} [$_{NP (SC)}$ ~~DP~~ NP]]]]

3.4. The existential root

As for the form *ësc'* (Table 5.1), I assume that this is an exponent of an existential root, √EXIST (the allomorphy between this root and the copula is left aside until section 5.2). This root represents an existential function 'from properties to sets of properties' (Keenan 1987: 291).²⁴ According to Partee & Borschev (2007: 152), 'existence is always relative to a "LOCation", which may be implicit'. Their LOC is a broad concept, not just a physical location; it is generally defined as location in a spatiotemporal domain (cf. 'contextual domain' in Francez 2007: 70–71). I use *LOC* in (37) as a generic placeholder for functions that map individuals to a function of type <s, t> (where *s* stands for the semantic type of eventualities, which are spatiotemporal particulars). The existential function, as defined in (37), asserts the existence of a subset of individuals that have both a given property P and a given spatiotemporal location *LOC*.²⁵

(37) $[[\sqrt{EXIST}]] = \lambda P_{<e, t>}.\lambda LOC_{<e, <s, t>>}. \exists x. P(x) \wedge LOC(x)(e)$

Note that EXIST is an existential function, without being an existential determiner. By definition, a root is acategorial, and the product of Merge in (38) is labelled as a category-neutral existential phrase, ∃P (cf. Kondrashova 1996).

(38)

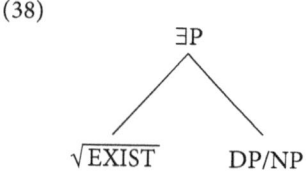

4. Definition of possession

Returning to possession, I will now provide its conceptual definition, relying on a unified cognitive representation of various possessive relations. As widely acknowledged in the typological literature, linguistic possession is a difficult concept to define. In most cases, the easiest way to proceed is to have an extensional definition that enumerates different types of structures or semantic relations (ownership, part-whole, kinship, etc.). Thus, possession can be defined as a list of surface-structural frames or event schemas (Heine 1997; Stassen 2009), or it can be described in terms of semantic features/parameters defining the possessor, the possessee and the relation itself (see Mazzitelli 2015: 22–26). Alternatively, possession can be defined at a cognitive level, where it is conceptualized in an image-schematic form used in cognitive grammar (Johnson 1987; Lakoff 1987).

More specifically, Langacker (1993: 6, 2009: 82) proposes to define possession as a relation between a reference point (R), its domain ('dominion' in Langacker's terms) and a target point (T). Somewhat simplifying Langacker's symbolic representation, and labelling R's domain as $d(R)$, I define possession as a relation of inclusion that holds between $d(R)$ and T, as shown in Figure 5.1, $d(R)$ includes T.

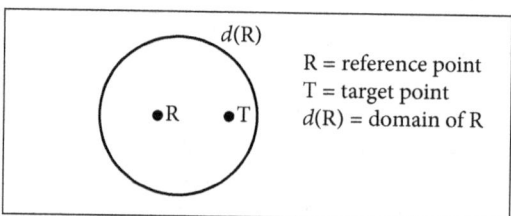

Figure 5.1 Conceptual representation of possession.

In Langacker's (1993: 6) original formulation, $d(R)$ corresponds to 'the conceptual region (or *the set of entities*) to which a particular reference point affords direct access (i.e. the class of potential targets)' (emphasis mine). Depending on the animacy of R, $d(R)$ consists of a certain number of zones (strata). For inanimate objects, $d(R)$ consists of R's physical body and its immediate physical space. For humans (or sentient individuals), $d(R)$ is much larger; in addition to the body and the immediate physical space, it also contains R's mental space, living space, personal belongings, personal relations, and finally the events and situations that fall under R's sphere of influence (Matushansky et al., forthcoming). Crucially, inclusion is not understood in its narrow sense as a part-whole relation that holds between a physical body and one of its parts, but it is a broader relation encompassing several types of more specific relations, which hold at each particular stratum/zone inside $d(R)$.

Interestingly, Bjorkman & Cowper (2016) have recently suggested that inclusion is encoded as an interpretable morphosemantic feature, INCL, on a light verb, represented here as little *v*. The head bearing INCL, labelled as v_{HAVE} in (39), relates two DPs in an asymmetric X-bar structure, in which the possessee (the target point) falls within the syntactic domain of the possessor (the reference point). In this case, the reference point and the target point are inferred from an asymmetric syntactic structure.

(39)

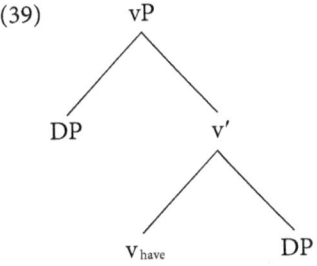

I will not discuss the details of Bjorkman & Cowper's analysis, which is primarily designed to establish a parallel between possession and modal necessity.[26] Nevertheless, using their proposal, I would like to make a tentative suggestion that INCL as a feature of little *v* is the definitional property of canonical HAVE languages, for example French or English. Being a feature, it can proliferate to the higher functional domain of the clause, giving rise to the aspectual auxiliary HAVE.[27] In such languages, a possessive HAVE sentence is 'a light-verb construction [...] that contains a v but no root' (Myler 2016: 24). In BE and BE/HAVE languages, such as Russian and Belarusian, INCL is a semantic function of a lexical root.

5. Analysis and discussion

5.1. Inclusion encoded in a spatiotemporal root

More precisely, I assume that inclusion is encoded in a spatiotemporal root, $\sqrt{AT}$, which has the denotation in (40): it denotes a relation of inclusion between an individual x and a set of individuals y with some property P.[28]

(40) $[[\sqrt{AT}]] = \lambda P_{<e,t>}.\lambda y_e.\lambda x_e.\lambda e_s.$ INCL$(P(y))(x)(e)$

In (41), $\sqrt{AT}$ is categorized by a prepositional head (P), which bears a genitive case feature encoding a domain: $\lambda y_e.\ d(y)$ ('domain **of** y' as defined in section 4; see Figure 5.1). The product of Merge in (41) is not a syntactic primitive, but it would still project when merged with a DP (it would share its case feature with the selected DP).[29] Thus, I label it as *u*-P for convenience. On the SEM side, Functional Application[30] yields a more specific function, whereby the first argument is interpreted as a reference point having a domain. In a more general function such as (40), the reference point has to be inferred as follows: since $P(y)$ is a non-referential property, y cannot be a reference point; therefore, the reference point is x, which should have a domain. The merger in (41) just inverses this inference. On the PHON side, $\sqrt{AT}$ is spelled out as *u* 'at', unless it is verbalized by v_ϕ, in which case it is spelled out as one of the HAVE forms (Table 5.2); see (42).

(41)

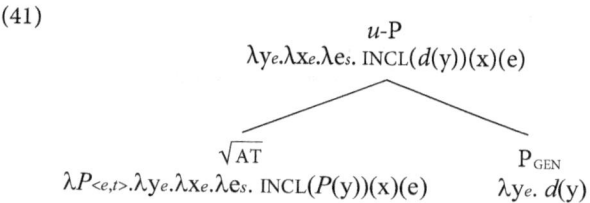

(42) a. $\sqrt{AT} \leftrightarrow$ HAVE / ___$v\phi$
 b. $\sqrt{AT} \leftrightarrow u$ / ___(elsewhere)

Functional heads v_{be}, Voice and $v\phi$ do not introduce any semantic roles. The copula and Voice are assumed to be 'type-neutral identity functions', as in (43a)–(b) (following Myler 2016: 42–43). They have different syntactic functions, but semantically either of these heads 'simply passes the denotation of the complement up the tree' (Myler 2016: 43). As for v_ϕ, it is subject to contextual allosemy. In the context of $\sqrt{AT}$, v_ϕ is neither a causative event nor activity. All it does is to mark transitivity, introducing a set of unvalued ϕ-features. These features are interpreted as a variable of type *e* once they are valued (43c).

(43) a. $[[v_{be}]] = \lambda y.\ y$
 b. $[[\text{Voice}]] = \lambda y.\ y$
 c. $[[v_\phi]] = y_e$ (iff ϕ-features are valued)

5.2. Deriving BE/HAVE possession

5.2.1. HAVE possession

For illustration, I will use the 1SG possessor (**me´**) and the demonstrative possessee *hètaja kniha* 'this book' (**this.book´**) from section 2.4. The annotated tree in (44) shows the first two applications of Merge. As you can see, this derivation yields a free variable in the denotation of the vP node. Generally, a variable resulting from valued φ-features would not be part of the logical form. However, in this particular case, it participates in the semantic composition and must be interpreted as an integral part of the denotation. At this point, there are two options: this variable is either existentially closed or licensed contextually.

(44)

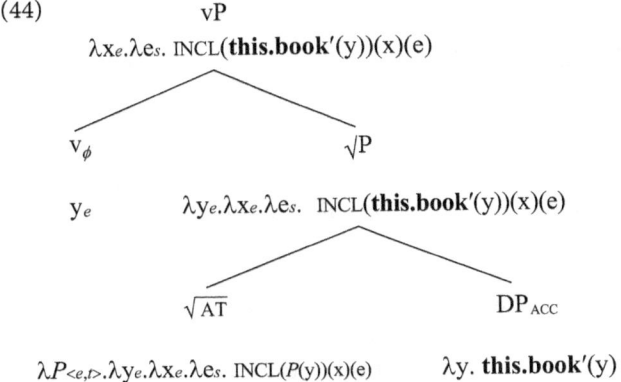

In an extended structure below (see (45)), I represent existential closure at the vP level (vP phase), using a first-order existential operator in [Spec,vP]. As it stands, this structure is a perfect candidate for GoN. Under the scope of sentential Neg (merged above VoiceP), we would obtain the desired logical form: ¬∃y. **this.book'**(y)... (cf. (24)). I will not delve into a detailed analysis of GoN here. Just for the sake of illustration, suppose that the object DP (before its merger with the root) already has a semantic case value, genitive.[31] Also, suppose that this genitive marks DP's non-referentiality in polarity contexts and, for independent reasons, requires the existential closure under the scope of a clausal Neg. In these circumstances, Agree (relating v_ϕ and the object DP) becomes impossible. However, as assumed in section 3.1, this situation does not make the derivation to crash: φ-features would still receive default values. It means that we would have exactly the same semantic composition as in (45), regardless of a different (genitive) case value and different (default) values in v_ϕ.

(45)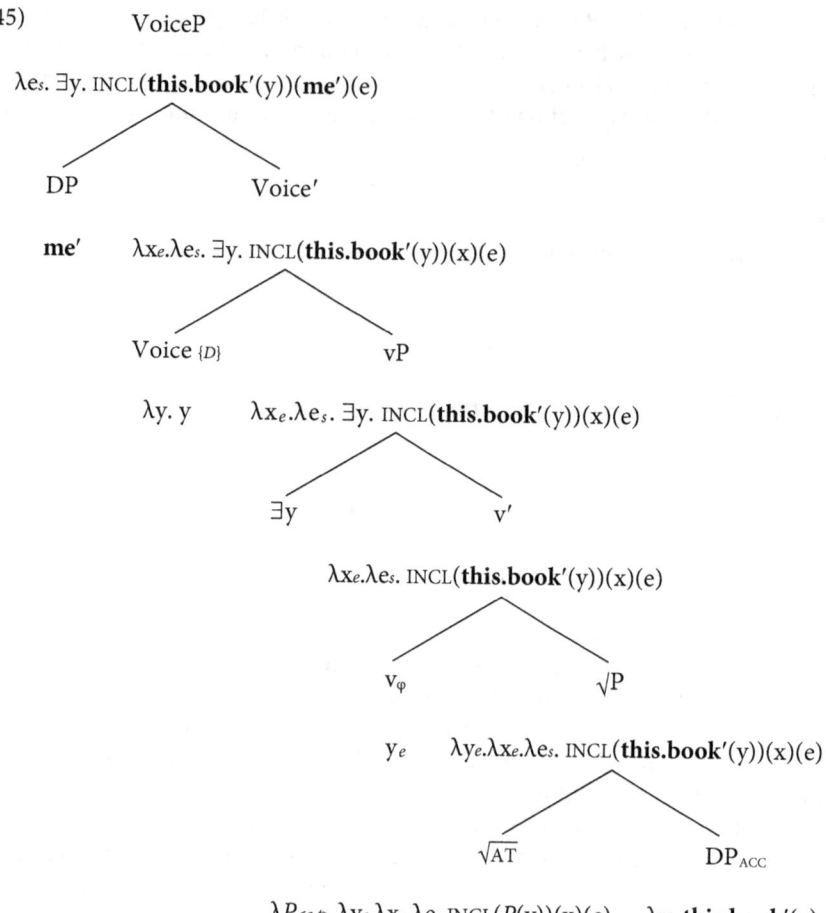

If the structure in (45) did not have an existential operator, the free variable would have to be contextually licensed. In (46), y^c stands for a contextually bound variable, as opposed to the existentially closed one in (45) (such a contextual licensing can be observed in (21)[32]).

(46) [[VoiceP]] = λe_s. INCL(**this.book'**(y^c))(**me'**)(e)

It is inferred that **me'** must have a possessive domain, d(**me'**), which is defined as a set of entities/individuals (see Langacker's original definition provided in section 4). The formulas in (45) and (46) can now be recast in set-theoretic terms. In fact, each of the options (existential closure vs. contextual binding) is associated with one of the two following set-theoretic possibilities. The first one is an intersection of d(**me'**) with another non-singleton set, **this.book'**(y) (Figure 5.2). The second possibility is the inclusion of a singleton set, **this.book'**(y^c) (Figure 5.3). In this case, there is no presupposition that there is a larger set of books extending beyond the possessive domain of the speaker. That is, existential closure always carries a presupposition that there is a larger set (partial inclusion). Contextual binding does just the opposite: it reduces a potentially large set to a singleton set (maximal inclusion).

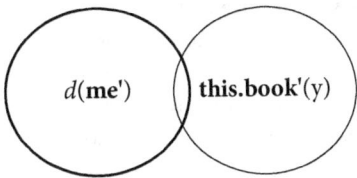

Figure 5.2 Possession as intersection of two sets (partial inclusion).

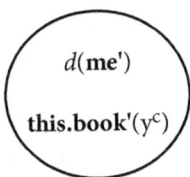

Figure 5.3 Possession as inclusion of a set (maximal inclusion).

Recall from section 4 that *d*(**me'**) is a multistratal conceptual region. If a set is alienable, it is conceptualized within the stratum of the immediate physical space surrounding the individual, inducing a physical control (temporary possession) reading.

With body parts, it is also possible to have an intersection of two non-singleton sets, as in (47a), or the inclusion of a singleton set, as in (47b)[33] (repeating (7b)). In (47a), it is presupposed that eyes are not Hanna's exclusive feature; they also exist in other human beings and they are used for seeing (thus, Hanna can use them as well). In this case, a body part has an instrumental reading. In (47b), the DP *pryhožyja vočy* 'beautiful eyes' is a definitional property of Hanna's body; there is no presupposition that beautiful eyes exist in other human beings.

(47) a. Hanna mae vočy (jana sama ŭsë ŭbačyc').
Hanna.NOM has eyes.ACC (she self everything will.see)
'Hanna has eyes (she will see everything herself).'

b. Hanna mae pryhožyja vočy.
Hanna.NOM has [beautiful eyes].ACC
'Hanna has beautiful eyes.'

The sentence in (47a) has an existential closure, as in (45). The existential closure always leads to an instrumental reading of a body part. What about the sentence in (47b), which supposedly does not have an existential operator? For that matter, body parts are different from alienable objects. In order to be a singleton set, a body part does not have to be contextually salient but needs a definitional property. The latter is usually expressed by an adjectival modifier (in (47b), it is *pryhožyja* 'beautiful'). In this case, the possible values for the variable are restricted by a set of definitional properties of Hanna's body. In other words, the context is not a salient situation in the discourse but Hanna's body. Thus, I can keep the same formula as in (46) but use a different superscript (y^{def}), indicating that the free variable is to be interpreted in the context of Hanna's definitional properties (the context is very local in this case).

(48) [[VoiceP]] = λe_s. INCL(**beautiful.eyes**'(y^{def}))(**hanna**')(e)

The same analysis extends to inanimate part-whole relations and, finally, yields the last peculiarity of HAVE, namely its incompatibility with the nouns denoting diseases and psychological conditions (Table 5.3). Diseases are arguably singleton sets within an individual (e.g. one cannot have several flus simultaneously). At the same time, diseases are not definitional properties of an individual. Thus, whenever diseases are to be interpreted as inalienable entities, the free variable cannot be properly interpreted in the context of a part-whole relation. That is, it cannot be contextually licensed. The only way to interpret it is to bind it by the existential quantifier, as in (45). Existential closure, however, entails a presupposition that there is a larger set outside the body, which leads to a contradiction (a possessee cannot be alienable and inalienable at the same time). Thus, the literal meaning of *ja maju hryp* is not 'I have flu', but 'I have a flu in my possession'. The same reasoning would apply to psychological conditions.

To summarize, v_ϕ introduces a variable of type e, which participates in the semantic composition and yields a free variable in the denotation of VoiceP. It is either existentially closed or contextually licensed. Existential closure entails a non-singleton set intersecting with the possessive domain of a reference point. Contextual licensing entails a set maximally included in the possessive domain of a reference point. Diseases and psychological conditions are singleton sets within an individual, but they are not definitional properties of an individual. Thus, the free variable cannot be contextually licensed; it is interpreted as a member of an intersecting set, yielding a contradiction between alienable and inalienable possession. Therefore, I conclude that the reduced functionality of HAVE clauses built from a lexical root, as in (40), is due to a free variable in their logical form. With this in mind, I turn to *u*-P.

5.2.2. BE possession

u-P selects a DP of type e, as shown in (49). This product of Merge, deriving *u mjane* 'at me', roughly means that, at some point in time and space, d(**me**') includes an individual x. The derived *u*-PP is a spatiotemporal function of type $<e, <s, t>>$, which cannot semantically compose with DPs of type $<e, t>$.

(49)   *u*-PP

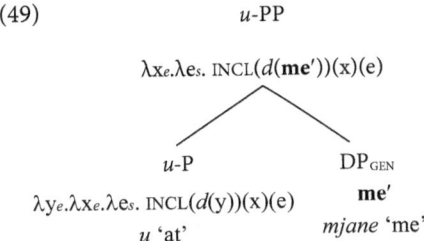

λx_e.λe_s. INCL(*d*(**me'**))(x)(e)

u-P — λy_e.λx_e.λe_s. INCL(*d*(y))(x)(e) — *u* 'at'

DP_GEN — **me'** — *mjane* 'me'

In order for a DP to be directly merged with *u*-PP, the semantic type of that DP has to undergo a type-shifting operation to be of type *e* (Partee 1986). A direct merger between *u*-PP and DP is shown in (50a). This structure corresponds to one of the set-theoretic options associated with the possessive meaning, namely possession as inclusion of a set (maximal inclusion). The structure in (50a) applies to body parts (and part-whole nouns) with a unique definitional property and diseases (and psychological conditions) as inalienable entities (see Table 5.3). But what about possession as an intersection of two sets? This option is also available but not through the direct merger with a DP. It must be mediated by the existential root (from section 3.4), as in (50b). Recall from section 5.2.1 that existential closure carries the presupposition of a larger set. Both structures are in complementary distribution, and both are verbalized by v_{be}.

(50) a. *Possession as inclusion of a set (maximal inclusion)*

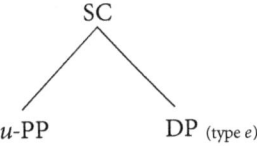

SC — *u*-PP — DP (type *e*)

b. *Possession as intersection of two sets (partial inclusion)*

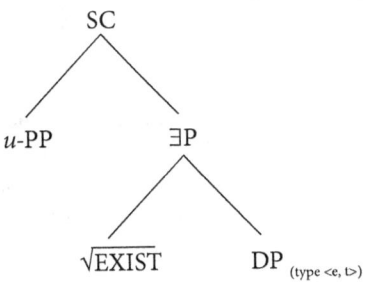

SC — *u*-PP — ∃P — √EXIST — DP (type <e, t>)

In (51), I show a vP structure of (50a). The iota operator (ιx) indicates a definite description of type *e* that can compose with *u*-PP. This structure illustrates what I previously referred to as 'copular BE', and it corresponds to the example in (19b). The definite DP will subsequently move to Spec,TP and the SC node will be labelled as PP (cf. (36)).

(51)

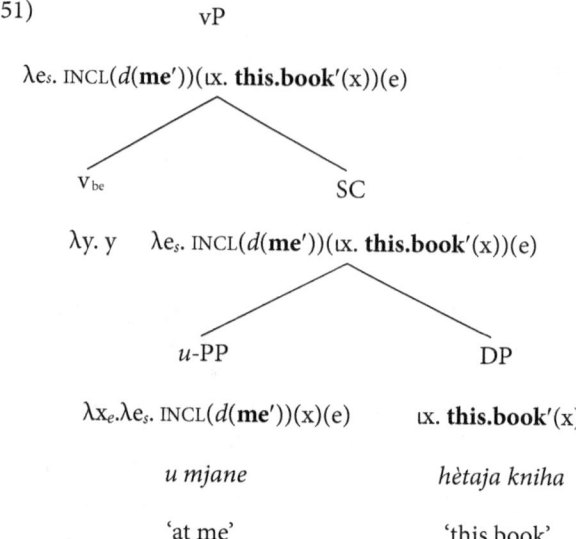

From a semantic point of view, the inclusion of an alienable singleton set into $d(\mathbf{me'})$ is conceptualized within the physical space associated with the speaker, and we obtain a temporary possession reading. In fact, the specific type of relationship between *u*-PP and the sister DP strongly depends on animacy of that DP. If it denotes a human, we do not get a possessive but purely locational reading (see (52b) in the context of (52a); cf. (19)).

(52) a. Ty   vedaeš   hdze   Mikola?
         you   know   where   Mikola.NOM?
         'Do you know where Mikola is?'

     b. Mikola   zaraz   u   mjane.
         Mikola.NOM   now   at   me.GEN
         'Mikola is at my place right now.'

In the case of (52b), *u*-PP is interpreted as 'locational' rather than 'possessive'. However, the syntactic structure or the lexical meaning of the predicate does not have to be changed. In fact, there is nothing in the formula itself – $\lambda x_e.\lambda e_s.$ INCL$(d(\mathbf{me'}))(x)(e)$ – that says 'possessive'. It is just a matter of how we label different relationships within $d(\mathbf{me'})$. Possession is derived from inclusion. The only change in (52b) is that the speaker and *Mikola* are both human. It yields exactly the same structure as in (51) (with the same denotations, except for *Mikola*).

I will now turn to the existential structure in (50b). Just like v_{be} verbalizes the structure in (50a), nothing in principle would prevent it from performing exactly the same function with (50b). The resulting vP is shown in (53), presenting a fully annotated structure of the existential BE. I am now in position to say something about the allomorphic forms observed in Table 5.1. Under the current proposal, it is not a mere lexical coincidence coming from nowhere. Now it can be claimed that the spell-out of √EXIST strictly depends on the spell-out of its verbalizer, following the rules in (54) (repeating (35)) and (55) (see Tsedryk, forthcoming, for a similar proposal for Russian).

(53)

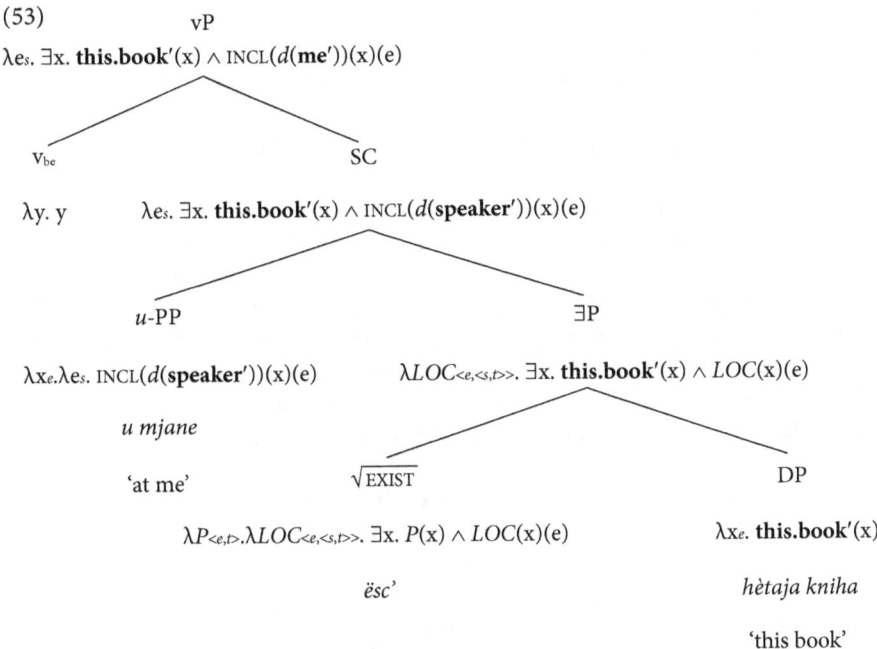

(54) a. v_be ↔ by- / __T[past] or [infinitive]
     b. v_be ↔ bud(z)- / __T[future]
     c. v_be ↔ Ø / __(elsewhere)

(55) a. √EXIST ↔ ësc' / __(54c)
     b. √EXIST ↔ Ø / __(elsewhere) (i.e. v_be has a phonetic form)

Interestingly, (53) can also generate a human DP. However, the relationship between *u*-PP and this DP would not be a physical location of an individual within *d*(**me'**) (i.e. the inclusion of a singleton set) but a more abstract type of relationship. This is shown in (56), illustrating a so-called 'availability reading' (Partee & Borschev 2007: 175). More precisely, *Mikola* is interpreted as an individual who can perform a certain task.[34]

(56) U mjane   ësc'   Mikola.   (Začym mne hèta rabic' samamu?)
     at me.GEN be.EXIST Mikola.NOM   why   me   this to.do   myself
     'I have Mikola. (Why should I do it myself?)'

The existential root can only quantify over a set of properties. *Mikola* as an individual does not provide the proper domain for quantification. Thus, √EXIST forces the proper name to instantiate a property that can be retrieved from discourse (*Mikola* as a person that can perform a discursively salient task).[35] The crucial point here is that √EXIST is able to quantify over a discursive domain outside the clause. In fact, examples such as (56) show that √EXIST does not quantify over individuals but rather over functions (non-local quantification). Thus, it is plausible to recast its analysis in terms of an existentially closed choice-function, along the lines of (57) (following Reinhart 1997).

(57) [[√EXIST]] = ∃*f*. CH(*f*) ∧ λ*LOC*$_{<e, <s, t>>}$. *LOC*(*f*(NP/DP))(e)

The details have yet to be worked out, but √EXIST should be able to compose with both properties and individuals. If it merges with an NP/DP denoting a property, it would lift the nominal type from <*e*, *t*> to *e*, assigning an individual to a given set (denoted by that NP/NP). If it merges with a DP of type *e*, as in (56), it would still be able to quantify over properties in the discursive domain and assign a given individual (*Mikola*) to a non-empty set. Full implementation of this idea is left for future research. The only remark that I would like to add here is that HAVE does not have the same existential force as √EXIST. This can be observed in the example below.

(58) *Ja   maju   Mikolu.   (Začym   mne   hèta   rabic'   samamu?)
      I.NOM have.1SG   Mikola.ACC   why   me   it   to.do   myself
      'I have Mikola. (Why should I do it myself?)'

According to my analysis, HAVE also has an existential operator. However, as was shown in section 5.1, the presence of this operator in a HAVE structure is contingent on a free variable of type *e*. That is, an existential operator quantifies over a local domain of individuals and cannot quantify over the choice-functions beyond the clausal domain. This yields yet another functional limitation of a HAVE structure, as opposed to a BE structure with √EXIST.

6. Conclusion

In this chapter, I proposed a unified analysis of predicative BE and HAVE possession in Belarusian. I showed (i) that there are two BE-possessive constructions, an existential and a non-existential one, and (ii) that HAVE is not derived from BE. HAVE alternates with both types of BE, and the actual alternation is not between BE and HAVE, but between *u* 'at' and HAVE. According to my analysis, HAVE is not a result of incorporation of a locative P into BE (Freeze 1992; Kayne 1993). A HAVE form is a verbalized/transitivized version of a spatiotemporal root, √AT, which is otherwise realized as *u* 'at' (its elsewhere phonological form). The logical form derived from the transitivized variant of √AT (i.e. its verbalization by v_ϕ) ends up with a free variable of type *e* (individual) in the denotation of the clause. This variable is either existentially closed or contextually bound. Both the strategies correlate with two set-theoretic possibilities, arising from the definition of possession as inclusion into a domain (or Langacker's 'dominion', which is 'the set of entities' or 'the class of potential targets'; see section 4). That is, possession can be either an intersection of two sets (partial inclusion entailed by existential closure) or inclusion of a set (maximal inclusion entailed by contextual binding). A non-transitivized version of √AT is a result of its categorization by head P that bears a semantic genitive case, yielding *u*-PP (a prepositional variant of √AT). The two set-theoretic possibilities are distributed between two derivational options: (i) *u*-PP is merged with an existential phrase embedding a DP of type <*e, t*> (intersection of two sets), or (ii) *u*-PP is directly merged with a DP of type *e* (inclusion of a set). Each of these two scenarios features a small clause that is subsequently verbalized by a copula. This is how a copular BE, on the one hand, and the existential BE, on the other, are derived. Both are in strict complementary distribution and show consistent allomorphy in the attested BE forms.

For reasons of space, the differences between Belarusian (a mixed BE/HAVE system) and Russian (a BE system) were not discussed here. Russian also has the same spatiotemporal root realized as *u* 'at'. Like in Belarusian, this root can also be transitivized by v_ϕ, yielding a HAVE form/structure. However, the use of the verbalized variant of √AT is much more restricted than the use of its prepositional variant. As I pointed out, a HAVE structure has a reduced functionality due to the occurrence of a free variable. For this reason, HAVE has ended up in very restrictive contexts (e.g. administrative discourse), and most HAVE constructions in Russian have either an idiomatic or a quasi-idiomatic meaning (see Mazzitelli 2015: 168–170 for further discussion and examples).

Notes

1. *Abbreviations:*

ACC	accusative case	FUT	future tense	NEG	negation
COND	conditional mood	GEN	genitive case	NOM	nominative case
DAT	dative case	INF	infinitive	PL	plural number
EMPH	emphatic marker	INST	instrumental case	PRS	present tense
EXIST	existential	LOC	locative case	PST	past tense
F	feminine gender	M	masculine gender	REFL	reflexive
FOC	focus marker	N	neuter gender	SG	singular number

2. I would like to thank Inna Livitz and two anonymous reviewers for their remarks on the previous draft. Many thanks to the editors of this volume and Gréte Dalmi in particular for a critical eye, support, and encouragement. I am the only one responsible for any remaining inconstancies.
3. The transliterated *ë* and *e* are pronounced as [jɔ] and [jɛ], respectively. Their non-palatalized counterparts are *o* [ɔ] and *è* [ɛ].
4. The instrumental case marking of the predicate is also possible in the past and the future (see section 3.3).
5. In Belarusian, *u* can also mean 'in', which is signalled by the locative case (compare *u Minsku* 'in Minsk.LOC' with *žyxar Minska* 'inhabitant Minsk.GEN' [lit. 'inhabitant of Minsk']).
6. The past tense marker has two allophones -*ŭ*- [w] and -*I*-, depending on the presence of a word-final vowel (the masculine form has a zero realization).

7   The final affricate -dz- [dz̑] in the future stem is conditioned by the palatalized vowel e [jɛ] (e.g. budz-eš 'be.FUT-2SG' is pronounced as [budz̑-jɛş]).
8   Available online: http://resurs.by/files/nn/1997/34/07.htm (accessed 21 April 2018).
9   The observed contrast applies to all diseases (curable as well as chronic and lethal).
10 Russian had a strong presence during the Soviet period and remains the dominant language in Belarus (see Mazzitelli 2015: ch. 4 for a comprehensive overview of the sociolinguistic situation in Belarus).
11 There is a noun *maëntak* 'estate', 'property' (of noble origin), which is etymologically related to HAVE, but it is not a productive derivation in modern Belarusian (cf. *imenie* in Russian). In fact, there is no way to derive a noun meaning 'owner' from HAVE. The verb *valodac'*, on the other hand, shares a suppletive root with *uladal'nik* 'owner', derived from *ulada* 'power'.
12 The token reading is facilitated by the focal stress falling on the subject of the clause.
13 Mazzitelli (2015) observes that HAVE in Belarusian is a unpreferred option to express temporary possession (hence the question mark in (21b)). I think that, with a proper context and intonation, (21b) is acceptable, but further investigation of the constraints applying to this use of HAVE is required. In section 5.2.1, I propose that the token reading with HAVE arises from a contextually bound variable, which is otherwise existentially closed by default. The ownership reading is thus a preferred option with HAVE, while temporary possession is a marked choice.
14 See Witkoś, Chapter 2 in this volume, and Kagan, Chapter 4 in this volume.
15 Lexical case cannot alternate with GoN:
    (i) Hanna   kirue   biznesam.
         Hanna.NOM   manages   business.INST
         'Hanna manages a business.'
    (ii) Hanna   bolej   ne   kirue   biznesam   / *biznesu.
         Hanna.NOM   anymore   NEG   manages   business.INST   /business.GEN
         'Hanna does not manage a business anymore.'
16 These features are observed with the subject agreement. I do not commit to possible differences between subject and object agreement, nor do I make a difference between a full-fledged and a defective v.
17 I diverge from Pesetsky & Torrego (2007), who assume that a feature can be valued but uninterpretable.
18 In (31a)–(31b), the verbs are in the past tense impersonal form (with neuter agreement -*a*). When the inflection is unstressed, the neuter form is homophonous with the feminine -*a*.
19 Available online: https://poembook.ru/poem/120269 (accessed 20 August 2018).
20 Available online: https://kurjer.info/2012/02/15/kaxanne-na-syo-zhyccyo/(accessed August 2018).
21 Wood & Marantz (2017) have recently proposed a single argument-introducing head, *i**. This head does not have its own categorial value and inherits one from the projection it merges with. This head could be used in (32), which would call for an extended v*P. For the sake of simplicity, I use Voice.
22 Dalmi (2012) suggests that the structure with the instrumental case involves an alternative operator in Tense.
23 Movement is not a separate syntactic operation but another application of Merge to a syntactic object that is already present in the structure (i.e. Internal Merge).
24 More precisely, 'a function f from properties to sets of properties is *existential* iff for all properties p, q $p \in f(q)$ iff $1 \in f(q \wedge p)$' (Keenan 1987: 291).

25 Myler (2016: 44) uses an existential expletive in his analysis, and he separately assumes an existential little v, which is semantically undistinguishable from the copula. In an appendix, Myler offers a possible way of recasting his analysis in terms of an implicit contextual argument used by Francez (2009). I leave the evaluation of such an implementation within the current proposal for future research.

26 Bjorkman & Cowper (2016) use the term 'possessive modality' (e.g. *I have a car* and *I have to buy a car*). In a nutshell, they claim that inclusion may not only hold between individuals, but also between sets of worlds. The modal use of *mec'* is illustrated below (see Mazzitelli 2011 for further data and discussion):

(i) Ja   meŭ-sja   byc'   vol'nym mastakom.
     I.NOM   have.PST.M-REFL   to.be   [free artist].INSTR
     'I should have been a free artist.'
     (*Litaratura i mastactva*, 27 April 2012)

27 In the higher functional domain, the reference time includes the event time (Klein 1994).

28 The denotation in (40) is similar (but not identical) to the denotation of a DP-internal possessive head (Poss) proposed by Myler:
    (i) $[[Poss]] = \lambda P_{<e,t>}.\lambda y_e.\lambda x_e.\lambda e_s. P(x) \wedge Poss(y)(x)(e)$ (Myler 2016: 52).

29 Category P could be derived from Wood & Marantz's (2017) single argument introducer, *i**. It would have a selectional D feature coupled with the genitive case. In Tsedryk (forthcoming), I assume that $\sqrt{AT}$ has an inherent (lexical) genitive case, but this assumption contradicts the general assumption that roots do not contain grammatical features.

30 *Functional Application*: 'If α is a branching node, {β, γ} is the set of α's daughters, and [[β]] is a function whose domain contains, [[γ]] then [[α]] = [[β]]([[γ]])' (Heim & Kratzer 1998: 44).

31 It may be assumed that a quantificational head (Q) is a case-assigner (Bailyn 2012: 207), but the details of the implementation of this assumption are not crucial.

32 Geist (2015) assumes that the determiner introduces a situation variable. Nothing prevents the determiner to have its own variable under the current proposal.

33 Strictly speaking, Hanna (like other humans) has a set of two eyes (anatomically, it is not a singleton set). However, eyes (whatever is their physical number within a body) define a body part as a unit. That is, the property of being beautiful applies to a body part in its totality, hence a singleton set in the context of a part-whole relation.

34 Compare with a similar example from Barwise & Cooper (1981: 183).
    (i) Who could possibly play Hamlet?
        Well, there's John.

35 McNally's (1998) BE-INSTANTIATED could be applied in this case (see Kagan, Chapter 4 in this volume), but we would have to assume that *Mikola* in (56) is not an individual but a property.

References

Abbott, B. 1997. Definiteness and existentials. *Language* 73: 103–108.

Alexiadou, A. & Lohndal, T. 2017. On the division of labor between roots and functional structure. In: D'Alessandro, R., Franco, I. & Gallego, Á. (eds), *The Verbal Domain*, 85–102. Oxford: Oxford University Press.

Bailyn, J. F. 2012. *The Syntax of Russian*. Cambridge: Cambridge University Press.
Barwise, J. & Cooper, R. 1981. Generalized quantifiers and natural language. *Linguistics and Philosophy* 4: 159-219.
Bjorkman, B. & Cowper, E. 2016. Possession and necessity: from individuals to worlds. *Lingua* 182: 30-48.
Borschev, V., Paducheva, E. V., Partee, B. H., Testelets, Y. & Yanovich, I. 2006. Sentential and constituent negation in Russian BE-sentences revisited. In: Lavine, J., Franks, S. L., Tasseva-Kurktchieva, M. & Filip, H. (eds), *Proceedings of Formal Approaches to Slavic Linguistics 14*, 50-65. Ann Arbor, MI: Michigan Slavic Publications.
Borschev, V., Paducheva, E. V., Partee, B. H., Testelets, Y. & Yanovich, I. 2008. Russian genitives, non-referentiality, and the property-type hypothesis. In: Antonenko, A., Bailyn, J. F. & Bethin, C. (eds), *Proceedings of Formal Approaches to Slavic Linguistics 16*, 48-67. Ann Arbor, MI: Michigan Slavic Publications.
Chomsky, N. 2000. Minimalist inquiries: the framework. In: Martin, R., Michaels, D. & Uriagereka, J. (eds), *Step by Step*, 89-155. Cambridge, MA: MIT Press.
Chomsky, N. 2001. Derivation by phase. In: Kenstowicz, M. (ed.), *Ken Hale: A Life in Language*, 1-52. Cambridge, MA: MIT Press.
Chomsky, N. 2013. Problems of projection. *Lingua* 130: 33-49.
Dalmi, G. 2012. Copular sentences as Kimian states in Irish and Russian. *Canadian Journal of Linguistics* 57: 341-358.
Den Dikken, M. 2014. On feature interpretability and inheritance. In: Kosta, P., Franks, S. L., Radeva-Bork, T. & Schürcks, L. (eds), *Minimalism and Beyond: Radicalizing the Interfaces*, 37-55. Amsterdam: John Benjamins.
Embick, D. & Marantz, A. 2008. Architecture and blocking. *Linguistic Inquiry* 39: 1-53.
Embick, D. & Noyer, R. 2007. Distributed morphology and the syntax/morphology interface. In: Ramchand, G. & Reiss, C. (eds), *The Oxford Handbook of Linguistic Interfaces*, 289-324. Oxford: Oxford University Press.
Francez, I. 2007. Existential propositions. PhD dissertation. Stanford University, Stanford, CA.
Francez, I. 2009. Existentials, predication, and modification. *Linguistics and Philosophy* 32: 1-50.
Freeze, R. 1992. Existentials and other locatives. *Language* 68: 553-595.
Geist, L. 2015. Genitive alternation in Russian: a situation semantics approach. In: Zybatov, G., Biskup, P., Guhl, M., Hurtig, C., Mueller-Reichau, O. & Yastrebova, M. (eds), *Slavic Grammar from a Formal Perspective*, 157-174. Berlin: Peter Lang.
Halle, M. & Marantz, A. 1993. Distributed morphology and the pieces of inflection. In: Hale, K. & Keyser, S. J. (eds), *The View from Building 20: Essays in Linguistics in Honor of Sylvain Bromberger*, 111-176. Cambridge, MA: MIT Press.
Heim, I. & Kratzer, A. 1998. *Semantics in Generative Grammar*. Oxford: Blackwell.
Heine, B. 1997. *Possession*. Cambridge: Cambridge University Press.
Isačenko, A. 1974. On *Have* and *Be* languages: a typological sketch. In: Flier, M. (ed.), *Slavic Forum: Essays in Linguistics and Literature*, 43-77. The Hague: Mouton.
Johnson, M. 1987. *The Body in the Mind: The Bodily Basis of Meaning, Imagination, and Reason*, Chicago, IL: Chicago University Press.
Kagan, O. 2013. *Semantics of Genitive Objects in Russian: A Study of Genitive of Negation and Intensional Genitive Case*. Dordrecht: Springer.
Kayne, R. 1993. Towards a modular theory of auxiliary selection. *Studia Linguistica* 47: 3-31.

Keenan, E. L. 1987. A semantic definition of 'Indefinite NP'. In: Reuland, E. J. & Meulen, A. (eds), *The Representation of (In)definiteness*, 286–317. Cambridge, MA: MIT Press.
Klein, W. 1994. *Time in Language*. New York: Routledge.
Kondrashova, N. 1996. The syntax of existential quantification. PhD dissertation. University of Wisconsin, Madison.
Lakoff, G. 1987. *Women, Fire, and Dangerous Things: What Categories Reveal about the Mind*. Chicago, IL: Chicago University Press.
Langacker, R. 1993. Reference-point constructions. *Cognitive Linguistics* 4: 1–38.
Langacker, R. 2009. *Investigations in Cognitive Grammar*. Berlin: Mouton De Gruyter.
Lavine, J. 2010. Case and events in transitive impersonals. *Journal of Slavic Linguistics* 18: 101–130.
Marantz, A. 1997. No escape from syntax: don't try morphological analysis in the privacy of your own lexicon. In: Dimitriadis, A., Siegel, L., Surek-Clark, C. & Williams, A. (eds), *University of Pennsylvania Working Papers in Linguistics 4*, 201–225. Philadelphia, PA: University of Pennsylvania.
Marantz, A. 2013. Locality domains for the contextual allomorphy across the interfaces. In: Matushansky, O. & Marantz, A. (eds), *Distributed Morphology Today: Morphemes for Morris Halle*, 95–115. Cambridge, MA: MIT Press.
Matushansky, O. 2000. The instrument of inversion: instrumental case in the Russian copula. In: Billerey, R. & Lillehaugen, B. D. (eds), *Proceedings of the 19th West Coast Conference on Formal Linguistics*, 288–301. Somerville, MA: Cascadilla Press.
Matushansky, O., Boneh, N., Nash, L. & Slioussar, N. Forthcoming. To PPs in their proper place. In: Ionin, T. & MacDonald, J. (eds), *Proceedings of Formal Approaches to Slavic Linguistics 26*. Ann Arbor, MI: Michigan Slavic Publications.
Mazzitelli, L. F. 2011. Possession, modality and beyond: the case of *Mec'* and *Mecca* in Belarusian. In: Nomachi, M. (ed.), *Grammaticalization in Slavic Languages: From Areal and Typological Perspectives*, Slavic and Eurasian Studies 23, 179–202. Sapporo: Slavic Research Center of the Hokkaido University.
Mazzitelli, L. F. 2015. *The Expression of Predicative Possession: A Comparative Study of Belarusian and Lithuanian*, Studia Typologica, Volume 18. Berlin: Mouton De Gruyter.
Mazzitelli, L. F. 2017. Predicative possession in the languages of the Circum-Baltic area. *Folia Linguistica* 51(1): 1–60.
McNally, L. 1998. Existential sentences without existential quantification. *Linguistics and Philosophy* 21: 353–392.
Milsark, G. 1974. Existential sentences in English. PhD dissertation. Massachusetts Institute of Technology.
Milsark, G. 1977. Toward an explanation of certain peculiarities of the existential construction in English. *Linguistic Analysis* 3: 1–29.
Myler, N. 2016. *Building and Interpreting Possessive Sentences*. Cambridge, MA: MIT Press.
Partee, B. H. 1986. Noun phrase interpretation and type-shifting principles. In: Groenendijk, J., de Jongh, D. & Stokhof, M. (eds), *Studies in Discourse Representation Theory and the Theory of Generalized Quantifiers*, 115–143. Dordrecht: Foris.
Partee, B. H. 1999. Weak NPs in HAVE sentences. In: Gerbrandy, J., Marx, M., de Rijke, M. & Venema, Y. (eds), *JFAK, a Liber Amicorum for Johan van Benthem on the Occasion of his 50th Birthday*, 39–57. Amsterdam: University of Amsterdam.
Partee, B. H. & Borschev, V. 2004. The semantics of Russian Genitive of Negation: the nature and role of perspectival structure. In: Toman, J. (ed.), *Proceedings of Formal Approaches to Slavic Linguistics 10*, 181–200. Ann Arbor, MI: Michigan Slavic Publications.

Partee, B. H. & Borschev, V. 2007. Existential sentences, BE and the Genitive of Negation in Russian. In: Comorowski, I. & von Heusinger, K. (eds), *Existence: Semantics and Syntax*, 147–191. New York: Springer.

Partee, B. H., Borschev, V., Paducheva, E. V., Testelets, Y. & Yanovich, I. 2011. Russian Genitive of Negation alternations: the role of verb semantics. *Scando-Slavica* 57: 135–159.

Pereltsvaig, A. 2007. *Copular Sentences in Russian: A Theory of Intra-Clausal Relations*. New York: Springer.

Pesetsky, D. & Torrego, E. 2007. The syntax of valuation and the interpretability of features. In: Karimi, S., Samiian, V. & Wilkins, W. K. (eds), *Phrasal and Clausal Architecture*, 262–294. Amsterdam: John Benjamins.

Reinhart, T. 1997. Quantifier scope: how labor is divided between QR and choice functions. *Linguistics and Philosophy* 20: 335–397.

Richardson, K. 2007. *Case and Aspect in Slavic*. Oxford: Oxford University Press.

Ritter, E. & Rosen, S. T. 1997. The function of Have. *Lingua* 101: 295–321.

Roy, I. 2013. *Nonverbal Predication: Copular Sentences at the Syntax–Semantics Interface*. Oxford: Oxford University Press.

Stassen, L. 2009. *Predicative Possession*. Oxford: Oxford University Press.

Tham, S. W. 2004. Representing Possessive predication: semantic dimensions and pragmatic bases. PhD dissertation. Stanford University, Stanford, CA.

Tham, S. W. 2006. The Definiteness Effect in English *Have* sentences. In: Denis, P., McCready, E., Palmer, A. & Reese, B. (eds), *Proceedings of the 2004 Texas Linguistic Society Conference*, 137–149. Somerville, MA: Cascadilla Proceedings Project.

Tsedryk, E. forthcoming. Introducing possessors in Russian: a new perspective based on the single argument introducer. In: Ionin, T. & MacDonald, J. (eds), *Proceedings of Formal Approaches to Slavic Linguistics 26*, 398–416. Ann Arbor, MI: Michigan Slavic Publications.

Ward, G. & Birner, B. 1995. Definiteness and the English existential. *Language* 71: 722–742.

Wood, J. & Marantz, A. 2017. The interpretation of external arguments. In: D'Alessandro, R., Franco, I. & Gallego, Á. (eds), *The Verbal Domain*, 255–278. Oxford: Oxford University Press.

6. Predicative possession as a clause type in Finnish

Maria Vilkuna

1. Introduction[1,2]

In the typological classification of predicative possession patterns defined by Heine (1997) and Stassen (2009), the basic possessive predication in Finnish is represented by the locational possession type. The verb is *olla* (be), which can also function as the copula in copular sentences. The possessor is marked by an oblique case, adessive, which also has straightforwardly locative uses, often corresponding to 'at' or 'on'. The possessee argument has traditionally been seen as the subject of the clause. At the same time, the possessive clause is a subtype of the existential clause (or sentence) and shares most of its central properties with this prototype. One of the common definitional properties of existential and possessive clauses is their unmarked order, LOC/POSS V NP. Unlike other clause types such as transitive or copular, the existential/possessive type has the locative/possessor element in the subject position, while the putative subject follows the verb. Simple examples of the clause types referred to in this chapter are given in (1) with their abbreviations.

(1) a. POSSESSIVE (PossCl)
Anna-lla   on   koira   / koir-i-a   / raha-a.
Anna-ADE   be.3SG   dog.NOM / dog-PL-PAR / money-PAR
'Anna has a dog / dogs / money.'

b. EXISTENTIAL (ExCl)
Sohva-lla / Anna-n   syli-ssä   on   koira
sofa-ADE / Anna-GEN   lap-INE   be.3SG   dog
'There is a dog on the sofa / in Anna's lap.'

c. LOCATIVE (LocCl)
Koira   on   sohva-lla   / Anna-n   syli-ssä.
dog   be.3SG   sofa-ADE   / Anna-GEN   lap-INE
'The dog is on the sofa / in Anna's lap.'

d. TRANSITIVE
Anna hala-a koira-a.
Anna hug-3SG dog-PAR
'Anna is hugging a/the dog.'

It is well known that the locational possessive pattern is typical of Uralic languages. The main features of the Finnish pattern are shared by Baltic-Finnic and also essentially by the Saami languages. Unlike Finnic and Saamic, several other Uralic languages use a genitive or dative case for the marking of the possessor, as in the Udmurt example (2) (Laakso & Wagner-Nagy, forthcoming).[3] In this sense, the term locational is more appropriate for the Finnic pattern than for those that have a case dedicated for possessor-like semantic roles, also used in the adnominial position. In addition, the languages outside the Baltic-Finnic group typically exhibit possessor indexing (Stassen 2009: 70–79; Laakso & Wagner-Nagy, 2019). In Finnish, the possessee can have a possessive suffix bound by the possessor (3), but unlike in possessor-indexing languages such as Hungarian (see Stassen 2009: 76) or Udmurt (2), this special option introduces extra implications.

(2) so-len końdon-ez vań
    3SG-GEN money-3SGPOSS be.PRS
    '(S)he has money.' (Udmurt, Edygarova 2015: 276)

(3) Anna-lla on koira-nsa.
    Anna-ADE be.3SG dog-3POSS
    'Anna has her dog [e.g. she is not in need of other company].' (Finnish)

A further difference between the Finnic-Saamic and most other Uralic existential/possessive clauses is that the former do not employ a special marker of negation but are negated with the general means, viz. the negative auxiliary (Veselinova 2015; Vilkuna 2015). On the other hand, Finnish differs even from its closest relatives and departs from the locational type as defined by Stassen (2009) when it comes to the function of the possessee, namely whether the possessee can be taken to be the subject of the clause.

This chapter adopts a constructional approach to grammar, i.e. a surface-oriented, declarative view of grammar as a network of constructions, conventionalized pairings of form and meaning (Goldberg 1995, 2006; Fried 2015, among others). From the typological point of view, taking predicative possession as a 'comparative concept' (Haspelmath 2010), it is clear that Finnish has a predicative possessive clause, PossCl, with the above properties. But is PossCl also a construction in Finnish grammar based on Finnish internal criteria and, if it is, what is its position among Finnish clausal constructions? The constructions discussed here are clause types, syntactic patterns that may show idiosyncratic properties over and above regular phrase structure and grammatical functions. My aim in this chapter is to describe the PossCl and to explicate – in an informal manner – its relations to neighbouring constructions. This requires taking into account the whole semantic range expressed by PossCl, much of which is outside prototypical possession.

The basic facts of the Finnish PossCl described here are well known and have been recorded in grammars, most recently in Hakulinen et al. (2004). To support my observations on some issues, especially in section 5, I use electronic corpora, mainly the corpus of internet discussions Suomi24.fi.[4] The study is not data-based in the strict sense, however, and simplified examples are used for illustration.

The chapter is structured as follows. Section 2 introduces the concept of clause type in the constructional framework. Sections 3 and 4 analyse the properties of ExCl and their realization in PossCl and ask what, if anything, separates the two. In section 5, case marking under negation is subjected to closer examination, touching upon some borderlines between PossCl and other specialized clause types. The conclusions are presented in section 6.

2. Clause types: General and restricted

For several decades, Finnish syntacticians have placed much weight on the notion of clause type (Hakanen 1972; Hakulinen & Karlsson 1979; Hakulinen et al. 2004; Huumo & Lindström 2014; Huumo & Helasvuo 2015[5]; Kajander 2013, among others). This stems from the complications arising from attempts to handle central syntactic phenomena in terms of traditional grammatical functions. The main distinction is between clausal constructions whose description involves some implementation of syntactic subjecthood and those in which subjecthood is problematic. The simplest formal definition of the syntactic subject for Finnish is the nominal constituent with nominative (morphologically unmarked) case that triggers person and number agreement on the verb ('basic subject' in Hakulinen et al. 2004), and this is seen as the only type of subject by Huumo & Helasvuo (2015). Taking subject agreement as an abstract schematic construction of its own (see Hoffman 2013: 310–311), clausal constructions that admit it will here be called GENERAL CLAUSE TYPES, in line with Hakulinen et al. (2004: §891). Examples are the locative and the transitive clause in (1). The general clause types contrast with several RESTRICTED CLAUSE TYPES, which have more specific functions, one of which is the possessive clause. The finite verb in the restricted clause types is always in third-person singular. Since grammatical constructions can define the grammatical relations in them (Croft 2001), there is no need to define the subject for restricted clause types, and no such attempt is made here.

There are naturally many ways of grouping clausal constructions (see Hoffmann 2013). The notion of clause type that is of interest here can be identified as a type of argument structure construction in the sense defined by Goldberg (1995, 2006), but with a more inclusive scope. Clause types in the present sense are schematic argument structure constructions that make crucial reference to the status of the most prominent argument (or lack of it) in the construction. Their meaning is more abstract in nature than the meaning of the narrower argument structure constructions such as, for example the English ditransitive construction (Goldberg 1995: 141–151). Clause types are neutral with respect to illocution-based clausal constructions (declarative, interrogative etc.), discourse-based 'dropping' of constituents and variation of constituent order. They are also neutral with respect to finiteness, i.e. they can be instantiated in finite and non-finite clauses, albeit with restrictions in the case of restricted clause types. Thus, the general clause types do not directly refer to subject-verb agreement as such, as this is restricted to finite clauses, but to the specific argument type that is also referred to by the subject agreement construction. This argument is also central in the linearization of clause types, as it is the default filler of the preverbal Topic position (Vilkuna 1989: 40–50). In restricted clause types, some other constituent performs this role. Thus, in PossCl it is the possessor phrase.

As is known from the extensive literature on subject properties, subjecthood has other syntactic consequences besides agreement. Thus, the PossCl in (3) with a reflexive possessive suffix in the possessee phrase indicates that the possessor is the dominating element in this configuration. Further, the ability of non-finite clauses – complements, adjuncts, participial modifiers – to accommodate the PossCl or other restricted clause types is heavily restricted, which is at least partially attributable to the lack of a grammatically controllable (PRO) subject argument in the restricted types. Thus PossCl can be instantiated by non-finite complements of 'raising' verbs, in which case the possessor appears in its normal adessive case (4), but this is not possible for complements of control verbs (5). With them, possessor case cannot be preserved (5a), and applying subject control either to the possessee ('dog') or to the possessor ('Anna') does not yield a PossCl but a predicate complement pattern (5b) or a LocCl (5c), both representing general clause types that take a basic subject.

(4) Anna-lla   sattu-u   ole-ma-an   koira.
    Anna-ADE   happen-3SG   be-INF$_M$ dog
    'Anna happens to have a dog.'

(5) a. *Anna-lla   halua-a   ol-la   koira.
       Anna-ADE   want-3SG   be-INF$_A$ dog
       Intended: 'Anna wants to have a dog.'

   b. Anna   halua-a   ol-la   koira.
       Anna   want-3SG   be-INF$_A$ dog
       'Anna wants to be a dog.'

   c. Koira   halua-a   ol-la   Anna-n   syli-ssä.
       dog   want-3SG   be-INF$_A$ Anna-GEN   lap-INE
       'The dog wants to be in Anna's lap.'

Things are also complicated by the fact that individual instances can be vague as to clause type, as will become apparent below, but it is clear that with the PossCl reading, neither the possessor nor the possessee can be read as the controlled element.

If taken as grammatical constructions proper, clause types may seem to lack a crucial property, a clear meaning or function. Especially the general clause types, i.e. transitive, intransitive and copular (Hakulinen et al. 2004: §891), seem to have very little schematic meaning. But as emphasized by Fried (2015), constructional meaning need not be *meaning* in the sense of semantic content. What is constructional, or non-compositional in the sense of not being reducible to its parts, may be, for instance, the functional relationship between the constituents (Fried 2015: 981). I take the PossCl to be a schematic construction that is an entrenched part of the language and whose basic use expresses a possessive relation but which can also be used for many rather abstract stative relations between a dominating entity and another entity in its domain. In such a relation, the dominating entity has some sort of control over the other one, has essential access to it, or sometimes (even more abstractly) is just somehow characterized by it (see Mazzitelli 2017 for the semantic range of the PossCl in Finnic languages). The limits of the relations which an abstract PossCl such as (6) can express are hard to define.

(6) Päätökse-llä ol-i kauaskantoise-t seuraukse-t /
 decision-ADE be-PST.3SG far_reaching-PL consequence-PL /

 paljon vastustaj-i-a.
 much opponent-PL-PAR
 'The decision had far-reaching consequences / many opponents.'

It should be mentioned that predicative possession can also be expressed in Finnish by constructions belonging to the general clause types. There are transitive constructions with the possessor as the subject, and intransitive and copular constructions with the subject as the possessee. The two transitive verbs are *omistaa* (own), typically pertaining to legal possession, and the more marginal *omata* often used to avoid the restrictions on using the PossCl in participial constructions. The intransitive verb *kuulua* (belong) typically expresses possession rights, and there are copular clauses containing the possessor in the genitive case ('the dog is Anna's') or as the genitive modifier X of a locative-marked nominal meaning 'in possession of X'. All these patterns have their own distributions, restrictions and semantic nuances, which may reveal something about the function of PossCl if compared with it. In contrast, the PossCl is the basic, unmarked construction for predicating core possession but also accommodates relations that would not normally be called possession.

3. The possessive clause as an existential clause

Finnish ExCls have no dedicated marker such as a 'there'-like expletive or a specific predicate. Therefore, it can be suggested that Finnish does not have a grammaticalized existential construction but this function is served by an 'inverted' information structure variant of LocCl (Creissels 2014). Still, what is called ExCl in the literature is one of the most discussed syntactic phenomena among Finnish linguists (see Huumo 2003 and the references therein), and this clause type is anchored in grammatical properties such as case marking and agreement. I take the Finnish ExCl to be a superordinate construction schema that is inherited by the PossCl, which supplies it with further properties such as the adessive case and (concrete or metaphorical) animateness of its locative-marked participant, the possessor. I share the common view of linguistically relevant existence not as existence as such but as presence in a location (see Borschev

& Partee 1998; Partee & Borschev 2008; Creissels 2014, among others; for Finnish, see Ikola 1954; Vilkuna 1989: 164; Huumo 1995, 2003). Possessive predication is a similar construal in the domain of person-like 'locations'. Despite some unfortunate connotations, I will occasionally refer even to possession as 'existence' in this sense for the sake of simplicity.

The essential ingredients of an ExCl are a concrete or abstract locative (LOC) phrase, a verb and a noun phrase referring to the located entity or possessee.[6] My abbreviation for the latter in this chapter is *E*, a mnemonic for 'entity' or 'existant'.[7] The properties of core ExCl are the following (Hakulinen et al. 2004: §893):

i) Neutral constituent order: LOC V E.
ii) Function: Introduces a new referent in the discourse.
iii) E case, affirmative clause: Partitive indicating cumulative (non-bounded) reference; otherwise nominative.
iv) E case, negated clause: Normally partitive.
v) Verb agreement with E: None.
vi) Verb: *olla* (be).

Each of these properties can be violated, the number of violations increasing the distance of the expression from the core ExCl. In what follows, I will discuss these properties mainly as they apply to the PossCl. It is natural to start with the morpho-syntactic properties iii) – v) before proceeding to i) – ii). Property vi) and the nature of the LOC will be discussed in section 4, as they are the features that most clearly differentiate the PossCl and ExCl.

3.1. Possessee case and agreement

Partitive marking is a common property of the E and the object of a transitive clause, but it is more extensive in the object, with aspectual effects that do not extend to partitive E (see Kiparsky 1998; Huumo 2010). The partitive E in ExCl (see (1a)) is restricted to measurable entities such as substances and sets, i.e. plural and mass referents and abstract entities grammatically treated as substances. E is nominative when it refers to a singular countable entity. The partitive-marked E refers cumulatively, allowing further specification by adverbs of quantity such as 'little' and 'a lot'. The reading is non-exhaustive, or rather not necessarily exhaustive; 'part of' is not a necessary component although this implication often arises in context. Partitive in ExCl conveys indefiniteness as a consequence of its cumulative reference, as semantic definiteness presupposes exhaustivity.[8] However, partitive does not rule out anaphoric reference to a previously mentioned type of substance or set (7a). With singular countable E arguments, non-exhaustive reference is naturally ruled out, and indefiniteness is a default implication that can be overruled for example by determiners, as in (7b).

(7) a. Halu-at-ko omen-i-a? Minu-lla on nii-tä liikaa.
   want-2SG-Q apple-PL-PAR I-ADE be.3SG 3PL-PAR too.much
   'Do you want some apples? I have too much of them.'

b. Anna-lla on edelleen se sama musta koira.
   Anna-ADE be.3SG still 3SG same black dog
   'Anna still has that same black dog.'

The E constituent can also be in plural nominative form and refer exhaustively while still maintaining semantic indefiniteness. This happens with *plurale tantum* words and in general with nouns that have a conventionalized plural use, such as paired body parts and clothes as well as a sizable group of abstract nouns such as *olosuhteet* 'circumstances' and *mahdollisuudet* 'possibilities' (8a). The use of nominative plural also extends to sets presented exhaustively, when the totality in question is a generic property of the possessor referent. An example is (8b), where the totality of worthy products and customers is presented as characterizing the possessor company; the point of the utterance is the quality introduced by the modifier (cf. section 5). There is also a subtype where the possessee set is exhaustively distributed among the possessor set (8c).

(8) a. Anna-lla on lenkkitossu-t / hyvä-t mahdollisuudet voittaa.
   Anna-ADE be.3SG sneaker-PL / good-PL possibility.PL win-INF$_A$
   'Anna has [a pair of] sneakers / good possibilities to win.'

   b. Mei-llä on hyvät tuotteet ja tyytyväiset
      we-ADE be.3SG good.PL product.PL and satisfied.PL
      asiakkaat.
      customer.PL
      'We have good products and satisfied customers.'
      (https://www.hs.fi/talous/art-2000005651316.html, accessed 22 April 2018)

   c. Tytö-i-llä ol-i punaise-t meko-t.
      girl-PL-ADE be-PST.3SG red-PL dress-PL
      'The girls had red dresses [each girl had a red dress].'

As for partitive marking of (even countable) NPs under negation, is an essentially exceptionless feature of the object; in ExCl, it is the default (9).[9] Since the circumstances of not applying the partitive in negated clauses are relevant for the closer investigation of PossCl, I postpone further discussion to section 5.

(9) Anna-lla ei ole koira-a / *koira.
    Anna-ADE NGV.3SG be dog-PAR / koira.NOM
    'Anna has no dog.'

Non-agreement with E is a powerful but vulnerable ExCl criterion[10]. Lack of plural agreement in an ExCl such as (8) is a norm in standard Finnish, where the basic subject triggers number agreement without exception. However, number agreement is widely omitted in most spoken varieties (see Helasvuo & Laitinen 2006). The same third-person singular verb form is widely used in LocCL as well as in all other general clause types and does not therefore properly distinguish ExCl from LocCl in informal language. On the other hand, hypercorrection and perhaps also dialectal systems with more agreement may result in occasional use of the plural verb form even in PossCl.[11]

In contrast to third person, non-third person strongly requires agreement. If a non-third-person pronoun occurs as the located argument in the LOC V NP pattern, it triggers agreement, as in (10a), and the pattern is a LocCl with a marked order (section 3.2) rather than an ExCl. In contrast, PossCl readily admits personal pronoun possessees but marks them with accusative case (10b).[12]

(10) a. Ahaa,   täällä   ole-tte   te.
         PRT$_D$ here   be.2PL   you.PL
         'Oh, it's you here.'

   b.   Onneksi   minu-lla   on   teidä-t.
         fortunately   I-ADE   be.3SG   you-ACC
         'I'm lucky to have you.'

That non-agreeing nominative variants (*oli te 'be-PST.3SG you.PL') are avoided reflects both the strength of the Finnish person agreement (in contrast to number agreement) and the strength of the non-agreement in PossCl.[13] At the same time, the accusative marking could be taken as a sign of incipient transitivization or 'Have Drift' (Stassen 2009) of possessive predication in Finnish, a development that Stassen (2009: 230–239) considers typologically exceptional from a locational possessive source. As has often been noted, the case-marking options of the possessee are indeed identical with those of the object, although the actual conditions of the marking differ. I will not pursue this idea here, but note that there is no sign of the possessor taking on subject marking or triggering agreement like a subject.

3.2. Word order, perspective and information structure

The normal constituent order of ExCl/PossCl reflects its function, taking LOC as the starting point and presenting its content as new information (Huumo & Helasvuo 2015). Syntactically, the LOC can be treated as a 'default topic' with a privilege to the topic position, which is neutrally occupied by the subject in the general clause types (Vilkuna 1989; see Holmberg & Nikanne 2002 for a generative account). However, the E V LOC/POSS order is also possible (11).[14] This marked choice can for example be made to present the possessor as the focus; the result is informationally similar to the transitive OVS order (Vilkuna 1989: 178–187).

(11) a. Samanlais-i-a   kokemuks-i-a   on   minu-lla=kin.
         same.kind-PL-PAR   experience-PL-PAR   be.3SG   I-ADE=CL
         'I, too, have similar experiences.'

   b.   Illa-n   tyylikkä-in   asu   oli   Anna-lla.
         evening-GEN   elegant-SUP   outfit   be-PST.3SG   Anna-ADE
         '(It was) Anna (who) had the most elegant outfit of the evening.'

In (11a), the focus clitic particle *-kin* (too) supports the focus interpretation of the possessor. The partitive case conveys indefiniteness and shows that the example is an ExCl/PossCl. However, when the E is nominative, the structure of an ExCl/PossCl with a marked order overlaps with that of a LocCl with an unmarked order such as (1c) above, and vice versa. This is in principle the case with (11b). The decision between an ExCL-type reading and a LocCl-type reading must rely on context. In (11b), the PossCl reading is supported by the superlative in the E constituent. In a situation where people's elegance is being compared, an 'elegance scale' can be presented as given and the 'winner' as the information focus.

The idea that ExCl are not just information structure variants of locative predications has received support from different directions. In a series of publications on the Russian patterns – which show considerable similarities with the Finnic ones – Partee & Borschev (2002, 2008) suggest a model-theoretic distinction they call perspectival structure. The difference between a locative and an existential sentence is what is chosen as the perspectival centre: the figure (the located entity) or the ground (LOC). This suggestion is not unlike Langacker's cognitivist view as applied to Finnish ExCl by Huumo (2003) and Huumo & Helasvuo (2015). In this theory, the E differs from the subject in not being construed as the semantic and discursive starting point that opens up the perspective on the situation described, although it shares with the subject the status of the first argument.

It should be noted at this point that 'being presented as new information' does not equal being indefinite or unidentifiable, although that is the default interpretation in PossCl/ExCl (recall example (7b) above). What is new is the relation that is construed between the possessor and the possessee. Usage-based research on the referents of clausal constituents in conversational language (Helasvuo 2001: 85–103) has shown that the E in ExCl typically does bring a new referent into the discourse. Interestingly, however, being introduced as a new referent does not typically lead to continuing relevance of the referent. It is not impossible to continue the discourse about the E referent, but it seems more common that the role of the E is just to describe the LOC by describing some of its contents or possessions. In contrast, as shown by Helasvuo (2001), the subject referent is typically under discussion and therefore mentioned more than once, i.e. 'tracked' in discourse. As for the possessor of the PossCl, even if calculations such as those by Helasvuo (2001) have not been made, it is more likely than the E to have the discourse properties of the subject. As a typically animate entity with at least some control over the E, the possessor is naturally topical. Thus the PossCl resembles the general clause types in information structure more than in grammatical structure.

4. The special character of the possessive clause

This far we have seen how several factors combine in a clause type, ExCl, which is considerably different from the general clause types, even though it may be difficult for an analyst to distinguish each individual occurrence. The ExCl/PossCl distinction is not always clear-cut, either. Although the core ExCl properties are not directly specific to PossCl, one property, viz. accusative marking of the personal pronoun E, is at most marginal in ExCl and, therefore, a strong marker of the distinctness of ExCl and PossCl. On the other hand, personal pronoun possessees are in themselves a somewhat peripheral phenomenon in the possessive domain. In this section, I will discuss two more pervasive distinctive characteristics of PossCl.

4.1. Possessor case

The possessor is marked with the adessive case, while the locative in an ExCl can be in any local case ('in Anna's lap' in (1b)), or consist of an adposition phrase or an adverb. Adessive is part of the Finnish locative case paradigm, the stative member in the three-direction system including allative (direction 'to') and ablative (direction 'from'). These so-called 'outer' locative cases, or L-cases, contrast with three 'inner' cases, of which inessive is the stative counterpart of adessive. As adessive is also used for concrete locative relations, it can sometimes give rise to both ExCl and PossCl readings. However, the circumstances for this ambiguity are rather restricted, consider the examples in (12).

(12) a. Tamperee-lla   on   paljon   opiskelijo-i-ta.
         Tampere-ADE   be.3SG   much   student-PL-PAR
         'There are a lot of students in Tampere.'

   b. Anna-lla   on   aurinkovoide-tta.
       Anna-ADE   be.3SG   sun.cream-PAR
       'Anna has some suntan cream.'

   c. Tamperee-lla   on   uusi   joukkoliikennesuunnitelma.
       Tampere-ADE   be.3SG   new   public.transport.plan
       'Tampere has a new public transport plan.'

   d. Mei-llä   on   uusi   auto.
       we-ADE   be.3SG   new   car
       'We have a new car.'

   e. Mei-llä   on   kärpäs-i-ä.
       we-ADE   be.3SG   fly-PL-PAR
       'We have flies. / There are flies in our place.'

The use of adessive, or the L-cases in general, to mark properly locative relations is in many ways idiosyncratic; example (12a) is a typical ExCl with a place name requiring an L-case. In contrast, an important generalization is that L-cases on human or animate nouns do not yield locative but possessive and dative-like meanings such as Recipient and Beneficiary (Kotilainen 1999). Thus (12b) is unambiguously possessive and does not directly convey that there is suntan cream on Anna's skin. Potential in-between cases can be found with nouns that can be interpreted both as locations and as institutions with such properties as ability of intention and action. This yields the possessive reading in (12c). The most prototypical animates, the discourse partners referred to by personal pronouns, are also the prototypical possessors (12d). However, personal pronouns and human nouns in L-cases sometimes stand for the home or personal surroundings of the person(s) in question, resulting in a type of locative meaning as in example (12e), which is more likely to be read as an ExCl about 'our place' than a PossCl about 'us'.

As was shown above, an ExCl with a nominative E and an inverted order of constituents has an exact counterpart in LocCl. With animate adessives, the same is possible if a non-possessive interpretation is available. Thus, (13) can convey either temporary location or a legal status, the latter relation coming close to possession in the social domain, but note that in this case the binding of the possessive suffix shows that the clause is a LocCl. With a plural subject, plural agreement would also be expected in standard language.

(13) Lapsi on isä-llä-än.
    child be.3SG father-ADE-3POSS
    'The child is at his father's place / in his father's custody.'

It seems that genuine occurrences of this kind of structure are rather restricted because of the restricted readings of the animate adessive, especially since the options 'A is B's' and 'A is in B's possession' mentioned in section 2 are also available.

Even the choice of possessor case can bring about some vagueness in the ExCl/PossCl distinction. One example is the expression of inalienable parts of inanimate objects such as buildings and other artefacts, which typically have inessive rather than adessive form when used as 'possessors' (14a). It is hard to find real criteria for deciding whether the pattern in (14a) represents a PossCl or an ExCl, but the predication of inherent part-whole relations has a clear connection to the expression of possession (see Mazzitelli 2017). On the other hand, more abstract relations involving non-animate 'possessors' are expressed with the adessive case, i.e. in a clear PossCl format (14b); conversely, some notions such as character features may be construed using the inessive even for animate referents (14c). Applying the cognitive metaphor theory (Lakoff & Johnson 1980), a person can be construed either as a container (inessive) or a possessor (adessive) in cases such as (14c) (Kotilainen 1999).

(14) a. Rakennukse-ssa on iso-t ikkuna-t.
        building-INE be.3SG big-PL window-PL
        'The building has big windows.'

    b. Rakennukse-lla on kiinnostava historia.
        building-ADE be.3SG interesting history
        'The building has an interesting history.'

    c. Minu-ssa / minu-lla on varmasti ärsyttäv-i-ä piirte-i-tä.
        I-INE / I-ADE be.3SG certainly irritating-PL-PAR feature-PL-PAR
        'I certainly have some irritating features.'

It should be made clear at this point that the core PossCl is not the only context for animate adessive constituents with a possessive meaning. An interesting extension of PossCl is the pattern in (15). The adessive possessor is a neutral topic position holder, and the E has the possessee role but is also the argument of a secondary predicate, which indicates the location or state of the E.

(15) a. Anna-lla   on   haava   sorme-ssa / takki päällä.
        Anna-ADE   be.3SG   cut   finger-INE / coat on.top
        'Anna has a cut on her finger / a coat on.'

    b. Anna-lla   on   koira   mukana / syli-ssä / turva-na-an.
       Anna-ADE   be.3SG   dog   along /   lap-INE / protection-ESS-3POSS
       'Anna has a dog with her / in her lap / for her protection.'

As can be observed from (15), a possessive relation is also understood between the possessor and the secondary predicate; this is sometimes made explicit by a possessive suffix. Given that the examples can also be paraphrased with an ExCl that has the counterpart of the secondary predicate as the head of the LOC phrase (*Annan sormessa on haava* [Anna-GEN finger-INE be.3SG cut] 'There is a cut in Anna's finger', etc.), the construction type could be taken as an external possessive construction (e.g. Haspelmath 1999). Examples such as (16) demonstrate that the role of an animate adessive is actually wider; it may also express the person affected by the state of affairs (Seržant 2016).

(16)   Minu-lla loppu-u akku.
        I-ADE   end-3SG battery
        'My battery is running out.'

Patterns such as (15) and (16) are enough to show that the adessive-marked animate participant is a strong candidate for the topic position even outside core PossCls (see also Vilkuna 1989: 169–175). The pattern in (15) displays more PossCl properties than (16); the Partitive of Negation is common (but not exceptionless) in the former but ruled out in the latter, and the personal pronoun E would require the *-t* accusative in (15). Pattern (15) can therefore be seen as an extended PossCl. However, it does not completely obey the PossCl property discussed in the following section.

4.2. The verb

The verb in the PossCl is *olla* (be). This is not always the case with the Finnish ExCl, although *olla* is by far most frequently encountered. Other typical verbs are *tulla* (come) as well as verbs of presence or appearance, such as *löytyä* (be found), *esiintyä* (occur) or *ilmestyä* (appear). The general minimal requirement for a verb in ExCl is intransitivity (see Huumo 2018 for exceptions), but the range of eligible verbs is hard to delimit. A contentful verb in ExCl can be interpreted as reflecting the character of the E, such as 'sparkling' in the case of a ring in (17a) below, or its typical way of 'being' in the location at hand (Vilkuna 1989: 163). Thus, true agentive verbs are admitted, for example *työskennellä* (work) when the location is a workplace or *leikkiä* (play) when a park with children playing is discussed. There is a consensus that even when the verb is agentive, the actual point of the message is to describe a location via its contents rather than an action as such (see Huumo & Helasvuo 2015), but openness to a wide set of verbs is still an important property of the ExCl. It is also part of the motivation for the representation of ExCl as an argument structure construction, as the construction does not depend on individual verbs but affects the interpretation of the verbs.

That PossCl can only involve the verb *olla* (be) is partly a matter of definition, since predicative possession is defined as the bare expression of the stative possessive relation between two entities.[15] Still, it is a mark of specialization of the PossCl (17b) that it does not seem to admit contentful verbs such as *kiilteli* (sparkled) like the ExCl, as shown by the contrast between (17a) and (17b). Note that the 'extended PossCL' discussed above does accept such verbs (17c).

(17) a. Anna-n   sorme-ssa   ol-i   / kiiltel-i
       Anna-GEN   finger-INE   be-PST.3SG   / sparkle-PST.3SG

       upouusi   sormus.
       brand.new   ring
       'On Anna's finger there was / there sparkled a brand-new ring.'

   b. Anna-lla   oli   / *kiiltel-i   upouusi   sormus.
      Anna-ADE   be-PST.3SG   / sparkle-PST.3SG brand.new   ring.
      'Anna had a brand-new ring.'

   c. Anna-lla   kiiltel-i   sorme-ssa   upouusi   sormus.
      Anna-ADE   sparkle-PST.3SG   finger-INE   brand.new   ring
      'Anna had a brand-new ring sparkling on her finger.'

As implied by verbs such as *tulla* (come) and *ilmestyä* (appear) mentioned above, the Finnish ExCl can also be dynamic, i.e. express change. In this case, the LOC constituent has directional case. Such patterns can involve an animate, possessor-like LOC, as in (18).

(18)   Minu-lle tul-i   viesti   / päänsärky.
        I-ALL   come-PST.3SG   message   / headache
        'I got a message / a headache.'

Instances such as (18) can be seen to involve more or less clear modifications of the possessive relation, but they are not possessive predications. Although they show that the Finnish ExCl includes variants expressing human-oriented changes and states of affairs, the presence of a human adessive-marked constituent is in itself not a criterion of the PossCl (see (16)).

In summary, we have seen that the Finnish PossCl shares its main properties with the ExCl but displays different tendencies of case and verb choice. The phenomenon to be discussed in the following section also seems to be characteristic of PossCl.

5. Negation and the borderlines of the possessive clause

One of the most conspicuous features separating ExCl/PossCl from the general clause types is Partitive of Negation, which is normally an object phenomenon (section 3.1). However, unlike the object, the E can escape this effect and stand in the nominative even under negation, as in (19a); the semantic difference between nominative and partitive in this example will be discussed below. Superficially, the nominative E looks more like the basic subject in the general clause types, which are not affected by negation even in the post-verbal position, as shown in (19b).

(19) a. Minu-lla ei ole punainen mekko /
I-ADE NGV.3SG be red.NOM dress.NOM /
punais-ta mekko-a.
red-PAR dress-PAR
'I don't have a red dress.'

b. Minu-lle ei sovi punainen mekko /
I-ALL NGV.3SG suit red.NOM dress.NOM /
*punais-ta mekko-a.
red-PAR dress-PAR
'A red dress does not suit me.'

Although negative instances with nominative E cannot perhaps be said to belong to the core PossCl, they do not belong to general clause types, either. Non-agreement is still the norm (see (20d) below), and the nominative pattern does not extend to the personal pronoun E. Moreover, part of the nominative instances are more akin to impersonal clause types expressing general circumstances, as will be seen at the end of this section.

Both intuition and corpus data suggest that negation has a narrow focus when the E is nominative. A notable pattern of this type involves possessees that can normally be assumed, such as body parts, i.e. inalienable possession. In simple clause negation, partitive is chosen ((20a) and (20b)), but nominative is normal (although not obligatory) when only some of the possessee's properties are targeted ((20c) and (20d)).[16] The existence of an entity with the targeted property is denied but the existence of an entity of the same type with other properties is implied.

(20) a. Minu-lla ei ole nenä-ä / *nenä.
I-ADE NGV.3SG be nose-PAR / nose.NOM
'I don't have a nose.'

b. ... vanhemp-i-a / *vanhemma-t.
parent-PL-PAR / parent-PL.NOM
'I don't have (any) parents.'

c. ... iso nenä / iso-a nenä-ä.
big.NOM nose.NOM / big-PAR nose-PAR
'I don't have a big nose.'

d.   ...   varakkaa-t   vanhemma-t   / varakka-i-ta
           wealthy-PL.NOM   parent-PL.NOM   / wealthy-PL-PAR

vanhemp-i-a.
parent-PL-PAR
'I don't have wealthy parents.'

Nominative is also possible with inalienable parts of inanimate referents such as windows of houses (see (14a) in section 4.1). Apart from inalienable possession, nominative E is not common but its limits are difficult to set.[17] One factor that favours the nominative pattern is the modifier *sama* (same) in the E, especially with its sentence-internal reading, i.e. when the members of the possessor group share identical 'possessions' (21).

(21)   Laps-i-lla   ei   ole   sama   isä.
       child-PL-ADE   NGV.3SG   be   same   father
       'The children do not have the same father.'

The nominative option in cases such as (19a) and (21) involves an exhaustiveness assumption concerning the implied possessee. An E such as 'a wealthy aunt' in (20d) instead of 'wealthy parents' is likely to stand in the partitive, as people are not normally assumed to have a single unique aunt. In inalienable possession, exhaustiveness is interpreted in relation to the possessor referent, but in the case of (19a) the implication is contextual: the sentence is felicitous in a context where the colour of the dress the speaker is wearing on the particular occasion has been misrepresented but not when the speaker is discussing the contents of her wardrobe. I take this to mean that the Partitive of Negation, basically a negative polarity item, always activates the set (or substance) in question and negates the existence of even the minimum member (or particle), in the case of (19a), one red dress. This is in accord with the fact that minimizing negative polarity elements such as the adverb *ollenkaan* (at all) or negative quantifiers such as *yksikään* ('(not) a single one') are possible with partitive E ((22a)–(22c)). When E is nominative, the adverb can only be interpreted as attaching to the modifier (22b), and quantifiers such as *yksikään* are ruled out (22c). In contrast, the quantifier *yksikään* would be fine in the subject phrase of (19b).

(22) a.   Minu-lla ei   ole   ollenkaan   nenä-ä.
          I-ADE   NGV3SG be   at.all   nose-PAR
          'I have no nose at all.'

     b.   ... ollenkaan   iso   nenä.
              at.all   big   nose
          'I don't have a big nose at all [my nose is not at all big].'

     c.   ... yh-tä-kään   punais-ta   mekko-a /
              one-PAR=CL   red-PAR   dress-PAR /

          *yksi-kään   punainen   mekko.
          one-CL   red.NOM   dress
          'I don't have a single red dress.'

Although the full semantics of the phenomenon is not well understood, it can be concluded that the cumulative meaning of the partitive case makes itself felt even under negation.

Finally, it can be observed that quite a few of the nominative instances contain an abstract E, which is often conventionally plural in form (23).

(23) Mei-llä   ei   ole   huono maku / suuret-t
      we-ADE   NGV.3SG   be   bad   taste / big-PL

      tulo-t /   läheise-t väli-t /   mukava-t   olosuhtee-t.
      income-PL /   close-PL   relation-PL / comfortable-PL circumstance-PL
      'We don't have a bad taste / a big income / a close relationship / comfortable circumstances.'

While such predications take the general PossCl form, they are somewhat exceptional as possessive predications. The plural nominative instances belong to the PossCl with exhaustive E discussed in section 3.1; recall (8b), a pattern with nominative E found to have an essentially characterizing function. A sign of this function is that some kind of restricting modifier is pragmatically necessary. This is true of (23) as well as in the affirmative versions 'I have a taste/an income/a relationship/circumstances'. Whether the clause is negated or not, the focus is not so much on the E as on its characteristics and, thereby, on characterizing the possessor. This type of PossCl, together with the option of nominative E, speaks for a certain distance from core possessives. This is even more true of the following set of examples.

(24) a. Minu-lla ei   ole   vapaapäivä.
         I-ADE   NGV.3SG be   day.off
         'I don't have a day-off [It's not my day off].'

     b. ...   flunssa /   krapula
                flu /   hangover
         'I don't have a flu / a hangover.'

     c. ...   kiire
                haste
         'I'm not in a hurry.'

     d. ...   kuuma / jano /   nälkä /
                hot /   thirst / hunger /

                paha / olo /   paha mieli
                bad /   state / bad mind
         'I'm not hot / thirsty / hungry / unwell / upset.'

The naturalness of a partitive E in (24) varies, but partitive is ruled out in group (24d). Example (24a) again gives rise to a reading that is distinct from the partitive-marked version. While the nominative-E pattern in (24a) is about the special nature of a particular day for me, the partitive E would elicit an interpretation such as 'I won't have a single day off (for a time)'. This distinction is the same as discussed in connection with (19a), but note that (24a) also has clear parallels in patterns such as (25):

(25)   Nyt   on   torstai.
       now   be.3SG   Thursday

       Tänään   on /   ei   ole   minu-n   vapaapäivä-ni.
       today   be.3SG / NGV.3SG   be   I-GEN   day.off-1POSS
       'It's Thursday today. It's / It's not my day off today.'

The sentences in (25) represent what is called the State Clause in the clause type classification of Hakulinen et al. (2004: §900–901). This is a cover term for a somewhat heterogeneous set of syntactically impersonal, often idiomatic patterns that describe circumstances and natural conditions prevailing in some location or time frame. Instead (or together with) the locative, many State Clause predicates contain an adessive animate constituent expressing the person affected by the state. As they also often involve the verb 'be', the clauses resemble ExCl (26a) or PossCl (26b), even though they cannot be claimed to introduce a referent.

(26) a. Täällä   on   kuuma   / tylsä-ä.
        here   be.3SG   hot   / boring-PAR
        'It is hot / boring here.'

   b.   Minu-lla on   kuuma   / tylsä-ä.
        I-ADE   be.3SG   hot   / boring-PAR
        'I am hot / bored.'

   c.   Mei-llä   on   kamala-n   sekais-ta.
        we-ADE   be.3SG   terrible-GEN   messy-PAR
        'It's a terrible mess in our place.'

Huumo & Helasvuo (2015) argue that the noun or adjective phrase in the state clause has the same syntactic role as the E of ExCl/PossCl. From the present point of view, the question is rather whether the clause type is the same. This question cannot be answered in the present discussion, but a negative answer is suggested by the observation that the case marking of the predicating noun or adjective (nominative *kuuma* but partitive *tylsää* and *sekaista* in (26)) is idiosyncratic (Hakulinen et al. 2004: §954) and does not depend on reference, quantification or negation as it does in ExCl/PossCl. In the borderline cases, such as the physical states in (24b), the potential E can be construed either as an abstract referent or just a state predicate. Marking the E with partitive makes explicit the former interpretation.

Partitive of Negation is the default case in the PossCl in the sense that partitive is not ruled out in the examples in this section unless they overstep the boundaries of PossCl, as in (24) and particularly in (24d). However, we have seen that the use of nominative E under negation does not bring the utterance closer to a general clause type, not even in cases where nominative is used to indicate that a possession relation holds (although not for the negated type of possessee). These occurrences are presuppositional in that they have to do with possessions that can normally be assumed. Since PossCl inherit many of their properties from the more general ExCl schema, it remains to be asked whether nominative E is also an option in this larger schema. The answer to this question is complicated by the overlap of ExCl with LocCl and other intransitive clauses, but my impression based on corpus data is that nominative is less typical in the non-possessive ExCl. Occurrences with nominative E analogous to possessives such as 'I don't have a big nose/wealthy parents' are most easily found in expressions of inanimate whole-part relations such as 'The building does not have big windows' ((14a) in section 4.1), which suggests that the latter are indeed a type of PossCl.

6. Conclusions

In this chapter, we have seen that the Finnish possessive clause shares most of its properties with the existential clause. In addition, the possessive clause has some unique properties, most notably the adessive marking of the possessor, the exclusion of verbs other than 'be' and the conventionalized use of accusative with personal pronoun possessees. Although the more problematic aspects of the differentiation of ExCl as opposed to general clause types have not been reviewed here, it is clear that the PossCl is a more easily observable and arguably more entrenched construction, both by virtue of its case choices – both possessor and possessee marking – and in verb choice. Abstract PossCl patterns show that the general form of the construction is productive, but the abstract instances do not necessarily have all the properties that constitute the core of the PossCl, most notably the animate possessor.

In this study, I did not attempt to give a formal exhaustive classification of Finnish clause types. It is possible that further research in the constructional framework brings to light reasons for a more fine-grained analysis of both ExCl and PossCl. As partitive marking of the E and its subtle exceptions in negative clauses indicate, clause types form a tight-knit network with several cross-cutting phenomena.

There is good evidence that the possessor (even though it is not a grammatical subject) is the dominant element in the PossCl. It can bind a reflexive element in the E, and it also determines the interpretation of the E in the cases when the latter is exhaustively construed. It is also typically animate and highly likely to be topical. The E referents are presented as controllable entities and are often introduced as personal attributes of the possessor. All these facts, together with the lack of agreement in the verb and the accusative case marking animate, i.e. otherwise most subject-like possessees, speak against the subject status of the E. As for the subject properties in Finnish PossCl, they are distributed between the possessor and the possessee. A construction-based treatment need not define a subject for each clausal construction.

Notes

1. Abbreviations

ABL	ablative case	NGV	negative auxiliary
ACC	accusative case	NOM	nominative
ADE	adessive case	POSS	possessive suffix
ALL	allative case	POSSCL	possessive clause
CL	clitic particle	PAR	partitive case
E	entity	PL	plural
ESS	essive case	PRS	present tense
EXCL	existential clause	PST	past tense
GEN	genitive case	PRT_D	discourse particle
INE	inessive case	SUP	superlative
INF_A	*A*-infinitive	SG	singular
INF_M	*mA*-infinitive	Q	interrogative clitic
LOCCL	locative clause		

2. I would like to thank Gréte Dalmi and Jaakko Leino for valuable literature hints and the Construction Grammar Circle at the University of Helsinki for comments on this chapter and interesting discussion over the years.
3. Finnish has a genitive case that is used, among other things, for adnominal possession, but no dative, whose typical functions are served by the locative cases as explained in section 4.1.
4. Aller Media ltd. (2014). *The Suomi 24 Sentences Corpus (2016H2)* [text corpus]. Kielipankki. Available online: http://urn.fi/urn:nbn:fi:lb-2017021505. The search interface used is korp.csc.fi.
5. My reading of Huumo & Helasvuo (2015) is partially based on the authors' earlier treatment in Helasvuo & Huumo (2010).
6. The LOC constituent can be missing, indicating existence in the universe of discourse. This can be seen as another subconstruction; yet another one is without LOC but with a preverbal partitive E and postverbal quantifier or measure phrase (see Hakulinen et al. 2004: §899, 902).
7. Huumo & Helasvuo (2015) use the term *E-NP*; I simplify this to *E* as I am not committed in this chapter to their definition.
8. In the Finnish tradition, the kind of indefinite meaning conveyed by the partitive *E* is called *quantitative indefiniteness* (Siro 1957; Hakulinen et al. 2004: §1421). Huumo & Helasvuo (2015) use the term *unbounded quantity*.
9. The object can avoid the partitive only in utterances with a clear positive implication, such as negative yes/no questions seeking for positive confirmation. Note that the effect of negation can only be attested when the partitive-marked NP in question is countable.
10. Only a nominative-marked argument triggers verb agreement in Finnish, so lack of agreement is only relevant for the nominative E. If agreement is taken to be the formal criterion for subjecthood, partitive E is never a subject (Huumo & Helasvuo 2015). Note that in the closely related Estonian, the nominative counterpart of E does trigger agreement: *Ta-l ol-i-d uue-d king-ad* [s/he-ADE be-PST-3PL new-PL shoe-PL] ('(S)he had new shoes') (Erelt, Metslang & Plado 2017: 249). The verb 'be' does not have third-person plural forms in present tense indicative, though.

11 An example from the internet corpus: *Mummu-i-lla o-vat piene-t eläkkee-t* [grandma-PL-ADE be.3PL small-PL pension-PL] 'Old women have small pensions [so they pay small taxes].'

12 Finnish personal pronouns have a specific accusative marker *-t*, while other singular objects are marked with *-n* and plural objects are in the nominative. The *-n* marking is not known to occur in ExCl/PossCl. Sporadic accusative marking of personal pronouns is also attested in core ExCl (see Hakulinen et al. 2004 §923 and Inaba 2015: 93), but the extent of the phenomenon is not known and speaker intuitions about it vacillate.

13 Another reflection of the strength of non-third-person agreement can be observed with impersonal modals such as *täytyy* (must) which only have third-person singular forms. Simplifying somewhat, these generally take their subject in genitive case but also allow nominative, especially in low-transitivity contexts. This non-agreeing nominative is ruled out with personal pronouns. (See Laitinen & Vilkuna 1993.)

14 In principle, the same holds for any other permutation of constituents, most notably the pre-LOC position of either E or the finite verb from. These alternatives do not affect the topic position.

15 There are two other potential verbs with very abstract meaning that could be argued to occur in PossCl. One is *riittää* (be enough), when used in the PossCl format with a plural or mass E to express that the quantity possessed is notable, for example *Sinu-lla riittä-ä energia-a* [you-ADE be.enough-3SG energy-PAR] ('You have lots of energy'). The second is *puuttua* (lack), which can be taken as a way of negating possession. It requires ablative case, for example *Sinu-lta puuttu-u energia-a* [you-ABL lack.3SG energy-PAR] '(You lack (sufficient) energy).' These expressions are quite restricted in use compared with the general PossCl format.

16 The E in such cases thus normally contains a restrictive modifier, but a modifier is, strictly speaking, not required, since the same effect may be achieved by the first part of a compound noun or a pro-form anaphoric to a quality mentioned before.

17 In the Suomi24 corpus, both nominative and partitive body part E's occur with roughly similar frequency, while phrases such as '(does not have) wealthy parents' clearly favour partitive E. On the basis of the discussion forum data alone, it cannot be judged whether the alternatives reflect different intended meaning.

References

Borschev, V. & Partee, B. 1998. Formal and lexical semantics and the genitive in negated existential sentences in Russian. In: Bošković, Ž., Franks, S. & Snyder, W. (eds), *Formal Approaches to Slavic Linguistics 6: The Connecticut Meeting 1997*, 75–96. Ann Arbor: Michigan Slavic Publications.

Creissels, D. 2014. Existential predication in typological perspective. *Paper presented at the 46th Annual Meeting of the Societas Linguistica Europaea*. Revised version. Available online: http://www.deniscreissels.fr/index.php?pages/autres-documents-téléchargeables.

Croft, W. 2001. *Radical Construction Grammar: Syntactic Theory in Typological Perspective*. Oxford: Oxford University Press.

Edygarova, S. 2015. Negation in Udmurt. In: Miestamo, M., Tamm, A. & Wagner-Nagy, B. (eds), *Negation in Uralic Languages*. Typological Studies in Language 108, 265–291. Amsterdam: John Benjamins.

Erelt, M., Metslang, H. & Plado, H. 2017. Alus [Subject]. In: Erelt, M. & Metslang, H.(eds), *Eesti keele Süntaks* [The Syntax of the Estonian Language], 240–257. Tartu: Tartu Ülikooli kirjastus.

Fried, M. 2015. Construction grammar. In: Alexiadou, A. & Kiss, T. (eds), *Syntax. Theory and Analysis. An International Handbook*, vol. 2, 974–1003. Berlin: De Gruyter Mouton.

Goldberg, A. 1995. *Constructions: A Construction Grammar Approach to Argument Structure*. Chicago: University of Chicago Press.

Goldberg, A. 2006. *Constructions at Work: The Nature of Generalization in Language*. Oxford: Oxford University Press.

Hakanen, A. 1972. Normaalilause ja eksistentiaalilause [Normal sentence and existential sentence]. *Sananjalka* 14: 36–76.

Hakulinen, A. & Karlsson, F. 1979. *Nykysuomen lauseoppia* [Syntax of Modern Finnish]. Helsinki: Suomalaisen Kirjallisuuden Seura.

Hakulinen, A., Vilkuna, M., Korhonen, R., Koivisto, V., Heinonen, T. R. & Alho, I. 2004. *Iso suomen kielioppi* [Comprehensive Finnish grammar]. Helsinki: Suomalaisen Kirjallisuuden Seura. Available online: http://scripta.kotus.fi/visk/.

Haspelmath, M. 1999. External possession in a European areal perspective. In: Barshi, I. & Payne, D. (eds), *External Possession*, 109–135. Amsterdam: John Benjamins.

Haspelmath, M. 2010. Comparative concepts and descriptive categories in crosslinguistic studies. *Language* 86(3): 663–687.

Heine, B. 1997. *Possession: Cognitive Sources, Forces, and Grammaticalization*. Cambridge: Cambridge University Press.

Helasvuo, M-L. 2001. *Syntax in the Making: The Emergence of Syntactic Units in Finnish Conversation*. Studies in Discourse and Grammar 9. Amsterdam: John Benjamins.

Helasvuo, M-L. & Huumo, T. 2010. Mikä subjekti on? [On the subject of subject in Finnish]. *Virittäjä* 114(2): 165–195.

Helasvuo, M-L. & Laitinen, L. 2006. Person in Finnish: paradigmatic and syntagmatic relations in interaction. In: Campbell, L. & Helasvuo, M-L. (eds), *Grammar from the Human Perspective. Case, Space and Person in Finnish*, 173–207. Amsterdam: John Benjamins.

Hoffmann, T. 2013. Abstract phrasal and clausal constructions. In: Hoffmann, T. & Trousdale, G. (eds), *The Oxford Handbook of Construction Grammar*, 307–328. Oxford: Oxford University Press.

Holmberg A. & Nikanne, U. 2002. Expletives, subjects, and topics in Finnish. In: Svenonius, P. (ed.), *Subjects, Expletives, and the EPP*, 71–105. Oxford: Oxford University Press.

Huumo, T. 1995. Bound domains: a semantic constraint on existentials. In: Hokkanen, T., Leinonen, M. & Shore, S. (eds), *SKY 1995: The 1995 Yearbook of the Linguistic Association of Finland*, 7–46. Helsinki: Linguistic Association of Finland.

Huumo, T. 2003. Incremental existence: the world according to the Finnish existential sentence. *Linguistics* 41 (3): 461–493.

Huumo, T. 2010. Nominal aspect, quantity, and time: the case of the Finnish Object. *Journal of Linguistics* 46: 83–125.

Huumo, T. 2018. The partitive A: on uses of the Finnish partitive subject in transitive clauses. In: Seržant, I. & Witzlack-Makarevich, A. (eds), *The Diachronic Typology of Differential Argument Marking*, 423–453. Berlin: Language Science Press.

Huumo, T. & Helasvuo, M-L. 2015. On the subject of subject in Finnish. In: Helasvuo, M-L. & Huumo, T. (eds), *Subjects in Constructions – Canonical and Non-Canonical*, 15–41. Amsterdam: John Benjamins.

Huumo, T. & Lindström, L. 2014. Partitives across constructions: on the range of uses of the Finnish and Estonian 'partitive subjects'. In: Luraghi, S. & Huumo, T. (eds), *Partitive Cases and Related Categories*, 153–175. Berlin: De Gruyter Mouton.

Ikola, O. 1954. Suomen lauseopin ongelmia I-III [Problems of Finnish syntax]. *Virittäjä* 58(3): 209–245.

Inaba, N. 2015. *Suomen datiivigenetiivin juuret vertailevan menetelmän valossa* [The roots of the Finnish dative genitive in the light of the comparative method]. Mémoires de la Société Finno-Ougrienne 272. Helsinki: Suomalais-ugrilainen Seura.

Kajander, M. 2013. Suomen kielen eksistentiaalilause toisen kielen oppimisen polulla [Paths of learning Finnish existential sentences]. PhD dissertation. Jyväskylä Studies in Humanities 220. University of Jyväskylä.

Kiparsky, P. 1998. Partitive case and aspect. In: Butt, M. & Geuder, W. (eds), *The Projection of Arguments: Lexical and Compositional Factors*. CSLI Lecture Notes 83, 265–307. Stanford CA: Center for the Study of Language and Information.

Kotilainen, L. 1999. Ihminen paikkana. Henkilöviitteisten paikallissijailmausten semantiikkaa [Person as place. On the semantics of human locative expressions]. MA Thesis. University of Helsinki, Department of Finnish Language.

Laakso, J. & Wagner-Nagy, B. forthcoming. Existential, locational, and possessive sentences. In: Bakró-Nagy, M., Laakso, J. & Skribnik, E. (eds), *Oxford Guide to the Uralic Languages*. Oxford: Oxford University Press.

Laitinen, L. & Vilkuna, M. 1993. Case-marking in necessive constructions and split intransitivity. In: Holmberg, A. & Nikanne. U. (eds), *Case and other Functional Categories in Finnish Syntax*, 23–48. Berlin: Mouton de Gruyter.

Lakoff, G. & Johnson. M. 1980. *Metaphors We Live by*. Chicago, IL: University of Chicago Press.

Mazzitelli, L. F. 2017. Predicative possession in the languages of the Circum-Baltic area. *Folia Linguistica* 51(1): 1–60.

Partee, B. & Borschev, V. 2002. Genitive of Negation and Scope of Negation in Russian existential sentences. In: Toman, J. (ed.) *Annual Workshop on Formal Approaches to Slavic Linguistics: the Second Ann Arbor Meeting 2001* (FASL 10), 181–200. Ann Arbor, MI: Michigan Slavic Publications.

Partee, B. & Borschev, V. 2008. Existential sentences, BE, and the Genitive of Negation in Russian. In: Comorovski, I. & von Heusinger, K. (eds), *Existence: Semantics and Syntax*, 147–190. Dordrecht: Springer.

Seržant, I. 2016. External possession and constructions that may have it. *Sprachtypologie und Universalienforschung* 69(1): 131–169.

Siro, P. 1957. Suomen kielen subjektista kielen rakenteen osana [On the subject in Finnish as part of the language structure]. *Virittäjä* 61(2): 181–190.

Stassen, L. 2009. *Predicative Possession*. Oxford: Oxford University Press.

Veselinova, L. 2015. Special negators in the Uralic languages. In: Miestamo, M., Tamm, A. & Wagner-Nagy, B. (eds), *Negation in Uralic Languages*. Typological Studies in Language 108, 547–599. Amsterdam: John Benjamins.

Vilkuna, M. 1989. *Free Word Order in Finnish. Its Syntax and Discourse Functions*. Helsinki: Suomalaisen Kirjallisuuden Seura.
Vilkuna, M. 2015. Negation in Finnish. In: Miestamo, M., Tamm, A. & Wagner-Nagy, B. (eds), *Negation in Uralic Languages*. Typological Studies in Language 108, 457–485. Amsterdam: John Benjamins.

7. The argument structure of BE-possessives in Hungarian

Gréte Dalmi

1. Segregating existential/possessive BE from copular BE[1,2]

Languages show a great diversity in the syntactic functions of BE-predicates. Apart from the temporal/aspectual auxiliary function (which will not be discussed here), three main manifestations of BE are mentioned in the literature: the copular function, the existential function and the possessive function (see Freeze 1992; Moro 1997, 2017; Den Dikken 1997, 2006). These functions are demonstrated in (1)–(3) for Russian and in (4)–(6) for Hungarian:

$BE_{COP} <[_{SC} DP\ XP]>$ *(where XP = NP/AP/PP/AdvP)*
(1) Ivan Ø   [studěnt / inteligentnyj / v škoľe].   (Russian)
    Ivan COP   student / intelligent / in school
    'Ivan is a student/intelligent/at school.'

BE_{EXIST} <(DP/PP), DP>
        LOCATION   THEME
(2) V ogoroďe   jesť   pťitsy.
    in garden BE_{EXIST} birds
    'In the garden there are (some) birds.'   (Russian)

BE_{POSS} <(DP/PP), DP>
       POSSESSOR THEME
(3) U Ivana   jesť   mašina.
    at Ivan-GEN BE_{EXIST} car
    'Ivan has a car.'   (Russian)

$BE_{COP} <[_{SC} DP\ XP]>$ *(where XP = NP/AP/PP/AdvP)*
(4) A császár   Ø   bölcs.
    the emperor   COP   wise
    'The emperor is wise.'   (Hungarian)

BE_{EXIST} <(DP, DP)>
(5) A kert-ben   VAN-NAK   virág-ok.
    the garden-in BE_{EXIST}-3PL   flower-PL
    'There are flowers in the garden.'   (Hungarian)

BE_{POSS} <DP, DP>
(6) A császár-nak   VAN   új   ruhá-ja.
    the emperor-DAT BE_{EXIST}.3SG   new   clothes-POSS3SG
    'The emperor has new clothes.'   (Hungarian)

The differences between copular BE vs. existential/possessive BE are perhaps less clear-cut in languages such as English. In the two languages demonstrated above, the three main functions of BE are fairly easy to segregate, as they manifest a whole range of distinct syntactic and semantic properties.

(i) *Semantic interpretation*
Existential and possessive BE-sentences state the existence of an individual in a given location or relation (x EXISTS in y) (see Chvany 1975; Milsark 1979; Freeze 1992; Paducheva 2000, 2008). By contrast, copular BE (whether lexical or null) is merely the mediator of predication relation between the non-verbal predicate, denoting a property, and the subject, denoting an individual (see Partee 1998). Copular BE, in addition, carries grammatical functions such as tense, mood, aspect and person/number/gender agreement in copular BE-sentences (see Moro 1997, 2017; Partee 1998; Bowers 2001; Rothstein 2001; Den Dikken 2006; Błaszczak 2007, 2010; Geist 2008; Partee & Borschev 2008 for details).

(ii) *Definiteness Restriction*
Existential and possessive BE-predicates impose the so-called Definiteness Restriction (DR)[3] on their Theme argument in several languages (Milsark 1979). This property sets apart these predicates from copular BE, which does not impose such semantic restrictions on its sole argument. This is illustrated in (7)–(8) for English, (9a)–(c) for Russian and (10a)–(10c) for Hungarian:

(7) Peter / Every student / This student / My student is a genius / clever BE_{COP}
    / in the room.

(8) There is *Peter/*every student/*this boy/*my student in the room. BE_{EXIST}

(9) a. Pjotr   / Každyj student / Etot student / Moj student   byvaet BE_{COP}
       Peter   / every student / this student / my student   BE.HAB.PRES3SG
       pjan-ym.
       drunk.INST
       'Peter /every student / this student / my student is (habitually) drunk.'

b. Na ulitse jest'   *Pjotr / *každyj student / *etot student /   BE_EXIST
    on street BE_EXIST.3SG   Peter / every student / this student /

*moj student.
my student
'There is Peter / every student / this student / my student in the street.'

c. U menja   jest'   *Pjotr / *každyj student / *etot student   BE_POSS
   at me   BE_EXIST   Peter / every student / this student

/*moj student.
my student
'I have *Peter/*every student/*this student/*my student.'

(10) a. Péter / Minden diák / Ez a diák   ∅   okos.
       Peter / every student / this the student   BE_COP   clever.
       'Peter / Every student / This student is clever.'   BE_COP

   b. Az   utcán   VAN⁴   *Péter / *minden diák / *ez a diák.
      the   street-on   BE_EXIST   Peter / every student / this the student
      'There is *Peter / *every student / *this the student in the street.'   BE_EXIST

   c. *Nekem   VAN   Péter-em   /   minden diák-om
       I-DAT   BE_EXIST   Peter-POSS1SG   /   every student-POSS1SG
      / ez a diák-om.
      / this the student-POSS1SG
      'I have Peter / every student / this student.'   BE_POSS

(iii) Quantifier floating (Q-Float)
Copular BE-sentences allow Q-Float (see Koopman & Sportiche 1991), while existential and possessive BE/HAVE sentences never do.⁵ This is problematic if existential and possessive sentences are derived from copular BE-sentences but follows automatically if the syntactic structure assigned to copular BE-sentences is distinguished from the one assumed for existential and possessive BE-sentences.

As is well known, Q-Float is possible if and only if the quantifier is part of the subject noun phrase. The quantifier remains inside the DP, while the rest of the subject DP moves to [Spec,IP]:

(11) [IP These men_i [VP t_i are [both t_i doctors]]].   BE_COP

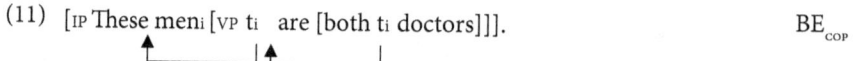

If we wanted to maintain the structural parallelism between the copular BE-sentence in (11) on the one hand, and the existential and possessive BE-sentences in (12) and (13), on the other, we would have to force the quantified DP *both these men* into the subject position of the non-verbal predicate *doctors*:

(12) *[IP There are [VP these meni [both ti] doctors]].   BE_EXIST

(13) *[IP Wej have [VP tj these men]k [both tk] doctors]].   HAVE_POSS

Under the assumption that existential and possessive sentences are structurally identical to copular BE-sentences, a view that pops up in the generative syntactic literature from time to time[6], the quantified DP would have to originate as the subject of the non-verbal predicate, and Q-Float ought to give grammatically correct sentences. The fact that Q-Float is impossible in such sentences indicates that the quantified DP *both these men* does not originate as the subject of the non-verbal predicate in them.

(iv) Clause negation in copular, existential and possessive BE-sentences
While copular sentences in Russian are negated by the negative particle *ne* 'NEG', existential and possessive sentences require the negative form *net* 'NEG' in the present indicative. This form is claimed to be the contraction of NEG+BE_EXIST (Chvany 1975; Paducheva 2000, 2008).

Notice that only the negated existential predicate *net* 'NEG+BE_EXIST' licences Genitive of Negation (GEN NEG) on the Theme argument[7]; the negated copula never does:

Negated copular BE-sentence
(14) Ivan   ne   ∅   profesor.
     Ivan   NEG   COP   professor
     'Ivan is not a professor.'

(15) *Ivan-a   ne   ∅   profesor.
      Ivan-GEN NEG   COP   professor
      Intended: 'Ivan is not a professor.'

Negated existential BE-sentence
(16) V našem   otd'elenii   net   profesor-a.
     in our   department   NEG+BE_EXIST   professor-GEN
     'At our department there is no professor.'

(17) *V našem   otd'elenii   ne   ∅   profesor-a.
      in our   department   NEG   COP   professor-GEN
      Intended: 'At our department there is no professor.'

Negated possessive BE-sentence
(18) U Ivana   net   mašin-y.
     at Ivan   NEG.BE_EXIST   car-GEN
     'Ivan has no car.'

(19) *U Ivana   ne   ∅   mašin-y.
      at Ivan   NEG   COP   car-GEN
      Intended: 'Ivan has no car.'

As we can see in (20)–(21), the negated copular verb imposes no such requirement on the Theme argument even if it takes a locative DP as its small clause complement. The clause negator is invariably *ne* (not) in copular BE-sentences. As opposed to negated existential BE-sentences, here the clause-initial DP can only be interpreted as definite and GoN is illicit:

Negated locative copular BE-sentence
(20) Profesor$_i$ ne   ∅   [t$_i$ v našem   otd'elenii].
     professor   not   COP   in our   department
     'The professor is not at our department.'

(21) *Profesor-a   ne   ∅   v našem   otd'elenii.
     professor-GEN   not   COP   in our   department
     Intended: 'The professor is not at our department.'

A similar difference between negated copular BE-sentences vs. negated existential and possessive BE-sentences can be observed in Hungarian.[8] In the present indicative, the negative particle *nem* (not) is only licit in negated copular sentences. In negated existential and possessive BE-sentences, the negative existential verb forms *nincs/nincsenek*, 'there is no…/there are no', must be used[9]:

Negated copular BE-sentence
(22) Péter   nem   ∅   fogorvos.
     Peter   NEG   COP   dentist
     'Peter is not a dentist.'

(23) *Péter   nincs   fogorvos.
     Peter   NEG.BE$_{EXIST}$ dentist
     Intended: 'Peter is not a dentist.'

Negated existential BE-sentence
(24) A falu-ban   nincs-(e)-nek   fogorvos-ok.
     the village-INESS   NEG.BE$_{EXIST}$-3PL   dentist-PL
     'There are no dentists in the village.'

(25) *A falu-ban   nem   ∅   fogorvos-ok.
     the village-INESS   NEG   COP   dentist-PL
     Intended: 'There are no dentists in the village.'
     Negated possessive BE-sentence

(26) Péter-nek   nincs   fogorvos-a.
     Peter-DAT   NEG.BE$_{EXIST}$ dentist-POSS3SG
     'Peter has no dentist.'

(27) *Péter-nek   nem   ∅   fogorvos-a.
     Peter-DAT   not   COP   dentist-POSS3SG
     Intended: 'Peter has no dentist.'

Table 7.1 *Differences between copular BE-sentences and existential BE-sentences in Russian and Hungarian.*

Russian and Hungarian	Copular BE-sentences	Existential/Possessive BE-sentences
Q-Float	YES	NO
Definiteness Restriction	NO	YES
GoN	NO	YES
Zero BE in present tense	YES	NO
Clause NEG and focus NEG are identical	YES	NO

The above facts lend support to a syntactic analysis that segregates existential and possessive BE-sentences from copular BE-sentences in these two languages. The differences between existential/possessive BE-sentences and copular BE-sentences are summarized in Table 7.1. The present proposal adopts the lexicalist view that existential BE and possessive BE select two eventuality participants, hence they are dyadic unaccusatives (see Paducheva 2000, 2008; Partee & Borschev 2008), while copular BE (whether lexical or null) is a monadic unaccusative predicate taking a single small clause. Copular BE serves as the mediator of predication relation between the non-verbal predicate and the subject (see Stowell 1981; Bowers 2001; Rothstein 2001; Den Dikken 2006; Błaszczak 2007, 2010; Geist 2008; Partee 1998; Partee & Borschev 2008; Maienborn 2005; Dalmi 2010, 2012, 2016).

2. BE-possessives in Hungarian

2.1. BE-possessives vs. HAVE-possessives: Conventional wisdom

When possessive sentences are discussed, it is almost obligatory to cite Benveniste's (1966) famous claim concerning predicative possession: '*avoir* n'est rien autre qu'un *être+à* inverse' (*avoir* is nothing other than inverted *être+à*). This view is often echoed in current syntactic theories, the most influential of which is perhaps Kayne's (1993) derivational analysis, inspired by Szabolcsi's (1983, 1985, 1992) work. In Kayne's theory, possessive sentences across languages are special instances of copular BE-sentences, in which the possessor and the possessee form a syntactic unit, and the possessor is moved from its post-verbal position to the canonical subject position (see Myler 2016 for a reformulation of this idea in Minimalist terms):

(28) a. Le/*Un livre$_i$ est [t$_i$ à Jean].
 the/a book is to Jean
 'The/*A book is Jean's.'

(28) b. Jean$_i$ a   [t$_i$ un / le livre].
     Jean   has   a / the book
     'Jean has a / the book.'

HAVE-possessives under this approach are analysed as *Raising*-constructions in which HAVE takes a small clause complement, just like copular BE (see Kayne 1993; Den Dikken 1997; Jung 2011; Myler 2016). This places possessive HAVE and its cousins among monadic unaccusatives.

The arguments listed in favour of segregating existential BE from copular BE in section 1 extend to possessive BE/HAVE. Q-Float, Definiteness Restriction, GoN and clause negation make it unquestionable that possessive BE and HAVE pattern with existential BE, and not with copular BE. Apart from the fact that copular BE and existential BE differ in a number of ways syntactically, the obvious semantic differences between permanent and *ad hoc* possession, indicated by the indefinite vs. definite article in (28a) and (28b), would remain unexplained under this approach. In addition, it would be difficult to extend such an analysis to languages in which the copular verb does not materialize at all in the present indicative and negating existential/possessive BE-sentences differs lexically from negating copular sentences (see Partee & Borshev 2008; Jung 2011; Arylova 2012 and Myler 2016 for recent analyses of BE-possessives Russian).[10]

Paducheva (2000) and Partee & Borschev (2008) advocate the view that existential and possessive BE-sentences denote a state predicated of two eventuality participants: BE$_{EXIST}$ <x in y>. This urges a rethinking of the canonical ways of analysing possessive BE/HAVE sentences in the generative syntactic literature.

2.2. Possessive DPs vs. BE-possessives in Hungarian

Standard analyses of Hungarian BE-possessives draw a parallel between possessive DPs and possessive BE-sentences (see Szabolcsi 1992, 1994; Alberti 1995; Alberti & Farkas 2018).[11] In order to show why this parallelism is not feasible, it is inevitable to make a short digression to the structure of possessive nominals.

Hungarian possessive DPs come in two types. In one, the possessor appears in the nominative case and forms an inseparable syntactic unit together with the possessee:

(29) [$_{DP}$ [$_{NP}$ a lány   új   lakás-a]]
         the girl.NOM new   flat-POSS3SG
     'the girl's new flat'

In the other, the possessor bears the dative case and is separated from the possessee by the definite article, as a result of possessor extraction (see Szabolcsi 1983, 1985, 1992, 1994; Szabolcsi & Laczkó 1992; Bartos 1999, 2000; Alberti & Farkas 2018 for the details of the standard analysis):

(30) [$_{DP}$ a lány-nak$_i$ [$_D$ *az* [$_{NP}$ t$_i$ új   lakás-a]]]
         the girl-DAT   the   new   flat-POSS3SG
     'the girl's new flat'

The nominative possessor must move together with the possessee as a single syntactic unit at clause level. As is typical in Uralic languages (see Wagner-Nagy, Chapter 10 in this volume, for Selkup; and see Simonenko, Chapter 8 in this volume, for Meadow Mari) the possessive suffix on the possessee indicates the person/number of the possessor in Hungarian:

(31) Fel-avat-ták   [$_{DP}$ [$_{NP}$ a lány   új   lakás-á-t]].
     PFX-inaugurate-PAST3PL   the girl.NOM new   flat-POSS3SG-ACC
     'They inaugurated the girl's new flat.'

(32) [A lány   új   lakás-á-t]   fel-avat-ták.
     the girl.NOM new   flat-POSS3SG-ACC   PFX-inaugurate-PAST3PL
     'They inaugurated the girl's new flat.'

(33) *A lány$_i$ fel-avat-ták   [t$_i$ új   lakás-á-t].
     the girl.NOMP   PFX-inaugurate-PAST3PL   new   flat-POSS3SG-ACC
     Intended: 'They inaugurated the girl's new flat.'

In Szabolcsi's (1994) analysis, whenever the possessor is extracted from the possessive NP, it must move through [Spec,DP], where it acquires the dative case. On these occasions, the definite article *a/az* 'the' is inserted between the dative possessor and the possessee:

(34) Fel-avat-ták   [$_{DP}$ a lány-nak$_i$ [$_D$ *az*] [$_{NP}$ t$_i$ új lakás-á-t]].
     PFX-inaugurate-PAST3PL   the girl-DAT   the   new flat-POSS3SG-ACC
     'They inaugurated the girl's new flat.'

Definite article insertion is obligatory also when the possessor is moved to the left periphery:

(35) [$_{TOPP}$ A lány-nak$_i$] fel-avat-ták   [$_{DP}$ t$_i$ [$_D$ *az*] [$_{NP}$ t$_i$ új lakás-á-t]].
     the girl-DAT   PFX-inaugurate-PAST1PL   the   new flat-POSS3SG-ACC
     'They inaugurated the girl's new flat.'

Possessive BE-sentences in Szabolcsi's derivational model receive a treatment analogous to that of possessive DPs. Existential BE in her account selects a single possessive DP, including both the possessor and the possessee. Given that this DP must be [-DEF] by the Definiteness Restriction, the possessor must be evacuated from it. Some problems raised by Szabolcsi's analysis of BE-possessives will be discussed in the next section.

2.3. Some problems raised by Szabolcsi's approach to BE-possessives

Szabolcsi's (1992, 1994) claim that possessive sentences in Hungarian consist merely of an existential BE plus a possessive DP rests on three main premises. *Premise 1*: existential/

possessive BE is a monadic unaccusative predicate; *Premise 2*: obligatory agreement between the possessor and the posseesse indicates that they form a syntactic unit; *Premise 3*: the Definiteness Restriction (DR) in BE-possessives is fulfilled by evacuating the possessor from the possessive DP. These premises will be briefly reviewed below.

Premise 1: BE_{EXIST} is a monadic unaccusative predicate
Crucial for Szabolcsi's theory is that existential BE is a monadic unaccusative predicate (see Kayne 1993 and Den Dikken 1997, 2006 for a similar view). In her account, the only difference between monadic BE-existentials and monadic BE-possessives in Hungarian is that in the latter, the Theme argument is the possessive DP itself. Under this view, possessive/existential BE has the same argument structure as the monadic unaccusative verb *elveszni* 'get lost', with the only difference that the former imposes the Definiteness Restriction on the Theme, whereas the latter does not:

(36) *Péter-nek   VAN   [$_{DP}$ t$_i$ [$_D$ **a**]   [$_{NP}$ t$_i$ bicikli-je]].
     Peter-DAT   BE EXIST   the   bicycle-POSS3SG

Intended: 'Peter has his bicycle.'

(37) Péter-nek   el-veszett   [$_{DP}$ t$_i$ [$_D$ **a**]   [$_{NP}$ t$_i$ bicikli-je]].
     Peter-DAT   PFX-got_lost   the   bicycle-POSS3SG

'Peter has lost his bicycle.'

Premise 2: Obligatory possessor extraction

In Szabolcsi's derivational analysis, the possessor is moved out of the possessive DP by an obligatory extraction rule, in order to avoid DR violation. The agreement suffix on the possessee reflects the person/number features of the moved possessor.[12]

(38) VAN   [$_{DP}$ a fiú-nak$_i$ [$_D$ [$_{NP}$ t$_i$ bicikli-je]]].
     BE EXIST.3SG   the boy-DAT   bicycle-POSS3SG

'The boy has a bicycle.'

In the case of DR-verbs, obligatory possessor movement is not accompanied by definite article insertion, as this would induce DR violation.[13] The possessor is extracted to the non-thematic [Spec,DP] position,[14] within the extended possessive construction. Here, it receives the dative case and, subsequently, it moves further up to the left periphery of the clause.

Premise 3: Obligatory agreement between the possessor and the possessee
Szabolcsi draws a parallel between the architecture of BE-possessives and possessive DPs. Her main argument for this parallelism is that the possessive suffix on the possessee

must agree in person/number with the possessor in both cases. Such agreement would be unexpected, she argues, if the possessor and the possessee were two distinct arguments of existential BE, as arguments do not normally show such person/number/gender agreement with each other.[15] She derives the obligatory agreement requirement from the DP-internal origin of the possessor, where agreement features are immediately licensed.[16] Thus, under Szabolcsi's account, this is an instance of DP-internal person/number agreement rather than agreement between two distinct arguments of the verb.

2.3.1. Obligatory possessor extraction out of the possessive DP

One reason why Szabolcsi's account of possessive DPs became so popular among generative linguists in the 1980s and 1990s was the structural analogy she established between Hungarian possessive constructions and the clausal architecture of configurational languages. In her account, the possessor corresponds to the subject and the possessee represents the predicate. The possessor is extracted from the possessive DP in the same way as subjects are extracted from the clause.[17]

Obligatory possessor extraction takes place in two steps: first, the possessor moves to an intermediate, non-thematic position where it acquires dative case; next, it moves further to the left periphery of the clause. Dative case on the possessor is therefore an indicator that obligatory possessor extraction has taken place.

Notice that crossing the DP boundary in itself does not violate Subjacency. However, crossing both the DP and the IP clause boundary in one step ought to result in ungrammaticality by standard considerations, as they are both maximal projections. Yet, the sentence in (41) is perfectly grammatical:

(39) * [$_{TOPP}$ [$_{IP}$ VAN   [$_{DP}$ ∅   [$_{NP}$ Péter   új   ruhá-ja]]]].
           BE$_{EXIST}$-3SG   DET   Peter.NOM   new   clothes-POSS3SG
   Intended: 'Peter has new clothes.'

(40) ...[$_{TOPP}$ [$_{IP}$ VAN   [$_{DP}$ Péter-nek$_i$ ∅   [$_{NP}$ t$_i$ új   ruhá-ja]]]].
            BE$_{EXIST}$.3SG   Peter-DAT   DET   new   clothes-POSS3SG

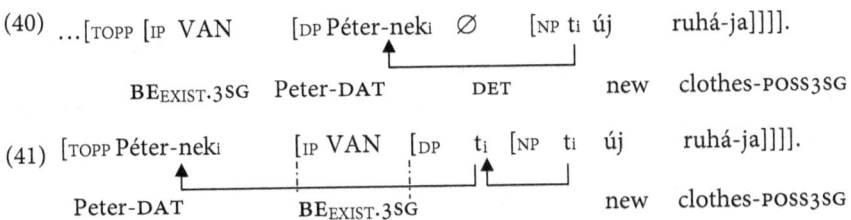

(41) [$_{TOPP}$ Péter-nek$_i$ [$_{IP}$ VAN   [$_{DP}$ t$_i$ [$_{NP}$ t$_i$ új   ruhá-ja]]]].
       Peter-DAT   BE$_{EXIST}$.3SG   new   clothes-POSS3SG

Thus, movement of the possessor to the left periphery must take place in two steps, to avoid subjacency violation.

Long operator movement is a syntactic operation that moves the possessor from the subordinate clause to the left periphery of the main clause through an empty DP position normally reserved for the referring word *az* 'it' (see Kenesei 1994):

(42) [$_{FOCP}$ PÉTER-NEK$_i$ mond-tad [$_{DP}$ t$_i$ [$_{CP}$ hogy [$_{IP}$ VAN [$_{DP}$ t$_i$ [$_{NP}$ t$_i$
   Peter-DAT   say-PAST2SG   that   BE$_{EXIST.}$3SG

új   ruhája]]]]]]?
new clothes
'Did you say that PETER had new clothes?'

Cyclic movement and long operator movement are familiar syntactic manoeuvres in Hungarian (see É. Kiss 1994, 2002 and the references cited therein); thus, the fact that they are possible also out of possessive DPs is not surprising. What is unusual is that they are claimed to be obligatory in the case of possessive DPs, although they are optional at sentence level. The situation is further complicated by the fact that the whole DP can also be moved to the left periphery of the main clause as a syntactic unit, (43), but even in this case, movement is optional. The other option, i.e. extracting the possessor to the left periphery of the main clause (see Kenesei 1994; É. Kiss 2002) and leaving the rest of the DP behind is illustrated in (44):

(43) [$_{FOCP}$ Ki-nek a   lány-á-t]$_i$ mondtad [$_{DP}$ t$_i$[$_{CP}$ hogy
   who-DAT   the   daughter-POSS3SG-ACC   say-PAST2SG   that

[$_{IP}$ elvesz-ed [$_{DP}$ t$_i$]]]]?
marry-2SG
'Whose daughter did you say that you would marry?'

(44) [$_{FOCP}$ Ki-nek$_i$ [$_{IP}$ mond-tad [$_{DP}$ t$_i$ [$_{CP}$ hogy [$_{IP}$ elvesz-ed
   who-DAT   say-PAST2SG   that   marry-2SG

[$_{DP}$ t$_i$ a [$_{NP}$ t$_i$ lány-á-t]]]]]]]?
the daughter-POSS3SG-ACC
'Whose daughter did you say that you would marry?'

Cyclic movement and long operator movement are syntactic operations that can move the possessive DP to the left periphery of the sentence, in general. Notice, however, that BE-possessives diverge from this general pattern as they disallow moving the whole DP (including the dative possessor) to the left periphery of the sentence.

(45) *[[$_{FOCP}$ PÉTER-NEK$_i$ új   ruhája]   mond-tad [t$_i$][$_{CP}$ hogy
    Peter-DAT   new clothes-POSS3SG   say-PAST2SG   that

[$_{IP}$ VAN [$_{DP}$ t$_i$]]]]?
BE$_{EXIST}$
Intended: 'Did you say it was Peter who had new clothes?'

(46) *[[$_{FOCP}$ KI-NEK$_i$ új   ruhá-ja]   mond-tad [t$_i$][$_{CP}$ hogy [$_{IP}$VAN [$_{DP}$ t$_i$]]]?
    who-DAT   new clothes-POSS3SG say-PAST2SG   that BE$_{EXIST}$
Intended:'Who did you say that had new clothes?'

The empirical generalization to make here is that while [+DEF] possessive DPs can freely travel to the left periphery of Hungarian sentences as a single unit, [-DEF] possessive DPs in Hungarian BE-possessives cannot do so. This asymmetric behaviour is unexpected, given the intermediate landing site designed for the possessor within the extended possessive DP projection (see Szabolcsi 1983, 1992, 1994) or in POSSP (see É. Kiss 2002).

In the present study, possessive BE selects two distinct arguments with a distinct thematic role each. This excludes the possibility of analysing BE-possessives on a par with possessive DPs, and leaves us with the 'dyadic unaccusative' analysis. Syntactic tests on pronominal binding, fronting pronominal vs. *wh*-possessors, agreement and lack of anti-agreement on the possessee are presented in support of this claim in the next subsections.

2.3.2. Pronominal binding

Under Szabolcsi's analysis, the possessor leaves a trace whenever it is moved to the left periphery. The trace is co-indexed with the moved possessor. The possessive suffix on the possessee agrees in person/number with the possessor:

Obligatory possessor extraction
(47) [A fiú-k-nak$_i$ VAN   [$_{DP}$ t$_i$ [$_{NP}$ t$_i$ lemez-ük]]].
    the boy-**PL-DAT**   BE$_{EXIST}$·3SG   record-POSS3PL
    'The boys have a record.'

This coreference requirement, however, is not as strict as it may seem at first. In the appropriate context, the possessive suffix may also agree with some external possessor, as in (48):

(48) [$_{TOPP}$ A fiú-k-nak$_j$ van   [$_{DP}$ *pro*$_k$ lemez-e]].
    the boy-**PL-DAT**   BE$_{EXIST}$·3SG   (his) record-POSS3SG
    'The boys$_j$ have got a record of his$_k$.' (speaking of Elvis Presley and his fans.)

The occurrence of the disjoint reference is problematic for Szabolcsi's movement analysis, which rests on the DP-internal origin of the dative possessor. The contrast between the coreferential vs. disjoint referential interpretations of the possessor can be further accentuated by adding the possessive reflexive pronoun *saját* (one's own):

(49) [$_{TOPP}$ A fiú-**k**-nak$_j$ van   [$_{DP}$ *pro*$_j$ saját   lemez-ük]].
    the boy-**PL-DAT**   BE$_{EXIST}$·3SG (3PL)   own   record-POSS3PL
    'The boys$_j$ have got a record of their$_j$ own.'

(50) [$_{TOPP}$ A fiú-k-nak$_j$ van   [$_{DP}$ *pro*$_k$ saját   lemez-e]].
    the boy-**PL-DAT**   BE$_{EXIST}$·3SG (3SG)   own   record-POSS3SG
    'The boys$_j$ have got a record of his$_k$ own.' (speaking of Elvis Presley's authentic record owned by the boys).

It is clear that the silent pronominal possessor requires an antecedent, whether it be the dative possessor, (49), or some contextually interpreted possessor, as in (50). The agreement morphology on the possessee reflects the *phi* features of the actual antecedent. In (50), the possessive suffix can only take the contextually interpreted 3SG possessor as its antecedent. Such sentences are problematic not only for the movement analysis but also for the analogy between possessive DPs and BE-possessives in Hungarian.

The complex structure of the DP-internal pronominal possessor is revealed by examples where possessive BE is replaced by its prefixed counterpart, *meg-van* (be obtained), (51)–(52). Here, the pronominal possessor is overtly expressed and is accompanied by the possessive reflexive pronoun *saját* (own). The pronominal possessor shows anti-agreement, that is, it shows up in the default singular form[18]:

(51) A fiú-k-nak$_i$ meg-van   [$_{DP}$ az ő$_i$ saját   lemez-ük].
 the boy-PL-DAT   PFX-BE$_{EXIST}$-3SG   the he.NOM   own   record-POSS3PL
 'They boys have got a record of their own.'

(52) A fiú-k-nak$_j$ meg-van   [az ő$_k$ saját   lemez-e].
 the boy-PL-DAT   PFX-BE$_{EXIST}$-3SG   the his own   record-POSS3SG
 'The boys have got a record of his own.' (speaking of Elvis Presley and his fans).

The fact that a disjoint reference between the DP-internal (lexical or null) anaphoric possessor and the dative possessor is possible makes the obligatory possessor extraction rule in BE-possessives untenable. Another piece of evidence against the obligatory possessor extraction rule comes from pronominal and *wh*-possessors. This will be discussed in the next subsection.

2.3.3. Misbehaving pronominal and *wh*-possessors

Nominative and dative pronominal possessors show a striking asymmetry when moved to the left periphery of the clause[19]:

(53) [$_{FOCP}$ A   TE   ÚJ   RUHÁ-D-AT$_i$ [$_{IP}$ látta Mari [$_{DP}$ t$_i$]]].
  the   you.NOM   new clothes-POSS2SG-ACC   saw Mary
 'Mary saw YOUR NEW CLOTHES.'

(54) *[$_{FOCP}$ (Te)-nek-ed$_i$ az   új   ruhá-d-at]   látta Mari.
  (you)-DAT-POSS2SG   the   new clothes-POSS2SG-ACC saw   Mary
 Intended: 'It was your new clothes that Mary saw.'

The inability of the dative pronominal possessor and the possessee to move together to the left periphery is surprising under Szabolcsi's account, as the DP is claimed to be the extended projection of possessive noun phrases, analogous to CP in the clausal architecture. Thus, the analogy with CP seems to break down at this point. In Szabolcsi's analysis, the possessor becomes a distinct syntactic unit as soon as it acquires the dative case in [Spec,DP]. By the same token, replacing the pronominal possessor by a *wh*-possessor gives us exactly the opposite scenario, (55)–(56). The dative *wh*-possessor forms a syntactic unit with the rest of the possessive construction and they can subsequently move to the left periphery of the clause together. This is not true for the nominative *wh*-possessor[20]:

(55) [_FOCP Ki-nek az új ruhá-já-t] látta Mari?
who-DAT the new clothes-POSS3SG-ACC saw Mary
'Whose new clothes did Mary see?'

(56) *[_FOCP Ki ∅ új ruhá-já-t] látta Mari?
who.NOM DET new clothes-POSS3SG-ACC saw Mary
Intended: 'Whose new clothes did Mary see?'

Wh-words in Hungarian have to move to FocP on the left periphery of the clause (see É. Kiss 2002 and the references therein). The dative *wh*-possessor can pied-pipe the rest of the possessive DP in (55) but the nominative *wh*-possessor in (56) cannot. This asymmetry is explained by obligatory possessor extraction in Szabolcsi's analysis. The *wh*-possessor is forced to move through [Spec,DP] and to receive the dative case there, or else the DR would be violated. If possessive BE is a dyadic unaccusative predicate taking a dative possessor and a nominative theme argument, as will be proposed in section 3, no obligatory possessor extraction needs to be postulated.

2.3.4. Lack of anti-agreement in BE-possessives

Anti-agreement (i.e. agreement of the possessive suffix with the possessor in person but not in number) is common in Hungarian possessive DPs (see Den Dikken 1998, 1999) but absent in BE-possessives.[21] As the contrast between (57) and (58) indicates, the possessive suffix on the possessee shows anti-agreement with the 3PL possessor; in BE-possessives, however, the possessive suffix on the possessee must agree with the 3PL possessor, hence anti-agreement is absent[22]:

(57) [_DP a fiú-k-nak_i [_D a] [_NP t_i kalap-**ja** / *a kalap-j-uk]].
the boy-PL-DAT the hat-POSS / the hat-POSS-3PL
'the boys' hat'

(58) VOLT [_DP1 a fiú-k-nak] [_DP2 kalap-j-**uk** / *kalap-ja].
BE_EXIST PAST3SG the boy-PL-DAT hat- POSS-3PL / hat-POSS
'The boys had a hat each.'

Den Dikken (1999) distinguishes three groups of Hungarian speakers (colloquial, conservative and liberal) and calls them Dialect A, B and C, respectively. He claims that strict agreement is required only by a conservative minority of Hungarian speakers. Notice, however, that 3PL pronominal possessors require 3PL agreement marking on the possessee in BE-possessives in all three dialects. The absence of the plural agreement marker -(V)**k** would be ungrammatical for Hungarian speakers in general:

(59) (Ő)-nek-i**k**   VAN   kalap-j-**uk** /*-ja.
    they-DAT-3PL   BE$_{\text{EXIST}}$3SG   hat- POSS-3PL / POSS
    'They have a hat-POSS3PL/*-POSS.'

These facts undermine the analogy between possessive DPs and BE-possessives. If possessive BE is taken to be a monadic unaccusative verb with a possessive DP argument, we would expect this possessive DP to show anti-agreement. Lack of anti-agreement in BE-possessives remains mysterious under the movement analysis.

We have seen that obligatory possessor extraction can be dispensed with once we accept that (a) possessive BE and existential BE are dyadic unaccusatives, and (b) there is a silent pronominal possessor within the Theme argument in Hungarian BE-possessives, for which the coreference requirement with the dative possessor is forced by Binding Theory.

3. The proposal

The present proposal breaks up with the traditional view that existential and possessive BE are monadic unaccusatives. Instead, they are taken to be dyadic unaccusative predicates with two internal arguments. Existential BE takes a Location and a Theme argument, while possessive BE takes an oblique Possessor and a Theme (see Freeze 1992; Paducheva 2000; Partee & Borschev 2008; Blaszczak 2007, 2010). This makes the VP-internal structure of existential/possessive BE look extremely similar to that of *psych*-predicates, which are arguably dyadic unaccusatives (see Belletti & Rizzi 1988 Grimshaw 1990; Harley 2002). Neither argument of *psych*-predicates qualifies as a canonical, agentive subject because neither of them is VP-external. This is exactly the case in BE-existentials and BE-possessives in Hungarian. The two arguments move to the left periphery due to discourse-semantic considerations and the Location/Possessor argument originates in a more prominent VP-internal position than the theme. Under this approach, possessor extraction does not arise, as the dative Possessor is a distinct argument of possessive BE.[23]

3.1. The argument structure of BE-possessives and BE-existentials

Before turning to Hungarian BE-possessives and BE-existentials, it is worth looking at the internal structure of dyadic unaccusatives, in general, and the *piacere* 'please'-class of *psych*-predicates, in particular. Dyadic unaccusative predicates are known to have two VP-internal arguments, an Experiencer and a Theme (Belletti & Rizzi 1988). In Minimalist terminology (Chomsky 1995), this translates into saying that their VP-layer does not project. The highest projection is the intransitive VP-shell in which either the Experiencer or the Theme argument occupies the [Spec,VP] position. Depending on which of the two arguments is more prominent, we get two classes of *psych*-predicates, the *fear*-class and the *frighten*-class (see Grimshaw 1990).[24] The truncated structure of dyadic unaccusatives for the *fear*-class of *psych*-predicates is given in (60):

(60)
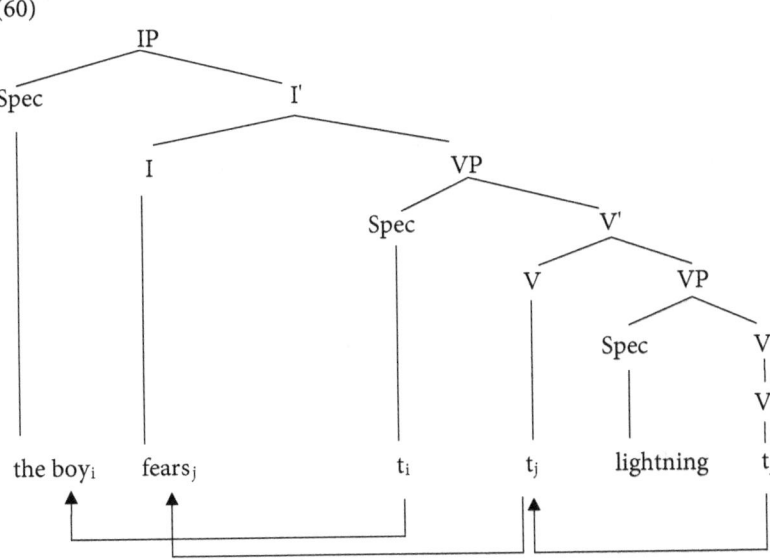

Here, the Experiencer argument is in a more prominent VP-internal position than the Theme and, therefore, it becomes the subject. In the *frighten*-class, the Theme argument is more prominent due to the causative VP-layer ('x causes y to fear'), while the Experiencer stays in the lower VP-internal position (see Grimshaw 1990 for details). Finally, there is a third class of *psych*-predicates, the *piacere*-class, where the Experiencer bears oblique case and has a more prominent VP-internal position than the Theme.[25] In non-null subject SVO languages, such as English, German or Dutch, the more prominent argument occupies the structural subject position. In V-initial languages (e.g. Greek, Spanish, Welsh), the oblique Experiencer must move to a higher position reserved for non-canonical subjects (see Cardinaletti 1997, 2004).

(61)

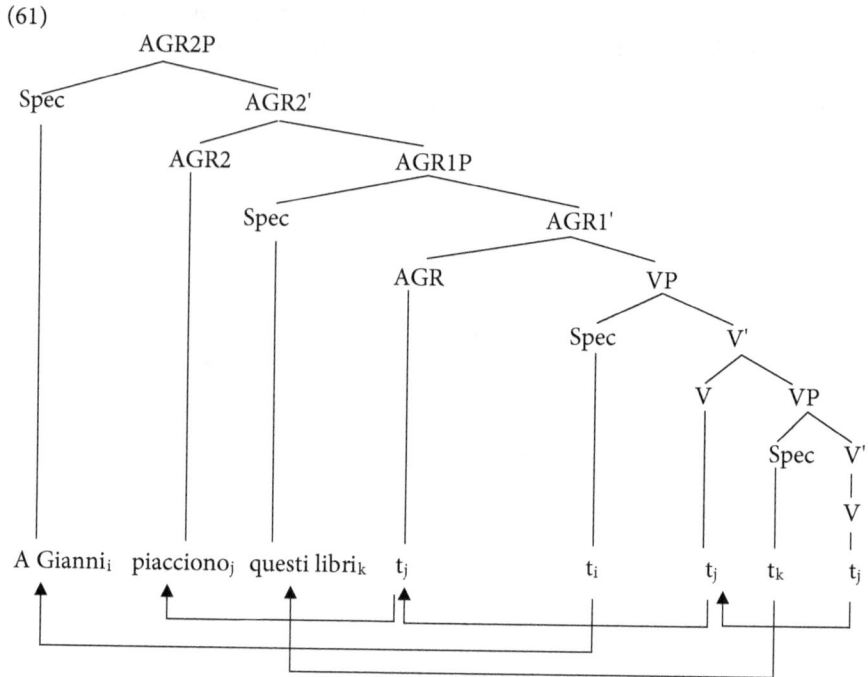

'to Gianni please these books'

The propositional part of Hungarian sentences is arguably V-initial in the sense of Alexiadou & Anagnostopoulou (1998).[26] In such languages, [Spec,IP] does not project and the arguments of the verb receive their theta role and case VP-internally (see Dalmi 2005, 2010, 2016 for a cartographic approach[27] to Hungarian syntactic phenomena along these lines). They move to the left periphery of the clause due to discourse-semantic principles (see É. Kiss 2002 and the references therein).

Hungarian BE-possessives resemble the *piacere*-class of *psych*-predicates in that the Possessor bears the dative case and has a more prominent VP-internal position than the Theme. This can be shown by introducing the possessive reflexive pronoun *saját* (own), which is always bound by the most prominent argument[28]:

(62) [$_{TopcP}$ A professzor-nak$_j$] [$_{IP}$VAN-NAK [$_{POSSP}$ t$_j$][$_{DP}$ *pro*$_j$ **saját** diák-ja-i]]].
 the professor-DAT BE$_{EXIST}$-3PL (3SG) own student-POSS3SG-PL
 'The professor$_i$ has students of his$_i$ own.'

(63) ??[$_{TopcP}$ Diák-ja-i$_k$] [$_{FocP}$VAN-NAK$_l$ [$_{IP}$ t$_l$ [$_{POSSP}$ t$_k$ [$_{DP}$ a *pro*$_j$ **saját** professzor- nak$_j$]]]].
 student-POSS3SG-PL BE$_{EXIST}$-3PL the (3SG) own professor-DAT
 'Their own professor has students.'

Binding the possessive reflexive by the nominative theme is far worse than binding the same possessive reflexive by the dative possessor. This is taken to indicate that the dative possessor is more prominent.

3.2. The source of agreement in Hungarian BE-possessives

On the basis of the agreement facts found in Hungarian possessive constructions, Szabolcsi (1983, 1985, 1992, 1994) rejects the idea that the possessor and the possessee originate as two distinct arguments of the existential predicate in Hungarian BE-possessives. As she argues, arguments within clauses do not normally agree with each other in person/number. The fact that the possessor and the possessee do show such agreement is taken to be evidence for the DP-internal origin of the possessor in her account.

As was mentioned in 2.2, syntactic configurations in which two arguments show person/number agreement are not common except for that of reflexivization. The present study adopts Den Dikken's (1999) proposal that possessive DPs in Hungarian host a (lexical or null) pronominal possessor,[29] which is bound by the DP-external dative possessor. Under this proposal, the dative possessor need not be 'externalized', as it does not originate DP-internally at all:

(64) [$_{DP}$ az ő$_i$ / pro$_i$ [$_{NP}$ problémá-ja]]]
      the he.NOM / (he.NOM) problem-POSS3SG
      'his problem'

The null pronominal possessor optionally takes the possessive reflexive pronoun *saját* (own) as its complement[30]:

(65) VAN   (én)-nek-em$_i$ [$_{DP}$ *pro$_i$* saját   munká-m   éppen elég]!
    BE$_{EXIST}$ (I)-DAT-POSS1SG   (my) own   work-POSS1SG   just enough
    'I have just enough work of my own!'

Replacing BE$_{EXIST}$ by its prefixed counterpart turns it into an achievement verb, meaning 'be obtained'. The difference between them is that the prefixed counterpart allows both possessors to be overt. This is problematic under the obligatory possessor extraction approach. Namely, under Szabolcsi's analysis, the extracted possessor leaves a trace in [Spec, NP], and that would make it impossible to insert a lexical pronominal possessor in that position in examples such as (66):

(66) Meg-van   Péter-nek$_i$ [$_{DP}$ az ő$_i$ saját   baj-a].
    PFX-BE$_{EXIST}$ Peter-DAT   the he.NOM own   trouble-POSS3SG
    'Peter has got trouble of his own.'

The reflexive possessive pronoun can alternate with the true reflexive pronoun *maga*. In such cases the DP-internal pronominal possessor cannot be overt (see Rákosi 2014):

(67) Mindenki-nek_i megvan [_DP a *pro*_i maga családi problémá-ja].
    everyone-DAT PFX-BE_EXIST the(3SG) self.NOM family problem-POSS3SG
    'Everyone has got family problems of his own.'

This further supports the claim that there is a (lexical or null) pronominal possessor[31] within the possessive DP that can optionally take the possessive reflexive pronoun *saját* (own) as its complement:

(68)

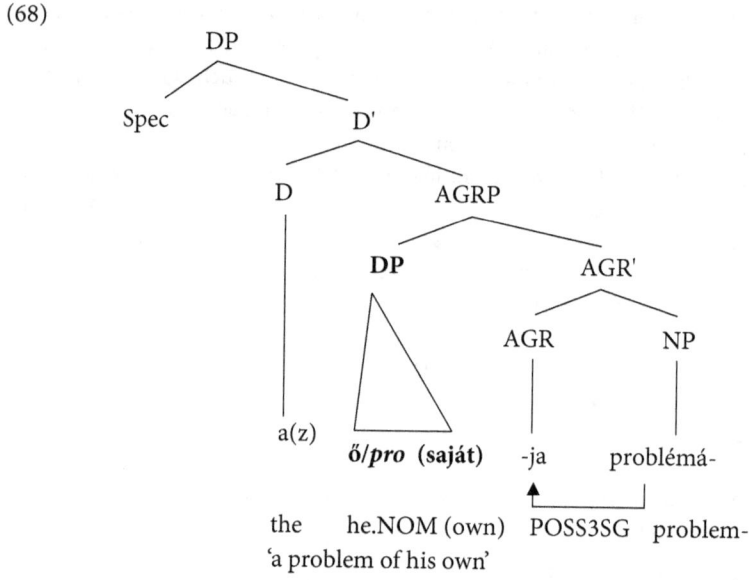

  the   he.NOM (own) POSS3SG problem-
  'a problem of his own'

The coreference requirement is necessary to exclude sentences such as (69):

(69) *Péter-nek_j VAN [Mari_k lemez-e].
    Peter_j-DAT BE_EXIST Mari-NOM_k record-POSS3SG
    *'Peter_j has got the record of Mary_k.'

The prefixed counterpart of BE_EXIST, *meg-van* (be obtained), however, imposes no such requirement, i.e. it allows the disjoint reference between the DP-internal pronominal possessor and its antecedent:

(70) A fiúk-nak_j MEG-VAN [_DP az ő_k / a *pro*_k saját lemez-e].
    the boys-DAT_j PFX-BE_EXIST the he.NOM_k / the (he.NOM)_k own record-POSS3SG
    'The boys_j have (obtained) his_k (own) record.' (speaking of John Lennon)

The DP-internal (lexical or null) pronominal possessor in Hungarian BE-possessives makes the movement analysis untenable; as a result, obligatory possessor extraction and article deletion become unnecessary. In addition, it relates BE-possessives to a huge class of verbs denoting the physical, psychological or mental circumstances of the Experiencer, i.e. the *piacere* 'please'-class of *psych*-predicates, where the Experiencer typically bears the dative case.

4. Conclusion

The chapter presents evidence in support of the view that the BE-predicate in Hungarian possessive and existential BE-sentences is a dyadic unaccusative verb whose VP-internal structure resembles that of the *piacere*-class of *psych*-predicates. Under this approach, obligatory possessor extraction can be dispensed with, as the dative possessor does not originate inside the possessee. The possessive DP theme hosts a lexical or null anaphoric possessor that is bound by the dative possessor. The anaphoric possessor may take the possessive reflexive pronoun *saját* (own) as its complement. The person/number agreement suffix on the possessee indicates coreference between the DP-internal anaphoric possessor and the dative possessor.

Notes

1. *Abbreviations*

ACC	accusative case	NEG	negative marker
CL	clitic pronoun	NOM	nominative case
COP	copula	PAST	past tense
DAT	dative case	PFX	prefix
DET	determiner	POSS	possessive marker
DR	Definiteness Restriction	SG	singular number
FOCP	focus phrase	PL	plural number
GEN	genitive case	POSSP	possessive phrase
ILLAT	illative case	TOP$_C$P	contrastive topic phrase
INESS	inessive case	Ø	zero copula/lack of article

2. This chapter benefitted from comments made by András Bárány, Marcel Den Dikken, Iliyana Krapova and Edith Moravcsik, which is gratefully acknowledged here. I wish to thank Olga Kagan and Inna Livitz for sharing their judgements concerning the Russian examples. I am also indebted to the anonymous reviewers and to the editors of the volume for their comments and questions that helped me formulate my claims in a more appropriate way. All remaining errors are mine.
3. The Definiteness Restriction (DR) requires that the Theme argument of verbs of *existence, creation, destruction* or *consumption*, etc. should be [-definite] and [-specific] (see Milsark 1979). On DR in Hungarian see Szabolcsi (1986); Bende-Farkas & Verkuyl (1997); É. Kiss (1995).
4. In (8b)–(8c) existential BE bears focus stress and the preverbal XP is topicalized (see É. Kiss 2002 and the references therein for the syntactic properties of topicalization and focusing in Hungarian).
5. This fact is closely related to the Definiteness Restriction (DR) imposed by existential/possessive BE on the Theme argument. DR is often masked away in languages without articles; in such languages, the copular vs. existential BE distinction can only be indirectly detected (see Geist 2015). Nonetheless, the fact that DR always applies to the Theme argument excludes the BE+Small Clause analysis of BE-possessives and BE-existentials cross-linguistically.
6. See Freeze (1992); Kayne (1993); Den Dikken (1997); Moro (1997, 2017).

7   Genitive of Negation in Russian is assigned to non-specific Theme arguments of transitive and unaccusative verbs *iff* the existential presupposition (or the existential entailment) is absent (see Partee & Borschev 2008; Kagan 2013):
    (i) Na lekci-i   ne   pojavilos student-ov.
        on lecture-LOC   not   appeared   student-GEN.PL
        'At the lecture no students appeared.'
    (ii) Student-y   ne   prinesli   knig   na lekciju.
         student-PL.NOM   not   brought   book.GEN.PL   on lecture
         'The students did not bring any books to the lecture.'
8   See Dalmi (2010, 2012, 2013, 2016) on the syntactic structure of Hungarian copular sentences in a cartographic framework.
9   Negated locative copular sentences also require *nincs/nincsenek*, just like locative existential sentences:
    (i) A fiúk   nincsenek   otthon.
        the boys NEG.BE$_{EXIST}$.PL at_home
        'The boys are not at home.'
    The reason for this is that there is no phonologically visible verb form to which the negative particle could cliticize in the present indicative, as copular BE in 3SG/3PL present indicative is zero (see Dalmi, 2010, 2012, 2013, 2016). In such cases negated existential BE is used as a suppletive form (see Laczkó 2012 for a similar view).
10 Recent derivational approaches establish a close connection between copular BE, existential BE and possessive HAVE (Freeze 1992; Den Dikken 1997; Jung 2011; Arylova 2012; Myler 2016) and introduce an ApplP, AnchorP or VoiceP functional projection responsible for the transitivization of copular BE in possessive HAVE-sentences.
11 For ease of exposition, section 2 of this chapter uses Szabolcsi's (1994) labelling of possessive DPs, in which both the possessor and the possessee originate DP-internally. This approach will be abandoned in section 3 for reasons explicated there.
12 Szabolcsi's model of possessive constructions has been criticized by Bende-Farkas & Verkuyl (1997); Den Dikken (1999); É. Kiss (2002) and Coppock & Wechsler (2012).
13 The Definiteness Restriction (DR) (originally called the Definiteness Effect by Milsark 1979) in Hungarian applies to verbs containing the [EXIST] component. This includes existential BE and its semantic derivatives, i.e. verbs of creation, destruction, consumption and production (see Szabolcsi 1986 for an early formulation of this claim).
14 Bartos (1999) introduces an AGRP functional projection as the locus of nominative case licensing for possessors, and retains DP as the intermediate landing site in the course of possessor extraction. He introduces further functional projections such as QP and NumP within the possessive DP, which are, however, not relevant for the present exposition.
15 Except for anaphoric pronouns, which must agree with their antecedent in person/number in several languages:
    (i) The girl saw *herself* in the mirror.
    (ii) The girls saw *themselves* in the mirror.
16 See Bartos (1999, 2000) for a detailed analysis of agreement within possessive DPs in Hungarian.
17 From the semantic perspective, this is rather the other way round, i.e. it is predicated of x that x is in y's possession.
18 See Den Dikken (1998, 1999) on anti-agreement in Hungarian possessive DPs.

19 The dative pronominal possessor is equally bad in post-verbal position:
    (i) *Ki látta   [_POSSP (te)-nek-ed]   [_DP az új ruhá-d-at]]?
         who saw   (you)-DAT-POSS3SG   the new clothes-POSS3SG-ACC
         'Who saw your new clothes?'
20 Kindergarten age children are not aware of this ban; they can move nominative *wh*-possessors together with the possessee to the left periphery as a single syntactic unit quite naturally:
    [_DP Ki   mackó-ja]   van   a pad-on?
         who-NOM teddybear-POSS3SG   BE_EXIST   the bench-ILLAT
    'Whose teddybear is on the bench?'
21 É. Kiss (2014) makes a claim to the contrary.
22 Apparently, number agreement on the possessee is subject to microparametric variation (see Den Dikken 1998; and also Alberti 1995 on the various semantic restrictions on the person/number agreement suffix of the possessee). Although lack of number agreement in (ii) is analysed as optional anti-agreement by Den Dikken (1999), for speakers of the conservative dialect, (ii) is unacceptable under the intended reading (see Dalmi, in prep.):
    (i) A fiúk-nak   VAN   labdá-**j-uk**.
         the boy-PL-DAT   BE_EXIST   ball-POSS-3PL
         'The boys have a ball each.'
    (ii) *A fiú-k-nak   van   labdá-**ja**.
         the boy-PL-DAT   BE_EXIST   ball-POSS
         'The boys have a ball each.'
23 In most Finno-Ugric languages, the possessor in BE-possessives may show up in various oblique cases but not in the dative (see Stassen 2009). Nikolaeva (2002) attributes the dative case on the Hungarian possessor to some European, presumably Slavic, influence.
24 Harley (2002) also relates possessive predicates and *psych*-predicates but she assumes an abstract P preposition for each of these verb classes.
25 The opposite order is also possible in Italian, however, it is derived by left dislocation. This is indicated by the fact that the olbique exoeriencer precedes the clitic pronominal theme under clitic placement (see Cardinaletti 1997, 2004):
    (i) Questi libri   (essi)   piacciono   a Gianni.
         these books   they   please   to Gianni
         'As for these books, they please Gianni.'
26 See É. Kiss (2013) for a similar claim.
27 In the cartographic approach (see Rizzi 1997, 2004, 2013), all sentences are assigned a tripartite clausal architecture. The C-domain hosts discourse-semantic projections such as ForceP, TOPP, FocP, the T-domain takes care of grammatical functions such as T(ense), Asp(ect) and Agr(eement), and the V-domain is the lexical layer, where the verb checks the case and the theta role of its arguments.
28 On the syntactic properties of the possessive reflexive *saját* (own), see Rákosi (2014).
29 Den Dikken (1999) proposes that the null possessor is a resumptive pronoun.
30 Lexical and null pronouns with the individual or generic reference interpretation are nowadays taken to be full DPs made up of hierarchically arranged feature bundles (see Harley & Ritter 2002). Reflexive pronouns, as well as generic pronouns, tend to be more complex than those with the individual reference interpretation (see Krzek 2012 on the Polish impersonal SIĘ). Dalmi (2017) proposes that the DP-internal

pronominal possessor is a complex DP in which the possessive reflexive pronoun *saját* (own) is a complement.

31 Den Dikken (1999) introduces a null resumptive pronoun à la Rouveret (1991) and correlates this feature of Hungarian possessive DPs to the basic VSO order, found also in Welsh clauses. In Welsh, as in other Celtic languages, overt subject agreement and overt pronominal subjects are in complementary distribution (see Tallerman 2005). Given that in Hungarian BE-possessives the DP-internal pronominal possessor can co-occur with the overt dative possessor in emphatic contexts, this analogy with Welsh and other VSO languages cannot be maintained.

References

Alberti, G. 1995. Role assignment in Hungarian possessive constructions. In: Kenesei, I. (ed.), *Approaches to Hungarian* 5, 11–29. Szeged: József Attila University Press.

Alberti, G. & Farkas, J. 2018. Modification. In: Alberti, G. & Laczkó, T. (eds), *A Syntax of Hungarian. Nouns and Noun Phrases*, vol. 2, 775–891. Amsterdam: Amsterdam University Press.

Alexiadou, A. & Anagnostopoulou, E. 1998. Parametrizing AGR: word order, V-movement and EPP-checking. *Natural Language and Linguistic Theory* 16: 491–539.

Arylova, A. 2012. AnchorP: argument structure of the Russian be-possessive. *Proceedings of CONSOLE* 19: 25–48.

Bartos, H. 1999. Morfoszintaxis és interpretáció. Az inflexiós jelenségek szintaktikai háttere. PhD dissertation. Eötvös Loránd University, Budapest.

Bartos, H. 2000. Az inflexiós jelenségek szintaktikai háttere. [The syntactic background of inflectional phenomena]. In: Kiefer, F. *Strukturális magyar nyelvtan 4. Morfológia*. [The Syntactic Structure of Hungarian 4. Morphology], 653–761. Budapest: Akadémiai Kiadó.

Belletti, A. & Rizzi, L. 1988. *Psych*-verbs and Theta-theory. *Natural Language and Linguistic Theory* 6: 291–352.

Bende-Farkas, Á. & Verkuyl, H. 1997. *On Hungarian Noun Phrase Structure*. UIL OTS Publication. Utrecht University.

Benveniste, E. 1966. *Être* et *avoir* dans leurs fonctions lingistiques. In: Benveniste, E. (ed.), *Problèmes de linguistique générale*, vol. 1, 187–207. Paris: Gallimard.

Błaszczak, J. 2007. *Phase Syntax. The Polish Genitive of Negation*. Habilitation treatise. University of Potsdam.

Błaszczak, J. 2010. A spurious genitive puzzle in Polish. In: Hanneforth, T. & Fanselow, G. (eds), *Language and Logos. Studia Grammatica* 72, 17–47. Berlin: Akademieverlag.

Bowers, J. 2001. Predication. In: Baltin, M. & Collins, C. (eds), *The Handbook of Contemporary Syntactic Theory*, 299–333. Oxford: Blackwell.

Cardinaletti, A. 1997. Subjects and clause structure. In: Haegeman, L. (ed.) *The New Comparative Syntax*, 33–64. London: Longman.

Cardinaletti, A. 2004. Toward a cartography of subject positions. In: Rizzi, L. (ed.) *The Structure of CP and IP. The Cartography of Syntactic Structures*, vol. 2, 115–166. Oxford: Oxford University Press.

Chomsky, N. 1995. *The Minimalist Programme*. Cambridge, MA: MIT Press.

Chvany, C. 1975. *On the Syntax of BE-sentences in Russian*. Cambridge, MA: Slavica.

Coppock, E. & Wechsler, S. 2012. The objective conjugation in Hungarian: agreement without *phi* features. *Natural Language and Linguistics Theory* 30: 699–740.

Dalmi, G. 2005. *The Role of Agreement in Non-finite Predication*. Amsterdam: John Benjamins.
Dalmi G. 2010. *Copular Sentences, Predication and Cyclic Agree*. Saarbruecken: Lambert Academic Publishing (VDM Verlag).
Dalmi, G. 2012. Copular sentences as Kimian states in Irish and Russian. *Canadian Journal of Linguistics* 57: 341–358.
Dalmi, G. 2013. The meaning of the zero copula in multiple BE-system languages. In: Bondaruk, A. & Malicka-Kleparska, A. (eds), *Ambiguity: Multi-Faceted Structures in Syntax, Morphology and Phonology*. SLAM 5, 169–200. Lublin: KUL.
Dalmi, G. 2016. What does it take to be a copula? *YPLM* 2: 1–28. Berlin: De Gruyter.
Dalmi, G. 2017. Little *pro*'s but how many of them? – On 3SG generic inclusive null pronominals in Hungarian. *LingBaW Journal* 3: 61–73.
Dalmi, G. (in prep.). The distribution and semantic content of 3SG vs 3PL possessive suffixes in Hungarian possessive sentences. Manuscript.
Den Dikken, M. 1997. The syntax of possession sentences and the verb have. *Lingua* 101: 129–150.
Den Dikken, M. 1998. Anti-agreement in DP. In: Bezooijen, R. & Kagen, R. (eds), *Linguistics in the Netherlands*, 95–107. Amsterdam: John Benjamins.
Den Dikken, M. 1999. On the structural representation of possession and agreement: the case of anti-agreement in Hungarian possessed nominal phrases. In: Kenesei, I. (ed.), *Crossing Boundaries: Theoretical Advances in Central and Eastern European Languages*, 137–178. Amsterdam: John Benjamins.
Den Dikken, M. 2006. *Relators and Linkers*. Cambridge, MA: MIT Press.
É. Kiss, K. 1994. Sentence structure and word order. In: Kiefer, F. & É. Kiss, K. (eds), *The Syntactic Structure of Hungarian*. Syntax and Semantics, vol. 27, 1–84. New York: Academic Press.
É. Kiss, K. 1995. Definiteness Effect revisited. In: Kenesei, I. (ed.) *Approaches to Hungarian* 5, 63–89. Szeged: JATE.
É. Kiss, K. 2002. *The Syntax of Hungarian*. Cambridge: Cambridge University Press.
É. Kiss, K. 2013. From proto-Hungarian *SOV* to old Hungarian *Top, Foc, V X**. *Diachronica* 3(2): 202–231.
É. Kiss, K. 2014. Ways of licensing external possessors. *Acta Linguistica Hungarica* 61(1): 45–68.
Freeze, J. 1992. Existentials and other locatives. *Language* 68(3): 553–595.
Geist, L. 2008. Predication and equation in copular sentences: Russian vs. English. In: Comorowski, I. & K. von Heusinger (eds), *Existence: Semantics and Syntax*, 79–105. New York: Springer.
Geist, L. 2015. Genitive alternation in Russian: a situation semantics approach. In: Zybatov, G., Biskup, P., Guhl, M., Hurtig, C., Mueller-Reichau, O. & Yastrebova, M. (eds), *Slavic Grammar from a Formal Perspective*, 157–174. Berlin: Peter Lang.
Grimshaw, J. 1990. *Argument Structure*. Cambridge, MA: MIT Press.
Harley, H. 2002. Possession and the double object construction. In: Pica, P. & Rooryck J. (eds), *The Yearbook of Linguistic Variation*, vol 2, 29–68. Amsterdam: John Benjamins.
Harley, H. & Ritter. E. 2002. Person and number in pronouns: a feature geometric analysis. *Language* 78(3): 482–526.
Jung, H. 2011. *The Syntax of BE-Possessives: Parametric Variation and Surface Diversities*. Amsterdam: Benjamins.

Kagan, O. 2013. *Semantics of Genitive Objects: A Study of Genitive of Negation and Intensional Genitive Case.* New York: Springer.

Kayne, R. 1993. Towards a modular theory of auxiliary selection. *Studia Linguistica* 47: 3–31.

Kenesei, I. 1994. Subordinate clauses. In: Kiefer, F. & É. Kiss, K. (eds), *The Syntactic Structure of Hungarian. Syntax and Semantics*, vol. 27, 275–375. New York: Academic Press.

Koopman, H. & Sportiche, D. 1991. The position of subjects. *Lingua* 85: 211–258.

Krzek, M. 2012. The syntax of impersonal constructions in Polish. PhD dissertation, The University of Newcastle.

Laczkó, T. 2012. On the (un)bearable lightness of being an LFG-style copula in Hungarian. In: Bhutt, M. & Holloway-King, T. (eds), *Proceedings of LFG12 Conference*, 341–361. Stanford, CA: CSLI Publications.

Maienborn, C. 2005. On the limits of the Davidsonian approach: the case of copular sentences. *Theoretical Linguistics* 31(3): 275–316.

Milsark, G. 1979. *Existential Sentences in English.* London: Routledge.

Moro, A. 1997. *The Raising of Predicates.* Cambridge: Cambridge University Press.

Moro, A. 2017. *The Brief History of the Verb To Be.* Cambridge, MA: MIT Press.

Myler, N. 2016. *Building and Interpreting Possession Sentences.* Cambridge, MA: MIT Press.

Nikolaeva, I. 2002. The Hungarian external possessor in a European Perspective. In: Hasselblatt, C. & Blokland, R. (eds), *Finno-Ugrians and Indo-Europeans: Linguistic and Literary Contacts.* Maastricht: Shaker.

Paducheva, E. 2000. Definiteness Effect: the case of Russian. In: von Heusinger, K. & Egli, U. (eds), *Reference and Anaphoric Relations*, 133–146. Dordrecht: Kluwer.

Paducheva, E. 2008. Locative and existential meanings of Russian byt'. *Russian Linguistics* 32: 147–158.

Partee, B. 1998. Copular inversion puzzles in English and Russian. In: Dziwirek, K., Coats, H. & Vakareliyska, C. (eds), *Formal Approaches to Slavic Linguistics*, 361–395. Ann Arbor: Michigan Slavic Publications.

Partee, B. & Borschev, V. 2008. Existential sentences, BE and GEN NEG in Russian. In: Comorowski, I. & von Heusinger, K. (eds), *Existence: Semantics and Syntax*, 147–191. New York: Springer.

Rákosi, Gy. 2014. Possessed by something out there: on anaphoric possessors in Hungarian. *Argumentum* 10: 548–559.

Rizzi, L. 1997. The fine structure of the left periphery. In: Haegeman, L. (ed.), *Elements of Grammar*, 281–337. Dordrecht: Kluwer.

Rizzi, L. 2004. On the cartography of syntactic structures. In: Rizzi, L. (ed.), *The Structure of CP and IP: The Cartography of Syntactic Structures* vol. 2, 1–16. Oxford: Oxford University Press.

Rizzi, L. 2013. Topic, focus, and the cartography of the left periphery. In: Luragi, S. & Parodi, C. (eds), *The Bloomsbury Companion to Syntax*, 435–451. London: Bloomsbury.

Rothstein, S. 2001. *Predicates and their Subjects.* Dordrecht: Kluwer.

Rouveret, A. 1991. Functional categories and agreement. *The Linguistic Review* 8: 353–387.

Simonenko, A. 2020. Existential possession in Meadow Mari. In: Dalmi, G., Witkoś, J. & Cegłowski, P. (eds), *Approaches to Predicative Possession: The View from Slavic and Finno-Ugric*, 167–190. London: Bloomsbury.

Stassen, L. 2009. *Predicative Possession.* Oxford: Oxford University Press.

Stowell, T. 1981. The origin of phrase structuee. PhD dissertation. Massachusetts Institute of Technology.
Szabolcsi, A. 1983. The possessor that ran away from home. *Linguistic Review* 3: 89–102
Szabolcsi, A. 1985. Functional categories in the non phrase. In: Kenesei, I. (ed.), *Approaches to Hungarian* 2, 167–189.
Szabolcsi, A. 1986. From the Definiteness Effect of lexical ingtegrity. In: Abraham, W. & Meij, S. de (eds), *Topic, Focus and Configurationality*, 321–348. Amsterdam: Benjamins.
Szabolcsi, A. 1992. *A birtokos szerkezet és az egzisztenciális mondat* [Possessive constructions and existential sentences]. Budapest: Akadémiai kiadó.
Szabolcsi, A. 1994. The noun phrase. In: É. Kiss, K. & Kiefer, F. (eds), *The Syntactic Structure of Hungarian*, 179–274. New York: Academic Press.
Szabolcsi, A. & Laczkó, T. 1992. A főnévi csoport szerkezete. [The structure of the noun phrase]. In: É. Kiss, K. & Kiefer, F. (eds), *Strukturális magyar nyelvtan*. [The Structure of Hungarian], 179–299. Budapest: Akadémiai Kiadó.
Tallerman, M. 2005. The Celtic languages. In: Cinque, G. & Kayne, R. (eds), *The Oxford Handbook of Comparative Syntax*, 839–880. Oxford: Oxford University Press.
Wagner-Nagy, B. 2020. Predicative possessive constructions in Selkup dialects. In: Dalmi, G., Witkoś, J. & Cegłowski, P. (eds), *Approaches to Predicative Possession: The View from Slavic and Finno-Ugric*, 211–227. London: Bloomsbury.

8. Existential possession in Meadow Mari

Alexandra Simonenko

1. Introduction[1]

This chapter is concerned with the syntax and semantics of possessive sentences in Meadow Mari.[2] Mari is a Uralic language spoken by several hundred thousand speakers in the Volga and Ural Regions of the Russian Federation. Meadow Mari, spoken in the western part of Mari El, the titular republic of the Mari, is one of four main dialects (besides Hill Mari, Northwestern Mari, and Eastern Mari), and is the basis of the dominant literary norm for Mari, the Meadow-Eastern literary language. Compared to other minority Finno-Ugric languages, Meadow Mari is relatively well studied, including a number of traditional grammatical descriptions (Alhoniemi 1993; Tuzharov 1987) and a series of more focused works dealing with particular aspects of the grammar, such as the morpho-syntax of case (Luutonen 1997; McFadden 2002; Caha 2013), reflexives (Volkova 2014), possessive suffixes (Fraurud 2001; Kuznetzova 2012; Simonenko 2014), and the structure of the noun phrase (Simonenko & Leontjev 2012).[3]

To the best of my knowledge, an analysis of the existential possessive sentences of Meadow Mari (or any variety of Mari, for that matter) has not yet been proposed. This chapter aims at filling this gap and, at the same type, contributing to a better understanding of sentential possession, in general, by providing the basis for a comparative study. The data on which this study draws come from the dialect of Staryj Torjal (the district of Novy Torjal, Mari El).

Assuming for a moment an informal working definition of possessive construction as a type of sentence whose propositional content expresses a relation between two entities such that one entity exercises some sort of control over another, Meadow Mari features two possessive sentence types. The first one, illustrated in (1), which I will dub existential possessive construction, features a possessor noun phrase (NP) in genitive case, a possessee in nominative, and a predicate *ulo* agreeing in number with the possessee argument.[4,5] The possessee may bear a possessive suffix agreeing with the possessor NP in person and number. The distribution of the suffix has to do with the partial/total nature of the possessive relation, as will be discussed below.

Existential possessive construction
(1) myj-yn aka-m ulo.
 I-GEN sister-POSS1SG be.PRES3SG
 'I have a sister.'

This type of possessive construction can be preliminarily characterized as introducing the existence of an entity (denoted by *akam*, 'my sister') and asserting a possessive relation between the entity and the possessor (in this case, the Speaker). This chapter is concerned mostly with this type.

The second type, which I will refer to as a predicative possessive construction, is instantiated by sentences such as (2), where the possessee NP is in nominative case, the possessor is again expressed by an NP in genitive, and the copula is phonologically overt in past tense only.[6]

Predicative possessive construction
(2) a. tide pört myj-yn
   that house I-GEN
   'That house is mine.'

 b. tide pört myj-yn yle.
   that house I-GEN be.PST3SG
   'That house was mine.'

Predicative possessive constructions serve to introduce a possession relation between an entity whose existence has already been established (*tide pört*, 'that house') and a possessor (the Speaker in (2b)). In other words, while an existential possessive construction in (1) introduces both an individual and a relation between that individual and the possessor, a predicative construction in (2) does only the latter.

Configurations illustrated in (1) and (2a)–(2b) contrast with respect to the so-called Definiteness Effect (DE), the ban on certain types of quantifiers in existential constructions first identified in Milsark (1974). The DE, dealt with by Barwise & Cooper (1981), Higginbotham (1983), Keenan (1987), Zucchi (1995), Paducheva (2000), Leonetti (2008) and Fischer, Kupisch & Rinke (2016), among others, has been characterized as a ban on quantifiers associated with a presupposition of existence (in the relevant situation) of some entities from the quantification domain (i.e. the set of entities with the nominal property) (see De Jong 1987; Diesing 1992; Szabolcsi 1994). In English, the DE is illustrated for an existential construction and for a relational *have*-construction in (3) and (4).

(3) *There is/are the/every/all/most/both/all mistakes   (Zucchi 1995: 46)

(4) *I have the/my/every/both sister(s).   (based on Szabolcsi 1983, 1994)

In contrast, non-presuppositional quantifiers are allowed in existential '*there is*' and possessive *have*-constructions, as shown in (5) and (6).

(5) There is/are a/some/three/zero/many/a lot of/no mistakes.   (Zucchi 1995: 46)

(6) I have a/three/no sister(s).

Meadow Mari existential possessive constructions, but not predicative ones, pattern with English existential *'there is'* and possessive *have*-constructions in that their nominative argument cannot contain quantifiers of the types listed in (3) and (4). This is illustrated in (7), where the nominative argument *tide aka* contains a demonstrative, a determiner commonly assumed to trigger the presupposition that there exists an entity with the property denoted by the noun.

(7) *myj-yn   tide   aka   ulo.
    I-GEN   that   sister   be.PRES3SG
    Intended: '*I have that sister.'

Example (8) makes the same point for a non-relational noun.

(8) *myj-yn   tide   pört   ulo.
    I-GEN   that   house   be.PRES3SG
    Intended: '*I have that house.'

In what follows, I will present a semantico-syntactic analysis of the existential possessive constructions in Meadow Mari, arguing that they pattern with Meadow Mari existential sentences in general. More specifically, I will propose that possession is expressed in such constructions in two loci and in two different flavours. First, I will propose that existential possessive sentences, as a subclass of existential constructions, make an existential assertion that is restricted to a situation where everything is controlled by the possessor. Second, I will argue that due to the semantics of possessive suffixes, such constructions also convey information about whether there is a salient relation, other than that of control, which holds between the possessor and the possessee and which applies exhaustively to the possessor's situation. That is, I will argue that existential possessive constructions in Meadow Mari convey information about both an instantaneous control and a more permanent possession. My account derives the DE on the assumption that there is a grammatical ban on utterances whose felicity conditions, such as an existential presupposition, are in a permanent conflict with the informativity condition (cf. Zucchi 1995 for declaratives; Oshima 2007 and Schwarz & Simonenko 2018, for interrogatives).

In the next section of the chapter, I will present existential possessive constructions in greater detail, with special focus on the distribution of possessive suffixes. In section 3, I lay out an analysis whereby the two main ingredients of the semantics of an existential possessive construction are an existential predicate, which introduces existential quantification, and a possessive suffix, which introduces a salient relation. In section 4, I give an account of the Definiteness Effect in Meadow Mari. Section 5 is a conclusion.

2. Existential possessive constructions: Basic patterns

The core ingredients of the class of constructions in Meadow Mari that I label *existential possessive constructions* are a possessor NP in genitive, a possessee NP in nominative and an existential predicate agreeing with the latter in number. As most other Finno-Ugric languages, Meadow Mari has a paradigm of possessive suffixes, which appear on the possessee.[7] Whether the suffix is obligatory depends on whether the relevant relation is partial or total with respect to the situation of the possessor, to be clarified in what follows.

2.1. Total vs. partial possession

With existential predicates in present tense and first- and second-person genitive possessor NPs, it may appear that certain nouns obligatorily receive a possessive suffix, as in (9)[8], whereas with others it is either optional, as in (10), or even unpreferred, as in (11).

(9) myj-yn pij*(-em) ulo.
    I-GEN dog-POSS1SG be.PRES3SG
    'I have a dog.'

(10) kyzyt myj-yn peš šuko paša(-m) ulo.
     now I-GEN very much work-POSS1SG be.PRES3SG
     'I have a lot of work now.'

(11) myj-yn pört(#-em) ulo.
     I-GEN house-POSS1SG be.PRES3SG
     'I have a house.'

In what follows I will argue that the suffix is obligatory in those cases where the relevant relation encompasses all the subparts of the current situation of the possessor and where the lack of overt marking would give rise to the inference that the contrary is true (i.e. that the relation holds only partially or does not hold at all). Example (9), without the suffix, illustrates such a scenario, whereas the one in (10) illustrates the possibility of a licit omission of the suffix. (11) is the most complicated case. There, I suggest, the use of the suffix is unpreferred since the non-totality inference associated with the omission is very unlikely. Before moving to the formal aspects of my analysis, I will add to the empirical database the patterns found in Giellatekno corpus of Meadow Mari.[9]

There are thirty-seven clauses of the *myjyn (modifier) (modifier) possessee ulo* type. In ten cases the possessive suffix is absent.[10] Examples (12) and (13) form almost a minimal pair with respect to the use of the suffix.

(12) nine   krepost'-vlak-ym   yštyme   šotyšto
     these   fortress-PL-ACC   making   about

     myj-yn   ške   **šonymaš-em**   ulo
     I-GEN   own   idea-POSS1SG   be.PRES3SG
     'I have my own idea about making these fortresses.'

(13) myj-yn   ik   **šonymaš**   ulo
     I-GEN   one   idea   be.PRES3SG
     'I have one idea.'

For the 1PL genitive phrase, there are five clauses found in the corpus, two of which do not have a possessive suffix. Examples (14) and (15) illustrate configurations with and without a possessive suffix, respectively.

(14) tide   surty-što   memnan   kažnyn-an
     this   farm-INESS   we.GEN   each-GEN

     iktör   **paj-na**   ulo
     equal   share-POSS1PL   be.PRES3SG
     'We all have equal shares in this farm.'

(15) tide   jodyš-lan-at   memnan   **vašmut**   ulo.
     this   question-DAT-FOC   we.GEN   answer   be.PRES3SG
     'We have an answer to this question.'

There are twenty-one existential possessive clauses with a present tense predicate and a second-person genitive phrase (*tyjyn (modifier) (modifier) possessee ulo*), all of which have a possessive suffix. There are nine clauses with a second-person plural genitive phrase, again, all with a possessive suffix. All twenty-eight constructions with a third-person singular genitive phrase have a possessee that bears a possessive suffix. Finally, there are twelve present tense clauses with a third-person plural genitive phrase, again, all with a possessive suffix on the possessee. The numbers are summarised in Table 8.1, which shows that possessive suffix omission in clauses with a present tense existential predicate is found only with the first person genitive NPs. Elicitation shows that omission is also possible with second- and third-person genitive NPs, which illustrates

Table 8.1 Possessive suffix use in existential possessive constructions in Giellatekno corpus.

Genitive phrase	Possessee with a suffix/total
1SG	27/37
1PL	3/5
2SG	21/21
2PL	9/9
3SG	28/28
3PL	12/12

the limited reliability of a (relatively) small corpus sample. The sample provides us, however, with some nice, naturally occurring examples. Returning to the elicitation data, consider the contrast between (16) (=9) and (17), where (17) is only felicitous on a 'warning' interpretation.

(16) myj-yn   pij*(-em)   ulo.
     I-GEN   dog-POSS1SG be.PRES3SG
     'I have a dog.'

(17) myj-yn   pij   ulo!
     I-GEN   dog be.PRES3SG
     '(Beware) I have a dog!'[11]

The sentence in (18) constitutes a parallel example for the third-person genitival possessor.

(18) Eskeryza,   tudyn   küzö   ulo!
     beware,   he.GEN   knife be.PRES3SG
     'Beware, he has a knife!'

I take it that what distinguishes the 'warning' scenario is the instantaneous or partial nature of the association between the possessor and the possessee. Consider a similar pair in (19)–(20).

(19) myj-yn   **joča-m**   ulo.
     I-GEN   child-POSS1SG be.PRES3SG
     'I have a child.' ['I have my own child.']

(20) myj-yn   **joča**   ulo.
     I-GEN   child be.PRES3SG
     'I have a child.' ['A friend asked me to babysit.']

The contrast in the partial/total nature of the possessive relation turns out to be limited to the context of present tense existential predicates.

2.2. The tense factor: Present vs. non-present

Non-present tense in existential possessive sentences makes the possessive suffix omissible with all noun types. Consider examples (21) and (22), which contrast with all of the possessive existential sentences introduced above in that the existential predicate is in the past tense.

(21) myj-yn   aka(-m)   **yle.**
     I-GEN   sister-POSS1SG be.PAST3SG
     'I had a sister.'

(22) tyj-yn   aka(-t)   **yle.**
     you-GEN   sister-POSS2SG   be.PAST3SG
     'You had a sister.'

The possessor in (21) and (22) cannot be interpreted as predicate giving a translation such as 'this sister was mine/yours'. Such an analysis would predict that (21) and (22) do not show the DE, contrary to the facts, as the ungrammaticality of (23) shows.

(23) *myj-yn   tide   aka-m   yle.
     I-GEN   that   sister-POSS1SG   be.PAST3SG
     Intended: '*I had that sister.'

A corresponding, grammatical predicative possessive construction is presented in (24).

(24) tide myj-yn   aka-m   yle.
     that I-GEN   sister-POSS1SG   be.PAST3SG
     'That was my sister.'

The meaning of the possessive suffix should thus be sensitive to the temporal dimension of the possessive relation, limiting it to the ongoing situations.

Just like the first- and second-person possessive suffix, the third-person possessive suffix on the possessee is optional in the past tense. Compare (25a) and (25b) as well as (26a) and (26b).

(25) a. myj-yn   ava-m-yn   nyl joča*(-že)   **ulo.**
        I-GEN   mother-POSS1SG-GEN   four child-POSS3SG   be.PRES3SG
        'My mother has four children.'

     b. myj-yn   ava-m-yn   nyl joča(-že)   **yle.**
        I-GEN   mother-POSS1SG-GEN   four child-POSS3SG   be.PAST3SG
        'My mother had four children.'

(26) a. aka-m-yn   pyrys*(-še)   **ulo.**
        sister-POSS1SG-GEN   cat-POSS3SG   be.PRES3SG
        'My sister has a cat.'

     b. aka-m-yn   pyrys (-še)   **yle.**
        sister-POSS1SG-GEN   cat-POSS3SG   be.PAST3SG
        'My sister had a cat.'

To sum up the distributional facts, the possessive suffix is obligatory with first- and second-person possessors in the present tense only on the total possession reading.

2.3. The range of expressible relations

The situations covered by the truth conditions of existential possessive constructions with animate genitival possessors seem to be limited to those where the possessor exercises a degree of control over the possessee. I take it that the assertion of a control relation entails a possibility of losing control, which corresponds to selling/giving away/losing (for an object) or losing (for a person).[12] Consider the following English pairs, where (27a) and (28a) entail (27b) and (28b), respectively. In contrast, there is clearly no entailment relation between (29a) and (29b) and (30a) and (30b).

(27) a. I have a house.
     b. I may sell it/give it away.

(28) a. I have a dog.
     b. I may lose it.

(29) a. I see a house.
     b. #I may sell it/give it away.

(30) a. I stand by a tax officer.
     b. #I am afraid to lose him.

Consider now the example in (31), which is false unless the Speaker owns a village. In contrast, the possessive morpheme in (32) is used in the context where the relevant relation can be described as 'being an inhabitant of'.

(31) #myj-yn   ola   ulo.
     I-GEN   village   be.PRES3SG
     Intended: '#There is a village where I was born' Attested: 'I have a village.'

(32) ola-m   peš   kugu.
     village-POSS1SG   very   big
     'My village (i.e. where I live) is very big.'

It thus appears that a possessive suffix by itself covers a wider range of relations than just possession proper, where possession is understood as involving a relation of control. Typologically, this is not an exceptional case. Søgaard (2005) shows on the basis of a sample of languages from different families that adnominal possessive constructions encode a wider range of relations that clausal possessive configurations.[13]

With inanimate possessors the only expressible relation is that of membership. Consider the unacceptable example in (33) where the intended reading is that the village has a school.

(33) #jal-yn   škol-že   ulo.
     village-GEN   school-POSS3SG   be.PRES3SG
     Intended: 'The village has a school.'

A grammatical way of expressing this meaning involves using a noun phrase in inessive case, as in (34).

(34) jal-yšte škol ulo.
 village-INESS school be.PRES3SG
 'The village has a school. / There is a school in the village.'

A minimal difference in meaning contribution of the genitive and inessive marking is illustrated by the following sentence pair, where the second utterance can only be interpreted in the sense that a table is part of the kitchen as a furniture set, rather than a kitchen as a spatial location.

(35) kuhni-što / *kuhn'-yn üštembal ulo.
 kitchen-INESS / kitchen-GEN table be.PRES3SG
 'There is a table in the kitchen.'

(36) kuhn'-yn üštembal-že ulo.
 kitchen-GEN table-POSS3SG be.PRES3SG
 'The kitchen (set) has a table (in it).'

The goal of the next section is to sketch an analysis capturing the above-mentioned patterns with a minimal number of special assumptions.

3. Existential possessive constructions: An analysis

3.1. Possessor-location link

In order to capture the fact that existential and proper locative constructions in Meadow Mari feature exactly the same paradigm of existential predicates (*ulo/yle/uke*, 'is/was/is not', etc.) and show the DE, I will assume that both constructions assert the existence of an individual with a nominal property relative to a particular domain. A parallel between existential possessive and existential locative constructions was drawn already in Freeze (1992), who argued, based on a typological sample, that the two involve essentially the same syntactic structure. The structure Freeze proposes for a head-final language (Hindi) is given in (37), where the predicate, heading the I(nflectional) projection, takes as its complement a prepositional predication. The latter introduces the possessor or locative phrase as the complement of P and the possessee as the specifier of P.' Freeze (1992: 579) also assumes that P' (denoting the possessor or location) fronts to [Spec, IP].

(37)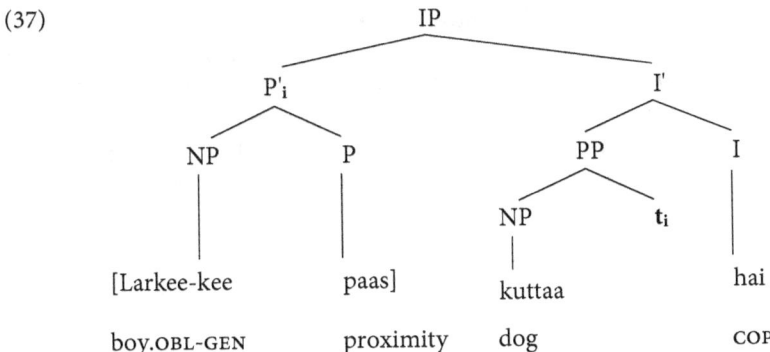

'The boy has a dog.'

Freeze (1992) argues that the possessor NP in existential possessive constructions is in fact a location that, by virtue of its [+animate] feature, slightly differs morphologically from inanimate locations. Namely, it has zero or different types of prepositions and/ or case marking. Even earlier, Szabolcsi (1981: 276) proposed to see Hungarian dative possessors as locative expressions.

In what follows, I will build on these insights by making the possessor-location link more explicit. It seems clear that a possessor cannot be literally taken as equating the physical location of a particular individual since this would not match the truth conditions of a sentence such as *myjyn pyrysem ulo* ('I have a cat'), which do not require that there be a cat literally on or even near the Speaker's body in order to be judged true. I will argue instead that in the case of existential possessive constructions, the location in question is a situation in which all individuals are related by a control relation to an (atomic or group) individual, traditionally called the possessor, and that such situations are contributed by the genitive phrase. Interpreting possession in terms of a control relation has a long tradition (see Baron & Herslund 2001; Stassen 2009; Levinson 2011; Arylova 2013 and references to earlier works therein).

3.1. Main predicate: Existential closure relative to a situation

The role of an existential predicate on this account is to introduce existential quantification relativized to a particular domain: the domain of the possessor or the domain given by a locative NP in existential possessive and existential locative constructions, respectively. I thus extend to existential possessive constructions in Meadow Mari a principle of relative existence developed in a series of works by Partee & Borschev and given in (38) (Partee & Borschev 2007: 155).

(38) *Principle of Relative Existence*
Existence (in the sense relative to affirmative existential sentences and negated existential sentences) is always relative to a LOC(ation).

I argue that a specific feature of existential possessive constructions is that location is defined via an individual, namely, as a set of situations where the individual in question controls other individuals and objects (in the sense defined below).

A sketch of the structure for the example in (39) is given in (40), where the genitive phrase corresponding to the possessor situation is introduced in the Specifier of the Topic projection, and the possessee phrase in nominative occupies [Spec, TP] (the vP level is omitted for the sake of clarity).[14]

(39)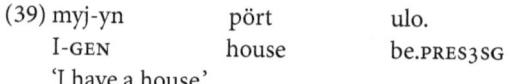
    myj-yn   pört   ulo.
    I-GEN   house   be.PRES3SG
    'I have a house.'

(40)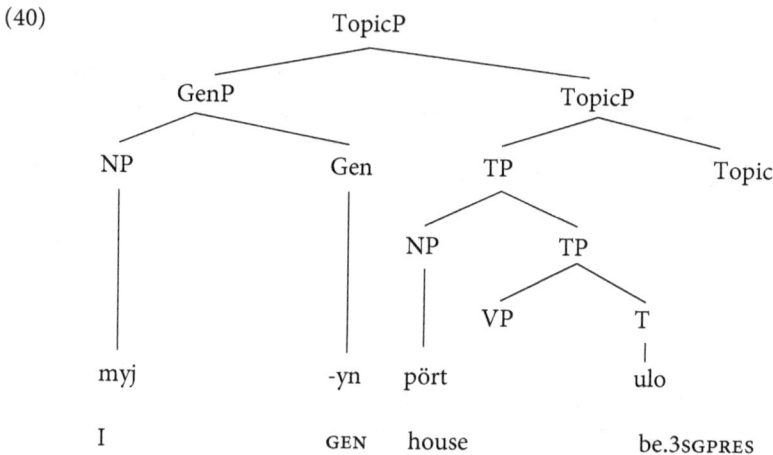

I assume that in general the Topic projection is responsible for introducing an Austinian situation or situations that restrict the proposition denoted by the complement of the Topic projection (cf. Schwarz 2009: 87). In existential possessive structures the Topic projection hosts a possessor phrase (i.e. genitive NP), which delimits the set of relevant situations.

The existential predicate in present tense denotes a function that takes a property (the denotation of the nominal predicate) and a situation variable s as its arguments and returns truth in case there exists an individual with the relevant property in the situation s at the time that equals the time of the utterance, as in (41). This analysis is similar to the treatment of existentials in McNally (1992), who proposes that an existential predicate introduces an assertion that there exists an individual instantiating the property supplied by the nominal predicate at a given spatio-temporal index.[15]

(41) $[[ulo]]^{g,c} = \lambda P_{<e,<\sigma,t>>}. \lambda s_\sigma. \exists x_e \exists t_\tau [P(x)(s)$ at $t = $ utterance time$]$

The existential predicate combines with the denotation of the nominal predicate by Functional Application (Heim & Kratzer 1998), binding the situation argument of the latter.

(42) $[[\textit{pört ulo}]]^{g,c} = \lambda s_\sigma. \exists x_e \exists t_\tau [x \text{ is a house in situation s at t = utterance time}]$

The situation argument of the existential predicate can be restricted by the denotation either of a locative phrase or, I argue, of a genitive one. First, I assume that the genitive morpheme is a relational predicate, in line with a vast tradition (e.g. Partee & Borschev 1998 and references therein), and that it encodes a control relation, (43).

(43) $[[\text{gen}]]^{g,c} = \lambda x_e. \lambda y_e. \lambda s_\sigma. y \text{ is controlled by x in s}$

If the second argument is closed under universal quantification, as I claim is the case when a genitive is merged in the Topic projection, it generates–with respect to an individual–a set of situations in which everything is controlled by that individual. The corresponding lexical entry is given in (44).

(44) $[[\text{gen}]]^{g,c} = \lambda x_e. \lambda s_\sigma \forall y_e \text{ in s}[y \text{ is controlled by x}]$

This solution is similar in spirit to the analysis of implicit (scope) restrictors in existential constructions put forth in Francez (2010), where the restrictor set correspond to a set of individuals standing in a particular context-specified relation to a salient antecedent. On the present analysis, the relevant relation is that of control. In contrast to Francez' analysis, I propose that in existential possessive constructions a possessor generates a set of situations, which makes it resemble a coda modifying the spatio temporal parameters of the existential predication on the analysis of McNally (1992).

The genitive phrase then denotes a set of situations in which every individual is controlled, to an extent sufficient to license a 'losing' entailment (see section 2.4), by the individual denoted by the complement of the genitive morpheme (a pronoun in the case at hand). This set of situations serves to restrict the existential assertion, as will be shown further.

The semantics in (44) predicts that genitive NPs cannot be used to simply express existence of an entity/individual in some location associated with the Speaker, as it crucially involves a control condition. This prediction is borne out: in order to convey the meaning 'Your sister is with me/at my place', a postpositional comitative phrase has to be used rather than a genitive one, as (45) shows. Being in a physical proximity of an individual does not necessarily imply control on the part of that individual, and so the use of a genitive phrase, introducing a control relation, is infelicitous in this case.

(45) myj   dene-m / *myj-yn   aka-t   ulo.
     I   with-1SG / I-GEN   sister-POSS2SG   be.PRES3SG
     'Your sister is with me/in my house.' [ZV 14 March 2018]

The composition of the former is given in (46), where the denotation of the genitive morpheme in (44) combines, by FA, with the denotation of the pronoun *myj* (the possessor in context c).

(46) $[[\text{gen}]]^{g,c}([[myj]]^{g,c}) = \lambda s_\sigma . \forall y \text{ in } s[y_e \text{ is controlled by the Speaker in } c]$[16]

The resulting set of situations intersects with the set of situations denoted by the predicate in (42). The utterance *myjyn pört ulo* ('I have a house') then has the following denotation:

(47) $[[myjyn\ pört\ ulo]]^{g,c} = \lambda s_\sigma . \exists x_e \exists t_\tau [x \text{ is a house in situation } s\ \&\ \forall y \text{ in } s[y \text{ is controlled by the Speaker in } c] \text{ at } t = \text{utterance time}]$

3.2. Possessive suffixes: Relationality, maximality and temporal independence

Let us now turn to the contribution of the possessive suffixes. A particularly interesting issue is whether they add anything to the semantics in (47). Given that possessive suffixes appear to cover a wider range of relations than genitive possessors (see section 2.4), I assume that one extra meaning component they add is a contextually defined relation variable. A preliminary version of a lexical entry for the 1SG possessive morpheme is given in (50). Following Simonenko (2017), I assume a Logical Form in (48) (corresponding to a tree diagram in (49)), where *i* is the index of a silent individual pronoun with an interpretation range restricted by person and number features (1st, 2nd or 3rd).

(48) i_{1sg} POSS NP

(49)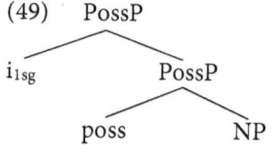

(50) $[[\text{POSS}]]^{g,c} = \lambda P_{<e,<\sigma,t>>} . \lambda y_e . \lambda x_e . \lambda s_\sigma . P(x)(s)\ \&\ R_c(x)(y)(s)$
PRELIMINARY I where R is contextually defined.

The combination of a possessive morpheme, a nominal predicate and a silent pronoun is interpreted as in (51).

(51) $[[i_{1sg}\ \text{POSS NP}]]^{g,c} = \lambda x_e . \lambda s_\sigma . [[\text{NP}]](x)(s)\ \&\ R_c(x)(g(i_{1sg}))(s)$

The possessive morpheme thus restricts the denotation of the noun phrase to the individual that stands in a particular relation to the referent of the pronoun.

The preliminary semantics of the possessive suffix in (50) does not capture the patterns in section 2.1, which I described as reflecting a total/partial nature of a possessive relation. In (52) I model this by introducing exhaustive quantification over the subparts of the possessor's situation as part of the possessive suffix semantics.

(52) $[[\text{POSS}]]^{g,c} = \lambda P_{<e,<\sigma,t>>} . \lambda x_e . \lambda y_e . \lambda s_\sigma . \forall s' \leq f_c(x)[R_c(y)(x)(s')]\ \&\ P(y)(s)$
PRELIMINARY II
where f_c is a function which maps an individual to a maximal situation ('possessor's situation') encompassing all minimal situations involving that individual.

The semantics in (52) is meant to capture contrasts such as the one between (16) and (17), repeated here as (53) and (54), respectively.

(53) myj-yn   pij*(-em)   ulo.
     I-GEN   dog-POSS1SG   be.PRES3SG
     'I have a dog.' [ZV: 15 March 2018]

(54) myj-yn   pij   ulo!
     I-GEN   dog   be.PRES3SG
     '(Beware) I have a dog!' [ZV: 15 March 2018]

The possessive suffix, on its updated semantics in (52), adds to the truth conditions a clause that the relevant relation between the possessor and an individual with the nominal property holds in all the subparts of the possessor's maximal situation, as opposed to just *a* situation in which the possessor has control. The contrast between the semantic contribution of a genitive possessor and a possessive morpheme, in addition to the nature of the relation (control vs. free variable), thus involves existential vs. universal quantification over relevant situations. In (55)–(56) I give the interpretation of (53), assuming a possessive suffix semantics in (52) and an existential predicate semantics in (41).

(55) $[[i_{1sg} \text{ POSS } pij]]^{g,c} = \lambda x_e . \lambda s_\sigma . \forall s' \leq f(\text{Speaker})[R_c(x)(\text{Speaker})(s')]$ & $[[\text{dog}]](x)(s)$

(56) $[[ulo]]^{g,c}[[i_{1sg} \text{ POSS } pij]]^{g,c} = \lambda s_\sigma . \exists x_e \exists t_\tau [\forall s' \leq f(\text{Speaker})[R_c(x)(\text{Speaker})(s')]$ & $[[\text{dog}]](x)(s)$ at t = utterance time]

(57) $[[myjyn\ pijem\ ulo]]^{g,c} = \lambda s_\sigma . \exists x_e \exists t_\tau [\forall s' \leq f(\text{Speaker})[R_c(x)(\text{Speaker})(s')]$ & $[[\text{dog}]](x)(s)$ & $\forall y$ in s[y is controlled by the Speaker in c] at t = utterance time]

In contrast, the denotation of (54) is as in (47) (modulo the nominal predicate).

I have so far proposed that an existential possessive construction without a possessive suffix conveys the existence of an entity with the nominal property in a situation where everything is controlled by the possessor at the time of the utterance. A possessive suffix makes a stronger contribution, viz. a statement that the entity in question is related to the possessor by some salient relation that holds in *all* the subparts of the Speaker's situation.

Since a possessive morpheme restricts the nominal denotation, in an upward entailing environment a structure with a possessive morpheme makes an utterance more informative than the one without. I assume that the logical forms with and without a suffix form structural alternatives (Fox & Katzir 2011) and that, by a Gricean expectation that the Speaker makes a maximally informative contribution if it is true, the non-use of a possessive suffix gives rise to an implicature that there is no relation that holds in all the subparts of the possessor's maximal situation. If such an inference is counterfactual, that is, if the context does support the stronger truth conditions involving the possessive suffix, an utterance without a suffix is perceived as deviant. The only context in which the omission is predicted to be permissible even if the no-total-relation inference is counterfactual are those where the inference itself is highly implausible, as in (11) where it is very unlikely that a house is being possessed just instantaneously, as a knife or an apple.

In contrast, in a downward entailing environment (e.g. under negation), a structure with a possessive morpheme is not necessarily more informative (there not being any dogs related to the Speaker by a salient relation in all subparts of the Speaker's maximal situation does not entail there not being any dogs controlled by the Speaker at the utterance time). In such environments, possessive morphemes are predicted to be omissible. Example (55) shows that this prediction is borne out:

(58) myj-yn   šüžar(-em)   uke.
     I-GEN   sister-POSS1SG   be.NEG.PRES3SG
     'I don't have a sister.'

The remaining pattern unaccounted for by the entry in (52) is the omissibility of the possessive suffix in past tense. A declarative statement about events in a past situation is an upward entailing environment, just as its present tense counterpart, and thus is predicted to require the use of a possessive morpheme in order to avoid the inference about the absence of an all-encompassing salient relation. I therefore relativize the possessive relation to a temporal parameter, namely, the possessor's current situation. This amendment is reflected in (59), where the function f_c from individuals to their maximal situations now returns only those situations that are ongoing at the utterance time.

(59) $[[POSS]]^{g,c} = \lambda P_{<e,<\sigma,t>>} . \lambda x_e . \lambda y_e . \lambda s_\sigma . \forall s' \leq f_c(x)[R_c(y)(x)(s')] \& P(y)(s)$
where f_c is a function that maps an individual to a maximal situation ('possessor's situation') encompassing all situations involving that individual and holding at t = utterance time.

Notice that this function does not have any kind of definedness conditions. This reflects the empirical fact that in Meadow Mari the felicity conditions on the use of possessive suffixes do not require that there exist an individual with the property denoted by an extended nominal projection. That is, they do not trigger an existential presupposition. Unlike English possessive pronouns, which are commonly assumed to presuppose the existence of an individual satisfying the nominal description and standing in a possessive relation to the possessor, Mari possessive suffixes occur both in interrogative and negative existential statements, as (60) and (61) show. Compare these to their ungrammatical English counterparts in (62) and (63).

(60) Tyj-yn   aka-t   ulo?
     you-GEN   sister-POSS2SG   be.PRES3SG
     'Do you have a sister?'

(61) myj-yn   aka-m   uke.
     I-GEN   sister-1SG   NEG
     'I don't have a sister'

(62) *Do you have your sister?

(63) *I do not have my sister.

Consider the effect of the amended entry in (59) on the interpretation of a past tense existential possessive claim. The sentence *myjyn pijem yle* ('I had a dog') has the denotation in (65), assuming the semantics of the past tense existential predicate in (64).

(64) $[[yle]]^{g,c} = \lambda P_{<e,<\sigma,t>>} . \lambda s_\sigma . \exists x_e \exists t_\tau [P(x)(s) \text{ at } t < \text{utterance time}]$

(65) $[[myjyn\ pijem\ yle]]^{g,c} = \lambda s_\sigma . \exists t_\tau \exists x_e [\forall s' \le f_c(\text{Speaker})[R_c(x)(\text{Speaker})(s')]$ & $[[dog]]$ $(x)(s)$ & $\forall y \text{ in } s[y \text{ is controlled by the Speaker in } c] \text{ at } t < \text{utterance time}]$
where f_c is a function that maps an individual to a maximal situation ('possessor's situation') encompassing all situation involving that individual and holding at t = utterance time

This past tense existential possessive sentence denotes a property of situations, which holds of a situation if there exists an individual that is a dog in that situation and that situation one where everything is controlled by the Speaker *at the time preceding the utterance time* and that individual is related by a salient relation to the Speaker in all the subparts of the Speaker's maximal *ongoing situation*.

If there is *currently* no salient relation between the dog-individual and the Speaker, this sentence would be false with the suffix and we then expect the suffix omission. We thus have derived the non-present tense obviation effect from the situational independence of the relation introduced by possessive suffixes. Independently of the times or situations introduced higher up, they signal a relationship in the Speaker's or addressee's current situation.

4. The Definiteness Effect

The DE seems to be a distinctive feature of a particular class of constructions at the core of which we find an existential assertion. As mentioned in section 1, existential possessive constructions in Meadow Mari show the DE in that Milsark's strong quantifiers are excluded from the position of the argument of the existential copula. This is illustrated again in (66).

(66) *myj-yn   tide   pij-em   ulo.
     I-GEN   that   dog-POSS1SG   be.PRES3SG
     Intended: '*I have that dog.' (On an existential reading.)

Building on Zucchi's (1995) account of the DE in English existential constructions, I propose that it arises in Mari as a result of an irreparable conflict between two felicity conditions, namely, the informativity condition and the existential presupposition introduced by an NP in the argument position. The informativity condition on existential sentences was formulated in Zucchi (1995: 69) as a requirement that the context neither entail that the denotation of the argument DP is empty nor that it is non-empty. This is a more general version of the felicity condition put forth in McNally (1992: 77), which requires that the individual whose existence is asserted by an existential construction be novel. These are essentially construction-specific versions of a yet more general informativity condition of Stalnaker (1978), invoked implicitly in Oshima (2007) and explicitly in Simonenko (2016) and Schwarz & Simonenko (2018) to account for the ungrammaticality of referential and factive islands, respectively. The condition can be stated as follows, where c is Stalnaker's (1978) context set:

(67) INFORMATIVITY CONDITION (Schwarz & Simonenko 2018)
Proposition p is felicitous with respect to a context c iff $c \nsubseteq p$

The informativity condition requires that the proposition concerned not be entailed by the context set. Below I give an example of how a clash between the informativity condition and an existential presupposition arises by going through the truth and felicity conditions of an offending configuration in (66).

I assume the structure in (68) for demonstrative phrases, where s_r is a Kratzerian resource situation relative to which a DP is interpreted. I also assume that the demonstrative head itself is interpreted as in (69), following Elbourne (2008) and Schwarz (2009).

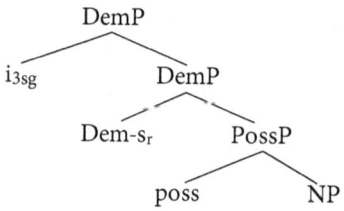

(69) $[[tide]]^{g,c} = \lambda s_\sigma . \lambda P_{<e,<\sigma,t>>} . \lambda y_e : \exists!x[P(x)(s) \& x = y] . \iota x[P(x)(s) \& x = y]$

The denotation of the demonstrative phrase is then as in (67), assuming that PossP meaning is as in (66). Importantly, the demonstrative (as presumably all other Milsark's strong quantifiers) introduces an existential presupposition.

(70) $[[i_{1sg} POSS\ pij]]^{g,c} = \lambda x_e . \lambda s_\sigma . \forall s' \leq f_c(Speaker)[R_c(x)(Speaker)(s')] \& [[dog]](x)(s)$

(71) $[[tide\text{-}s_r\ i_{1sg} POSS\ pij]]^{g,c} = \lambda x_e : \exists!x[\forall s' \leq f_c(Speaker)[R_c(x)(Speaker)(s')] \& [[dog]](x)(s_r) \& x = y] . \iota x[\forall s' \leq f_c(Speaker)[R_c(x)(Speaker)(s')] \& [[dog]](x)(s_r) \& x = y]$

Once the denotation in (70) combines with the denotation of the third-person silent pronoun (68), a demonstrative phrase, if defined (i.e. iff ∃!x[∀s'≤f$_c$(Speaker)[R$_c$(x)(Speaker)(s')] & [[dog]](x)(s$_r$) & x = g(i$_{3sg}$)]), denotes the referent of that pronoun, g(i$_{3sg}$) (i.e. the unique individual x that satisfies the condition x = g(i$_{3sg}$)).

Before we try to interpret an existential statement containing *tide pijem*, notice that there is a type mismatch between [[i$_{3sg}$ *tide-s$_r$* i$_{1sg}$ POSS *pij*]] (individual type e) and the first argument slot of [[*ulo*]] (property type <e<s,t>>), whose semantics is given in (44), repeated here as (72).

(72) [[*ulo*]]^{g,c} = λP$_{<e,<σ,t>>}$. λs$_σ$. ∃x$_e$∃t$_τ$[P(x)(s) at t = utterance time]

Let us assume for the sake of argument that this conflict is resolved via an intensional version of Partee's (1986) *ident* type-shifting and that [[i$_{3sg}$ *tide-s$_r$* i$_{1sg}$ POSS *pij*]]^{g,c}, following such type-shifting, denotes a function from individuals to propositions that are true just in case the individual is identical to g(i$_{3sg}$) in a given situation. Let us also assume that the function *ident*$_{intens}$ comes with a requirement that there exist an individual identical to the input of the function in the relevant situation, as in (73).

(73) *ident*$_{intens}$ ([[i$_{3sg}$ *tide-s$_r$* i$_{1sg}$ POSS *pij*]]^{g,c}) = λx$_e$. λs$_σ$: ∃!x[x = g(i$_{3sg}$) in s]. x = g(i$_{3sg}$) in s.

(74) [[*ulo*]]^{g,c} (*ident*$_{intens}$([[i$_{3sg}$ *tide-s$_r$* i$_{1sg}$ POSS *pij*]]^{g,c})) = λs$_σ$: ∃!x[x = g(i$_{3sg}$) in s]. ∃x$_e$∃t$_τ$[x = g(i$_{3sg}$) in s at t = utterance time]

Intersecting it with the denotation of the genitival phrase in (44), repeated in (75), we get a proposition in (76).

(75) [[*gen*]]^{g,c}([[*myj*]]^{g,c}) = λs$_σ$. ∀y in s[y is controlled by the Speaker in c]

(76) ([[*myjyn*]]^{g,c})([[*ulo*]]^{g,c} (*ident*$_{intens}$([[i$_{3sg}$ *tide-s$_r$* i$_{1sg}$ POSS *pij*]]^{g,c}))) = λs$_σ$: ∃!x[x = g(i$_{3sg}$) in s & ∀y in s[y is controlled by the Speaker in c]] . ∃x$_e$∃t$_τ$[x = g(i$_{3sg}$) in s & ∀y in s[y is controlled by the Speaker in c] at t = utterance time]

The hypothetical (but empirically ungrammatical) existential possessive construction with a demonstrative carries a presupposition that there exists a unique individual identical to g(i$_{3sg}$) in a situation where everything is controlled by the Speaker, while the assertion states that there exists an individual, identical to g(i$_{3sg}$), in a situation where everything is controlled by the Speaker at a time identical to the utterance time. It follows that any context set *c* which entails the presupposition will entail the assertion as well. I propose that the source of the Definiteness Effect in Mari existential possessive constructions is the same as in the case of English existential constructions (Zucchi 1995), referential DP islands (Simonenko 2016) and factive islands (Oshima 2007; Schwarz & Simonenko 2018), namely, an irreconcilable conflict between the requirement for the utterance to be informative and the existential presupposition.[17] Given the existence presupposition triggered by the demonstrative determiner and the semantics of existential constructions, the informativity condition in (67) cannot be satisfied in any context in which the existence presupposition is satisfied, and vice versa.

The DE in existential possessive constructions is of course not limited to demonstratives. (77) and (78) replicate it for two so-called strong quantifiers, 'both' and 'all'.

(77) *myj-yn   koktynat   pij-em   ulo
      I-GEN   both   dog-1SG   be.PRES3SG
      Indended: '*I have both dogs.'

(78) *myj-yn   čyla   pij-em   ulo.
      I-GEN   all   dog-POSS1SG   be.PRES3SG
      Intended: '*I have all the dogs.' (On an existential reading.)

What makes Meadow Mari existential possessive constructions typologically interesting, especially in comparison with their European counterparts, is that possessive suffixes, unlike possessive pronouns in European languages, do not trigger DE. I have argued that this is expected, given the independent evidence that they do not trigger an existential presupposition, a crucial ingredient of the DE on the account I have adopted here.

In the general case, in an existential possessive construction with a determiner triggering an existential presupposition, the following pattern obtains: both the presupposition and the assertion establish the existence of an individual with the nominal property relative to the same domain. This is because the existential predicate binds the situational argument of its complement both at the level of presupposition and at the level of assertion and 'passes on' to it the restrictions introduced by the genitive possessor. This is not the case in predicative possessive constructions, such as the one in (2a), repeated here as (79).

(79) tide   pört   myj-yn
     that   house   I-GEN
     'That house is mine.'

In a predicative construction, a certain property is predicated of the denotation of the subject. In (80) it is the property of belonging to the Speaker. I assume that the predicative zero copula has the following semantics. That is, it is identical to its overt existential counterpart in (41) with the exception that there is no existential closure this time.

(80) $\lambda P_{<e, \sigma t>} . \lambda x_e . \lambda s_\sigma . P(x)(s)$

Recall that a genitive morpheme, without a universal closure, denotes a relation of control, as in (43), repeated here as (81).

(81) $[[\text{gen}]]^{g,c} = \lambda x_e . \lambda y_e . \lambda s_\sigma .$ y is controlled by x in s

A combination of the predicative copula with the denotation of the genitival phrase, $\lambda x_e . \lambda s_\sigma . x$ *is controlled by the Speaker in s*, results in an identical predicate:

(82) $\lambda x_e . \lambda s_\sigma$ x is controlled by the Speaker in s

With the denotation of the demonstrative phrase in (83) (based on the entry in (69)) as the final argument, this gives the proposition in (84).

(83) $[[i_{3sg} \; tide\text{-}s_r \; pört]]^{g,c}$ = is defined iff $\exists ! x[x$ is a house in $g(r)$ and & $x = g(i_{3sg})]$ if defined, $[[i_{3sg} \; tide\text{-}s_r \; pört]]^{g,c} = \iota x[x$ is a house in $g(r)$ & $x = g(i_{3sg})]$

(84) $[[tide\text{-}s_r \; pört \; myj\text{-}yn]]^{g,c} = \lambda s_\sigma : \exists ! x[x$ is a house in $g(r)$ and & $x = g(i_{3sg})]$. $\iota x[x$ is a house in $g(r)$ & $x = g(i_{3sg})]$ is controlled by the Speaker in s

Unlike an existential possessive construction which asserts the existence of an individual in a domain controlled by the possessor, a predicative possessive construction actually conveys a relational information about an individual whose existence has already been established. It is also easy to see that there is no entailment relation between the presupposed and asserted content in (84), and thus this sentence can satisfy the informativity condition in (67) even in those contexts that satisfy its presupposition. The DE is thus correctly predicted not to arise.

5. Conclusion

In this chapter I presented an analysis of existential possessive constructions in Meadow Mari, which includes an analysis of the role of genitive possessors and possessive suffixes as well as the emergence of the Definiteness Effect. I have proposed that genitive possessors yield a relation of control co-temporary with the time of the existential predicate, while possessive morphemes introduce a salient relation, possibly different from that of control and holding in all the ongoing situations involving the possessor. I argued that the genitive phrase assumes either the semantics of a relation or, if one of the arguments is universally closed, of a property to be a controller in a given situation. This flexibility allows it to provide a domain restriction in existential possessive constructions and a property in the predicative possessive constructions.

I also proposed a fully compositional account of the contrast in the Definiteness Effect between existential possessive constructions on the one hand and predicative possessive constructions on the other. I showed that in the latter case an existential presupposition trigger contributes to the sentence presupposition being equivalent or stronger than the assertion, leading to a permanent conflict between presupposition satisfaction and informativeness.

Notes

1. *Abbreviations*

ACC	accusative case	PL	plural number
DE	Definiteness Effect	PRES	present tense
GEN	genitive case	PST	past tense
INESS	inessive case	SG	singular number
INF	infinitive		
NEG	negative marker		

2. I am very thankful to Zinaida Vetkeevna Klutcheva, Yulia Ivanovna Soboleva and Galina Gennadyevna Pushkina for sharing with me their knowledge of Mari. I am grateful to the editors of the present volume, an anonymous reviewer, Itamar Francez and Jeremy Bradley for extremely helpful comments and suggestions. Needless to say, I am responsible for all the remaining flaws. This work has been supported by Research Foundation Flanders and Ghent University as well as CNRS grant 'Multimodal analysis of the noun phrase in Finno-Ugric languages: Referential continuity and encoding of the informational structure of the sentence' (PIs Benjamin Fagard & Natalya Serdobolskaya).

3. Unlike many other minority Finno-Ugric languages, Meadow Mari enjoys rich, recently created linguistic resources, such as large on-line dictionaries (https://www.univie.ac.at/maridict/site-2014/dict.php?int=0 and http://marlamuter.com/en/), morphological analysers (http://giellatekno.uit.no/cgi/index.mhr.eng.html and https://www.univie.ac.at/maridict/site-2014/index.php?int=0), and a corpus (http://gtweb.uit.no/u_korp/?mode=mhr).

4. The infinitival form of this copula is *ulaš*.

5. I do not discuss in this chapter the question about the syntactic structure of nominal expressions in Mari and use the term NP, in Grimshaw's (1991) sense, as an extended nominal projection.

6. A zero copula in present tense in predicative constructions is by no means specific to Meadow Mari. The pattern is also found, for instance, in Hungarian (Dalmi 2010), Russian (Pereltsvaig 2007; Partee & Borschev 2007), Turkish (Zwart 2002), among other languages (Stassen 1996).

7. The distribution of these suffixes goes well beyond what could be sensibly put under the umbrella of possessive constructions. For a brief overview of non-possessive uses in different Finno-Ugric languages, see Simonenko (2014). The paradigm looks as follows, where brackets indicate possible allomorphy:

1SG (e)m	1PL (ə)na
2SG (e)t	2PL (ə)da
3SG že	3PL (ə)št

8. I use the term *animate nouns* to refer to NPs denoting animate beings.

9. SIKOR 2016.

10. I use the following three queries [(word = 'мыйын')] [(pos = 'N')] [(word = 'уло')]; [(word = 'мыйын')][] [(pos = 'N')] [(word = 'уло')]; [(word = 'мыйын')][][][(pos = 'N')] [(word = 'уло')].

11. There is similar pattern in Russian where the presence/absence of an existential predicate in a possessive construction corresponds to the permanent/instantaneous interpretation contrast, as (i) and (ii) illustrate.

    (i) U menja est' ružje.
       at. I.GEN be.PRES3SG rifle.NOM
       'I have a rifle.' (In general, at home.)

(ii) U menja ružje!
    at.I.GEN   rifle.NOM
    'I have a rifle!' ('On me, in the current situation.')

12   Evans (1995: 46) gives the following definition of control: 'X [the possessor] can expect Y [the possessee] to be in the same place as X when X wants, and X can do with Y what X wants.' I will limit myself to a more straightforwardly tested entailment, without claiming that it is the only one valid.

13   Pleshak (2018) makes an inventory of the relations expressible by adnominal possessive constructions in Mari, Mordvin and Permic languages.

14   I am not committing myself here to a specific layout of the clausal left-periphery, focusing on the projection that matters for the semantic analysis at hand, namely, the topic phrase. This is also a highly simplified representation with regard to the derivation of the tense-final order. For approaches to SOV involving left-branching TP and remnant VP movement, see Haegeman (2001). The simplified representation in (40) will suffice as an LF for my purposes here.

15   More specifically, in McNally's system the existential predicate takes as its argument a nominalized function–the result of mapping a property onto its entity correlate–and maps it to truth in case there exists an individual in the extension of the nominalized function at a given spatio temporal index.

16   Naturally, the person of the controller depends on the features of the complement of the genitive morpheme.

17   Partee (1999) suggests that 'the interaction of strong NP's with the predicate *exist*, which is true of every entity in the domain, makes existential sentences containing strong NP's come out either tautologous, contradictory, or else asserting or denying something they already presuppose'.

References

Alhoniemi, A. 1993. *Grammatik des Tscheremissischen (Mari): Mit Texten und Glossar.* Buske Verlag.

Arylova, A. 2013. *Possession in the Russian clause: towards dynamicity in syntax.* Groningen: s.n.

Baron, I., & Herslund, M. 2001. Semantics of the verb HAVE. In: Herslund, M., Baron, I. & Sørensen, F. (eds), *Dimensions of Possession*, 85–98. Amsterdam: John Benjamins.

Barwise, J. & Cooper, R. 1981. Generalized quantifiers and natural language. *Linguistics and Philosophy* 4: 159–219.

Caha, P. 2013. Explaining the structure of case paradigms by the mechanisms of Nanosyntax. *Natural Language & Linguistic Theory* 31: 1015–1066.

Dalmi, G. 2010. *Copular Sentences, Predication and Cyclic Agree.* Saarbruecken: Lambert Academic Publishing (VDM).

De Jong, F. 1987. Generalized quantifiers: the properness of their strength. In: van Benthem, J. & Ter Meulen, A. (eds), *Generalized Quantifiers in Natural Language*, 21–45. Dordrecht: Foris.

Diesing, M. 1992. *Indefinites.* Cambridge: MIT Press.

Elbourne, P. 2008. Demonstratives as individual concepts. *Linguistics and Philosophy* 31(4): 409–466.

Evans, N. 1995. *A Grammar of Kayardild.* Berlin: Mouton de Gruyter.

Fischer, S., Kupisch, T. & Rinke, E. 2016. *Definiteness Effects: Bilingual, Typological and Diachronic Variation*. Newcastle upon Tyne: Cambridge Scholars Publishing.

Fox, D. & Katzir, R. 2011. On the characterization of alternatives. *Natural Language Semantics* 19(1): 87–107.

Francez, I. 2010. Context dependence and implicit arguments in existentials. *Linguistics and Philosophy* 33(1): 11–30.

Fraurud, K. 2001. Possessives with extensive use. In: Baron, I., Herslund, M. & Sørensen, F. (eds), *Dimensions of Possession*, 243–267. Amsterdam: John Benjamins.

Freeze, R. 1992. Existentials and other locatives. *Language* 68(3): 553–595.

Grimshaw, J. 1991. Extended projections. Unpublished manuscript. Brandeis University.

Heim, I. & Kratzer, A. 1998. *Semantics in Generative Grammar*, vol. 1185. Oxford: Blackwell.

Haegeman, L. 2001. Antisymmetry and verb-final order in West Flemish. *Journal of Comparative Germanic Linguistics* 3(3): 207–232.

Higginbotham, J. 1983. The logic of perceptual reports: an extensional alternative to situation semantics. *Journal of Philosophy* 80: 100–127.

Keenan, E. 1987. On the semantic definition of 'indefinite NP'. In: Reuland, E. J. & Ter Meulen, A. G. B. (eds), *The Representation of (In)Definiteness*, 286–317. Cambridge, MA: MIT Press.

Kuznetsova, A. I. 2012. Kumuljatsija grammatititcheskih znatchenij v agglutinativnyh pokazateljah: deiktitcheskie funktsii posessiva v ural'skih jazykah [The cumulation of grammatical meanings in agglutinative markers]. In: Serdobolskaya, N. V., Toldova, C. Y., Say, S. S., & Kalinina, E. Y. (eds), *Finno-ugorskie jazyki. Fragmenty grammaticheskogo opisanija* [Essays on the grammar of Finno-Ugric languages], 262–339. Moscow: Languages of the Slavic cultures.

Leonetti, M. 2008. Definiteness effects and the role of the coda in existential constructions. In: Müller, H. H. & Klinge, A. (eds), *Essays in Nominal Determination: From Morphology to Discourse Management*, 131–162. Amsterdam: John Benjamins.

Levinson, L. 2011. Possessive WITH in Germanic: HAVE and the role of P. *Syntax* 14(4): 355–393.

Luutonen, J. 1997. *The Variation of Morpheme Order in Mari Declension*. Helsinki: Suomalais-ugrilainen seura.

McFadden, T. 2002. The morphosyntax of Finno-Ugric case-marking: a DM account. In: Hirotani, M. (ed.), *Proceedings of the 32nd Annual Meeting of NELS*, 347–364. Amherst, MA: GLSA Publications.

McNally, L. 1992. *An Interpretation for the English Existential Construction*. New York: Garland.

Milsark, G. 1974. Existential sentences in English. PhD dissertation. Massachusetts Institute of Technology.

Oshima, D. Y. 2007. On factive islands: pragmatic anomaly vs. pragmatic infelicity. In: Washio, T., Satoh, K., Takeda, H. & Inokuchi, A. (eds), *New Frontiers in Artificial Intelligence: Proceedings of JSAI 2006 (LNCS 4384)*, 147–161. New York: Springer.

Paducheva, E. 2000. Definiteness effect in Russian. In: von Heusinger, K. & Egli, U. (eds), *Reference and Anaphoric Relations*, 133–146. Dodrecht: Kluwer.

Partee, B. 1999. Weak NP's in HAVE sentences. In: Gerbrandy, J., Marx, M., de Rijke, M. & Venema, Y. (eds), *JFAK, a Liber Amicorum for Johan van Benthen on the occasion of his 50th Birthday*, 39–57. Amsterdam: University of Amsterdam.

Partee, B. & Borschev, V. 1998. Integrating lexical and formal semantics: genitives, relational nouns, and type-shifting. In: Cooper, R. & Gamkrelidze, Th. (eds), *Proceedings of the Second Tbilisi Symposium on Language, Logic, and Computation*, 229–241. Tbilisi: Tbilisi State University, Center on Language, Logic, Speech.

Partee, B. & Borschev, V. 2007. Existential sentences, BE, and the Genitive of Negation in Russian. In: Komorovski, I. & von Heusinger, K. (eds), *Existence: Semantics and Syntax*, 147–190. Dordrecht: Springer.

Pereltsvaig, A. 2007. *Copular Sentences in Russian: A Theory of Intra-Clausal Relations, Studies in Natural Language and Linguistic Theory*, vol. 70. Berlin/Heidelberg: Springer Science & Business Media.

Pleshak, P. 2018. Adnominal possessive constructions in Mordvin, Mari and Permic. *ESUKA – JEFUL* 9(1): 139–168.

Schwarz, F. 2009. *Two types of definites in natural language*. PhD dissertation. University of Massachusetts Amherst.

Schwarz, B. & Simonenko, A. 2018. Factive islands and meaning-driven unacceptability. *Natural Laguage Semantics* 26(3–4): 253–279.

Simonenko, A. 2014. Microvariation in Finno-Ugric possessive markers. In: Huang, H.-L., Poole, E. & Rysling, A. (eds) *Proceedings of the 43rd Annual Meeting of the North East Linguistic Society*, vol. 2, 127–140. CreateSpace Independent Publishing Platform. Amherst, MA: GLSA Publications.

Simonenko, A. 2016. Semantics of DP Islands: the case of questions. *Journal of Semantics* 33(4): 661–702.

Simonenko, A. 2017. Towards a semantic typology of specific determiners. In: Cremers, A. van Gessel, Th. & Roelofsen, F. (eds) *Proceedings of the 21st Amsterdam Colloquium*, 425–434. Amsterdam: ILLC.

Simonenko, A. & Leontiev, A. 2012. Morfo-syntax imennoj grupy v Finno-Ugorskych jazykach [Morphosyntax of the Noun Phrase in Finno-Ugric languages]. In: Serdobolskaya, N. V., Toldova, C. Y., Say, S. S. & Kalinina, E. Y. (eds), *Finno-ugorskie jazyki. Fragmenty grammatičeskogo opisanija* [Finno-Ugric languages. Fragments of grammatical description], 262–339. Moscow: Languages of Slavic Cultures.

SIKOR. 2016. UiT The Arctic University of Norway and the Norwegian Saami Parliament's Saami text collection, Version 8 December 2016. Available online: http://gtweb.uit.no/korp/.

Søgaard, A. 2005. The semantics of possession in natural language and knowledge representation. *Journal of Universal Language* 6(2): 85–115.

Stalnaker, R. 1978. Assertion. In: Cole, P. (ed.), *Syntax and Semantics 9*, 78–95. New York: Academic Press.

Stassen, L. 1996. The switcher's paradise: nonverbal predication in Maltese. *Italian Journal of Linguistics* 8(1): 275.

Stassen, L. 2009. *Predicative possession*. Oxford Studies in Typology and Linguistic Theory. Oxford: Oxford University Press.

Szabolcsi, A. 1981. The possessive construction in Hungarian: a configurational category in a non-configurational language. *Acta Linguistica Academiae Scientiarum Hungaricae* 31: 261–289.

Szabolcsi, A. 1983. The possessor that ran away from home. *The Linguistic Review* 3(1): 89–102.

Szabolcsi, A. 1994. The noun phrase. In: Kiefer, F. & É. Kiss, K. (eds), *The Syntactic Structure of Hungarian*, 179–274. New York: Academic Press.

Tuzharov, G. M. 1987. *Grammatičeskie kategorii imeni sushchestvitel'nogo v mariiskom iazyke* [Grammatical categories of the noun in Mari]. Yoshkar-Ola: Mariiskoe knizhnoe izdatel'stvo.

Volkova, A. 2014. *Licensing reflexivity: unity and variation among selected Uralic languages*. PhD dissertation. Utrecht University.

Zucchi, A. 1995. The ingredients of definiteness and the Definiteness Effect. *Natural Language Semantics* 3: 33–78.

Zwart, J. W. 2002. The antisymmetry of Turkish. *Generative Grammar in Geneva* 3: 23–36.

9. Predicative possession in Permic

Nikolett F. Gulyás

1. Introduction[1,2]

The present chapter discusses the syntactic and the semantic properties of predicative possession in two Permic languages, Komi-Permyak and Udmurt, from the viewpoint of linguistic typology (cf. Stassen 2009, 2013). While the domain of adnominal possession has received much attention in previous works (Bartens 2000; Winkler 2001; Ponomareva 2002; Hausenberg 1998), research on predicative possession has been of marginal interest. Since the two languages studied in this chapter are closely related both genealogically and typologically, one would expect that a certain number of similarities exist in the structural coding and syntactic properties they employ. Although Komi-Permyak and Udmurt share several characteristics in predicative possession, microvariation can be attested principally with respect to syntactic properties such as agreement or omission. In the present chapter, I discuss these similarities and differences in more detail on the basis of data elicited from native consultants.

The chapter is structured as follows. In section 1, I introduce the sociolinguistic and morphosyntactic profile of Komi-Permyak and Udmurt. I give a short overview on data and methods used in the study and then summarize the semantic and structural aspects and classification of predicative possession. Section 2 is dedicated to the description of predicative possession in Permic. I provide a classification of the construction with reference to coding properties as well as to syntactic and semantic features. In section 3 I summarize the findings.

1.1. The Permic languages

Komi-Permyak and Udmurt[3] belong to the Permic subgroup of the Uralic language family. The Komi-Permyak language is spoken in the Perm Region at the upper banks of the Kama river to the West of the Ural Mountains in the former Komi-Permyak Autonomous Okrug. Nowadays, the area belongs to the Perm Region. The All-Russia Population Census in 2010 (Perepis 2010) reported 94,456 ethnic Komi-Permyaks, while the number of native speakers was 63,106. Komi-Permyak has three major dialects, i.e. the northern, the southern and the eastern (Batalova 1975: 3; Bartens 2000: 31–32).[4]

Udmurt (also known as Votyak) is one of the official languages of the Udmurt Republic located at the western hills of the Ural Mountains, between the Kama and the Vyatka rivers. The majority of Udmurts live within the republic, but there are diasporas in the neighbouring republics, primarily in the Republic of Tatarstan and Bashkortostan as well as in the Perm Krai, the Kirov and the Sverdlovsk Oblast. In the 2010 national census in Russia, the number of the ethnic Udmurts was 552,299 and 342,963 people were reported as native speakers (Perepis 2010). The Udmurt language has four major dialectal groups: the northern, the central, the southern and the Beserman (cf. Kel'makov 2003), which can be divided into dialects and subdialects. Permanent contact with Russian speakers has influenced both languages and in Udmurt there are several features at all linguistic levels due to Turkic influence (cf. Bereczki 1998; Agyagási 2012).

Both languages are typically agglutinative, with an extensive verbal and nominal morphology (cf. Csúcs 1990, 1998; Batalova 1975; Bartens 2000). Komi-Permyak has eighteen and Udmurt has seventeen nominal cases (Ponomareva 2010; Kel'makov & Hännikäinen 2008) including accusative, genitive and several locative cases. The basic word order is taken to be SVO for Komi-Permyak and SOV[5] for Udmurt (Rédei 1978; Winkler 2001). Another well-known feature of these languages is that the second- and third-person possessive suffixes have additional functions beside the marking of possession. Earlier approaches (Rédei 1978; Csúcs 1990, 1998) consider these as markers of definiteness, while others (Nikolaeva 2003; Leinonen 2006; Tánczos 2016) claim that they refer to topicality, or indicate emphasis, contrast or associative relationship.

Nominal predicates show variation in the usage of the predicate they co-occur with (*em* in Komi-Permyak and *vań* in Udmurt)[6]. In copular clauses, there is no verbal element in the present tense, (1a), (2a), while the copula is present in other tenses, (1b), (2b), as well as in non-indicative clauses.

(1) a. Me velötiś.
      I teacher
    'I am a teacher.'

   b. Me völ-i velötiś.
      I COP-PST.1SG teacher
    'I was a teacher.' (Komi-Permyak, Permic, Uralic)

(2) a. Mon muso.
      I cute
    'I am cute.'

   b. Mon muso val.
      I cute COP.PST
    'I was cute.' (Udmurt, Permic, Uralic)

On the other hand, both in existential (3), (4) and predicative possessive clauses, the existential verb *em* 'be' and *vań* 'be' is generally used, even in the present tense (Bartens 2000: 292–293; Winkler 2001: 65).

(3) Žir-yn   em-öś   serpas-sez.
    room-INE   be.PRS-PL   picture-PL
    'There are pictures in the room.' (Komi-Permyak)

(4) Škola   gurt-ad   vań-a?
    school   village-2SG.LOC   be.PRS-Q
    'Is there a school in your village?' (Udmurt, Winkler 2001: 65)

1.2. Data and methodology of research

The data used in the present study were collected from various sources. On the basis of the previous literature (Csúcs 1990, 1998; Kel'makov & Hännikäinen 2008; Winkler 2001; Edygarova 2010; Bartens 2000; Batalova 1975; Ponomareva 2002, 2010), I compiled two questionnaires containing 130 sentences in Hungarian that were subsequently translated into the target languages by native speakers. The results were checked by means of pragmatic as well as acceptability judgement tests. For this study, I mainly used these elicited data with some additional information taken from previous works. Unless otherwise indicated, the glossed examples are taken from my own data collection.[7]

1.3. Theoretical background: The domain of predicative possession

The notion of possession is broad and diversified; however, there have been several attempts to create a unified definition of the phenomenon. Stassen (2009: 11) defines possession as a relationship between two entities called the possessor and the possessee. This relation is quite specific: one of the two entities, the possessee, belongs to the other one or, in other words, the possessor controls the possessee (Stassen 2009: 11). In many cases, the relationship between them is asymmetric in that the two entities included in the semantic concept are hardly interchangeable (cf. Langacker 2009). It seems to be a universal feature of human languages that they can distinguish between two main types of possession, i.e. adnominal and predicative. From a semantic point of view, Dixon (2010: 262–263) describes adnominal possession as a set of different types of relationship including ownership, part-whole relationship, kinship relations, associations, etc. Payne (1997: 111) discusses predicative possession under the term *predicate nominals*, by which he means 'clauses in which the semantic content of the predication is embodied in a noun.' In his classification, predicate nominals include existential ('somewhere there is an X'), locational ('X is in somewhere') and predicative possessive clauses ('someone has X'). Another approach describes possession as a state (not an event), considering constructions with a transitive verb such as *have* as atypical (Givón 2001: 134).

Stassen's (2009) typology of predicative possession takes into consideration the following factors:

i) semantic features of the possessor (human vs. non-human)
ii) semantic features of the possessee (animate vs. inanimate)
iii) type of relationship depicted in possession (alienable vs. inalienable)

Alienable possession is often cited as the prototype or a canonical type of possession, yet Stassen (2009: 16) considers it part of a larger CONCEPTUAL SPACE. Besides the prototypical cases, languages can distinguish between INALIENABLE, TEMPORAL AND ABSTRACT POSSESSION. These subtypes of possession can be determined by the values of CONTROL and PERMANENT CONTACT. Permanent contact means that the locational relation between the possessor and the possessee is permanent, while control refers to the 'power' that the possesor has over the possessee. The four subdomains of possession are characterized in Table 9.1:

The semantic criterion for inalienability varies across languages. In most cases, body parts, kinship terms (but in some languages also words denoting social relations or implements of material culture) belong to this subtype of possession (cf. Stassen 2009: 18). An example of inalienable possession can be found in (5).

(5) June has green eyes.

Temporal or physical possession represents another subtype. Example (6) is understandable in the context of a fight in a bar (Stassen 2009: 19).

(6) Look out! That guy has a knife!

In this case, the ownership of the possessee is not so relevant at the time of the utterance. In other words, temporary possession can hold at a certain point in time. In temporary possession, the relationship between the 'possessor' and the 'possessee' 'is typically seen as accidental, or at least as not necessarily permanent' (Stassen 2009: 19). The possessor has certain control over the possessee.

The last subtype of possession in terms of semantics is the abstract possession. The term is self-explanatory, since it refers to an abstract possessee, as illustrated in (7):

(7) I have a headache.

Stassen (2001, 2013) distinguishes at least four subtypes of predicative possession crosslinguistcally. In his classification, there is a fundamental division of the

Table 9.1 Semantic classification of predicative possession (Stassen 2009: 17).

Subtype of possession	Permanent contact	Control
Alienable	+	+
Inalienable	+	−
Temporal	−	+
Abstract	−	−

subtypes depending on transitivity. As it has already been mentioned, in possessive constructions containing a transitive verb, the syntactic subject is the possessor, while the possessee is the direct object of the verb. In the Uralic language family, only Ob-Ugric languages (cf. Havas 2015 and the references therein), Nganasan (see Wagner-Nagy, Chapter 10 in this volume) and South Saami (Kowalik 2016) use a transitive verb in predicative possessive clauses:

(8) Mīša   toŋkə jəm   rȳt   taj-aʌ.
    Misha very good boat   possess-PRS.3SG
    'Misha has a very good boat.' (Surgut Khanty, Ob-Ugric, Uralic; Csepregi 2015)

In turn, the first subgroup of intransitive possession is formally similar to an existential clause, as the verbal element has locational or existential meaning, interpreted as 'to be at', 'to be there', or 'to exist'. Thus, the difference between Stassen's four subtypes is based on the coding of the possessor and the possessed NP. In the first subtype, the possessee bears the role of the syntactic subject and the possessor is coded by an oblique case (often locative). This subgroup is called the locational type. It is important to mention that dative coding found in Hungarian also belongs to this group:

(9) Anná-nak   van   egy   jó   recept-je.
    Anna-DAT   be.PRS.3SGa   good   recipe-3SG
    'Anna has a good recipe.' (Hungarian)

This subtype involves also constructions where the possessor is marked by the genitive case. This is the structure we find in Permic languages (cf. Kondrateva 2011), as depicted in the Komi-Permyak example (10), and also in Mari.

(10) Nasta-lön   em   soj.
     Nastya-GEN   be.PRS.SG   sister
     'Nastya has a sister.' (Komi-Permyak)

Topic possessive clauses, which constitute the third subtype of possession in Stassen's (2009) typology, have the possessee as the syntactic subject, while the possessor is encoded as the topic of the construction. The possessor indicates the 'setting' or 'background' of the sentence that forms the discourse frame that restricts the truth value of the sentence that follows it. Its function can thus be paraphrased by the English phrases such as *given X, with regard to X, speaking about X, as far as X is concerned* (see Stassen 2013 and the references therein):

(11) Si   tuama   si   wewean   wale   rua.
     ANIM.SG   man   TOP   exist   house   two
     'The man has two houses.' (lit. 'As far as the man is concerned, there are two houses.') (Tondano, Northern Sulawesi, Austronesian; cited by Stassen 2013)

The fourth member of intransitive possession clauses is called the conjunctional (see Stassen 2013), or the *with*-type. Here, the possessor is the grammatical subject and the possessee is often encoded by a phrase with an associative or comitative meaning and the relation between the two NP-s describes simultaneity (cf. Stassen 2009: 54–55).

(12) lo   eke   na   bongo.
     3SG   be   and/with   garment
     'She has a garment.' (Sango, Adamawa-Ubangi; cited by Stassen 2013)

To sum up, the four subtypes of predicative possessive clauses in Stassen's (2001, 2009, 2013) typology are the *HAVE*-possessive, the locational possessive including clauses with a possessor marked by the dative or the genitive case, the topic possessive and the *with*-possessive.

2. Classification of predicative possessive clauses in Permic

2.1. Coding properties

The predicative possessive construction follows similar patterns in Komi-Permyak and Udmurt. Both languages use the genitive case for encoding the possessor followed by an existential verb meaning 'to be'. Possessive marking on the possessee, however, is different in the two languages. The possessee is usually unmarked in Komi-Permyak, while the possessive suffix is present in Udmurt:

(13) Nasta-lön   em   ńebög.
     Nastya-GEN   be.PRS.SG   book
     'Nastya has a book.' (Komi-Permyak)

(14) Ol'ga-len   umoj už-ez   vań.
     Olga-GEN   good work-3SG   be.PRS
     'Olga has a good job.' (Udmurt)

In the case of pronominal possessors, the encoding remains the same, i.e. the possessor is marked with the genitive case, and the possessee is usually unmarked in Komi-Permyak, while it bears the possessive suffix in Udmurt (Bartens 2000: 292–293):

(15) Tijan   em   kerku.
     you.PL.GEN   be.PRS.SG   house
     'You have a house.' (Komi-Permyak; Ponomarova 2010: 57)

(16) Mynam   puny-je   vań.
     I.GEN   dog-1SG   be.PRS
     'I have a dog.' (Udmurt)

Another characteristic feature of the Permic languages is differential possessor marking (cf. Winkler 2001: 71). When an adnominal possessive phrase, such as the one depicted in (17a) or (18a), is used as the grammatical object of the clause, the possessor is marked ablative instead of the standard genitive; while the possessee has a special accusative form of the possessive suffix, as shown in (17b) and (18b).

(17) a. Nasta-lön jurśi basök.
Nastya- GEN hair nice.
'Nastya's hair is nice.'

b. Ašyn me kyj-a Nasta-liś jurśi-sö.
tomorrow I braid-FUT.1SG Nastya-ABL hair- ACC.3SG
'I will braid Nastya's hair tomorrow.' (Komi-Permyak)

(18) a. Irina-len stakan-ez ǯök vylyn.
Irina-GEN glass-3SG table on
'Irina's glass is on the table.'

b. Mon tolon kur-i Irina-leś stakan-ze.
I yesterday borrow-PST.1SG Irina-ABL glass-ACC.3SG
'Yesterday I borrowed Irina's glass.' (Udmurt)

Examples (13)–(16) illustrate that the prototypical encoding of predicative possession in Permic languages belongs to the locational subtype in terms of Stassen's (2009) classification. However, the question arises whether there are additional clause types that can be considered as other subtypes of possession in these languages on the basis of his typology. According to my data, there are some candidates but, as we will see, these examples cannot be analysed as real instances of possession. In both languages there exists a transitive verb with the meaning 'to hold' that can appear in possessive-like clauses, as in the Udmurt example (19a). The direct object of the verb is indefinite and unmarked, but despite the rough similarity to *have*-possession, the only acceptable reading of the clause (19a) is a non-possessive one, where the verb has the meaning 'to raise'. An additional argument against the possessive interpretation of the construction stems from the lexical limitations of the verb, since the NP denoting the quasi-possessee is semantically always associated with agriculture. In the case of real possession, such a restriction cannot be formulated. When the possessee is marked by the overt accusative case form, the verb denotes the concrete event of holding (cf. (19b)):

(19) a. Andrej yž voź-e.
Andrey sheep hold-PRS.3SG
'Andrey raises sheep.' (Intended meaning: 'Andrey has a sheep.')

b. Andrej yž-ze voź-e.
Andrey sheep-ACC.3SG hold-PRS.3SG
'Andrey holds his sheep (in his hands).' (Udmurt)

Similar restrictions are observed with additional subtypes of intransitive possessive clauses, such as *with*-possessives. According to acceptability judgement tests provided by native consultants, the syntactic subject *ponö* (my dog) in example (20) can in principle be interpreted as a possessee but the whole clause does not represent predicative possession. While in true predicative possessive clauses the possessee is unmarked, this NP has the possessive suffix:

(20) Me-köt em pon-ö.
I-COM be.PRS.SG dog-1SG
'My dog is with me.' (Intended meaning: 'I have a dog.') (Komi-Permyak)

According to my database, there are no candidates in these languages that can be considered the representatives of further locational or topical possession types. To sum up, we can see that the only type of predicative possession belongs to the subgroup of genitive, and in a broader sence, locative possessives. The possible examples for transitive (*have*) or conjunctional (*with*) possessives do not, in fact, constitute instances of possession.

Yet another type of clauses denoting possession[8], which is usually not discussed as a separate subtype in typologies of possession, can be found in both the languages investigated here. In particular, it includes a possessor marked by the genitive case being the predicate of the clause, while the possessee does not appear in its default form, i.e. it is marked in Komi-Permyak and unmarked in Udmurt. In contrast to typical possessive constructions, instances of that type do not contain an existential verb and their semantic formula is 'x belongs to y'.

(21) a. Kin-lön eta *perna/perna-ys?
who-GEN this cross/cross-3SG
'Whose cross is this?'

b. Eta *perna/perna-ys Petra-lön.
this cross/ cross-3SG Peter-GEN
'This cross belongs to Peter.' (Komi-Permyak)

(22) a. Kin-len ta ly/*ly-ez?
who-GEN this bone/bone-3SG
'Whose bone is this?'

b. Ta ly/*ly-ez puny-len.
this bone/bone-3SG dog-GEN
'This bone belongs to the dog.' (Udmurt)

In the following sections, I will focus only on the most typical expressions of predicative possession in Permic languages, therefore the nominal clauses mentioned above will not be discussed.

2.2. Syntactic properties

2.2.1. Agreement

As was discussed in the previous section, the possessor agrees with the possessee in person and number. Despite being closely related languages, some variation can be observed between them with respect to verbal agreement. While in Komi-Permyak the predicate element *em* (be) agrees with the possessee in number (Ponomareva 2002, 2010), its Udmurt counterpart *vań* (be) is not sensitive to grammatical number (cf. Winkler 2001; Edygarova 2010).[9] However, in the second past tense the verb agrees with its subject also in number (Bartens 2000: 266).

(23) a. Nasta-lön   em   ńebög.
        Nastya-GEN   be.PRS.SG   book
        'Nastya has a book.'

  b. Nasta-lön   em-öś   ńebög-gez.
     Nastya-GEN   be.PRS-PL   book-PL
     'Nastya has books.' (Komi-Permyak)

(24) a. Pijaš-len   apaj-ez   vań.
        boy-GEN   sister-3SG   be.PRS
        'The boy has a sister.'

  b. Pijaš-len   apaj-jos-yz   vań.
     boy-GEN   sister-PL-3SG   be.PRS
     'The boy has sisters.' (Udmurt)

  c. Pijaš-len   apaj-ez   vylem.
     boy-GEN   sister-3SG   be.2PST.SG
     'The boy had a sister.'

  d. Pijaš-len   apaj-jos-yz   vyliľľam.
     boy-GEN   sister-PL-3SG   be.2PST.PL
     'The boy had sisters.' (Udmurt)

Winkler (2001: 65) considers Udmurt *vań* to be a particle not a verb. Other scholars, for example Csúcs (1990: 63), Rédei (1978: 96) and Kondrateva (2011: 79) define these elements either as copulas or as existential verbs. An argument against the interpretation of *vań* and *em* as particles is that they are both inflected for tense[10]:

(25)   Nasta-lön   völi   ńebög.
        Nastya-GEN   be.PST.SG   book
        'Nastya had a book.' (Komi-Permyak)

(26) Pijaš-len   apaj-ez   val.
      boy-GEN   sister-3SG   be.PST
      'The boy had a sister.' (Udmurt)

The fact that the Komi-Permyak predicative element agrees in number with the grammatical subject also supports the verbal interpretation of *em*. Both *em* and *vań* are considered to derive historically from the reconstructed Proto Finno-Ugric existential verb *wole* (to be) (cf. Bartens 2000: 265). On the other hand, the plural marking -*öś* used in predicative and existential clauses in Komi-Permyak is identical to the plural marker of adjectives (cf. Ponomareva 2002, 2010), which makes the verbal interpretation of the element controversial. This question requires further research but in this chapter I will accept the verbal interpretation of the above elements.

In Komi-Permyak predicative possessive clauses, agreement with numerals shows variation. Generally, cardinal numerals in Komi-Permyak require singular heads and do not trigger plural agreement either on the verb or on the possessee, while indefinite numerals, such as *una* (many), modify the possessee, which can appear in a plural form but the agreement in number is not obligatory. In this case, the predicative verb, again, generally agrees with the possessee in number.

(27) a. Petra-lön   em   una   kań.
         Peter-GEN   be.PRS.SG   many   cat
         'Peter has many cats.'

     b. Petra-lön   em-öś   una   kań-(ńez).
         Peter-GEN   be.PRS-PL   many   cat-PL
         'Peter has many cats.' (Komi-Permyak)

2.2.2. Omission

In this section, I discuss the possibility of omission with regard to different constituents of the possessive clause, namely the omission of the existential verb, the pronominal possessors and the possessive suffixes. Edygarova (2010: 238) finds that the existential verb can be omitted in Udmurt when the situation depicted by the verb is 'egophoric'[11] or refers to an abstract entity, cf. (28). However, my informants interpret this sentence as locative rather than possessive. In a similar vein, locational reading appears to be the only one available in the Komi-Permyak counterpart of (28), provided in (29).

(28) Miľam -   d'emokratija!
      we.GEN   democracy
      'We have democracy!'(Alternative translation: 'By us, there is democracy!')
      (Udmurt)

(29) Mijan-   d'emokrat'ija,   a   tijan   d'iktatura.
      we.GEN   democracy   but   you.PL.GEN   dictatorship
      'By us, there is democracy, by you, there is a dictatorship.'
      (Intended meaning: 'We have democracy but you have a dictatorship.') (Komi-Permyak)

Asztalos (2018) presents additional examples of predicative clauses without an existential verb in Udmurt. She claims that the the verb can be omitted in the present tense when the possessee or its modifier is focused, (30).

(30) Saša-len   kyk   nylpi-jez.
      Sasha-GEN   two   child-3SG
      'Sasha has two children.' (Udmurt; Asztalos 2018: 125)

While the omission of lexical possessors is usually ungrammatical in both languages, pronominal possessors can be left out of the construction. In examples (31)–(32) for Komi-Permyak and Udmurt, respectively, possessive agreement on the possessee is obligatory.

(31) a. (Menam)   em   una   ńebög-ö.
          I.GEN   be.PRS.SG   many   book-1SG
          'I have many books.'

      b. Em   una   *ńebög/ńebög-ö.
          be.PRS.SG   many   book/book-1SG
          'I have many books.' (Komi-Permyak)

(32) a. (Mynam)   tros   eš-e   vań.
          I.GEN   many   friend-1SG   be.PRS
          'I have many friends.'

      b. Tros   *eš/eš-e   vań.
          many   friend/friend-1SG   be.PRS
          'I have many friends.' (Udmurt)

The behaviour of possessive suffixes is different in the two languages. In Komi-Permyak, the possessee is generally unmarked,[12] while in Udmurt the possessive suffix can hardly be omitted. There are some cases when possessive agreement is restricted by syntactic or lexical criteria. In Komi-Permyak, for instance, when the possessee has a demonstrative modifier, the possessive suffix cannot be omitted (33a) but whenever it is modified by a cardinal numeral, the presence of the possessive suffix renders the sentence ungrammatical (33b):

(33) a. Nasta-lön   em   eta   perna-*(ys)?
          Nastya-GEN   be.PRS.SG   this   cross-3SG
          'Nastya has this cross.'

  b. Nasta-lön em ötik von/*von-ys da kyk soj/*soj-ys.
    Nastya-GEN be.SG one brother/brother-3SG and two sister/sister-3SG
    'Nastya has a brother and two sisters.' (Komi-Permyak)

On the other hand, the omission of possessive agreement usually results in an ungrammatical (or at least a degraded) clause in Udmurt (cf. Edygarova 2010):

(34) Puny-len *ly/ly-ez   vań.
   dog-GEN bone/bone-3SG be.PRS
   'The dog has a bone.' (Udmurt)

2.2.3. Negation

Negation in the present tense is expressed by the negative existential verb *abu* in Komi-Permyak and *övöl* in Udmurt. The structure of the clause remains the same as in affirmative sentences. The possessor is marked by the genitive case and agrees with the possessee. In Komi-Permyak (35a)–(35b) the possessee triggers number agreement on the predicative element, while in Udmurt clauses in the present tense, there is no verbal agreement in number.

(35) a. Nasta-lön abu   ućöt-žyk soj.
     Nastya-GEN NEG.PRS.SG small-COMP sister
     'Nastya has no younger sister.'

   b. Nasta-lön abu-öś   ućöt-žyk soj-jez.
     Nastya-GEN NEG.PRS-PL small-COMP sister-PL
     'Nastya has no younger sisters.' (Komi-Permyak)

(36) Eš-e-len   apaj-jos-yz övöl.
   friend-1SG-GEN sister-PL-3SG NEG.PRS
   'My friend does not have sisters.' (Udmurt)

In the past tense, both languages use the simple past form of the negative existential verb (37), (38a). Negation in the second past tense in Udmurt can be expressed either by the copula together with the negative existential verb *övöl*, or in a synthetic way by using a negative participle form of the existential verb (38b) (Bartens 2000: 247; Edygarova 2015: 277).

(37) Sylön   ńekör ez   vöv   kań-(ys).
   (s)he.GEN never NEG.PST.3SG be.CNG cat-3SG
   '(S)he never had a cat.' (Komi-Permyak)

(38) a. Tiľad   jyrviź-dy övöl vyl-em.
     you.PL.GEN brain-2PL NEG be-2PST.SG
     'Apparently you are foolish.' (Lit. 'Apparently you did not have a brain.')
     (Udmurt; cited by Edygarova 2015: 277)

b. Gurt-sy-len   ńim-yz   vyly-mte.
   village-3PL-GEN name-3SG   be-NEG.2PST.SG
   'Their village did not have a name.'

2.2.4. Word order

Traditionally, Komi-Permyak is classified as an SVO language, Udmurt is a non-rigid SOV language (Csúcs 1990; Winkler 2001; Rédei 1978; Vilkuna 1998). According to my database, the order of constituents in predicative possessive clauses follows the SVO pattern in Komi-Permyak, however the picture is more complicated in Udmurt. In Komi-Permyak, the possessor is typically clause-initial, followed by the existential verb, while the possessee is in a clause-final position. If the possessee has a modifier, several orders are possible. Example (39a) seems to be the most neutral order, clauses (39b) and (39c) both contain a focused constituent, and in examples (39d) and (39e), there is contrastive focus.

(39) a. Menam   em   una   blog.
        I.GEN   be.PRS.SG   many   blog
        'I have many blogs.'
        Context: Do you have only one blog?

   b. Menam   [una]_FOC   em   blog.
      I.GEN   many   be.PRS.SG   blog
      'I have MANY blogs.'

   c. Menam   [una blog]_FOC   em.
      I.GEN   many blog   be.PRS.SG
      'Many blogs I have.'

   d. Una   blog   menam   em   (a   ńe   ńevna).
      many   blog   I.GEN   be.PRS.SG and   NEG   few
      'I have many blogs (not just a few).'

   e. Una   blog   (a   ńe   ńevna)   em   menam.
      many   blog   and   NEG   few   be.PRS.SG   I.GEN
      'Many blogs I have (not just a few).' (Komi-Permyak)

The constituent order of affirmatives can be the neutral order for polar questions (40a). However, it is more neutral for the existential verb to be placed clause-initially (40b).

(40) a. Nasta-lön   em   (ja)   ur?
        Nastya-GEN   be.PRS.SG   Q   squirrel?
        'Does Nastya have a squirrel?'

b. Em   ja   Nasta-lön   ur?
   be.PRS.SG Q   Nastya-GEN   squirrel?
   'Does Nastya have a squirrel?' (Komi-Permyak)

As for Udmurt, the neutral order of the predicative possessive clause has been considered verb-final (cf. Csúcs 1990: 63; Winkler 2001: 71), but Edygarova (2010) and Asztalos (2018) provide examples in which the existential verb is not in the clause-final position. My data also support their findings. Both clauses in (41a) and (41b) can answer the question 'What is your friend doing?'. In (41c), the verb is placed in the clause-initial position and can be analysed as the focus of the clause:

(41) a. Eš-e-len   vań   blog-ez.
        friend-1SG-GEN   be.PRS   blog-3SG
        'My friend has a blog.'

     b. Eš-e-len   blog-ez   vań.
        friend-1SG-GEN   blog-3SG be.PRS
        'My friend has a blog.'

     c. [Vań]_FOC   blog-ez   eš-e-len.
        be.PRS   blog-3SG friend-1SG-GEN
        'My friend does have a blog.' (Udmurt)

To sum up, the neutral order within the predicative possessive clause is possessor–verb–possessee in Komi-Permyak and possessor–possessee–verb in Udmurt. Generally speaking, the word order in predicative possessive clauses follows the basic word order in the two languages.

2.3. Alienable and inalienable possession

In the previous sections I demonstrated the coding properties and some syntactic features of predicative possession in Permic. It can be seen from the examples above that semantic properties have no or just a limited effect on the formal structure (e.g. coding, negation, word order, etc.) of possessive clauses. As an illustration, we can compare some Udmurt clauses containing constituents with different animacy values. Example (42a) includes a possessor with [+animate, +human] features, while the possessor in (42b) is [+animate, -human]. Finally, example (42c) includes an inanimate possessor.

(42) a. Oľga-len   puny-jez   vań.
        Olga-GEN   dog-3SG   be.PRS
        'Olga has a dog.'

b. Puny-len   ly-jez   vań.
   dog-GEN   bone-3SG   be.PRS
   'The dog has a bone.'

c. Kńiga-len   vyli-jez   övöl.
   book-3SG-GEN cover-3SG   be.NEG.PRS
   'A/The book has no cover.' (Udmurt)

Alienability seems to have only a limited effect on the encoding of predicative possession in Komi-Permyak, since possessees denoting body parts (43a), kinship terms (43b) as well as abstract nouns (43c) can appear with or without a possessive suffix:

(43) a. Maša-lön   em   žir   ńoľ   ćuń-(ys).
        Masha-GEN   be.PRS.SG   only   four finger-3SG
        'Masha has only four fingers.'

     b. Mašha-lön   em   von-(ys).
        Masha-GEN   be.PRS.SG   brother-3SG
        'Masha has a brother.'

     c. Mašha-lön   em   kad-(ys).
        Masha-GEN   be.PRS.SG   time-3SG
        'Masha has time.' (Komi-Permyak)

In Udmurt, the possessive suffix can be omitted when the possessee is an abstract noun.

(44) ...noš miľam   syće   opyt   vań.
     but   we.GEN   such   experience   be.PRS
     '... but we have such an experience.' (Udmurt; Edygarova 2010: 235)

Microvariation can again be attested between the two languages. While the paradigm of possessive suffixes shows no formal alternation in Komi-Permyak, in Udmurt certain nouns denoting body parts (45a), kinship terms (45b) or even abstract concepts (45c) are marked by a possessive suffix containing the vowel -y (as opposed to the canonic marker including the vowel -e).

(45) a. So-len   ki-yz   övöl.
        (s)he-GEN   hand-3SG   be.NEG.PRS
        '(S)he has no hand.'

     b. So-len   vań   vyn-yz.
        (s)he-GEN   be.PRS   brother-3SG
        '(S)he has a brother.'

c. Mynam   ali   dyr-y   vań.
   I.GEN   now   time-1SG   be.PRS
   'I have some time now.' (Udmurt)

Edygarova (2010) proposes that there is a distinction between alienable and inalienable possession in Udmurt. However, the number of nouns taking the possessive suffix of the -y type is limited. Additionally, the alternation between -y and -e type of possessive suffixes can also be described as a morphonological rather than a semantic-based alternation.

3. Conclusion

In the present chapter I provided a description of predicative possession in two Permic languages, Komi-Permyak and Udmurt. We have seen that the prototypical encoding of possession belongs to the genitive (locational) type (Stassen 2013) in which the possessor is marked by the genitive case, the existential verb is inflected for tense (and also for number in Komi-Permyak), and the possessee is the grammatical subject of the clause. There is no clear evidence supporting the existence of other encoding types of predicative possession according to Stassen's (2009) typology, since clauses including a transitive verb with the meaning 'to hold' as well as constructions with an NP marked with the comitative case in Komi-Permyak are not real instances of possession. Despite close genealogic, typological and areal relationship between the two languages, microvariation still can be observed. With respect to the coding properties of predicative possessive clauses, possessees typically do not take a possessive suffix in Komi-Permyak, while possessive suffixes are generally present in Udmurt. In Komi-Permyak, the absence or presence of the possessive suffixes seems to depend on syntactic parameters, whereas semantic features do not affect coding properties. On the contrary, Udmurt possessive suffixes show sensitivity to semantic properties such as alienability, but the alternation is lexically limited and can be interpreted as a morphophonological variation instead of using a semantic criterion in the description. Further research on semantic features is required in order to provide a better understanding on the expression of predicative (and also adnominal) possession in Permic languages.

Notes

1   Abbreviations

1	first person	GEN	genitive
2	second person	INE	inessive
3	third person	LOC	locative
ABL	ablative	NEG	negative (existential) verb
ACC	accusative	NOM	nominative
ANIM	animate	OBJ	object marker
CNG	connegative	PL	plural

COM	comitative		PRS	present tense
COMP	comparative		PST	past tense
COP	copula		Q	interrogative clitic
DAT	dative		SG	singular
FOC	focus		TOP	topic
FUT	future tense			

2. I am grateful to the editors of the volume, in particular to Gréte Dalmi, for comments; to the members of the Typological Database of the Volga Area Finno-Ugric Languages research group at ELTE, Budapest, especially to Erika Asztalos, as well as the members of the Nominal Structures in Uralic Languages project at RIL-HAS, Budapest and in particular to Ekaterina Georgieva for the insightful conversations about the topic. I owe gratitude to the two anonymous reviewers for their extensive and inspiring comments on an earlier version of the chapter. I am also indebted to Larisa Ponomareva, Vasily Epanov and Yulia Speshilova for sharing their invaluable thoughts on the data with me. The present study was supported by the National Research, Development and Innovation Office under grant number NKFI K 125282 and NKFI 125206. Any remaining errors or misunderstandings are the sole responsibility of the author.

3. According to Ethnologue (Lewis, Simons & Fennig 2015), both languages are ranked as 'Developing (5)' on the EGIDS scale, which means that 'the language is in vigorous use, with literature in a standardized form being used by some though this is not yet widespread or sustainable.' Despite this, there are some differences between Komi-Permyak and Udmurt with respect to their sociolinguistic status. Udmurt is an official language, which means that it can be used – at least theoretically – in all formal and informal domains, while Komi-Permyak has no special status. Still it has primarily been used in intrafamiliar and educational communication to some extent (Leshchenko, Dotsenko & Ostapenko 2015).

4. General descriptions of Komi-Permyak and its closest relative, Komi-Zyrian, languages (Rédei 1978; Bartens 2000) usually mention differences in the grammatical properties in the two languages but they consider Komi-Permyak as a dialect of the Komi (or Komi-Zyrian) language. However, Batalova (1975) and Ponomareva (2002) offer sociolinguistic arguments against this view.

5. See Asztalos (2016), among others, for an alternative approach.

6. The verb *lony* (to be) in Komi-Permyak and *luyny* (to be) in Udmurt are used in the future tense, the imperative and the conditional.

7. I follow the conventions of the Leipzig Glossing Rules (https://www.eva.mpg.de/lingua/resources/glossing-rules.php).

8. These sentences can be analysed as nominal predicates although they inherently express the notion of possession.

9. This property is not restricted only to possessive clauses, there is no agreement in number in existential clauses in Udmurt, either (cf. Bartens 2000: 292). Moreover, the verb *luyny* (to be) used in predicative possessive clauses in the future tense is inflected for number.

10. Synchronically, these verb forms are suppletive but from a historical perspective it can be outlined that they developed from the same word stem (cf. Bartens 2000: 265).

11. She does not explain the meaning of the term but on the basis of her examples it may refer to possessors in the first person.

12. One of my informants (Larisa Ponomareva, personal communication) considers the frequent omission of the possessive suffix in Komi-Permyak to be the result of Russian influence. This seems to be a reliable explanation but it requires further research.

References

Agyagási, K. 2012. Language contact in the Volga-Kama area. *Studia uralo-altaica* 49: 21–37.

Asztalos, E. 2016. A fejvégű grammatikától a fejkezdetű felé: generációs különbségek a mai udmurt beszélőközösségben a szórendhasználat és -megítélés terén. [From head-final to head-initial grammar: generational differences among contemporary Udmurt speakers in the field of word order]. In: É. Kiss, K., Hegedűs, A. & Pintér, L. (eds), *Nyelvelmélet és kontaktológia*, 126–156. Budapest: Szent István Társulat.

Asztalos, E. 2018. Szórendi típusváltás az udmurt nyelvben. [Word order type change in Udmurt]. PhD dissertation. Eötvös Loránd Tudományegyetem, Budapest.

Bartens, R. 2000. *Permiläisten kielten rakenne ja kehitys* [The structure and development of the Permic languages]. Mémoires de la Société Finno-Ougrienne 238. Helsinki: Suomalais-Ugrilainen Seura.

Batalova, R. M. 1975. *Komi-permjatskaja dialektologija* [Komi-Permyak dialectology]. Moskva: Izdateľstvo Nauka.

Bereczki, G. [1983] 1998. A Volga–Káma-vidék nyelveinek areális kapcsolatai. [Areal contacts among the languages of the Volga–Kama region]. In: Rédei, K. (ed.), *Ünnepi könyv Bereczki Gábor 70. születésnapja tiszteletére*, 179–205. Budapest: ELTE Finnugor Tanszék.

Csepregi, M. 2015. Habitive constructions (Surgut Khanty). In: Havas, F., Csepregi, M., F. Gulyás, N. & Németh, Sz. *Typological Database of the Ugric Languages*. Budapest: ELTE Finnugor Tanszék. Available online: http://en.utdb.nullpoint.info/type/surgut-khanty/habitive-constructions/habposstrns.

Csúcs, S. 1990. *Chrestomathia Votiacica*. [Votyak Chrestomathy]. Budapest: Tankönyvkiadó.

Csúcs, S. 1998. Udmurt. In: Abondolo, D. (ed.), *The Uralic languages*, 276–304. London: Routledge.

Dixon, R. M. W. 2010. *Basic Linguistic Theory. Volume 2: Grammatical Topics*. Oxford: Oxford University Press.

Edygarova, S. 2010. *Kategorija posesivnosti v udmurtskom jazyke* [The category of possession in the Udmurt language]. PhD dissertation. University of Tartu.

Edygarova, S. 2015. Negation in Udmurt. In: Miestamo, M., Tamm, A. & Wagner-Nagy, B. (eds), *Negation in Uralic Languages*, 265–323. Amsterdam: John Benjamins.

Givón, T. 2001. *Syntax. A Functional-Typological Introduction*. vol. 1. Amsterdam: John Benjamins.

Hausenberg, A.-R. 1998. Komi. In: Abondolo, D. (ed.), *The Uralic Languages*, 305–326. London: Routledge.

Havas, F. (ed.). 2015. Habitive constructions. In: Havas, F., Csepregi, M., F. Gulyás, N. & Németh, S. (eds), *Typological Database of the Ugric Languages*. Budapest: ELTE Finnugor Tanszék. Available online: http://en.utdb.nullpoint.info/content/habitive-constructions.

Keľmakov, V. 2003. *Dialektnaja i istoricheskaja fonetika udmurtskogo jazyka* [Dialectical and historical phonetics of the Udmurt language]. Chast I. Izhevsk: Udmurt State University.

Keľmakov, V. & Hännikäinen, S. 2008. *Udmurtin kielioppia ja harjoituksia* [Grammar and exercise book of Udmurt], 2, korjattu painos. Helsinki: Suomalais-Ugrilainen Seura.

Kondrateva N. 2011. *Kategorija padezha imeni sushchestviteľnogo v udmurtskom jazyke* [The category of nominal case in the Udmurt language]. Izhevsk: Udmurt State University.

Kowalik, R. 2016. Predicative possession in South Saami. MA thesis. Stockholm University.
Langacker, R. W. 2009. *Investigations in Cognitive Grammar*. Berlin: Mouton de Gruyter.
Leinonen, M. 2006. Omistussuhteen ulokkeita: komin possessiivisuffiksin ei-possessiivisista funktioista. [Appendages of possession: Komi possessive suffixes in non-possessive function]. *Journal de la Société Finno-Ougrienne* 91: 93–114.
Leshchenko, Y., Dotsenko T. & Ostapenko T. 2015. Cross-linguistic interactions in bilingual mental lexicon and professional linguistic competence formation: an experimental research with native speakers of the Komi-Permyak and Russian languages. *Procedia - Social and Behavioral Sciences* 214: 1039–1047.
Lewis, M. P., Simons, G. F. & Fennig, Ch. D. (eds). 2015. *Ethnologue: Languages of the World*. Eighteenth edition. Dallas, TX: SIL International. Available online: http://www.ethnologue.com.
Nikolaeva, I. 2003. Possessive affixes in the pragmatic structuring of the utterance: evidence from Uralic. In: Suihkonen, P. & Comrie, B. (eds), *International Symposium on Deictic Systems and Quantification in Languages Spoken in Europe and North and Central Asia*, 130–145. Izhevsk: Udmurt State University; Leipzig: Max Planck Institute of Evolutionary Anthropology.
Payne, T. E. 1997. *Describing Morphosyntax. A Guide for Field Linguists*. Cambridge: Cambridge University Press.
Perepis. 2010. *Vserossijskoj perepis'i nasel'en'ija 2010 goda* [All-Russia census 2010]. Available online: http://www.gks.ru/free_doc/new_site/perepis2010/croc/perepis_itogi1612.htm.
Ponomareva, L. 2002. Fonetika i morfologija mysovskogo-lupinskogo dialekta Komi-permjatskogo jazyka. [Phonetics and morphology of the Mysovsky-Lupinsky dialect of Komi-permyak]. PhD dissertation. Udmurt State University, Izhevsk.
Ponomareva, L. 2010. *Komi-permják nyelvkönyv*. [Komi-Permyak textbook]. Budapest. Manuscript.
Rédei, K. 1978. *Chrestomathia Syrjaenica*. [Zyrian Chrestomathy]. Budapest: Tankönyvkiadó.
Stassen, L. 2001. Predicative possession. In: Haspelmath, M., König, E., Oesterreicher, W. & Raible, W. (eds), *Language Typology and Language Universals*, 2, 954–960. Berlin: de Gruyter.
Stassen, L. 2009. *Predicative Possession*. Oxford: Oxford University Press.
Stassen, L. 2013. Predicative possession. In: Dryer, M. S. & Haspelmath, M. (eds), *The World Atlas of Language Structures Online*. Leipzig: Max Planck Institute for Evolutionary Anthropology. Available online: http://wals.info/chapter/117.
Tánczos, O. 2016. Toward a unified account of the suffix -ez/-jez in Udmurt. Talk given at *the 49th Annual Meeting of Societas Linguistica Europae*, Naples.
Vilkuna, M. 1998. Word order in European Uralic. In: Siewierska, A. (ed.), *Constituent Order in the Languages of Europe*, 173–233. Berlin: Mouton de Gruyter.
Winkler, E. 2001. *Udmurt*. Munich: Lincom Europa.

10. Predicative possessive constructions in Selkup dialects

Beáta Wagner-Nagy

1. Introduction[1,2]

A possessive relation requires two entities, the possessor and the possessee. In a possessive construction, the possessee shows person/number agreement with the possessor (cf. Heine 1997: 3). With respect to the morpho-syntactic properties of the constructions, one can distinguish adnominal (or attributive) possession and predicative possession. The aim of this chapter is to discuss the variety of predicative possessive constructions manifested in Selkup and to show the different strategies employed for this purpose in various Selkup dialects. While the predicative possession strategies in Selkup have been widely investigated (N. Sebestyén 1957; Wagner-Nagy 2011; Budzisch 2015; Poljakova 2016; Kim-Maloney & Kovylin 2016, 2017, among others), the topic still requires further research.

The chapter is organized as follows. In section 1, a short introduction to the Selkup language is given (1.1) and the corpora used in the present study are discussed (1.2). In section 2, I outline the typological background of my study and discuss the types of predicative possessive constructions. In 2.2, I give an overview of the Selkup predicative possession constructions and define the most frequent types. It will be shown that the core predicative possessive construction is the existential construction of the locative type and, therefore, the possessor is locative-marked.

1.1. Overview of Selkup

Selkup (also known as Ostyak Samoyed) together with Nenets, Enets and Nganasan as well as the already extinct Kamas and Mator, belongs to the Samoyedic branch of the Uralic language family. With the latter two, i.e. Enets and Nganasan, Selkup builds the so-called Southern Samoyedic group. Thus, strictly speaking, it is not a Finno-Ugric but a Samoyedic language.

Selkup is spoken in South-Western Siberia, along the tributary rivers of Yenisei and Ob in the Tomsk Region, the Yamal-Nenets Autonomous District and the Krasnoyarsk Krai. There are numerous regional dialects of Selkup; they are commonly divided into three or four main dialectal groups: Northern Selkup, Central Selkup, Southern Selkup and Ket Selkup, but some researchers place the Ket dialects into the Southern Selkup group (for details relating to the dialectal classification, see Janurik 1978 and Bekker et al. 1995: 23). Northern Selkup is spoken in the Yamal Nenets Autonomous district. The Central dialect is spoken in the Krasnoyarsk Krai, while the Southern and Ket dialects are spoken in the Tomsk Region along the rivers Ob and Ket'. Table 10.1 shows the dialectal classification.

Selkup is a critically endangered language on the verge of extinction. In their original ethnic territory, Selkup people are now in a minority position, the majority of the inhabitants being speakers of Russian. While the statistical data show a slight increase in the number of people declaring themselves to be Selkup, the ratio of Selkup speakers is constantly decreasing. According to the latest official Russian census carried out in 2010,[3] there are only 3,527 people who claim to be ethnically Selkup. However, only about 29 per cent of them speak one of the Selkup varieties. It must be mentioned that only ten to fifteen speakers are estimated for the Central and Southern Selkup dialects. Concerning the age of the speakers, Selkup is only spoken by the elderly and the language is no longer being passed on to younger generations.

Selkup is a typical agglutinative language with the predominant SOV word order, however the pragmatic organization permits word order changes and, under the

Table 10.1 Selkup dialects.

Dialectal group	Dialect	Sub-dialect
Northern	Taz	Middle-Taz
		Upper Taz
	Baikha	
	Yelogui	
	Tolka	
Central	Tym	
	Narym	
	Vasyugan	
	Vakh	
Southern	Ob	Middle-Ob
		Upper-Ob
	Chaya	Lower Chaya
		Upper Chaya
	Chulym	
	Ket	Middle-Ket
		Upper-Ket

influence of Russian, the word order can be changed to SVO. This language typically employs postpositions. There are no prepositions recorded, but the development of preverbs can be observed. The modifier always precedes the head.

Selkup has a large inventory of cases; most scholars (Bekker et al. 1995; Kuznecova, Helimskij & Gruškina 1980, among others) distinguish thirteen or fourteen cases. The case inventory consists of three grammatical cases (nominative, accusative and genitive) and at least four cases denoting location (e.g. lative, elative, locative and prolative). There are two locative cases: the common locative (-qɨn/-qɨt), which is present in all dialects, and the so-called adessive case (-nan), which is used only in the Central and Southern dialects. The latter participates in the formation of possessive constructions (see section 2.1.1). Additionally, there are some minor cases such as dative, instrumental/comitative, translative, caritive and coordinative.

1.2. The data used in this study

This study is predominantly corpus-based, yet, occasionally, data from the existing grammatical and typological descriptions were used. Most of the examples were taken from the Selkup Language Corpus (SLC), which consists of only already published texts from Northern, Central and Southern dialects.[4] Actually, this corpus contains 127 morphologically glossed and further annotated texts with 6,512 sentences (38,738 tokens). The texts were collected from thirty-five different speakers. Additionally, I used some Northern Selkup examples that come from the Selkup Corpus compiled in the INEL-Project.[5] This corpus contains thirty-five transcriptions with 1,021 sentences (5,514 tokens). Table 10.2 shows the amount of the materials[6].

1.3. General characteristics of predicative possessive constructions

It is characteristic for possession expressed through a predicative construction that the sentence obligatorily includes a verbal predicate. Typologically, the constructions can be further divided into sub groups. However, there is no agreement among researchers as to their number (for further information see Stassen 2001: 954, 2009, 2013). According to Stassen's typology, the following sub groups of the predicative possessive relation can be differentiated: the so-called transitive constructions (*HAVE*-possessive) and the construction that is essentially based on the existential *be*-construction. Transitive constructions are not typical for the Uralic languages, but Khanty, Mansi and Nganasan use this kind of construction (see Wagner-Nagy 2011).

Table 10.2 Amount of the materials.

Dialectal Group	Sentences	Tokens
Northern	2,039	11,371
Central	1,490	10,265
Southern	3,934	22,164

The so-called existential-possessive construction is expressed by a sentence whose predicate is a verb meaning 'to be', 'to exist' or 'to be there'. The possessor normally does not have the subject function in the sentence. Based on how the possessor is coded, Stassen (2009) distinguishes the following sub types: oblique possessive, topic possessive and conjunctional possessive.

Uralic languages use the oblique possessive construction, which has at least two subtypes. The first expresses locational relation. It is characteristic of some Uralic languages that the possessor is marked locative case (e.g. lative, adessive, etc.). The second subtype is the so-called genitive possession. Under intensive Turkic influence, some Uralic languages developed a genitive possessive construction (e.g. Mari, Kamas or Udmurt). Especially the Samoyedic languages, such as Nganasan and Selkup, can code the possessor with nominative case (see section 2.1.2. below and Wagner-Nagy 2011, 2015).

Heine (1997, 2001) categorizes predicative possessive constructions slightly differently. He argues that possessive constructions are derived from other constructions via grammaticalization processes. All constructions describe the so-called event schemas. He identifies eight event schemas that underlie possessive constructions: Action, Location, Companion, Genitive, Goal, Source, Topic and Equation (Heine 1997: 47). For example, the Action Schema that describes the proposition 'X takes Y' may develop into a construction bearing the meaning 'X has Y' if it undergoes a conceptual transfer (semantic change).

The possessive construction retains some morpho-syntactic features of the source construction. Thus, the possessee of the Action Schema is typically encoded as the direct object of the sentence as in German: *Peter hat einen Tisch* ('Peter has a table'). The *habeo*-verb comes normally from a prototypical transitive verb with the meaning 'take, keep'. If the source is the Location Schema ('Y is located by X'), the possessor is the locative argument of the verb; the possessee is the grammatical subject of the sentence. In the case of the Goal Schema (X exists for/to Y), the possessor is the dative adjunct, while in the Genitive Schema ('X's Y exists'), it is a genitive modifier of the possessed NP. The situation is a little bit different in the Companion Schema ('X is with Y'), in which the possessor is the subject and the possessee is the comitative adjunct in the sentence. In the Topic Schema ('as for X, Y exists'), the possessor is the clausal topic. Heine argues that the possessor figures as a possessive modifier of the possessee. In this respect, this structure is similar to the Genitive Schema, but in the Genitive Schema, the possessor is encoded as a genitive modifier of the possessee, in the Topic Schema that is not the case. The Source Schema (Y exists from X) and the Equation Schema (Y is X's) do not occur in Uralic languages. In the following, I will use Heine's categorization, but in some cases I will refer to Stassen's categorization as well.

2. Possessive constructions in Selkup

Selkup uses the so-called existential (or intransitive) possessive construction. Thus, the predicate of the possessive sentence is the verb *e:qo* (be). In this sense, Selkup is a typical Uralic language. Specific existential verbs present in all Northern Samoyedic languages are unknown.

Before presenting the attested constructions that I consider typical, I give an overview of earlier research. I predominantly focus on Kim-Maloney & Kovylin's descriptions (2016, 2017), in which the authors postulate the following possessive constructions for Selkup: locational construction (Location Schema), genitive construction (Genitive Schema) as the core construction, conjunctional (this corresponds to Heine's Companion Schema) and HAVE-possessive (Action Schema) as peripheral constructions. In my opinion, there are only three possessive constructions in Selkup: Location, Topic and potentially Genitive Schema. Before I analyse the respective examples illustrating these types, I provide the reasons for which the other constructions are not present in Selkup.

Kim-Maloney & Kovylin (2016, 2017) assume the existence of the transitive construction with a grammaticalized verb 'have'. In their opinion, in the Southern dialects, the verb *war-* (in Northern dialects *wəri-*) with the primary meaning 'keep' can be interpreted as a 'have' verb. It is a well-known fact that among Uralic languages only Khanty, Mansi and Nganasan use the Action Schema (transitive possessive construction). However, the statement that other Uralic languages also apply transitive possessive constructions to express possession has occurred many times in the literature. For instance, Hajdú (1968) postulates the transitive construction also for Nenets, and Honti (2007, 2014), on the basis of Kim's description (1981), postulates it for Selkup, as well.

As it has already been mentioned, it is a typologically and historically well-known fact that the verbs 'keep', 'hold' and 'take' can be the source of the predicate in possessive constructions. It can undergo desemantization and, consequently, be used in a new context, namely in the possessive construction. Depending on the extent of the grammaticalization process, the verb might be used in both functions simultaneously, as, for example, in Nyulnyulan (cf. McGregor 2001: 69). However, at the end of the process the verbs typically lose their original meaning and they exclusively occur as the predicates of the construction, as in German. We can only view it as the end of the grammaticalization process if inalienable possession can also be expressed by the respective verb, i.e. provided the verb is used in both sentence types 'I have a father' (kinship terms as social inalienable possession) and 'I have blue eyes' (body parts). As opposed to Ob-Ugric languages, in which the verb 'keep' is indeed grammaticalized as the predicate of the transitive possessive construction, it is not the case in Nenets or in Selkup. In both the languages, the verb 'keep' is used only in sentences that deal with animal husbandry. Neither the examples given by Kim-Maloney & Kovylin (2016: 16), nor the data from the corpora corroborate the claim regarding the transitive construction. The following example shows the use of this verb in the Southern dialects (for examples from Nenets, see Wagner-Nagy 2011: 228).

(1) a. suːru-la-p war-za-t
wild.animal-PL-ACC keep-PST-3PL
'They kept the cattle.'
Middle Ob dialect [d_SEV_1981_SisterBrother_flk.007]

b. nadak neb warə-nda
girl duck keep-INFER.3SG
'It seems that the girl keeps a duck.'
Tym dialect [Kim-Maloney & Kovylin 2017: 31]

Speakers of the Northern dialects use this verb in connection with animals, as well. The following sentences, both taken from a corpus, illustrate this fact. In (2a), wild animals were introduced, and they are also the dropped object of in (2b).

(2) a. Imaqota ponä pakta, suːrɨ-ľaː-qi-p moːt
old.woman outwards jump.3SG wild.animal-DIM-DU-ACC tent
tultɛː-ŋɨ-tɨ.
bring-AOR-3SGOBJ$_C$
'The old woman went out on the street and carried two animals into the tent.'
Taz dialect [d_ NN_197X_YoungBoy_flk.012]

b. Wərɨ-q-olam-nɨ-tɨː.
keep-INF-begin-AOR-3DUOBJ$_C$
'They began to keep them.'
Taz dialect [d_ NN_197X_YoungBoy_flk.013]

In sum, it can be concluded that there are no transitive possessive predicate constructions (Action Schema) in Selkup.

As already observed, Selkup uses the existential construction, in which the possessor can be marked through several case markers. According to Kim-Maloney & Kovylin (2016, 2017), the conjunctional construction (Companion Schema) also occurs in Selkup, but the authors, as well as Budzisch (2015: 48), consider this structure marginal. According to Stassen (2009: 54fn)[7] this kind of construction is typical for languages of the Eastern Austronesian and Papuan area, the Northern part of South America or sub-Saharan Africa, but Heine (1997: 54) also provides an example from Portuguese. However, this construction is not typical of languages in Siberia, as it only occurs in some Altaic languages and Chukchi (Stassen 2009: 358–359). Therefore, if Selkup had this construction, it would be significantly typologically different from the other Uralic languages of the Ob-Yennisei area. A closer look at these sentences reveals that this construction is used only in a few lexicalized forms, which replace a non-verbal predicate. The sentence in (3a) represents an example given by Kim-Malony & Kovylin (2016) from the Ket dialect, and (3b), a construction from the Northern dialectal group, is taken from the corpus.

(3) a. i tʲumbane assɨ orup-se e-ŋ.
and wolf NEG force-INSTR be-3SG
'The wolf is not strong. (lit. the wolf is not with force)'
Ket dialect [Kim-Maloney Kovylin 2016:17]

b. Tat onɨ-ľ or-s ɛː-ŋa-ntɨ.
you yourself-ADJVZ force-INSTR be-AOR-2SG
'You are strong.' (lit. 'you are with your force.')
Taz dialect [a_KNK_1965_BearAndHare_flk.017]

The construction above can naturally have a possessive interpretation, as well, i.e. 'The wolf has force' and 'You have force', respectively. However, the main question is whether we can find examples illustrating a similar type of construction with another possessee. Are there any sentences with an inalienable subject, for example kinship or body part or permanent possessee? The answer to a question along these lines is 'no', as there are no examples for Companion Schema as a possessive construction in the corpora. In consequence, it can be claimed that this construction is highly unlikely to express possession in Selkup. At the same time, there are numerous examples in which the noun 'force' in the instrumental case appears in the sentence as an intensifying adverb modifying adjectives, (4a), or even as an adjunct adverbial, (4b).

(4) a. Filipp or-sa soma qum
  Philip force-INST good man
  'Philip is a very good man.'
  Ket dialect [a_AR_1965_RestlessNight_transl.027]

 b. ow-sʲe   zašiba-nu-ŋ
  force-INST knock-AOR-3SG
  'He hit (it) hard.'
  Ket dialect [d_KKN_1971_Itja_flk.023]

In the following sections, the properties for the coding of the possessor and the possessive schema used in Selkup will be described.

2.1. Coding of the possessor and the possessee in affirmative sentences

As mentioned above, Selkup uses more than one schema for the coding of the possessor. The most common is the Location Schema, which occurs in all dialectal groups. Beyond that, one finds the Genitive and the Topic Schemas as well. It is typical for Selkup predicate possessive sentences that if the possessor is can be elicited from the context, it is generally not overt in the sentence. In what follows, I present a construction in which the possessor is a locative argument of the predicate and, subsequently, I discuss the Topic and Genitive Schemas.

2.1.1. Location Schema

In this kind of construction, the predicate is a conjugated form of the verb *eːqo* (be), and the possessor NP is encoded by the locative case or with a locational postposition. The possessee NP is the grammatical subject of the predicate and appears in nominative. Dialectal groups differ according to the coding of the possessor. The common way to code the possessor in the Central and Southern dialects is coding with the adessive case *-nan*. The following sentences display a typical locative possession construction from these dialectal groups. Example (5a) shows a sentence with a noun as the possessor, and in (5b) and (5c) the possessor is pronominal. These two examples suggest that there are apparently no constraints regarding the word class of the possessor.

(5) a. ... tudo-n-nan šidɨ haj e-ja.
　　　crucian-GEN-ADES two eye be-AOR.3SG
　　'... the crucian has two eyes.'
　　Vasyugan dialect [d_ChND_1983_Nikita.007]

　b. tab-ɨ-štja-nan e-ppa kɨba mɨ-la
　　 s/he-EP-DU-ADES be-PST.REP.3SG small thing-PL
　　 'They had children.' (lit. 'small things.')
　　 Middle Ob dialect [d_TMR_1967_Pönege_flk.002]

　c. tab-ɨ-stja-n-naːn jeː-qa-n neː-t
　　 s/he-EP-DU-GEN-ADES be-AOR.3SG daughter-3SGPOSS
　　 'They have a daughter.'
　　 Middle Ob dialect [d_PMP_1961_Fairytale_flk.002]

The examples above also demonstrate that the possessee has to be marked with a possessive suffix if it is inalienable (kinship term or human body part). Although the possessee in (5b) is a semantically inalienable kinship term in the form of a metaphor (*small thing* meaning 'child'), that can be the reason why this word is not obligatorily marked with the possessive suffix. In (5a) *eye* is a body part, but it does not belong to a human being.

The Northern dialects do not have the locative-animate case (*-nan*), and, although the common locative case (*-qin*) is not used here as a possessor marker, the Location Schema appears as well. Possessor marking is carried out by the locative postposition *miqin/ miqit* (by, at, near to). This is the common locative case form of the noun *mi* (thing). This noun has been grammaticalized as a locational postposition. It is used mostly in possessive sentences, but there are a few examples in which the postposition is used in locational meaning, as in (6) below. In other dialects, as in Ket, the postposition is used in temporal expressions such as *qarimiqin* [*qari* (morning) + *mi-qin* (thing-LOC)] (in the morning), etc., though its usage in a possessive construction is not attested.

(6) təm ila košar mɨqɨt
　　 s/he live.3SG mammooth at
　　 'He lives at the mammooth.'
　　 Taz dialect [d_KaIA_1973_Natenka_flk.064]

The possessive construction with this postposition can typically be found if the possessor has already been mentioned in the text, and the speaker, possibly for the sake of emphasis, nevertheless repeats it. In most such cases, the possessor is referred to by a pronoun but the speaker also repeats the possessor noun. The construction in the Northern dialect is illustrated by a short text passage. Sentence (7a) introduces the possessor (a woman) and in (7b) she appears as the possessor.

(7) a. iːma ili-mpa ira-sɨmɨ-lʼ
　　 woman live-PST.REP.3SG husband-PROPR-ADJZV
　　 'There lived a married woman....'
　　 Taz dialect [a_KMG_1976_BriefVacation_nar.004]

b. iːma-n   mɨqɨt nɔːkɨr kɨp-l̥a   ija-iː-tɨ   ɛː-sa
   woman-GEN   at   three small-DIM   child-PLPOSS-3SGPOSS   be-PST.3SG
   'This woman had three small children.'
   Taz dialect [a_KMG_1976_BriefVacation_nar.005]

As was mentioned above, the pronominal possessor can also be marked by the postposition (8):

(8) ilɨ-mpa   imaqota,   təp-ɨ-n   mɨqɨn   ɛ-ppa
    live-PST.REP.3SG old.woman   s/he-EP-GEN   at   be-PST.REP.3SG
    iːja-tɨ,   Ičakɨčɨka
    child-3SGPOSS   Ichakychika
    'Once there was an old woman, she had got a son, Ichakychika.'
    Taz dialect [d_KVM_1977_IchaAndNenets_flk.001]

In the corpus, there are only sentences in which the possessee is inalienable and it is marked with the possessive suffix. A few examples with alienable possessee are found in the descriptions, as well. In these examples, the possessee never bears the possessive suffix:

(9) teb-ə-n   miɣɨt   qil̥   čeŋga
    s/he-EP-GEN   at   fish   EX.NEG.3SG
    'S/he does not have fish.'
    Taz dialect [Kim-Maloney & Kovylin 2017: 30]

2.1.2. Topic Schema

In this schema, the grammatical subject is the possessed NP. The possessor takes up the sentence-initial position and is unmarked, i.e. it stands in the nominative. Thus, the possessor is usually in topic position, and the possessee is the focus of the clause and represents new information. The sentence ends with the verb *ɛːqo* (be) agreeing with the possessee. The negative existential verb *čäːŋkɨqo* also has to agree in person and number with the possessee. This schema is not often used in positive sentences; most of the examples are negated sentences (see section 3.2 below). The following sentence shows this structure in affirmative sentences.

(10) a. ukkɨr   qup   27   kanak-tɨ   e-ŋa
         one   person   27   dog-3SGPOSS   be-AOR.3SG
         'A man has 27 dogs.'
         Taz dialect (Erdélyi 1969: 31/a)

     b. a   imaqota   qəːlɨ-tɨ   čäːŋka
         but   elderly.woman   fish-3SGPOSS   NEG.EX.3SG
         'But the elderly woman did not have any fish.'
         Taz dialect [d_BEP_1973_Itja2_flk.003]

c. puja-l'ʒi-ga   wargɨ   haj   ɛ-ja,   ug-ɨ-t   karɨn
   owl-DIM-DIM   big   eye   be-AOR.3SG   beak-EP-3SG.POSS   crooked
   ɛ-ja
   be-AOR.3SG
   'An owl had big eyes, had a crooked beak.'
   Vasyugan dialect [d_ChDN_1983_Time_flk.025]

As is demonstrated by these sentences, if the possessee is animate, (10a) and (10b), it must bear the possessive suffix. If the possessee is inanimate, as in (10c), it does not require the possessive suffix.

It is typical for Selkup possessive sentences that the possessor is not overt in the sentence if it is understood through the context. In this case, the possessed entity is obligatorily marked by the possessive suffix, which indicates the person and number of the possessor. This construction can be considered as a subtype of the Topic Schema and it appears in all dialects. The following examples illustrate the structure.

(11) a. nuŋa-tɨ   ɛ-ppa
         tambourine-3SGPOSS   be-PST.REP.3SG
         'He had a tambourine.'
         Vasyugan dialect [d_NN_1973_Shaman_flk.002]

   b.   nagur   neː-di   e-ku-nda
         three   daughter-3DUPOSS   be-DUR-INFER.3SG
         'It seems, they had three daughters.'
         Narym dialect [d_SAA_1971_ThreeSisters_flk.002]

2.1.3. Genitive Schema

Some researchers, such as Bekker et al. (1995), as well as Kim-Maloney & Kovylin (2016, 2017), argue that the possessor can also be marked by genitive in Selkup. At the same time, they point out that these constructions are very rarely used. Corpus data corroborate this claim. In Northern Selkup, we have only two examples of this kind of construction (12a) and (12b). Both sentences are recorded from the same speaker. Although they are from two different texts, they constitute the variants of the same text. In example (12b), the possessor does not precede the possessee. The speaker places it after the possessee as a kind of clarification. Here, the possessor functions as a post-modifier of the possessee:

(12) a. Ukkɨr   ɔːmti-ľ   qoː-t   ńaľa-tɨ   ɛː-ppi-nti
         one   horn-ADJVZ   chief-GEN   daughter-3SGPOSS   be-PST.REP-INFER.3SG
         (ɛː-ppa)
         be-PST.REP.3SG
         'A tsar has a daughter.'
         Taz dialect [a_NEP_1965_FoolInSackCoat_flk.007]

   b.   Ukkɨr   naľa-tɨ   ɔːmti-ľ   qoː-n, ….
         one   daughter-3SGPOSS   horn-ADJVZ   chief-GEN
         'The tsar has a daughter …'
         Taz dialect [a_NEP_1965_ThreeBrothers_flk.12]

The question arises whether this construction can be used with a pronominal possessor. There is no simple answer to this question, as the genitive form of some pronouns in Selkup dialects coincides with the nominative form; for example the genitive form of *man/mat* (I) is *man*. However, given that some variation can be observed in the nominative form, *man* cannot be unambiguously considered the genitive form. As opposed to this, the forms of the 3SG pronoun (Taz *tǝp* (s/he) vs. *tǝpin* (her/his)) do not coincide. Given that, the case of the possessor can be identified (for more information about the forms see Janurik 1975–1976). There are no examples in the corpus for any of the dialects that would support this view. The authors mentioned above also fail to cite examples that would unambiguously prove the genitive marking. As a result, the status of this construction is uncertain.

2.2. Negated constructions

As a rule, in the negative construction the negative existential verb, occupying the sentence-final position and agreeing with the possessee NP in number and person, has to be used. The form in the Northern dialects is *čäŋki-*, while in the Central and Southern dialects it is *tangu-/čangu-*, etc. The possessor is marked with nominative, locative or dropped entirely. In negated sentences, the possessor is seldom overt; it is typically referred to by the possessive suffix on the possessed. The possessor can always be omitted if it has already been mentioned previously in the text, since, in this case, a reference is sufficient. The negative existential verb can naturally take on mood or tense markers, too; for example the past marker as in (13c):

(13) a. taššu-k,   mi:-nan   po: ťa:g-wa
       cold-ADV   we.DU-ADES   tree   NEG.EX-AOR.3SG
       'It is cold and we do not have wood.'
       Middle Ob dialect [d_ILP_1981_ItjaGrandmother_flk.009]

   b. a   imaqota   qǝ:li-tɨ   čä:ŋka
      but   old.woman   fish-3SGPOSS   NEG.EX.3SG
      'And the old woman doesn't have fish.'
      Taz dialect [d_BEP_1973_Itja2_flk.003]

   c. ni   porqɨ-tɨ,   ni   pe:mɨ-tɨ   čä:ŋka-sa
      NEG   clothing-3SGPOSS NEG   footwear-3SGPOSS   NEG.EX-PST.3SG
      'He had neither clothing nor footwear.'
      Taz dialect [a_SAI_1965_LittleDoll_flk.002]

In the Central and Southern dialects, another negative existential predicate (*ńetu*) can be used as well (cf. Bekker et al. 1995b: 240). This element is definitely a Russian loanword. This negative predicate is so widely adopted in some dialects that it can combine with the 3SG verbal suffix and with the aorist marker, thus it is grammaticalized as a verb. Accordingly, the form of the particle is *ńetu-wa*, *ńetu-k*, *ńetu-ya* or *ńetu-pa*. The data from the Tym and Narym dialects show that the negative element *ńetu* can take both positions: it can occur sentence-final, as in Russian, and can also precede a noun, but in the possessive sentences, it obligatorily occupies the sentence-final position. The two negative existentials coexist in some dialects (e.g. Narym and Middle Ob) and can both occur in the same sentence. Sporadically, it also occurs in other dialects. It is typically attested in the language use of speakers who speak the so-called mixed dialect. In this case, the speakers relocated from the Ob region to other dialect areas, for example to the Tym river region, taking along the characteristics of their original dialect, including the negative particle ńetu. While this negative particle does not occur in the utterances of the speakers representing the pure Tym dialect, speakers of the mixed Narym-Tym dialect widely use it (for more details, see Kovylin 2016: 104).

(14) a. tab-nan   or-t   nʲetu-pa.
        s/he-ADES   force-3SGPOSS   NEG-AOR.3SG
        'He had no force.'
        Narym dialect [d_MNS_1984_DaughterOfEarth_flk.013]

   b. ti-nan   wadʒe-l   nʲetu,   nʲajo-m   čangu.
      you.PL-ADES   meat-2SGPOSS   NEG   bead-1SGPOSS   NEG.EX.3SG
      'You do not have meat, I do not have bread.'
      Narym dialect [Dulson-Archive, Volume 65:147]

2.3. Word order in possessive constructions

In the recent literature on the typology of predicative possession, the phenomenon has often been discussed together with existential and locational sentences (Freeze 1992; Payne 1997; Dryer 2007). The reason for this is that the three sentence types contain the same elements. The pivot element (or theme) of locatives and possessives is usually definite, while in existential sentences it is indefinite. Selkup does not have articles and, therefore, it expresses the definiteness of the NP by other means. It can be a possessive suffix or the word order. Some languages without articles, for example Russian, move the (unmarked) definite theme to the subject position in locative sentences. The questions that arise here are which word order is used in Selkup in the possessive constructions and what is the relation between the word order of locative, existential and possessive constructions? As we could see in the majority of the examples above, the sentence-initial position in possessive constructions expressed by the Locative Schema is occupied by the locative element (see section 2.1.1. above). Consequently, its word order is not identical to the word order of locative sentences; it is its direct opposite. We have seen above that in possessive sentences with a Location Schema the theme (pivot) element is unmarked. Example (15a) shows a possessive sentence with Loc-Th-Cop word order, while the word order in the locative (15b) is Th-Loc-Cop.

(15) a. Teb-i-sta-ɣe-nen   oqɨr   kɨbańaʒa   je-s.
        s/he-EP-DU-DU-ADES   one   boy   be-PST.3SG
        'They had a boy.'[8]
        Upper Ob dialect [d_PVD_1966_BoyDevil_flk.002]

b. Kɨba-qup   twe:-l   čebo-ɣɨt   e-ppa.
   small-person   birchbark-ADJVZ   cradle-LOC   be-PST.REP.3SG
   'The child was in the cradle.'
   Narym dialect [d_SAA_1984_MyGrandmother_nar.007]

It can be argued that in most cases, the order of the constituents is possessor-possessee. However, as Budzisch (2017: 49) points out, depending on the information structure of the sentences, the possessee can be shifted in the topic position, as well. In my opinion, though, this does not depend solely on information structure. The use of this word order is typical for texts produced by speakers using a heavily Russian-influenced syntax. The number of such sentences is rather small. I provide the Russian translation of the following examples ((16a) and (16c), respectively), in order to demonstrate the phenomenon.

(16) a. Lentu   ńego   ńet,
        ribbons   at him   NEG.EX.3SG

        ńikto   emu   žertvy
        nobody   him   sacrifice

        ńe   prinosit.
        not   brings

   b. *ržade*   tab-ɨ-n-nan   ťangu-k,   kudɨ-nnaj
        ribbons   he-EP-GEN-ADES   NEG.EX-3SG   who-EMPH

        tap-ə-n   ko-m   aya   pen-gu-d
        he-EP-DAT   sacrifice-acc   NEG   put-dur-3sg.obJ$_c$
        'He has no ribbons, no one sacrifices anything to him.'
        Vasyugan dialect [d_ChDN_1983_IdjasTown_flk.015]

   c. U ńix   byli   ďeti...
      at them   were   children

   d. tab-la-nan   ɛ-za:-dɨt   ɛlma:t-la...
      he-PL-ADES   be-PST-3PL   child-PL
      'They had children ...'
      Middle Ob dialect [d_ILP_1981_ItjaOneEyedDevil_flk.002]

As Budzisch (2017: 58) argues, sentences with the zero copula are also encountered, yet their use is not widespread. As the following sentence illustrates, the word order is the same as in the common structure, thus the order Loc-Th is preserved.

(17) tab-ɨ-n-nan   na:n   nɛ-j-qum-nan   okkɨr   i:-t
     s/he-EP-GEN-ADES   this   woman-ADJZV-person-ADES   one   son-3SGPOSS
     'She, this woman has a son.'
     Middle Ob dialect [d_PMP_1961_Fairytale_flk.044]

3. Summary

As we have seen above, Selkup uses two different schemas for the expression of possession, i.e. the Topic and the Location. In the former, the possessor can be covert in all dialectal groups. The possessee can be marked or unmarked, but the use of the suffix is not optional–it depends on the semantic characteristics of the possessee. In the latter, if the possessee belongs to the category of social inalienable possession (i.e. kinship), it is obligatorily marked with a possessive suffix. If the possessee belongs to other categories, such as body parts, it does not take the possessive suffix. In the case of the Topic Schema, the animate possessee is obligatorily marked with the possessive suffix. The third schema, i.e. the Genitive, is debatable. There is no evidence that would unambiguously confirm the existence of this construction. Table 10.3 gives an overview of the constructions and their characteristics.

Table 10.3 Selkup possessive construction.

	Location Schema		Topic Schema	Word order
	Case suffix	Postposition		
Northern dialect		√	√	LocThcop
Central dialect	√		√	LocThcop
Southern dialect	√		√	LocThcop

Notes

1 *Abbreviations*

ACC	accusative case	GEN	genitive case
ADES	adessive	HAB	habitual aspect
ADJVZ	adjectivizer	INF	infinitive
ADV	adverbial	INFER	inferential marker
AN	animate	INSTR	instrumental case
AOR	aorist tense	LOC	locative case
COP	copula	NEG	negative particle
DAT	dative case	OBJ$_c$	objective conjugation
DIM	diminutive marker	PL	plural number
DU	dual number	POSS	possessive marker
DUR	durative marker	PROPR	proprietive
EMPH	emphatic marker	PST	past tense
EP	epenthetic	REP	reportative marker
EXIST	existential	TH	theme

2 A part of this publication has been produced in the context of the joint research funding of the German Federal Government and Federal States in the Academies' Programme, with funding from the Federal Ministry of Education and Research and the Free and Hanseatic City of Hamburg. The Academies' Programme is coordinated by the Union of the German Academies of Sciences and Humanities (INEL project). The another port of the work leading to this publication was supported by the German Science foundation (Grant number WA3153/3-1).

3   http://www.gks.ru/free_doc/new_site/perepis2010/croc/Documents/Vol4/pub-04-0. pdf [accessed 30 January 2018].
4   The compilation of the Selkup data (Budzisch et al. 2019) is funded by the German Science Foundation (DFG), Grant no. WA3153/3–1; the contributors to this project are Josefina Budzisch and Anja Harder; in this chapter the glosses and translations were added by Beáta Wagner-Nagy.
5   This corpus (Brykina et al. 2018) contains texts recorded by Angelina Kuzmina in the 1970s. Her archive is saved at the Institute of Finno-Ugric/Uralic Studies at the University of Hamburg and will be digitalized and analysed in the course of INEL. The contributors to this project are Maria Brykina and Svetlana Orlova. The glosses and translations were carried out by them. This publication has been produced in the context of the joint research funding of the German Federal Government and Federal States in the Academies' Programme, with funding from the Federal Ministry of Education and Research and the Free and Hanseatic City of Hamburg. The Academies' Programme is coordinated by the Union of the German Academies of Sciences and Humanities.
6   Examples coded as [XYZ_ year_title of text.number of the sentence] refer to the texts from the Spoken Selkup language corpus (marked with d_) and the Selkup Corpus materials of the INEL project (marked with a_). XYZ stands for the abbreviations of the speaker. Sentences from grammars, descriptions or dictionaries are referred to by the source.
7   In Stassen's work, this schema is called the '*with*-possession'.
8   *kiba* means 'little, small', the word *ńaʒa* is not used as stem, the meaning is unknown.

References

Bekker, E. G., Alitkina, L. A., Bykonja, V. V. & Iljašenko, I. A. 1995. *Morfologija seľkupskogo jazyka. Južnye dialekty. časť* I [Morphology of the Selkup language. The Southern dialects. Part 1]. Tomsk: Tomskij gosudarstvennyj pedagogičeskij institute.

Brykina, M., Orlova, S. & Wagner-Nagy, B. 2018. INEL Selkup Corpus. Version 0.1. Publication date 2018-12-31. Archived in Hamburger Zentrum für Sprachkorpora. http://hdl.handle.net/11022/0000-0007-CAE5-3. In: Wagner-Nagy, B., Arkhipov, A., Ferger, A., Jettka, D. & Lehmberg, T. (eds), *The INEL corpora of indigenous Northern Eurasian languages*.

Budzisch, J. 2015. Possessive constructions in Southern Selkup dialects. *Tomsk Journal of LING & ANTHRO* 10: 45–50.

Budzisch, J. 2017. Locative, existential and possessive sentences in Selkup dialects. *Finnisch-Ugrische Mitteilungen* 41: 46–61.

Budzisch, J., Harder, A. & Wagner-Nagy, B. 2019. Selkup Language Corpus (SLC). Archived in Hamburger Zentrum für Sprachkoropra. Version 1.0.0. Publication date 2019-02-08. HYPERLINK "http://hdl.handle.net/11022/0000-0007-D009-4"http://hdl.handle.net/11022/0000-0007-D009-4.

Dryer, M. S. 2007. Clause types. In: Shopen, T. (ed.), *Language Typology and Syntactic Description. Volume I: Clause Structure*, 2nd edn, 224–275. Cambridge: Cambridge University Press.

Erdélyi, I. 1969. *Selkupisches Wörterverzeichnis. Tas-Dialekt*. Budapest: Akadémiai Kiadó.

Freeze, R. 1992. Existentials and other locatives. *Language* 68: 555–595.

Hajdú, Péter 1968. *Chrestomathia Samoiedica*. Budapest: Akadémiai Kiadó.

Heine, B. 1997. *Possession. Cognitive Sources, Forces, and Grammaticalization*. Cambridge: Cambridge University Press.
Heine, B. 2001. Ways of explaining possession. In: Baron, I., Herslund, M. & Sørensen, F. (eds), *Dimensions of Possession*, 311–328. Amsterdam: John Benjamins.
Honti, L. 2007. A birtoklás kifejezésének eszközei az uráli nyelvekben szinkrón és diakrón szempontból. [Ways of expressing possession from diachronic and synchronic points of view]. *Nyelvtudományi Közlemények* 104: 7–56.
Honti, L. 2014. *Uráli birtokos szerkezetek*. [Possessive constructions in Uralic languages]. Budapest: Magyar Tudományos Akadémia.
Janurik, T. 1975–1976. A személyes névmások birtokos névmási használata a középső-obi szölkup nyelvjárásban [Personal pronouns as possessive pronouns in the Middle-Ob dialect of Selkup]. *Néprajz és Nyelvtudomány* 19–20: 189–206.
Janurik, T. 1978. A szölkup nyelvjárások osztályozásához [On the classification of Selkup dialects]. *Nyelvtudományi Közlemények* 80: 77–104.
Kim, A. A. 1981. *Habeo*-konstrukcii v sel'kupskom jazyke. [*Habeo*-constructions in Selkup]. *Jazyki i toponimija* 8: 90–94.
Kim-Maloney, A. & Kovylin, S. 2016. Strategii formirovanija predikativnoj posesivnosti v sel'kupskih dialektah. [Strategies of predicative possession formation in Selkup dialects] *Tomsk Journal LING & ANTHRO* 14: 9–21.
Kim-Maloney, A. & Kovylin, S. 2017. Problemy semantičeskoj interpretacii konstrukcij s posesyvnym formantami v dialektax sel'kupskogo jazyka. [Semantic interpretation problems of constructions with possessive formants in the dialects of Selkup]. *Tomsk Journal LING & ANTHRO* 18: 29–41.
Kovylin, S. 2016. Otricanie i sposoby ego vyraženija v vachovskom i vasjuganskom dialekte khantyjskogo jazyka, i v central'nych i južnych dialektax sel'kupskogo jazyka. [Negation and ways of its expression in the Vakh and Vasyugan dialects of Khanty and in the Central and Southern dialects of Selkup]. PhD dissertation. University of Tomsk.
Kuznecova, A., Helimskij, E. & Gruškina, E. V. 1980. *Očerki po sel'kuskomu jazyku* [Sketch Grammar of Selkup]. Moskva: Izdatel'stvo Moskovskogo universiteta.
McGregor, W. 2001. The verb *have* in Nyulnyulan languages. In: Baron, I., Herslund, M. & Sørensen, F. (eds), *Dimensions of Possession*, 67–84. Amsterdam: John Benjamins.
N. Sebestyén I. 1957. Die possessiven Fügungen im Samojedischen und das Problem des uralischen Genitivs (I.) *Acta Linguistica Hungarica* 7: 41–71.
Payne, T. E. 1997. *Describing Morpho-Syntax*. Cambridge: Cambridge University Press.
Poljakova, N. V. 2016. Osnovnye sposoby vyraženija predikativnoj possessivnosti v dialektax sel'kupskogo jazyka. [Basic ways of expressing predicative possession in the dialects of Selkup]. *Tomsk Journal LING & ANTHRO* 14: 43–49.
Stassen, L. 2001. Predicative possession. In: Haspelmath, M., König, E., Oesterreicher, W. & Raible, W. (eds), *Language Typology and Language Universals*, vol. 2, 954–960. Berlin: de Gruyter.
Stassen, L. 2009. *Predicative Possession*. Oxford: Oxford University Press.
Stassen, L. 2013. Predicative possession. In: Dryer, M. S. & Haspelmath, M. (eds), *The World Atlas of Language Structures Online*. Leipzig: Max Planck Institute for Evolutionary Anthropology. http://wals.info/chapter/117.
Wagner-Nagy, B. 2011. *On the Typology of Negation in Ob-Ugric and Samoyedic Languages*. Helsinki: SUS.
Wagner-Nagy, B. 2015. Negation in Selkup. In: Miestamo, M., Tamm, A. & Wagner-Nagy, B. (eds), *Negation in Uralic Languages*, 133–158. Benjamins: Amsterdam.

11. Conclusion

Gréte Dalmi, Jacek Witkoś and Piotr Cegłowski

Writing a conclusive set of remarks summing up an enterprise that is by definition inconclusive is not an enviable task. This volume leaves open the grand-scale theoretical perspective of how possession is encoded in human language and what particular structures are employed to convey this semantic relation in particular languages. We believe that for the complete picture of the linguistic expression of the relation of possession to emerge, one would have to provide detailed analyses of a large number of languages representing diverse language groups and families, including various language-related historical factors, as diachronic changes may also affect these constructions. The current volume constitutes a modest beginning and an invitation for further discussion.

The chapters in the present volume investigate some aspects of predicative possession in two large language families, Slavic and Finno-Ugric. The common ground of these contributions is the attempt to place possessive sentences of the individual languages in a comparative perspective concerning the choice of the HABERE or ESSE types of possessive sentences. The contributions pick the relevant features characterizing predicative possession in the languages investigated here. Not surprisingly, these characteristic features are significantly alike in the two language families. The Definiteness Effect manifests itself in all of the languages presented in the volume. In some of them, this requirement materializes even in negated possessive sentences via genitive or partitive case on the possessee.

In this respect, the comparison between Russian and Polish is extremely interesting. They differ considerably in the application of the Genitive of Negation (GoN), an issue that has a long history of research (Partee & Borshev 2004, 2008; Bailyn 1997; Brown 1999; Kagan 2013; Witkoś 2003). In possessive constructions under the scope of sentential negation, the nonspecific/non-presupposed/indefinite possessee needs to change its case from nominative to genitive. The specific/presupposed/definite possessee remains nominative. This truly fascinating and finessed picture of the possessive construction in Russian can be juxtaposed with the morpho-syntax of Polish, which does not recognize any semantic distinctions in its HAVE-possessive construction and forces all possessees to shift from accusative to genitive under negation. It is striking that such a profound semantic distinction is encoded in the Russian mode of the GoN, while it is entirely absent from Polish (see Błaszczak 2007 and the references cited therein).

As was noted in the introductory chapter, Slavic languages tend to use HAVE-possessives (with the notable exception of Russian), while Finno-Ugric languages predominantly use BE-possessives with an oblique possessor. Here the possessive suffix on the possessee signals the person/number features of the possessor. In the latter language family, the connection between possessive BE-sentences and existential BE-sentences is strikingly obvious. While existential BE takes a Location and a Theme argument, the same existential BE selects an oblique possessor and a possessee in BE-possessives.

This raises the interesting question whether the choice between HAVE-possessives and BE-possessives in the individual languages is regulated by some universal principles of grammar. In this respect, languages where both types are represented are of crucial importance. Belarusian is a language in which the choice between the two types is subject to semantic restrictions (see Mazzitelli 2017; Tsedryk, Chapter 5 in this volume). In some Slavic languages, BE-possessives were gradually replaced by HAVE-possessives (see Grkovic-Major 2011).

While various aspects concerning the semantic and syntactic facets of the HAVE vs. BE distinction remain the leitmotif of the volume, the extractability of possessive (genitive) complements is also contemplated here in a way that highlights their potential implications for the comparative view of the syntactic composition of nominal structures (Progovac 1998; Bošković 2008, among others).

These days theoretical proposals abound and multiply almost by the dozen in the linguistic research community. New approaches do not necessarily start afresh, but they typically constitute creative combinations of strands of older proposals, borrowings, extensions and creative applications to and from neighbouring fields. Theoretical unification is the task of the future, when the main descriptive points are agreed on. New ideas, associations and connecting points between different proposals criss-cross and spring into the linguistic observer's alert eye as we speak, so we have high hopes for extensive continuations of the work presented here.

The exploration of the connections between these two major types of possessive sentences from a comparative point of view is still ahead of us. Although the comparative approach is widely used in synchronic and diachronic studies, these studies usually focus on a single language family (for Slavic, see McAnnalen 2011; for Finno-Ugric, see Miestamo, Tamm & Wagner-Nagy 2015; Bakró-Nagy et al. 2018). This book is therefore a unique collection, perhaps the first of its kind, which allows us to take a closer look at the ways of expressing predicative possession in two important, though genealogically unrelated, language families.

While Slavic languages have been relatively well described in formal theories, Finno-Ugric studies are still mostly done in a typological framework. Comparisons are possible to make across language families only if the data become available. The editors' primary intention was to promote such comparisons. We will leave it to the readers to decide whether the volume has served this noble purpose.

We whole-heartedly recommend this volume to theoretical, historical and corpus linguists working on predicative possession. It offers a whole range of facts and data that are hardly found in any other collection. The book may also serve as a useful source of reference for students of advanced courses in Linguistics.

References

Bailyn, J. F. 1997. Genitive of Negation is obligatory. In: Browne, W., Dornisch, E., Kondrashova, N. & Zec, D. (eds), *Annual Workshop on Formal Approaches to Slavic Linguistics: The Cornell Meeting*, 84–114. Ann Arbor, MI: Michigan Slavic Publications.

Bakró-Nagy, M., Laakso, J. & Skribnik, E. (eds). 2018. *The Oxford Guide to the Uralic Languages*. Oxford: Oxford University Press.

Błaszczak, J. 2007. *Phase Syntax. The Polish Genitive of Negation*. Habilitation treatise. Potsdam: University of Potsdam.

Bošković, Ž. 2008. What will you have, DP or NP? *Proceedings of the North East Linguistic Society* 37: 101–114.

Brown, S. 1999. *The Syntax of Negation in Russian: A Minimalist Approach*. Stanford, CA: CSLI Publications.

Grkovic-Major, J. 2011. The development of predicative possession in Slavic languages. In: Nomachi, M. (ed.), *The Grammar of Possessivity in South-Slavic Languages*, 35–54. Sapporo: Hokkaido University Press.

Kagan, O. 2013. *Semantics of Genitive Objects: A Study of Genitive of Negation and Intensional Genitive Case*. New York: Springer.

Mazzitelli, L. 2017. Predicative possession in the languages of the Circum-Baltic area. *Folia Linguistica* 51(1): 1–60.

McAnnalen, J. 2011. The history of predicative possession in Slavic: internal development vs. language contact. PhD dissertation. UCL, Berkeley.

Miestamo, M., Tamm, A. & Wagner-Nagy, B. (eds). 2015. *Negation in Uralic Languages*. Typological Studies in Language 108, 457–485. Amsterdam: John Benjamins.

Partee, B. & Borschev, V. 2004. The semantics of Russian Genitive of Negation: the nature and role of perspectival structure. In: Toman, J. (ed.), *Proceedings of Formal Approaches to Slavic Linguistics 10*, 181–200. Ann Arbor, MI: Michigan Slavic Publications.

Partee, B. & Borschev, V. 2008. Existential sentences, BE and GEN NEG in Russian. In: Comorowski, I. & von Heusinger, K. (eds), *Existence: Semantics and Syntax*, 147–191. New York: Springer.

Progovac, L. 1998. Determiner phrase in a language without determiners. *Journal of Linguistics* 34: 165–179.

Witkoś, J. 2003. Some notes on Single Cycle syntax and Genitive of Negation. In: Bański, P. & Przepiórkowski, A. (eds), *Generative Linguistics in Poland: Morphosyntactic Investigations*, 167–182. Warsaw: Instytut Podstaw Informatyki Polskiej Akademii Nauk.

Index

A
agglutinative language 187, 206
Agree 15, 20, 26, 29–32, 35 n. 19, 53, 93, 99
agreement
    anti- ~ 147–150, 156 n. 18, 157 n. 22
    person/number ~ 7, 145, 153, 155, 157 n. 22, 205
    ~ suffix 6, 144, 155, 157 n. 22
Anti-locality 43–45, 49, 54, 56, 57 n. 10
aorist 215
argument
    theme ~ 2–3, 7, 42, 137, 139–140, 144, 149–151, 155 n. 3, 155 n. 5, 156 n. 7, 222
    ~ chain (A-chain) 17, 35 n. 19
    ~ structure 3, 5, 115, 125, 136, 144, 150
aspectual
    ~ auxiliary 97, 136

B
Belarusian 2, 4–5, 80–83, 85–89, 91, 93–94, 97, 106–107, 107 n. 5, 108 n. 11, 108 n. 13, 222
Beneficiary 122
BE-possessive vii, 1, 3, 5–7, 74–76, 83, 106, 136, 141–144, 146–150, 152–154, 155 n. 5, 157 n. 23, 158 n. 31, 222
BE
    copular ~ 2–3, 5, 7, 81–91, 103, 107, 136–142, 156 n. 9, 156 n. 10
    existential ~ 2–3, 5, 73, 76 n. 2, 81–86, 88–91, 104, 107, 139–145, 150, 155, 155 n. 4, 155 n. 5, 156 n. 9, 156 n. 10, 156 n. 13, 207, 222
    ~ predicate 3, 5, 136–137, 155
body parts 81, 84, 101–103, 109 n. 33, 119, 126, 132 n. 17, 189, 200, 209, 211–212, 218

C
c(onstituent)-command 15–16, 25, 27–28, 31, 33 n. 5, 34 n. 7, 34 n. 12, 42, 53

case
    ablative ~ 122, 132 n. 15, 192
    accusative ~ 4, 11–12, 14, 23, 25–27, 29, 32, 33 n. 5, 34 n. 8, 35 n. 16, 35 n. 18, 66–67, 72, 76 n. 1., 89–91, 93, 107 n.1, 120, 122, 124, 130, 132 n.12, 187, 192, 207, 221
    adessive ~ 113, 116–117, 122–125, 129–130, 207–208
    allative ~ 122
    comitative ~ 25, 173, 191, 201, 207–208
    dative ~ 11, 14, 25, 27–29, 33 n. 5, 49, 114, 122, 131 n. 3, 142–147, 149, 152, 154, 157 n. 19, 157 n. 23, 190–191, 207–208
    genitive ~ 4, 6, 11–12, 14–17, 21–5, 27–8, 31–32, 33 n. 5, 34 n. 6, 34 n. 7, 34 n. 8, 34 n. 14, 35 n. 18, 40–42, 44–50, 52, 54–55, 63, 65–68, 70–73, 75–76, 89, 91, 98–99, 107, 109 n. 29, 117, 132 n. 13, 162–163, 165–166, 170–173, 180–181, 183 n. 16, 187, 190–193, 197, 201, 207–208, 211, 214–215, 218, 221–222
    inessive ~ 122–123, 131 n. 1, 170, 182 n. 1
    instrumental ~ 11, 25, 27, 49, 94–95, 107 n. 4, 108 n. 22, 207, 211
    locative ~ 21–22, 24, 28–29, 32, 35 n. 16, 106, 107 n. 5, 117–118, 122, 129, 131 n. 3, 140, 171, 173, 187, 190, 207–208, 211–212, 215–216
    nominative ~ 2, 4, 6, 15, 17–18, 21–25, 27, 32, 33 n. 5, 65–67, 72–73, 82, 89–90, 115, 118–121, 123, 126–130, 131 n. 10, 132 n. 12, 132 n. 13, 132 n. 17, 142–143, 148–149, 153, 156 n. 14, 157 n. 20, 162–165, 172, 207–208, 211, 213, 215, 221
    oblique ~ 2, 7, 15, 21–22, 24–25, 29, 32, 113, 150–151, 157 n. 23, 190, 208, 222
    partitive ~ 15, 33 n. 5, 121, 126–128, 221
    structural ~ 4, 15, 27, 29, 34 n. 13, 89, 93

~ overwriting 4, 11, 20–25, 28, 32
~ projection 4, 20, 25–26, 28, 32, 35 n. 17
~ valuation 26–27, 32, 93
clause
   ~ final position 198–199
   ~ initial position 140, 198–199
   existential ~ 5, 90, 113, 117, 130, 190, 195, 202 n. 9
   infinitival ~ 13, 19, 23, 30–32, 36 n. 19, 36 n. 21
   negated ~ 118
   restricted ~ 115–116, 118
Chukchee (Chukchi) 32, 210
coda 6, 61–62, 68, 71, 73, 75, 173
complement
   infinitival ~ 32, 116
   nominal (NP-) ~ 4, 22–24, 40, 43, 45–48, 50–52, 54–55, 57 n. 9
   small clause ~ 140, 142
Construction Grammar 5, 131 n. 2
Conceptual Space 189
copular
   ~ BE 2–3, 5, 7, 81–85, 88–91, 103, 107, 136–142, 156 n. 9, 156 n. 10
   ~ sentences 3, 113, 139–140, 142, 156 n. 8, 156 n. 9
   ~ verb 81, 140, 142
copy / copying 21–22, 31, 35 n. 19, 95

D

dative possessor 6, 143, 146–150, 153, 155, 158 n. 31, 171
definedness conditions 176
definite(ness) 3–4, 17–18, 33 n. 2, 34 n. 8, 36 n. 19, 51, 61–63, 65–67, 69–76, 77 n. 8, 77 n. 9, 87–89, 103, 118, 140, 142–144, 155 n. 3, 187, 216, 221
Definiteness
   ~ Effect 4, 6, 61–64, 68, 73–76, 81, 87, 156 n. 13, 163–164, 177, 181, 221
   ~ Restriction 3, 5, 7, 87, 137, 141–144, 149, 155 n. 3, 155 n. 5, 156 n. 13
determiner 6, 61–63, 87, 96, 109 n. 32, 118, 164, 180
discourse
   ~ -marking 52, 56, 57 n. 13
   ~ sensitive structures 57 n. 14
Distributed Morphology 5, 81, 92
DP Hypothesis 40, 53, 57 n. 6

dyadic
   ~ unaccusative predicate 6, 141, 147, 149–151, 155

E
Enets 205
English 15, 27, 41–43, 64, 68, 70, 73, 76, 81, 86–87, 97, 115, 137, 151, 163–164, 169, 176, 178–179, 190
entail(ment) 67–69, 71, 86, 89, 102, 107, 156 n. 7, 169, 173, 175–176, 178–179, 181, 183 n. 12
existential
   ~ closure 87, 99–103, 107, 171, 180
   ~ quantifier 64, 102
   ~ possessive constructions 6, 162–166, 169–173, 175, 177, 179–181, 208
   ~ presupposition 6, 16, 156 n. 7, 164, 176, 178–181
   ~ sentences 3–4, 6, 11, 16, 61–66, 68–69, 71–73, 76, 77 n. 6, 77 n. 9, 87, 121, 156 n. 9, 164, 167, 171, 178, 183 n. 17, 216
   ~ verb 15, 19, 68, 73, 140, 188, 191, 193–199, 201, 208, 213, 215
extraction
   ~ across numerals 4, 45–48
   deep ~ 4, 46, 49
   NP-complement ~ 4, 40, 43, 45–49, 54
   possessor ~ 142, 144–145, 147–150, 153–155, 156 n. 14
   sub- ~ 28–29

F
feature
   ~ assignment 21
Finnish 2, 5, 113–115, 117–122, 124–125, 130, 131 n. 3, 131 n. 8, 131 n. 10
Finno-Ugric
   ~ languages 1–2, 6–7, 157 n. 23, 162, 165, 182 n. 2, 182 n. 3, 182 n. 7, 195, 202 n. 2, 205, 219 n. 5, 221–222
Focus
   ~ marking 48, 57 n. 14
   Contrastive ~ 53, 198
   Narrow ~ 126

G
Genitive
   ~ Schema 208–209, 211, 214

~ of Negation 3–4, 7, 11–20, 22–23, 25–29, 32, 33 n. 2, 33 n. 4, 33n. 5, 34 n. 6, 34 n.7, 34 n. 8, 34 n. 12, 35 n. 18, 35 n. 19, 36 n. 20, 66–69, 72–76, 89–91, 108 n. 15, 139–142, 156 n. 7, 221
~ of Quantification 21–22, 23, 34 n. 7, 34 n. 15, 45
genitive constructions
   adnominal ~ 24
   partitive ~ 34 n. 15
German 28, 151, 208–209, 218 n. 2, 219 n. 4, 219 n. 5
(probe and) goal 15, 29, 32, 54–55
Goal (Schema) 208

H
HAVE-possessive 1, 3, 7, 80, 98, 106, 141–142, 191–192, 207, 209, 221–222
Hungarian 2, 5–6, 114, 136–137, 140–150, 152–154, 155, 155 n. 3, 155 n. 4, 156 n. 8, 156 n. 13, 156 n. 16, 156 n. 18, 157 n. 23, 158 n. 31, 171, 182 n. 6, 188, 190

I
inclusion 5, 81, 96–97, 100–101, 103–105, 107, 109 n. 26
indefinite(ness) 3–4, 17, 36 n. 19, 61–62, 66–67, 71–72, 75, 77 n. 8, 87–88, 118–119, 121, 131 n. 8, 142, 192, 195, 216, 221
information structure 117, 120–121, 217
informativity condition 6, 164, 178, 180–181

K
Kase
   ~ sequence (Kseq) 25–29
Khanty 190, 207, 209
kinship 81, 84, 91, 96, 188–189, 200, 209, 211–212, 218
Komi-Permyak 6, 186–188, 190–199, 201, 202 n.3, 202 n. 4, 202 n. 6, 202 n. 12

L
Left Branch Extraction 4, 41
left periphery
   ~ of the clause 144–150, 152, 157 n. 20
   ~ of the nominal domain 52, 54, 56, 143

locative
   agentive ~ 12, 16, 18–20, 32
   ~ existential 3, 11–12, 15–16, 18–20, 156 n. 9
   ~ possessive 193
locational
   ~ postposition 211
logical form 90, 92, 99, 102, 106, 174–175
Long Distance Genitive of Negation 4, 13–14, 29, 32, 35 n. 19

M
Mansi 207, 209
Meadow Mari 2, 6, 143, 162, 164–165, 170–171, 176–177, 180–181, 182 n. 3, 182 n. 6
Merge/merge 20–27, 29, 44, 81, 92, 95–96, 98–99, 102–103, 106, 108 n. 21, 108 n. 23, 173
Move 31–32, 44–45, 108 n. 23
movement
   A- ~ 18
   Cyclic ~ 31, 55, 146
   Long Operator ~ 145–146
   overt ~ 35 n. 19
   covert ~ 35 n. 19
   head ~ 36 n. 21
   QUANT-to-D ~ 22

N
nano-syntax 26
negative
   ~ operator 64, 67
Negative Polarity Item 34 n. 7, 42, 127
NEG
   ~ raisers 43
negation
   clause ~ 11–12, 126, 139, 142
   constituent ~ 11, 23
Nenets 205–206, 209
Nganasan 190, 205, 207–209
Northern Sulawesi 190
Nyulnyulan 209

O
Ob-Ugric 190, 209
OVS ~ 120
ownership 81, 86–89, 91, 96, 108 n. 13, 188–189

P
part-whole (relation) 84–85, 91, 96–97, 102–103, 109 n. 33, 123, 188
partitive
~ construction 34 n. 15, 62–63, 65, 73, 118–119, 126–130, 131 n. 6, 131 n. 8, 131 n. 9, 131 n. 10, 132 n. 17
Partitive of Negation 124, 126–130
Permic 2, 6, 183 n. 13, 186–187, 190–193, 199, 201
Phase Impenetrability Condition 29–32, 35 n. 19, 43–45, 49, 57 n. 10
phonological form 31, 92–93, 98, 105–106
pivot 4, 6, 61–62, 65–66, 68–69, 73, 75–76, 87, 216
Polish 2–4, 11–13, 15, 18, 20–22, 27, 30–32, 33 n. 2, 33 n. 4, 34 n. 8, 34 n. 12, 35 n. 18, 36 n. 20, 40–45, 48–51, 53–54, 56, 57 n. 7, 57 n. 14, 83, 85, 157 n. 30, 221
possessee 3, 5–6, 74, 76, 87–91, 96–98, 102, 113–114, 116–122, 124, 126–127, 130, 141–145, 147–149, 153, 155, 156 n. 11, 157 n. 20, 157 n. 22, 162–170, 172, 183 n. 12, 188–201, 205, 208, 211–215, 217–218, 221–222
possessive
conjunctional ~ 191, 193, 208–210
oblique ~ 208
topic ~ 190–191, 208
~ BE 2–5, 73, 76 n. 5, 83, 136–139, 141–144, 147–150, 155 n. 5, 222
~ binding 41–42
~ sentence 2–4, 6–7, 61, 73–76, 138, 138–139, 141, 143, 162, 164, 167, 177, 208, 211–212, 214–216, 221
~ suffix 6, 114, 116, 123–124, 143–144, 147–149, 162, 164–169, 174–177, 180–181, 187, 191–193, 195–196, 200–201, 202 n. 12, 212–216, 218
possession
abstract ~ 84–85, 189
adnominal (attributive) ~ 131 n. 3, 169, 183 n. 13, 188, 192, 201, 205
alienable ~ 86, 91, 101–102, 104, 189, 199, 201, 213
inalienable ~ 102–103, 123, 126–127, 189, 199, 201, 209, 211–213, 218
intransitive ~ 190–191, 193, 208

total vs. partial ~ 165, 169
permanent ~ 88, 164
predicative ~ 1–3, 5–6, 80–81, 83, 113–114, 117, 125, 141, 186, 188–189, 192–193, 199–201, 205, 216, 221–222
temporary ~ 87–91, 101, 104, 108 n. 13, 189
possessor
genitive ~ 49, 165, 174–175, 180–181
dative ~ 6, 143, 146–150, 153, 155, 158 n. 31, 171
nominative ~ 143
oblique ~ 2, 7, 150, 222
pronominal ~ 6, 148–150, 153–154, 157 n. 19, 157 n. 30, 158 n. 31, 191, 195–196, 213, 215
postposition 173, 207, 211–213, 218
predicate
intensional ~ 67
psych- ~ 6, 33 n. 5, 150–152, 154–155, 157 n. 24
unaccusative ~ 3, 141, 144, 149–150
prepositional object 12
pro
French-type ~ 15
probe
split ~ 14–16, 27, 29, 33 n. 5, 34 n. 12
presupposed
non- ~ 17, 221
property
~ denoting 4, 62, 67–68, 76
~ -type hypothesis 90
~ -type interpretation 66, 69, 72, 75
psychological conditions

Q
Q(uantifier)-Float 138–139, 141–142
quantifier
proportional ~ 62, 69–70
strong ~ 69–70, 76, 177–178, 180
question
polar ~ 198

R
Recipient 122
reconstruction 30
remnant
~ VP movement 183 n. 14

Russian 2–4, 6, 13, 16–17, 21, 24, 33 n. 2, 34 n. 6, 34 n. 8, 34 n. 15, 35 n. 19, 61–65, 67–73, 75–76, 77 n. 5, 77 n. 8, 82–83, 85, 89–90, 97, 105, 107, 108 n. 10, 108 n. 11, 121, 136–137, 139, 141–142, 155 n. 2, 156 n. 7, 182 n. 6, 182 n. 11, 187, 202 n. 12, 206–207, 215–217, 221–222

S

scope of negation 4, 12, 14, 27, 34 n. 8, 81, 89, 99, 221
Samoyedic 2, 205, 208
scrambling 41
Serbian/Croatian 41–44, 49, 57 n. 7,
Selkup
  ~ dialects 2, 6, 143, 205–211, 214–216, 218, 219 n. 4, 219 n. 6
Slavic
  ~ languages 1–4, 7, 20, 25, 33 n. 4, 57 n. 12, 66–67, 80, 93, 157 n. 23, 221–222
Skewed Distribution 46–48, 50
Small Nominal Hypothesis 40–41
South Saami 190
SOV ~ 183 n. 14, 187, 198, 206
Specifier 26, 29–30, 35 n. 16, 95, 170, 172
(non-)specific 3, 17, 34 n. 8, 35 n. 19, 62, 64, 66–67, 70–72, 74–76, 77 n. 8, 155 n. 3, 156 n. 7, 221
Spell-Out
  ~ domain 21–22, 24, 31
Standard Deviation 46–48
subcategorization 23
Surgut Khanty 190
SVO ~ 151, 187, 198, 207
syncretism 25, 49–50

T

Tondano 191
Topic
  Aboutness ~ 51–52, 57 n. 16
  Contrastive ~ 51–52, 57 n. 16
  default ~ 120
  Given ~ 51–52, 57 n. 16
  ~ interpretation 51–52, 55
  ~ phrase / projection 172–173, 183 n. 14
  ~ position 116, 120, 124, 132 n. 14, 213, 217
  ~ Schema 211, 213–214, 218
topicalization 35 n. 18, 155 n. 4
transitivity 93, 98, 124, 132, 190

U

Udmurt 2, 6, 114, 186–188, 191–201, 202 n. 3, 202 n. 6, 202 n. 9, 208
Ugric
  Ob- ~ 190, 209
Undermerge 22–23
Uralic
  ~ languages 1, 114, 143, 162, 186–187, 188, 190, 202 n. 2, 205, 207–210

V

Vergnaud-licensed
  ~ DP 24, 30
Volgaic
  ~ languages 6
VSO ~ 158 n. 31

W

word order 3, 57 n. 12, 120, 187, 198–199, 206–207, 216–218

www.ingramcontent.com/pod-product-compliance
Lightning Source LLC
Chambersburg PA
CBHW052037300426
44117CB00012B/1859